VICTORIAN FREAKS

VICTORIAN FREAKS

The Social Context of Freakery in Britain

EDITED BY

Marlene Tromp

The Ohio State University Press
Columbus

Library of Congress Cataloging-in-Publication Data
Victorian freaks : the social context of freakery in Britain / edited by Marlene Tromp.
    p. ; cm.
Includes bibliographical references and index.
ISBN-13: 978–0–8142–1086–4 (cloth : alk. paper)
1. Abnormalities, Human—Great Britain—History—19th century. 2. Freak shows—Great Britain—History—19th century. 3. Body, Human—Social aspects—Great Britain—History—19th century.
[DNLM: 1. Abnormalities—history—Great Britain. 2. History, 19th Century—Great Britain. 3. Social Conditions—history—Great Britain. WZ 308 V645 2008] I. Tromp, Marlene, 1966–
QM691.V53 2008
616.0430941—dc22
                    2007045057

This book is available in the following editions:
Cloth (ISBN 978–0–8142–1086–4)
CD-ROM (ISBN 978–0–8142–9166–5)

Cover design by Laurence J. Nozik
Text design by Juliet Williams
Type set in Adobe Goudy Old Style
Printed by Sheridan Books, Inc.

9 8 7 6 5 4 3 2 1

CONTENTS

ILLUSTRATIONS

FOREWORD

FREAKERY UNFURLED

ROSEMARIE GARLAND-THOMSON

THIS RICH and compelling collection is exemplary of what academics
do best. The cultural work of scholars is to create new knowledge in
the form of an ongoing critical conversation that considers and recon-
siders a subject in increasingly fresh and complex ways. During the
ten years between the publication of *Freakery: Cultural Spectacles of the
Extraordinary Body*,[1] the collection I edited in 1996, and this 2008 publication of *Victorian Freaks*, edited by Marlene Tromp, the conversation
about the display of human beings as curiosities for what Robert Bogdan
has called "amusement and profit" has expanded and deepened.[2]

In my view, the emergence of what has come to be called Freaks
Studies, a subfield within American Studies and Cultural Studies, begins
in 1978 with Leslie Fiedler's counterculture manifesto, *Freaks: Myths
and Images of the Secret Self*.[3] While Fiedler's study unearths the history
of the freak figure in new ways, it is rooted in the archetypal criticism
of the period and a 1970s sensibility that seeks to defend freaks against
the establishment. Fiedler aligns the freak figure with the hippie figure, arguing that freaks ought to be valued and allowed to exist in the
world because they teach "us" about "ourselves." Ten years later in 1988,
Robert Bogdan's *Freak Show: Presenting Human Oddities for Amusement
and Profit* brings a social constructivist reading to the freak figure that

focuses on the disparity between actual people who took on the role of freaks and the exaggerated performance of the displays. Bogdan's materialist analysis brings forward for the first time the social category of disability to demonstrate that freak shows are part of the labor history of people with disabilities, often augmented with racialization and gender ambiguity. By moving the freak figure from mythology to materialism, Bogdan begins the critical project of humanizing freaks.

Almost ten years after Bogdan published *Freak Show*, my edited collection, *Freakery*, expanded his constructivist approach by bringing forward the issue of representation more fully, often through literary analysis and historiography. Following Bogdan, *Freakery* and the various book-length studies that began in that volume rigorously grounded their analysis in the social systems of disability, race, gender, class, and sexuality. After Bogdan, freaks were always people who performed roles as freaks. Several very strong cultural studies about freaks, largely by historians and literary critics, emerged from Bogdan's tradition and *Freakery*. Rachel Adams, James W. Cook, Andrea Dennett, Alice Dreger, and Benjamin Reiss, among others, ranged across American freakery, dominated as it is by Barnum, the canny and outrageous entrepreneur who took us all to the cleaners with his humbugs, even as we delighted in the ride.[4]

My challenge in writing the foreword to *Freakery*—and in all the scholarly work I do on the representation of disability—is how to find precise language to talk about freaks and their display that unsettles the way we understand freaks as freakish, as on the far edge of human, as not "us." In other words, how do we talk about freaks without reinscribing the oppressive attitudes we attempt to critique? The most effective way to do this is to keep a steady focus on the materiality of the people who performed as freaks and the particular circumstances of their actual lives. Bogdan's sociological constructivist approach assures the freak's humanity by focusing on the social relations of enfreakment.

Victorian Freaks advances this project of according full humanity to the people who performed as freaks by shifting from a social constructivist understanding of freakery to a rigorous materialist analysis. This fine collection ranges across a wide spectrum of what might be called freak instances in a particular historical time and place: Victorian Britain. By turning the focus of freaked studies from American matters to concerns that emerge in the British context—while acknowledging the global and transnational implications that remain in play, even when reading from that British context—the authors here look to the alternative notions of the marketplace and economics in Britain, alongside the intellectual and social industry of medicine, the role of imperialism, and the peculiarly British set of social values presented in the period fiction. Thus, this collection when placed beside much of the other studies of freakery introduces a strong comparative aspect into our inquiry of these pervasive spectacles.

By materialist analysis, I mean not just economic relations of freakery but also how the material aspects of social categories such as race, gender, class, and—in particular—disability play out in the material world. This insistence on the specific materiality of freak performances refuses metaphor and insists on humanity. It expands from the material lives of freaks, their handlers, and their audiences to demonstrate how the shows were dramas that played out cultural anxieties in both the individual and national context. The virtue of this analysis is that the freaks cannot be relegated to metaphorical figures of otherness, but rather they are enfleshed as they are enfreaked, always particular people in particular lives at particular moments in particular places.

Victorian Freaks not only makes a splendid contribution to Freak Studies, Disability Studies, and Victorian Studies, it is one of the liveliest collections I have come across. It knows how to talk about freaks, to vivify and humanize the entire cast of characters involved in these marvelous and theatrical social rituals.

Notes

1. Rosemarie Garland-Thomson, ed., *Freakery: Cultural Spectacles of the Extraordinary Body* (New York: New York University Press, 1996).

2. Robert Bogdan, *Freak Show: Presenting Human Oddities for Amusement and Profit* (Chicago: University of Chicago, 1988).

3. Leslie Fiedler, *Freaks: Myths and Human Images of the Secret Self* (New York: Simon & Schuster, 1978).

4. Rachel Adams, *Sideshow U.S.A.: Freaks and the American Cultural Imagination* (Chicago: University of Chicago Press, 2001); James W. Cook, *The Arts of Deception: Playing with Fraud in the Age of Barnum* (Cambridge, MA: Harvard University Press, 2001); Andrea Stulman Dennett, *Weird and Wonderful: The Dime Museum in America* (New York: New York University Press, 1997); Alice Domurat Dreger, *Hermaphrodites and the Medical Invention of Sex* (Cambridge, MA: Harvard University Press, 1998); and Benjamin Reiss, *The Showman and The Slave: Race, Death, and Memory in Barnum's America* (Cambridge, MA: Harvard University Press, 2001).

ACKNOWLEDGMENTS

The editor would like to express her sincere gratitude to Sandy Crooms and Heather Lee Miller, both of whom were wonderful and supportive editors; Julie Anne Lambert, librarian at the John Johnson Collection of Printed Ephemera at the Bodleian; the librarians at Denison University; Sandy Spence and Tiffany Horton; and the anonymous readers for The Ohio State University Press.

INTRODUCTION

TOWARD SITUATING THE VICTORIAN FREAK

MARLENE TROMP,
WITH
KARYN VALERIUS

"**FREAKS**" have captivated our imagination since well before the Victorian period—we can trace records back to the public exhibition of freaks for centuries—but the nineteenth century was a time of significant social change, highly popular freak shows, and taxonomic frenzy; this nexus makes the period particularly rich for the study of the freak[1] phenomena. Nearly every critic writing on freaks has echoed this sentiment, pointing to the Victorian era as central in the establishment of freak shows and in the evolving understanding of "freaks" as a social construct. Indeed, it was in 1847 that the term developed its contemporary association with human anomaly.[2] This collection of essays considers the period Rosemarie Garland-Thomson has described as the epoch of "consolidation" for freakery.[3] The authors here focus on this period, highlighting several important patterns. They examine the struggle over definitions of freakery, the unstable and sometimes conflicting ways in which freakery was understood and deployed. They explore the ways in which the multiple constructs of freakery threatened to undermine definitions of normalcy—a notion in relation to which freakery was structured.

Centrally, the essays in this collection seek to understand the effects of individual and ideological relationships to freakery and to situate

1

freaks in their Victorian cultural context. In this way, we hope to flesh out the impact of freakery on mainstream culture, as well as some of the cultural investments that produced freakery. While this book only begins this project, the scholarship presented here helps us better understand not only freakery but also the period. To open the conversation, we have three aims in the introduction: first, to *locate* freakery. We talk about how, in general, freakery comes to be defined by its historical period, which makes comprehending freakery's context a vital process. We then ask broad-based questions about how it can be read in its social, political, and material context in the nineteenth century. Second, we *dislocate* freakery to examine the ways in which the malleability and fluidity of the concept amplified its importance in mainstream culture. Debates over the freak brought conversations about freakery into the mainstream in a way that again calls for attention to cultural and historical specificity. Finally, we look across the range of essays in the collection to identify how they will, with more specificity, identify some of the material effects of and relationships to freakery.

Locating the Freak: Social Context

Mary Russo has argued in her study of the "freak and the uncanny" that the "grotesque body is . . . irregular secreting, multiple, and changing," yet it is also "identified with . . . social transformation."[4] While she acknowledges that the carnivalesque and freakish can have a "complicitous place in dominant culture," she underscores the potential for social transformation from the locus of the freak, and indicates that, for this reason, studies of it have often been anthropological, culturally situated, and a source of information regarding social processes.[5] To a Victorianist, assessing the complex role of freakery in the nineteenth century means situating these disruptive and multivalent constructs. In her study of female disability in the nineteenth-century novel, Cindy LaCom argues that we must read bodily difference in its historical context to understand better how identity in the period—for both the "normative" and the "non-normative"—was constructed.[6] We can better comprehend constructions of femaleness, she argues, if we understand constructions of the woman as freak. It is not only scholars of freakery who have argued that context is crucial in terms of understanding social constructs and identity formation, but also theorists of culture and identity. Judith Butler laid much of the groundwork for such thinking when she argued that gender, sexuality, and, more generally, the body itself are "produced effects of [laws] imposed by culture"—in other words, that these structures are generated by and generate social meaning.[7] It follows, then, that we must understand the social context in which those "laws" are produced to evaluate this process and its outcomes.

Biologist Anne Fausto-Sterling concurs with Butler's claims about the social process of identity formation in her study of sexual "anomalies." She explains that the body is a "somatic fact *created* by cultural effect."[8] The body—whether normative or not—is structured by the cultural context. This does not mean that the "body" is simply discursive, that there is no body or potential bodily difference to comprehend or figure or that these constructs are not multiple and slippery. Rather, it suggests that the body and its characteristics only come to mean something within a particular social and conceptual system and that the body is, in fact, determined by context. Take, for example, a case tackled by both Butler and Fausto-Sterling—and one that can serve as a model for studying the social and bodily construct of freakery in the nineteenth century—that of biological sex.

Fausto-Sterling explains that those categories that seem so clear and foundational in contemporary culture are actually socially defined, and that we can see this evidenced in the response to intersexed or "hermaphroditic" bodies (bodies that blur the lines between the sexes by being neither "properly" male nor female). Intersexuals' bodies are often surgically restructured in Western culture to preserve traditional notions of gender, but these restructurings are based on highly capricious and culturally specific notions of what "counts" as male or female genitalia (i.e., the size or length of the phallus) or what is valued in that particular society. For example, children who are born with congenital adrenal hyperplasia—chromosomally XX ("female") babies who have "masculinized" genitalia (an apparent penis)—are almost always identified as boys at birth and then surgically altered to "look female" in the United States: the phallus is reduced, the tissue surrounding it cosmetically shaped, and the children raised as girls. In Saudi Arabia, however, where male births are highly valued, these children are often raised as male.[9] On the other hand, children with XY ("male") chromosomes who are androgen insensitive are born with "feminized" genitalia and are typically raised as female. In adulthood, with no intervention, they will be virtually indistinguishable from adult XX bodies, except for the lack of functional uterus and ovaries.[10] In the nineteenth century, these individuals would have been read as unquestionably female, though infertile. Today, a woman might unexpectedly discover this medical fact as an adult and have her whole life turned upside down, as Olympic athlete Maria Patiño did when she was barred from competing in 1988.

Both of these cases reveal the way in which social context drives our understanding of bodies and sex identity. By extension, we can see how this would relate to bodily definitions of normalcy and freakery. While we may have been trained to think of freakery as a self-evident physical anomaly with which someone is born, the essays here emphasize the ways in which freakishness is made, not just with biology, but with a social function in a social context. If people from different cultures and physical landscapes (e.g., Chinese or Africans) could be exhibited as freaks in the United States and Europe in the nineteenth century simply because they were culturally and socially different from Anglo-Americans and Anglo-Europeans, and if people with tattoos or very long hair or nails were (and remain) staples of freak shows, then we must recognize the way in which enfreakment is not just about nature's work but rather is created by the body, plus its context, plus individual choices. Social context has as much weight as physical difference. Even those differences we recognize as most overtly bodily, such as hirsutism or, even more subtly, hair on a woman's upper lip, are tolerated in various degrees depending upon the culture, and some clearly visible differences have almost no social valence at all—such as whether or not individuals have attached or detached earlobes—or very little social valence, such as extra toes or missing fingers. It is, in part, because we frame something as freakish that it becomes freakish to us, as Robert Bogdan has argued. For Bogdan, a freak is social construction, not a personal matter or condition of body—a "frame of mind and set of practices."[11]

This certainly does not mean we should elide the very real bodily differences that can affect individual lives. Disability and visible difference have often been central features in the construction of freakishness, and there is a politics to this phenomenon,[12] but we must ask in tandem what makes one difference freakish and not another in a particular cultural moment. To understand this process of enfreakment we must understand the social context in which it is defined. Moreover, most academics are scholars of particular periods and locations, and having "situated" information enriches our understanding of all other aspects of that physical and temporal landscape. Currently, however, the vast majority of the scholarship on freak shows and on the construction of freaks has been situated in the United States, in part because of colossal figures such as P. T. Barnum, who has been read almost exclusively in his native American context. There has been no sustained exploration that historically and physically situates the phenomenon in nineteenth-century Britain or examines its impact on British Victorian consciousness. The work on U.S. culture has served as a model for the kind of scholarship contained in this collection, particularly as it points to the ways in which American culture shaped and was shaped by the structure and content of circuses, sideshows, and their performers. Chief among these works is Rosemarie Garland-Thomson's *Extraordinary Bodies: Figuring Disability in American Culture and Literature* and her fine collection, *Freakery*, which spans history and genre to speak to largely American "cultural spectacles" shaped around the "extraordinary body." Other important and pivotal studies are Leslie Fiedler's *Freaks: Myths and Images of the Secret Self* and Robert Bogdan's *Freak Show: Presenting Human Oddities for Amusement and Profit*. Also significant are Rachel Adams's *Sideshow U.S.A.: Freaks and the American Cultural Imagination*, James W. Cook's *The Arts of Deception: Playing with Fraud in the Age of Barnum*, Benjamin Reiss's *The Showman and the Slave: Race, Death, and Memory in Barnum's America*, and Janet M. Davis's *The Circus Age: Culture and Society Under the American Big Top*.[13] This superb work on freakery has provided the springboard for this project, and the general precepts of these arguments are often enormously valuable.

These writers point to the ways in which the production of performers in a particular space and time emerges from and helps shape the circulating social concerns. For example, Barnum advertised performers whom he billed as former slaves, exhibitions that were marketed to appeal to American patriotism, to both exploit and speak to the ongoing anxieties about the history of slavery, and to participate in the production of a new sense of Americanness. As Benjamin Reiss has argued, studying the strategies of such exhibitions is like "tak[ing] a tour of [American] antebellum cultural history."[14] James W. Cook concurs, calling these exhibits "the birthday of modern American popular culture."[15] He traces its initial "quintessentially antebellum American[ness]" and its ultimate transformation into a Barnumesque game of questions of truth and performance, calling the latter a form of "artful deception"[16] that he reads as a particularly American phenomenon. There is no equivalent study that focuses on Britain. Another fine study, John Kuo Wei Tchen's *New York Before Chinatown*,[17] examines the role of Orientalism in the creation of Americanness. His research considers the range of Asian exhibits, from Chang and Eng, the "Siamese Twins," to those who simply appeared on stage in Asian dress. He argues that responses to such performers were based on American ideological constructions of Orientalism—structures that reflected American values of race, difference, and national identity, not British notions of the same.

We must take up the lead offered by scholars like these and move toward situating freakery in the British context for Victorian studies scholars. In spite of the heavily American focus of most previous research, many of the people who figure our understanding of freakery appeared frequently in Victorian Britain, and the British were voracious consumers and producers of freakery. Joseph Merrick, the "Elephant Man," was born in and spent most of his life in England; Charles Stratton, known as "General Tom Thumb," was a favorite in the royal courts; Julia Pastrana, "The Nondescript," inspired English poets and novelists; and Krao Farini, "The Missing Link," appeared at the Westminster Aquarium in London. As Mathew Sweet has pointed out in one of the few studies that even speaks to England's consumption of freakery, "In Britain, the exhibition of bizarre curiosities—some living, some dead, some animal, some human—was a thriving industry throughout the eighteenth and nineteenth centuries."[18] Though this collection cannot offer an exhaustive or complete response to the critical questions about the place of the freak in Victorian Britain—indeed, as a body, these essays suggest that any notion of "containment" or "completeness" would ignore the multiplicity and fluidity that they also describe—it does offer a significant and engaging conversation about these issues. It attempts, for the first time, to throw the door open to questions about the context of British Victorian freakery, to take seriously Rachel Adams's sense that imbricated in the freak shows were "ruptures in the anticipated order of things."[19] If we hope to gesture toward the ways in which these ruptures figured social structures and social power, and also may have participated in social evolution, we must place them in their context.

Of course, this does not mean that we should ignore the transnational pollination, and the essays here cross the borders of the time and space they intend to illuminate in order to flesh out the differences and similarities between the U.S. and British contexts in richer ways. There is real value in understanding cross-cultural dialogues and in drawing out these relationships, but the distinctions are relevant as well. Even a cursory look at the British handbills produced for performers evidences the way in which they often bore the mark of English concerns and anxieties. Perhaps performers and their managers may have even chosen the itinerary for their tour because the identity they were continually constructing better suited the context of a particular set of cultural concerns. For example, an Irish or Indian performer had a different sociopolitical valence in England than he would in America, and notions of class were figured very differently in the United States than in Britain. The essays in this collection, however, will begin to develop a conversation around this field of concerns. While this project calls for more work on British freakery, work that can more clearly illuminate both differences and similarities and offer the kinds of comparative analyses that will enrich our understanding of both "normalcy" and "deviance" in a British context, these essays seek to locate—and, as we explain below, to dislocate—the Victorian freak.

Dislocating the Freak: Social Ambiguity

While we have argued that locating the freak is crucial, we must also attend to dislocation as well, exploring freakery's fluidity, political ambiguity, and, in Rachel Adams's term, "plasticity." Freak exhibitions in the nineteenth century did not offer stable definitions of the freak. Instead, they employed hyperbole, misrepresentation, elaborate costuming and staging, and narrative modes from the fantastic to the sentimental. They paired farce with medical description and scientific theories. These strategies made the freak exhibition a mélange of ideas, of propositions; and these propositions invited a range of affective responses from curiosity and wonder to horror and disgust—but they always evoked conversation. Medical science may have attempted to minimize ambiguity and eliminate contradiction, but even scientific narratives were often in conflict, which generated more debate. Exhibited freaks and their managers often exploited the tensions in these conversations, generating multiple, even contradictory interpretations of bodily and social meaning for and with its audiences. As Rachel Adams has argued, both performers and audiences actively participated in generating meanings at freak shows—live events that privileged audience engagement. Audience and performers were engaging with one another in a climate that confused the boundaries between self and other, normal and pathological, authenticity and fraudulence.[20]

Ambiguous bodies were not only commodified to produce a profit; they were a traffic in such ambiguous social meanings and controversy as well. Although promotional hype often proclaimed that the "original," ithentic," "biggest," or "smallest" was represented at the show, the ₀₋al of such advertising was not necessarily to persuade the public of the veracity of such claims but to provoke *profitable* conjecture. Freak shows attracted audiences by inviting the public to engage in epistemological speculation. Was the Feejee Mermaid a fake? Was the bearded lady really a man? Audiences paid for the opportunity to take a look and decide for themselves. Significantly, this interrogatory practice made freak shows volatile interpretive spaces that repeatedly called the boundary between the imaginary and the real into question, and by extension challenged the authority of discourses like medical science to name and explain the significance of the human body, as well as that of mainstream culture to determine all notions of normalcy. While profitable, such tension also begins to help us understand how such widespread cultural dialogue could produce cultural effects.

Much scholarly analysis of freak shows within the rubrics of cultural studies and disability studies proceeds from a commitment to contest discourses that naturalize race, gender, sexuality, and disability as categories describing bodily attributes rather than as structures that emerge from social relationships. They focus on rendering visible the effects of culture on freakery and of freakery on culture. Bogdan and Garland-Thomson agree that the freak show both authorized and delegitimated identities, but they part ways on who is enabled in the encounter between the freak and the observer. For Robert Bogdan, the present-day condemnation of freak shows reflects well-meaning but condescending assumptions about disability that were not shared by nineteenth-century performers and audiences. Bogdan argues that the majority of performers did not understand themselves to be exploited but preferred making a living with freak shows to the limited alternatives available to them in the mainstream.[21] In a critique of Bogdan's study, historian David Gerber argues that unequal social relations severely constrained the choices available to the people who became freak show performers and therefore compromised the "consent" Bogdan reads there.[22] Garland-Thomson's work looks to the ways in which the "othered" body serves as a marker for normalcy and absorbs anxieties embedded in the production of normalcy, notions that shift from culture to culture and over time.[23] Each of them agrees, however, that the formation of freak identity was a process, and one that was complexly inflected by the culture in which the freak emerged.

Here, we emphasize, as many of the essays in this collection do, the ways in which freakery operates through partial, shifting identifications—rather than stable oppositions and objectification—and that freaks were marked, figured, and refigured by the social and national context that both Bogdan and Garland-Thomson perceive as crucial. This is not to elide the exploitation of freak performers or the asymmetrical power relations between audiences and performers. It does, however, challenge us to imagine that, while freak shows did help to materialize the politically invested distinction between the normal and the pathological, the relationship between the terms was not always simple and was always heavily inflected by social engagement. Freaks provoked both identification and disavowal. The ambiguity, rhetorical excess, and ambivalence mobilized by the freak could work to oppose the standard for normalcy—to destabilize its naturalized status—as well as to produce and confirm it.

This "uneven" process, in Mary Poovey's terms,[24] made the meaning of exhibits (and the audiences that visited them) a question for speculation. Freak shows encouraged debate, which drew audiences and, in turn, became a part of a larger cultural dialogue. Whether or not it was always a conscious strategy—Barnum clearly chose it and excelled at it[25]—the process engaged the public. The details of two of Barnum's cases provide perhaps the most vivid example of the ways in which the freak was defined by and engaged in social debate and dialogue. When Madame Clofullia, a bearded woman, first exhibited herself in the 1850s, an "audience member" employed by Barnum objected that she was actually a man in women's clothing and filed a lawsuit. Several doctors, her husband, and her father all verified that she was a woman, and the courts dismissed the suit. The media, of course, followed the entire affair with interest, arousing curiosity and attracting crowds.[26] Likewise, when Barnum exhibited the Feejee Mermaid (a stuffed creature constructed from the body of a monkey sewn to the tail of a fish) in 1842, several naturalists publicly denounced the mermaid as impossible, and Barnum exploited this to his benefit. His advertisements maintained the uncertainty of the matter: "[It] is decidedly the most stupendous curiosity ever submitted to the public for inspection. If it is artificial the senses of sight and touch are ineffectual—if it is natural then all concur in declaring it *the greatest Curiosity in the World.*"[27] Although the disagreement in this case was between scientific opinion and the claims of showmen, Barnum presented it to the public as a controversy among scientists and invited the general public to weigh in on the matter. "Who is to decide," an advertisement asked, "when *doctors* disagree?" These tactics render visible the social engagement: the showman, the performer, the journalist, the scientist, and the public all participate in the process. Clearly, this kind of richly inflected conversation can reveal Victorian ideological investments in a host of issues, including those beyond freakery itself.

For example, while the debates framing freak exhibitions and performances were driven by a desire for profit, rather than to challenge prevailing political structures, the social dialogue they produced often achieved both ends. These gestures tapped into the investments of audiences in ongoing social conflicts regarding "the Woman Question," the emergent hegemony of the professional class, empire, and scientific advances. While the marketing strategies for an exhibit such as the Feejee Mermaid were a means of preempting charges of fraud and producing an audience, they appealed in part because they challenged the exclusiveness of scientific opinion and publicly extended a general invitation to participate in what was constructed as a scientific debate. Bearded ladies such as Madame Clofullia and the famous Julia Pastrana supplied a level of double entendre to women's rights certainly not anticipated by nineteenth-century suffragists and their opponents. The claim that Clofullia was a fraud provoked speculation about her gender identity and, by implication, adamantly asserted two unambiguously distinct sexes, setting the stage for a spectacular announcement that she was indeed a woman with a full beard. This announcement unsettled prevailing assumptions about the distinctions between male and female bodies at a historical moment in which feminists and their opponents alike were invoking physiological explanations for sex difference to authorize their political claims.

Indeed, as Christopher Hals Gylseth and Lars O. Toverud suggest, the Victorians seemed to have been haunted by the figure of the bearded woman. These authors quote at length a poem by Arthur Munby called "Pastrana,"[28] in which the narrator describes an encounter with the bearded lady. His account suggests a gendered slipperiness that undermines not only notions of femininity, but also—perhaps as a corollary—notions of masculinity as well:

Perhaps she would get at me, after all!
If the links should break, I might well feel small,
Young as I was, and strong and tall,
    And blest with a human shape,
To see myself foil'd in that lonely place
By a desperate brute with a monstrous face,

And hugg'd to death in the foul embrace
   Of a loathly angry ape.[29]

Though the narrator is young and strong and tall, the very epitome of
masculinity, he is undone by the power of the bearded lady. In whatever way the culture attempts to manage and chain her into place,
"the links [might] break," and when she is set loose, the boundaries
of gender determinacy are crossed. She threatens the narrator with an
"embrace" so powerful that it would "foil" him, undo his masculine
power, make him feel "small." The imagined embrace, however, also
implies the eroticized attraction of Pastrana and other bearded women.[30]
This complex series of tensions offered more than simply the shock
value of this singular difference, as this poem suggests. They preoccupied
the Victorian imagination because they suggested a kind of slipperiness
of identity that threatened to undermine gender codes, a phenomenon
that was occurring in a host of ways culturewide. Where a discomfit-
ing cultural disruption was already taking place—every novel, book of
manners, and household guide was engaged in the struggle to define
gender—the bearded woman seemed to underscore a radical instability
of the norm. The narrator of the poem has no power against her; she is
only contained by the uncertain chains. Clearly, her size and strength
are metaphors for the danger—as well as the attraction—of boundary transgression. They reveal the allure and drama of the freak that
engaged the culture at large.

   The social tensions described in these examples could not have
existed in a vacuum. They exploited ideological tensions already in
place, as well as public interest in social conflicts. Some exhibits encouraged skepticism toward experts (like the Feejee Mermaid), but others
(like Julia Pastrana) utilized medical authority to assert their authenticity. Some performers were self-consciously complex in their presentation—and in a way challenged the overt characterization offered by
the freak show. Historian David Gerber proposes and then repudiates
the conclusion that the comedic self-parody of Charles Stratton's performances as the famous, diminutive General Tom Thumb might be
considered acts of defiance. However, it is precisely Stratton's refusal to
play his roles seriously and the self-referential dimension of this humor
that foregrounded his performances as performances that would have
worked to complicate the caricature of Tom Thumb, if not to create
a palpable distinction between "Stratton the man doing the performance" and Tom Thumb. Like Stratton, other quite famous freak show

performers turned the hyperbole and contradictions of freak show hype to parodic effect. For instance, Krao Farini, a Laotian woman covered with hair, was exhibited as a missing link at the London Aquarium, and a photograph of her as a child pictures her dressed in animal skins against a jungle setting. As a young adult she continued to be billed as a missing link—who spoke five languages and dressed in fine clothing. The irony of Farini's performances as an educated, well-dressed "missing link" with fine manners exposes the "missing link" narrative as a construction and insists on her humanity. At the very least, Farini called attention to her outrageous displays as performances rather than authentic representations. In doing so, she created a tension between her enfreakment and her humanity, and they exploited this tension as a source of entertainment. The practice of exhibiting people of color as "missing links" confirmed prevailing racial hierarchies that denied the humanity of nonwhite people, but these processes were never stable or complete. Farini's complexly inflected performances as a "missing link" enacted a reversal that makes the definition of humanness a question rather than the self-evident, natural result of evolution. These tensions make evolution recognizable as a political discourse.

Nineteenth-century freaks and freak shows generated multiple, often contradictory interpretations because freak show practices for exciting public interest put interpretation of the explicitly contradictory evidence in the hands of the culture at large. Moreover, the performers themselves refused to fall into simple categorizations. The freak exhibition was as likely to reproduce the status quo as it was to produce politically subversive effects (or to do both at once). While there were many gestures that attempted to codify normality and its difference from those at the margins with reference to the freak, the slipperiness of freakery made this reference disruptive and created a threatening dislocation of terms. Not only did this process draw in audiences, but it also reveals a rich array of culturally situated tensions and invites us to explore them, to understand what they might have meant in Victorian Britain.

Developing the Context, Examining the Effects

The essays in this collection plumb the question of context in many different ways, and their concerns spring from those precipitated by much early work on freakery. Whereas other critics have discussed the ways in which definitions of normalcy were generated by marginalizing various groups of people, these essays look to press this question further, opening an exploration of the ways in which freakery emerged in a particular social context and may have even participated in social change and in the politics of mainstream culture. As Rachel Adams has argued, the vast majority of criticism has assumed a kind of docile silence on the part of both the freaks themselves and their audience. This has even translated into a sensibility that imagines that freaks were distant from "ordinary" people and removed from everyday life. Adams resists the notion of freak show silence, however, arguing that "freaks talk back, the experts lose their authority, the audience refuses to take their seats."[31] This collection looks for this dialogue in subtle and explicit ways. The essays on imperialism, for example, look to the way in which discourses of science—from Darwinian theory to medicine—were joined to freakery and deployed to do scientific work and work of empire. These essays also explore and speak to the tensions in British self-definition between consumer desire and material self-control. Others look at the relationship between the freak and the audience and the use of freakishness as a metaphor in other culturally marginal contexts. In all of these ways, these essays ask how freaks "talked back" to mainstream culture in Britain and how this helped shape mainstream culture. The authors here examine freaks' pitch narratives, product advertisements, handbills, newspaper accounts, medical debates and texts, art, literature, cartes de visite, and diaries. Future research might explore the ways in which the British theater, museum, and publishing industries affected notions of freakishness and think about how British involvement in the West Indies and Africa also shaped cultural concepts of freakery.

Overall, the essays here attempt to centralize the question of cultural impact to move beyond individual psychology. When people watched Julia Pastrana—most of whose entire body was covered in coarse black hair—dance and sing on stage, they had more than simply an individual or personal experience. Those moments were also social events that affected life inside and outside the freak show. Poets, gentlemen, and prose writers such as Arthur Munby memorialized their experience of her for a Victorian audience. This cultural exchange was no less lively when her manager-husband had Pastrana and her infant embalmed, stuffed, encased in glass, and put on tour again after their birthing bed deaths. What this meant in Victorian Britain was something different from what it meant in America, or France, or any other part of the world.

The collection is structured to highlight and begin to flesh out several of these themes. It opens with part I, "Marketing and Consuming Freakery," in which the first essay, by Heather McHold, called "Even As You and I: Freak Shows and Lay Discourse on Spectacular Deformity," examines the way in which the medical community competed with freak shows for the right to define freakery, suggesting that the latter succeeded by incorporating bourgeois normalcy into freak show rhetoric. Joyce Huff's "Freaklore: The Dissemination, Fragmentation, and Reinvention of the Legend of Daniel Lambert, King of Fat Men" suggests that, though this seven-hundred-pound jailer died by the early nineteenth century, images of him proliferated decades later, and he became an icon in the shifting focus of economic theory from production to consumption and his eating a valorizing synecdoche for all consumer activity in Victorian England. Finally, Timothy Neil's "White Wings and Six-Legged Muttons: The Freakish Animal" discusses the exhibited animal in the Victorian period, contending that the predominance of a human narrative context constructed all such animals as freaks and helped figure human freakishness as well. Together these essays look at the evolution and use of the discourse of freakery in Victorian Britain, examining its deployment in mainstream culture from medicine to consumerism, religion, and entertainment.

In part II, "Science, Medicine, and the Social," Meegan Kennedy's "'Poor Hoo Loo': Sentiment, Stoicism, and the Grotesque in British Imperial Medicine" explores the role of imperial and Orientalist ideologies in understanding and responding to the medical anomaly of Hoo Loo, an Asian man with an enormous tumor. Mapping the medical discourse of the day against racial rhetoric provides insight into another aspect of Orientalism. Christine C. Ferguson examines Dr. Frederick Treves's famous case history of "Elephant Man" Joseph Merrick in the context of Victorian discourses of mutism and linguistic evolution. Ferguson argues that the narrative enacts a triumph of language in which the animality of the freak is (partially) abated through his cultivation of a voice and the linguistic skills—speaking, reading, and writing—foregrounded in Darwinian accounts of human identity. This section looks at how the medical and scientific worlds marked and were marked by freakery. By plumbing various concrete examples, it asks how freakery was a part of social institutions, such as medicine and science, that affected every Victorian's life. Nadja Durbach's "The Missing Link and the Hairy Belle: Krao and the Victorian Discourses of Evolution, Imperialism, and Primitive Sexuality" tackles the perceived evidence of Darwin's theories in the body of Krao. Durbach's careful examination reveals, however, that much more than scientific discourse was embedded in the rhetoric of evolution and the exhibition of Krao. Both were intimately linked to imperialism and the sexuality of the colonized woman.

Durbach's essay provides a fine transition to part III, "Empire, Race, and Commodity." In this section, Marlene Tromp's "Empire and the Indian Freak: The 'Miniature Man' from Cawnpore and the 'Marvellous Indian Boy' on Tour in England" explores the rendering of Indian freaks and reads their publicity materials and the scientific studies about them in the context of sociopolitical concerns regarding India as a colony. She argues that such performers and the rhetoric around them both exploited and undermined the beliefs that buttressed imperialism. Kelly Hurley's "The Victorian Mummy-Fetish: H. Rider Haggard, Frank Aubrey, and the White Mummy" investigates imperial Gothic fiction at the British fin de siècle, to ask how the mummy, particularly the white mummy in "lost white civilization" novels, comes to serve as an uncanny double for the Western subject, a process both fearsome and pleasurable, a process with parallels to that of enfreakment. Finally, Rebecca Stern's essay, "Our Bear Women, Ourselves: Affiliating with Julia Pastrana," explores popular depictions of Pastrana's live exhibitions in the 1850s alongside the subsequent exhibition of her embalmed corpse in the 1860s to explore national identity and gender. Pastrana's dark-complexioned, hair-covered body crystallizes in reverse a prescription for Victorian white womanhood, warning that one ought not to be a spectacle. The essays in this section suggest that we must reckon with freakery in order to enrich our understanding of Victorian imperialism.

Martha Stoddard Holmes's essay, "Queering the Marriage Plot: Wilkie Collins's *The Law and the Lady*," opens part IV, "Reading and Spectating the Freak," which begins to look at the role of artistic representation in the social work of freakery. Stoddard Holmes suggests that, though critics have argued that people with disabilities were publicly reinscribed as objects of charity by the end of the eighteenth century, the fiction of the nineteenth century demonstrates the ways in which disabled bodies keep alive erotic curiosity as much as they did sympathy. Melissa Free's "Freaks That Matter: The Dolls' Dressmaker, The Doctor's Assistant, and the Limits of Difference" also looks at fiction to explore the way in which Victorian culture valued at least some of the potential contributions of freaks—unless those figures were also marked by alternative sexualities. "Queer" figures were likely to be "sacrificed" for the social good. Finally, Christopher Smit deploys Levinas's idea of collaboration and "responsibility" to reconsider notions of the freak as an exploited or abused victim of the photographer. In "A Collaborative Aesthetic: Levinas's Idea of Responsibility and the Photographs of Charles Eisenmann and the Late Nineteenth-Century Freak-Performer," Smit argues that it was a much more mutually engaged process that valued physical difference rather than degrading it. In these artistic productions, we can see both how mainstream Victorian culture articulated freakery and how such notions were disseminated to the public.

As a body, these essays attempt to explore the impact of the freak on the nineteenth-century consciousness and social practices. While the concept of the freak and the practices associated with freakery were emerging across the world and had a visible (and critically traceable) relationship to the United States, freakery is no less crucial to understanding Victorian England. Though P. T. Barnum was an American son, his sideshows were in rich conversation with English past and present. Many of those figures who define our contemporary understanding of freaks—indeed, many of Barnum's "human curiosities"—came from England. Rather than eliding the differences between the United States and England, these essays seek to examine the fruitful exchange between the two continents and with lands across Asia, Africa, and South America. This little-explored landscape is illuminated here with the hope that it will open further dialogue on the role of freakery in England's evolving political and social world and the role of England in the evolving concept of freakery. The significant impact of disability studies, postcolonial studies, and queer studies on cultural, historical, and literary studies is also evident in these essays, and this collection seeks to speak to those fields as well as to scholars of the Victorian period to ask how freaks are situated in such a way as to reveal much about the culture and the period.

Notes

1. I have chosen to use this term—like Rosemarie Garland-Thomson, Elizabeth Grosz, and Rachel Adams—for an array of reasons. What Garland-Thomson calls "freak discourse" has particular resonance in the nineteenth century, but the word "freak" is also apt for two political reasons relevant to this study: first, because of the potentially political reclamation of the term, a concept I will discuss further below, and second, because of what Adams calls the "plasticity" of the word—"freaks" is so fluid that it "cannot be aligned with any particular identity or ideological position." See Rachel Adams, *Sideshow U.S.A.: Freaks and the American Cultural Imagination* (Chicago: University of Chicago Press, 2001), 10.

2. Rosemarie Garland-Thomson, ed., *Freakery: Cultural Spectacles of the Extraordinary Body* (New York: New York University Press, 1996), 4.

3. Ibid., 2.

4. Mary Russo, *The Female Grotesque: Risk, Excess and Modernity* (New York: Routledge, 1994), 8.

5. Ibid., 56.

6. Cindy LaCom, "'It Is More Than Lame': Female Disability, Sexuality, and the Maternal in the Nineteenth-Century Novel," in *The Body and Physical Difference: Discourses of Disability,* ed. David T. Mitchell and Sharon L. Snyder (Ann Arbor: University of Michigan Press, 1997), 199.

7. Judith Butler, *Gender Trouble* (New York: Routledge, 1990), 64; see also *Bodies That Matter* (New York: Routledge), 1993.

8. Anne Fausto-Sterling, *Sexing the Body* (New York: Basic Books, 2000), 21, emphasis in original.

9. Ibid., 58–59.

10. Actor Jamie Lee Curtis, whose womanhood few would question, is reportedly androgen insensitive.

11. Robert Bogdan, *Freak Show: Presenting Human Oddities for Amusement and Profit* (Chicago: University of Chicago Press, 1988), 24.

12. This body of essays acknowledges the critical role that disability studies has played in our understanding of freaks, from Garland-Thomson's work to Lennard J. Davis's *Enforcing Normalcy: Disability, Deafness, and the Body* and collections such as *The Body and Physical Difference,* edited by David T. Mitchell and Sarah L. Snyder. They also suggest that our responses might include and complicate these notions, particularly suggesting that the collapse of such binaries cannot accommodate all of the ways in which we might understand freakishness or its social effects.

13. Rosemarie Garland-Thomson, *Extraordinary Bodies: Figuring Physical Disability in American Culture and Literature* (New York: Columbia University Press, 1996); Leslie A. Fiedler, *Freaks: Myths and Images of the Secret Self* (New York: Simon and Schuster, 1979); James W. Cook, *The Arts of Deception: Playing with Fraud in the Age of Barnum* (Cambridge, MA: Harvard University Press, 2001); Benjamin Reiss, *The Showman and The Slave: Race, Death, and Memory in Barnum's America* (Cambridge, MA: Harvard University Press, 2001); and Janet M. Davis, *The Circus Age: Culture and Society Under the American Big Top* (Chapel Hill: University of North Carolina Press, 2002).

14. Reiss, 6.

15. Cook, 3.

16. Ibid., 13.

17. John Kuo Wei Tchen, *New York Before Chinatown: Orientalism and the Shaping of American Culture, 1776–1882* (Baltimore, MD: Johns Hopkins University Press, 2001).

18. Mathew Sweet, *Inventing the Victorians* (New York: St. Martin's Press, 2001), 140.

19. Adams, 13.

20. Peggy Phelan makes an argument for live performances as enacting a nonreproductive economy of meaning in "The Ontology of Performance: Representation

Without Reproduction," in *Unmarked* (New York: Routledge, 1993), 146–66; see especially 150–52.

21. Bogdan, 34.

22. David Gerber, "The 'Careers' of People Exhibited in Freak Shows: The Problem of Volition and Valorization," in Garland-Thomson, *Freakery*, 43.

23. Garland-Thomson, *Extraordinary Bodies*.

24. See Mary Poovey, *Uneven Developments* (Chicago: University of Chicago Press, 1988).

25. See Eric Fretz, "P. T. Barnum's Theatrical Selfhood and the Nineteenth-Century Culture of Exhibition," in Garland-Thomson, *Freakery*, 97–107.

26. Bogdan, 228.

27. Neil T. Harris, *Humbug: The Art of P. T. Barnum* (Boston: Little, Brown, 1973), 65. See also Cook on this important theme.

28. Christopher Hals Gylseth and Lars O. Toverud, *Julia Pastrana: The Tragic Life of the Victorian Ape Woman*, trans. Donald Tumasonis (Thrupp, UK: Sutton Publishing, 2003). They argue that after seeing Pastrana, Munby was "seriously shaken, mentally and physically" and feared she might "get [him]" (31–32).

29. Cited in ibid., 33.

30. The bearded lady not only undermined stable notions of gender identity but also evoked the ultimate marker of femaleness, the uncovered vagina. It was often figured, unsettlingly, however, as the "vagina dentata," a devouring and threatening version of femaleness that simultaneously seduces men and severs the "source" of their power. Julia Pastrana's case serves to illustrate this metaphor in the obsessive and inaccurate assertion—even taken up even by Charles Darwin—that Pastrana had a double set of teeth (see ibid.).

31. Adams, 13.

PART I

Marketing and Consuming Freakery

THE ESSAYS in this section are attempts to open some broader questions, through examination of particular material examples of freakery. Heather McHold's essay serves as an introduction to the debates about who had the authority to demand ownership of and talking rights on "freakery," examining P. T. Barnum in the context of his English reception. While her discussion reveals the role of performance advertisements and a rhetoric of middle-class respectability on medical discourse specifically, her argument also challenges us to think through what other British institutions might have been competing to create or might have been in part created by the discourse of freakery. Joyce Huff's essay on Daniel Lambert and cultural rhetoric of consumption speaks to specifically British notions of consumption and class dynamics. Her essay provides an English refiguration of scholarship on American consumer capitalism and freakery. Finally, Timothy Neil's essay offers a unique look at another freak discourse—that of animal freaks—to investigate the nineteenth-century English obsession with enfreakment. Based on rarely seen archival materials from the British National Fairgrounds Archive, his essay focuses on the role animal freaks played in relation to human freakishness.

EVEN AS YOU AND I

Freak Shows and Lay Discourse on
Spectacular Deformity

HEATHER McHOLD

But for one particular trick which Dame Nature has played each one of them, these sports of Fortune are just men and women, with the feelings and habits, the likes and dislikes, the occupations and amusements of the rest of the world.

—*The Strand Magazine* (February 1898)

Introduction

In the late 1880s an English poster announced the marriage of Patrick O'Brien and Christanna D. Dunz. It declared: "When the Reverend Mr. Ruoff began the marriage service [at the Protestant Church in New York City] there was perfect silence. The groom's response came in a sharp, clear voice, while the bride's was smothered by tears. When the service was over . . . the groom . . . fumbled around in a clumsy way . . . then gave [the veil] a quick twitch, and bending down, kissed the bride with a smack which resounded through the whole church, and caused a hearty round o[f] applause."[1] While Christanna's tears and Patrick's composure would have appealed to contemporary gender expectations that brides appear emotional and grooms brave, the O'Briens' marriage ceremony was controversial in other ways. Despite the fact that both the Episcopal and Anglican churches deemed marriage a sacrament, Patrick and Christanna reported that this New York wedding was the third time they had married each other.[2] Those who performed superfluous wedding ceremonies had vociferous critics, including, for example, a contributor to the *Brooklyn Eagle*, who complained that P. T. Barnum made a practice of "turning the solemn rites of marriage into a public entertainment for the gaping crowd of curiosity hunters."[3] Nevertheless, for the O'Briens and many other Victorian couples, the spectacle of the marriage ceremony and the fantasies it evoked were far more important than the wedding's liturgical importance.

The O'Briens had a special interest in spectacular marriage ceremonies because they were both close to eight feet tall and were exhibiting as giants in late-Victorian London. This account of their marriage also reported the dates and times that the couple would exhibit in London, and as a deliberate marketing document, this handbill is especially useful to historians of culture. The narratives that showmen put forward as they sought paying audiences for human oddities were shaped by contemporary ideologies and designed to temper historically specific tensions. Indeed, patterns within the advertisements for what Victorians called "freak shows" suggest that the market success of those exhibiting as freaks relied largely on their ability to encourage curiosity in physical oddness without aggravating intense British cultural anxiety about the spectacle trade, physical degeneration, and working-class leisure. Indeed, while Americans savored hucksterism and prized the sassy defiance that mass culture presented to the values of social and intellectual elites as essential elements of Jacksonian national identity, tomfoolery, crowds, and class insubordination caused considerably more social and cultural tension in late-Victorian Britain. In order to help alleviate intensifying British antipathy toward itinerate freak show stars and their display before working-class crowds, late-Victorian showmen consistently put new emphasis on how those exhibiting their physical deformities expressed respect for gender difference, domestic virtue, hard work, productivity, and consumerism.

This specific selection of qualities was significant, for these were the priorities of British Evangelicalism and had become the distinct markers of respectable middle-class identity.[4] Ultimately, the handbills, memoirs, posters, and journal articles publicizing Victorian human oddities reveal the expansion of middle-class ideologies and the British Evangelical tradition into one of the most unstable sectors of working-class society.

Using social reactions to human oddities and monsters in order to track contemporary cultural priorities is not new. Historians have shown that in ancient times, responses to severe deformity reflected contemporary notions of fate, and before the Enlightenment, most communities expressed their general feelings of human insignificance and lack of control by tracing human anomalies to supernatural forces, divine will, or excessive maternal imagination.[5] In the early Renaissance, Europeans expressed their growing faith in an omnipotent but benevolent God by arguing that God made monsters to punish humankind and to encourage penitence for sins such as greed, blasphemy, idleness, and insubordination.[6] In the seventeenth century, the intellectual connection between deformity and sin lessened to some extent, and Europeans began to value cases of remarkable deformity as fascinating products of the natural universe. In fact, Katherine Park and Lorraine Daston have used monstrosity's late seventeenth-century representations to track the growth of a Baconian, "catalogue everything," methodology in natural science.[7] They explain that by the eighteenth century, monsters had become desirable objects for curiosity cabinets and private museums, and they note that, on the popular level, the market in spectacular exhibitions flourished as communities flocked to see examples of "Nature's wonderful diversity." Dennis Todd adds that during this period of increasing social mobility, "men of taste" also expressed growing fears of social disorder and began to complain that the popular exhibition of monsters and other wonders of nature encouraged mental laziness and lawlessness.[8]

Unfortunately, modern European historians have largely ignored the cultural history of late-Victorian freak shows. Scholars who have looked at the subject have generally limited their research to the question, "What were the various kinds of freaks?" They have catalogued the kinds of human anomalies on exhibit, but most have failed to analyze the social construction of freak identity and its historical specificity. Two prevailing assumptions have discouraged research on European freak shows. First, many historians assume that spectacular exhibitions had lost their cultural significance by 1850 because an early-Victorian regulatory campaign had closed most of the traditional fairs where human anomalies had exhibited.[9] Second, historians have also assumed that modern medical knowledge had made freak shows obsolete by 1850 by removing the mysteries behind human deformity.

Both of these theories deserve review. Freak shows outlasted the legislative assault on the old fairs by developing a more corporate approach to their industry and moving exhibitions into grand halls such as Astley's Theatre, the Egyptian Hall in Piccadilly, the Alhambra in Leicester Square, the Royal Aquarium, Piccadilly Hall, and St. James' Hall.

Moreover, claims that medical knowledge quashed popular curiosity in human anomalies by 1850 also prove inaccurate. The scientific study of deformity's causes in a new field called teratology was far from secure at the end of the nineteenth century, and medical knowledge had only a marginal role in the popular culture of sideshows. In fact, sideshow managers used medical testimony selectively to increase wonder rather than dispel it, and audiences continued to flock to freak shows well into the 1890s.

Moreover, the late nineteenth-century cultural history of spectacular exhibitions deserves more attention specifically because, as the literary critic Mary Poovey argues, issues that contemporaries constitute as problems "mark the limits of ideological certainty,"[10] and because, while human anomalies had long contributed to concerns about the boundaries of normalcy and raised fears of social disorder, the French scientist B. A. Morel presented a theory of degeneracy in 1857 that created a new level of anxiety about deformity across Europe. Morel intensified Victorian uneasiness with deformity and exhibition culture by suggesting that physical weaknesses or degenerate traits (1) progressed and intensified with age, (2) were produced by intemperate living, and (3) were dominant in heredity.[11] By the 1880s Victorian degeneracy theorists were arguing that people with deformities were sure to become an increasing burden on society and that families showing physical oddities would undermine national stamina if their reproduction was not regulated through eugenics.[12] The rise of Morel's degeneracy theory meant that the deformed raised concerns about more than the bounds of normalcy; they also began to feed rising anxieties about Britain's racial and political decline.

At the same time, the long-standing complaints that spectacular exhibitions and popular fairs encouraged social anarchy, sexual license, and violence continued.[13] The deformed who exhibited themselves for profit sparked social anxiety because they were often itinerant show people who, as they traveled from fair to fair, seemed independent of society's stabilizing institutions: family and parish. Moreover, fair patrons themselves also inspired considerable anxiety. As licensing advocates were quick to point out, fairs had, since the mid-eighteenth century, been attracting fewer middle-class families while the overall number of working-class patrons grew.[14] This was a time when bourgeois writers described working-class men as "brutes . . . brought up in the darkness of barbarism," and reports of rowdy and promiscuous mobs of working-class fairgoers commonly made it into the press.[15]

Despite managerial attempts to secure the respectability of spectacular exhibitions by moving them from fairgrounds into grand halls, exhibition stars and their promoters remained on the outlying borders of decency. As Peter Bailey explains, "Next to the pub . . . the music halls became the most embattled institution in working-class life, as reform groups strove variously to close them, censor them or reproduce their essential appeal in facsimile counter-attractions purged of vulgarity."[16] As a result, articulating the respectability of human oddities became essential to profits.[17] Freak show promoters began to put unprecedented emphasis on the personal qualities of the exhibited deformed, and in 1898 the journalist Arthur Goddard clarified the common strategy for Victorian freak advertisers in a remarkably self-conscious article titled "'Even as You and I,' at Home with the Barnum Freaks."[18] Applying the relatively new form of the personal interview, Goddard constructed typical promotional biographies for several well-known exhibition figures and emphasized details such as marital status, work history, manners, and material possessions.[19] As he did so, Goddard argued explicitly that visiting these freaks at home made him especially able to conclude that these stars were "normal" despite their physical oddities. Notably, as Goddard insisted that "these sports of Fortune are just men and women, with the feelings and habits, the likes and dislikes, the occupations and amusements of the rest of the world," his "rest of the world" was not just the able-bodied but specifically those respectable folk who honored their families, respected gender boundaries, worked hard, and hoped for material success.[20] Ultimately, the narrative choices in late-Victorian freak show documents reveal that showmen believed that extending notions of bourgeois respectability to human oddities would draw audiences.

This trend was consistent with a cultural shift in the British working class more broadly. From mid-century, the notion of respectability had become increasingly popular among music hall performers and the working classes that made up the majority of freak show audiences, and these groups expressed respectability in specific ways. As Lois Rutherford reveals, from the 1860s music hall dancers and singers expressed their own respectability in terms of "acquiring a respectful independence by means of providential collective self-help, typically associated with upwardly mobile artisans and skilled workers."[21] Nevertheless, for regular-bodied entertainers, these claims were auxiliary to performance announcements. Handbills for these performers very rarely mentioned whether the dancer, singer, or musician was polite, nice, or well educated.[22]

In freak discourse, by contrast, the personal expression of respectability took center stage. In an attempt to moderate the intense social and cultural suspicion of the exhibited deformed, British showmen told stories about the exhibited freaks that elevated the values traditionally affiliated with the puritanical middle class. For example, show barkers sought status for the deformed by emphasizing how the exhibited expressed and valued a strong work ethic, self-sufficiency, gender propriety, and polite behavior.[23] That said, it is important to recognize that showmen were more concerned with profits than accurately representing how freaks actually lived. As advertisers presented the respectability of freaks in historically specific ways, they were most interested in exploiting the societal assumption that deformity precluded respectability. Show barkers traded in irony rather than accuracy. Yet however romantically ironic, and even specifically because of their self-conscious irony, the marketing biographies of late-Victorian freaks tell an important tale about the expansion of British middle-class ideologies into working-class consciousness.

Spinning Freak Biographies

The marriage ceremony figured centrally in late-Victorian advertisements for giants and dwarfs. Indeed, this advertising theme was so consistent that few remained single. In addition to the O'Brien wedding, other spectacular ceremonies featured the midget Don Santiago de Los Santos and a similarly small woman, the giants Colonel Bates and Anna Swan, the midgets General Mite and Lucia Zarate, and Minnie Warren (sister of Lavinia, who was married to General Tom Thumb) and fellow midget Commodore Nutt. In addition to recognizing that marriage had long been a marker of respectable bourgeois adulthood, freak show marriage ceremonies reflected the increasing popularity of formal marriage among the working class. Interestingly, as John Gillis points out, while registering a marriage became more attractive to the working class after mid-century, civil marriage was a more popular option for those who sought to save expenses.[24] Not surprisingly, for human oddities seeking to impress audiences, the church ceremony, with all of its implications for pomp and publicity, was the rule.

Showmen did more than emphasize the pairings themselves. They also bolstered the appeal of their investments by clarifying that the freak marriages functioned. For most couples, this meant that show barkers

reported that babies were born. Barnum so valued the legitimacy children gave to marriages that when Tom Thumb and his wife, Lavinia,
proved barren, Barnum rented a baby for them. When it became incon-
venient to keep up the ruse, Barnum reported that the child had died.
The appeal of this farce was remarkably long lasting. More than thirty
years later, an article in *The Strand Magazine* reported that "In 1866,
Mrs. Stratton presented her husband with a baby, which, however, died
early, of inflammation of the brain."[25] In the 1880s another giant named
O'Brien and his wife Annie joined their peers in spectacular parent-
hood. They increased the efficacy with which their "baby" promoted
their exhibition and marked their creation of a nuclear family by naming him Brian O'Brien.[26]

Productive work also figured as a marker of desirable normalcy in
late-Victorian freak show narratives to the extent that F. M. L. Thompson's description of the respectable working class applies to exhibition
freaks. Exhibited human anomalies wanted audiences to know that, like
other aspiring members of the lower working class, they were "fiercely
self-reliant and determined to live on their own resources and to not
suffer the indignities of poor relief, charity, or ruinous debt."[27] Those on
display expressed their shared faith in the respectable value of work by
recounting work histories, family traditions of employment, prejudice
against malingerers, and even pride in financial success. For example,
the biographers of Robert Hales, the Norfolk giant, reported that Hales
had worked as a wherryman before he "set up in the Craven Head
Tavern, Drury Lane."[28] There, in addition to being both exhibit and
licensed victualler, Hales claimed to be a "Professor of Galvanism."[29]
In a similar vein, Joseph Merrick, the Elephant Man, dedicated half of
his late-century, six-paragraph autobiography to his employment history
and reported that he had worked making cigars, peddling with a license,
and then "hawking on [his] own account."[30]

Other freak show stars emphasized that they came from families
that valued hard work. For example, Charles Tripp, a famous armless
man, reported that he was the son of an engineer who had worked on
the Grand Trunk Railway in Canada.[31] Eli Bowen, a legless success,
informed audiences that he had passed on a good work ethic to his
offspring by bragging that his son had become an attorney and justice
of the peace in America.[32] Joseph Merrick recounted the humiliation
he felt when his inability to find work brought censure from his family.
He wrote: "When I went home for my meals, my step-mother used to
say I had not been to seek for work. I was taunted and sneered at so

that I would not go home to my meals, and used to stay in the streets with an hungry belly rather than [suffer her criticism that] 'That's more than you have earned.'"[33] In fact, Merrick so valued his identity as an effective member of society that he failed to mention the time he spent in the Leicester workhouse (which was four years) and described himself only as a patient in the Leicester infirmary.[34]

Freak show texts also presented the deformed as "respectable and normal workers" by highlighting exhibited people's financial independence and trade success. For example, accounts of Millie-Christine, who were born as slaves in North Carolina, declared that the twins had purchased their own freedom with their profits from exhibiting and would soon emancipate their parents.[35] Tom Thumb's financial success was the most remarked upon, and in 1894 *The Strand* noted that Tom Thumb brought in more than 150,000 pounds during his European tour of 1845 and 1847.[36]

Victorian showmen also expressed the growing influence of middle-class ideology in what was largely a working-class discourse by emphasizing consumerism among freaks. Time and again, showmen used products to depict the deformed as respectable participants in British society and suggested that exhibited freaks shared the middle class's interest in domesticity, financial security, and leisure time. Notably, the growing significance of consumer goods in freak discourse was consistent with a larger cultural trend to affiliate products with success and other cultural values.[37] As they linked the deformed with possessions that held increasing cultural meaning, freak show promoters articulated both the growing national fascination with abundance and the fantasy that all Britons might come to enjoy a surplus of civilizing consumer products.[38]

The props of a comfortable domestic life figured most prominently and consistently. For example, Laloo, a boy with a parasitic twin, usually appeared seated on a fringed Victorian chair or standing with his arm resting on a fancy chair in a room adorned with wallpaper and a framed picture of a boat.[39] The joined twins Rosalie and Josephine Blazek, known as the Pygopagi twins, stood for their exhibition portrait on a plush ottoman in a well-appointed parlour.[40] Tom Thumb highlighted his disposable income and good taste by showcasing his miniature carriage.[41] Like Tom Thumb also, Millie-Christine appeared in a variety of outfits. While the twins' dresses ranged from simple smocks to well-tailored bodices and skirts in rich fabrics, they consistently wore double strands of pearls.[42] The armless Jeanne Rosalie Raymon also adorned herself well.[43]

She appeared with a watch as well as a feathered hat. Other commonly featured possessions included fine boots, jewels, and books.

In addition to paying homage to good taste and disposable income, product images appealed to the Victorian belief that leisure time distinguished the respectable. Not surprisingly, freak show narratives differentiated between how men and women ought to spend their free time. Representations of male exhibition figures often featured a variety of athletic activities. For example, illustrations of Chang and Eng showed them hunting, rowing, playing badminton, and fishing with the appropriate equipment and attire.[44] In a similar manner, Arthur Goddard sought to make his readers at home with a sword swallower, Delno Fritz, by noting that this exhibition star was "a devoted cyclist, and something of an amateur baseball player."[45] With such images, showmen took advantage of a growing cultural discourse that affiliated amateur athleticism with respectability.[46] As Peter Bailey explains, the mid-Victorian middle class, who had had access to sports through the public schools, became increasingly interested in how athletics might foster the nation's military preparedness and desirable capitalist values. These beliefs continued into the twentieth century, when one writer explained that "Manly sports, as they should be played, tend to develop unselfish pluck, determination, self-control and public spirit."[47]

The leisure activities that female freaks claimed to pursue were also gender appropriate. These, by contrast, tended to assert the human oddity's modesty and dedication to domesticity. The giant Leah May, for example, made a point of why she did not like to bicycle. Using irony to good effect, May explained that she had not joined many New Women in this activity because she did not wish to make a spectacle of herself. "I have always wanted to very much," she declared with presumed reserve, "but think what a machine for me would look like!"[48] Instead of bicycling, May filled her time with domestic pursuits, for example, "embroidering an intricate pattern for a tablecloth or some such piece of feminine handiwork."[49] Many female oddities claimed to have similar, domestic-centered interests. For example, when Goddard visited the bearded woman Annie Jones, he found her "finishing a lesson on the mandoline."[50] Anna Swan's pamphlet suggested that Miss Swan spent much of her time entertaining friends at home and declined to mention that this giant had, in fact, acted briefly on the New York stage.[51]

Finally, the most moving example of material culture's importance in the construction of respectable normalcy for audience-seeking

Victorian freaks comes from the life of Joseph Merrick. According to his doctor and patron, Dr. Frederick Treves, Merrick asked for a "silver-fitted dressing bag," which contained a silver-backed brush and comb, a shoe-horn, a hat brush, ivory-handled razors, and a silver cigarette case.[52] Treves was fascinated by this request since Merrick's deformities made him unable to use these items in a normal way. Ironically, Treves himself identified the symbolic power of the kit, but he underestimated it as he described the bag as "theatrical 'property.'" Consistent with his tendency to infantilize Merrick, Treves saw the kit only as a prop for Merrick's innocent "play acting" at being a "real swell."[53] In light of the interest in respectable normalcy across the freak discourse and the trend to link products with status, in particular, it seems probable that Merrick was interested in more than fantasy play. Most likely, Merrick valued the kit because, like his contemporaries, he had special appreciation for how products represented the possession of desirable qualities. This kit's contents announced that Merrick appreciated the bourgeois ideals of good taste, cleanliness, and financial comfort.

Conclusion

For the deformed on exhibit in Victorian England, the intellectual connection between respectability, behavior, and personal possessions was essential. Indeed, it was the secret to market success. Contrary to what historians have assumed thus far, the freak show industry did not fold under moral pressure or accede to medical incursion at mid-century. In fact, the freak show trade paid little attention to contemporary medical debate. Nineteenth-century showmen continued to advertise human oddities as remarkable examples of nature's majesty, as their eighteenth-century predecessors had done, and while the Victorian medical community was fascinated with how deformities came about, the freak show industry only spoke of deformity's causes in the most traditional way; they continued to champion the power of maternal emotions on the unborn even as many doctors were challenging maternal impression theory. Moreover, if freak show promoters were interested in the general medical community's growing professional status, it was because medical interest in freaks helped showmen counter claims that human oddities only appealed to the superstitious and uneducated crowds vilified by social reformers. For the most part, showmen referred to both real and imagined medical interest in exhibited human anomalies because medical patrons lent status to freaks in much the same way that elite and royal audiences had done for centuries.

By the mid-nineteenth century, however, these traditional advertising themes alone were not enough to promote human anomalies. The "moral revolution" that had closed many popular fairs did more than encourage showmen to move their shows into the grand exhibition halls.[54] To respond to the moral campaign to control popular leisure, rising cultural interest in respectability, fears that deformed bodies housed immoral characters, and growing concern about degeneracy, Victorian showmen put new emphasis on the humanity of freaks and their roles as cultural players. Personal histories that emphasized such things as marital status, dedication to work, and access to material comforts appeared increasingly alongside the old advertising themes. Ultimately, showmen in Britain made human oddities seem worthy of their spectators by insisting not only that the exhibited were remarkable examples of normal human development but also that these exhibition stars were exemplary participants in bourgeois culture.

Their attempt to make audiences feel comfortable with those on display by publicizing customarily private details was well calculated. The strategy was effective because it expressed and exploited two specifically Victorian phenomena. First, it took full advantage of contemporary belief in the ideology of separate spheres. Since the domestic world was considered sacrosanct and a protective haven from the public sphere where, on the other hand, competition and free trade wearied and corrupted men, there was an implicit understanding that information about the private lives of freaks was somehow more authentic than regular advertising material. Second, biographical narratives capitalized on the rising cultural dominance of the middle-class values that came out of the British Evangelical tradition. Showmen made human oddities attractive to audiences anxious about physical and moral degeneracy by conscientiously constructing personal histories for freaks that both highlighted well-recognized markers of middle-class respectability and established these qualities as the standards for normalcy. The workings of romantic irony in freak show biographies are historically significant, then, both because they reveal the growing cultural significance of Evangelical middle-class ideologies across Victorian society and because they helped extend the significance of those traditionally middle-class ideologies about gender difference, domesticity, hard work, and consumerism from markers of respectability within a class into markers of British normalcy across the boundaries of class and physical form. As

Arthur Goddard put it, when human oddities expressed the behaviors and beliefs traditionally recognized as part of middle-class Evangelical seriousness, they became the cultural peers of their diverse audiences, or "even as you and I."

Wonder was not dead in late-Victorian Britain. But the nature of wonder had changed since the early eighteenth century. While eighteenth-century audiences marveled at how freaks denoted nature's diversity and power, in the period after 1850 wonder rested in the extension of respectable normalcy to those on the boundaries of physical difference. Human anomalies marketed themselves by championing their physical oddities while simultaneously insisting on their cultural propriety. They did not yet describe themselves as patients with histories that doctors could best illuminate. As a result, even though their industry was under attack, the nineteenth century can be considered a good period for the exhibited deformed. Integrated into the natural world, they were better able to present themselves to audiences not simply as individuals with remarkable bodies but also as fellow citizens who shared a comforting set of values and were worthy of respect.

Notes

1. Arthur Goddard, "'Even as You and I': At Home with the Barnum Freaks," *The Strand Magazine* (February 1898): 493–96. Also in the John Johnson Collection of Printed Ephemera, Bodleian Library, Oxford, Freaks Collection, folder 1, hereafter cited as "J. J., Collection Folder number." The church was at Smithfield Street and Sixth Avenue.

2. Ibid. They had married in Pittsburgh on November 20, 1883, and also at an undisclosed date in Louisville before a crowd of three thousand.

3. "Marriage à la Barnum," *Brooklyn Eagle* (January 26, 1863), in *The Lost Museum*, http://chnm.gmu.edu/lostmuseum/lm/210. This editorial complained of P. T. Barnum's exploitation of the Episcopal Church when Bishop Potter performed the marriage of Charles Stratton (Tom Thumb) and Lavinia Warren.

4. In *Family Fortunes: Men and Women of the English Middle Class, 1780–1850* (Chicago: University of Chicago Press, 1987), Leonore Davidoff and Catherine Hall have described the restructuring of family relationships and identity according to a rising respect for evangelical seriousness, domestic morality, and gender division as central to the construction of the middle class. Dror Wahrman suggests that political language shifted from affiliating "middle classness" with studied and sensible public opinion to include "domestic virtue, . . . religiosity, . . . an evangelical impulse, [and] social control" after 1832. See *Imagining the Middle Class: The Political Representation of Class in Britain, c. 1780–1840* (Cambridge: Cambridge University Press, 1995), 378.

5. Dudley Wilson, *Signs and Portents: Monstrous Births from the Middle Ages to the Enlightenment* (London: Routledge, 1993).

6. Ibid., 47.

7. Katherine Park and Lorraine Daston, "Unnatural Conceptions: The Study of Monsters in Sixteenth- and Seventeenth-Century France and England," *Past and Present* 92 (August 1981): 20–54. They have added to the subject with *Wonders and the Order of Nature: 1150–1750* (New York: Zone Books, 1998).

8. Dennis Todd, *Imagining Monsters: Miscreations of the Self in Eighteenth-Century England* (Chicago: University of Chicago Press, 1995), 148–49.

9. Regulatory acts included the Vagrant's Act (1822), the Regulation of Fairs Acts (1823, 1848, and 1850), and the Theatre's Act (1843). See Peter Bailey, "Introduction," in *Music Hall: The Business of Pleasure*, ed. Peter Bailey (Philadelphia: Open University Press, 1986), ix.

10. See Mary Poovey, *Uneven Developments: The Ideological Work of Gender in Mid-Victorian England* (Chicago: University of Chicago Press, 1988), 12. Here Poovey draws on Jacques Derrida's "Structure, Sign, and Play in the Discourse of the Human Sciences," in *Writing and Difference*, trans. Alan Bass (Chicago: University of Chicago Press, 1978), 284, 285.

11. B. A. Morel, *Traité des Dégénérescences physiques, intellectuelles, et morales de l'espèce humain; et des causes qui produisent ces variétés maladives* (Paris, 1857).

12. Francis Galton and Karl Pearson headed the eugenics movement in Britain. Galton used the threat of progressive morbid heredity to justify social control of reproduction through interventionist and restrictive social policies, or "negative" eugenics. Hoping to segregate degenerates from the healthy breeding pool, he called for the extinction of degenerate lines through forced sterilization of epileptics, the feeble-minded, and others classed as "unfit." His follower, Karl Pearson, advocated less oppressive, "positive" interventions such as financial rewards for mothers of the educated classes and government control of health education. Both men included deformed persons in their lists of degenerates and had little hope for positive evolution among society's "undesirables."

13. Todd, 148.

14. Hugh Cunningham, "The Metropolitan Fairs: A Case Study in the Social Control of Leisure," in *Social Control in Nineteenth-Century Britain*, ed. A. P. Donajgrodzki (Totowa, NJ: Rowman and Littlefield, 1977), 311.

15. J. P. Kay, *The Moral and Physical Condition of the Working Classes Employed in the Cotton Manufacture in Manchester*, 2nd ed. (London, 1832), 580–81. Quoted in Robert D. Storch, "The Problem of Working-Class Leisure: Some Roots of Middle-class Moral Reform in the Industrial North, 1825–50," in Donajgrodzki, 141. For reports of brutish behavior see "Bow Fair" and "Fillinham Fair" (July 6, 1851), Fillinham Collection, The British Library, London, 1889 b, folder 10/4 Fairs, 7, 39; George Sanger, *Seventy Years a Showman* (New York: E. P. Dutton & Company, 1926), 59, 89.

16. Peter Bailey, *Leisure and Class in Victorian England: Rational Recreation and the Contest for Control, 1830–1885* (New York: Methuen, 1987 [1978]), 154.

17. Chris Waters describes the campaign against working-class entertainment as part of a "profound crisis in bourgeois ideology [and] self-perception in the city."

See "Manchester Morality and London Capital," in Bailey, *Music Hall*, 141–61, especially 151.

18. Goddard, 493–96.

19. Paul Starr suggests that American journalists invented the genre of the personal interview in the 1860s and that this mode of journalism and publicity came to England twenty years later. See *The Creation of the Media: Political Origins of Modern Communications* (New York: Basic Books, 2004), 148.

20. Goddard, 493.

21. Lois Rutherford, "Managers in a Small Way," in Bailey, *Music Hall*, 99–100.

22. See Evanion 1851 for an example of the brief presentation style that characterized advertisements for physically normal music hall performers. The bill simply lists the performers: "Sam Redfern, the Black Philosopher, The Mademoiselle Bertolto, Juvenile French Character Singer and Dancer . . . Miss Lillie Western, America's Greatest Versatile Musical Artiste."

23. On the middle class see F. M. L. Thompson, *Rise of Respectable Society* (Cambridge, MA: Harvard University Press, 1988), 199.

24. John Gillis traces working-class animosity to church weddings and a general inability to afford marriage licenses in the 1840s. He also suggests, however, that by the 1850s "the combined forces of economic, social, and political change had begun to alter the conditions of working-class life in such a way that the alternatives to legal matrimony no longer seemed feasible or attractive." By the 1880s, he continues, "marriage fees were no longer a real obstacle, and for those who did not wish to have to treat their neighbors . . . civil marriage was one inexpensive way of avoiding the publicity of wedding in a local church." See *For Better or for Worse: British Marriages, 1600 to the Present* (New York: Oxford University Press, 1985), 228, 235.

25. "Giants and Dwarfs," *The Strand* 8, no. 58 (September 1894): 434. Also in J. J., Freaks, 1.

26. Evanion 1870.

27. Thompson, 199–200.

28. He did so after touring with Barnum from 1848 to 1851. "Giants and Dwarfs," 433–34.

29. Ibid.

30. Thus, like other exhibited human anomalies, he emphasized his participation in the regular economy. See Joseph Merrick, "Autobiography," in Michael Howell and Peter Ford, *The Illustrated True History of the Elephant Man* (London: Allison & Busby, 1983), 224.

31. Goddard, 493.

32. Ibid.

33. Merrick, 224.

34. Ibid.

35. Handbill from Piccadilly Mall exhibition in February 1885, Evanion 2905.

36. "Giants and Dwarfs," 434. M. R. Werner notes that a London magazine reported this same figure on September 18, 1847. See *Barnum* (New York: Harcourt, Brace and Company, 1923), 96. (My thanks to Frederick Fleischer at the Barnum

Museum, Bridgeport, Connecticut, for this reference.) Daisy and Violet Hilton made up to five thousand dollars a week in the early twentieth century and, as Allison Pingree points out, socialized with Harry Houdini, Eddie Cantor, and Bob Hope. See "The Exceptions That Prove the Rule," in *Freakery: Cultural Spectacles of the Extraordinary Body*, ed. Rosemary Garland-Thomson (New York: New York University Press, 1996), 173.

37. See Thomas Richards, *The Commodity Culture of Victorian England: Advertising and Spectacle, 1851–1914* (Stanford, CA: Stanford University Press, 1990), 141. Also see Ann McClintock, "Soft-Soaping Empire: Commodity Racism and Imperial Advertising," in *Imperial Leather: Gender, Race and Sexuality in the Colonial Contest* (New York: Routledge, 1995), 207–31.

38. See Richards, and Annie E. Coombes, *Reinventing Africa: Museums, Material Culture and Popular Imagination in Late-Victorian and Edwardian England* (New Haven, CT: Yale University Press, 1994).

39. J. J., Freaks 1; Evanion 461. Also see Evanion 2526, another bill from the Nottingham Goose Fair, October 1887, which depicts Laloo seated inside next to a window.

40. The mother wore a dress that reminded readers of the girls' peasant background, but the father was drawn in more formal attire and held reading material that attested to his literacy. See Evanion 4552.

41. See J. J., Entertainments, folio 6.

42. In 1885 Millie-Christine's show pamphlet depicted them in diamond- and zigzag-patterned skirts under off-the-shoulder bodices. See Evanion 2905. Mr. and Mrs. Patrick O'Brien were also natty dressers. See Evanion 1870.

43. J. J., Entertainments, folio 6. An illustration of the stout dwarf "Chip," the Boy Wonder, offers another example of an exhibition figure possessing a fancy, silver- or bone-handled walking stick. See Evanion 715.

44. Other images showed them driving an open carriage, cutting trees, plowing a field, and playing instruments while wearing suits and sitting on a sofa. See Evanion 482.

45. Goddard, 495. Admittedly, Delno Fritz was not technically deformed, but Goddard thought it appropriate to group him with Barnum's other physical freaks, and, since he was a member of the exhibition trade, Fritz's public persona and status were certainly matters of concern.

46. Bailey, *Leisure and Class*, 143–44.

47. H. B. Philpott, *London at School: The Story of the School Board* (1904), 127, quoted in Bailey, *Leisure and Class*, 137.

48. Goddard, 496.

49. Ibid., 6.

50. Ibid., 495.

51. It declared that "Miss Swan has spent the greater portion of her life in her own home" and explained that her "genial amiability of disposition and pleasing intelligence" had won her many friends. Pamphlet on "The Novia-Scotia Giantess, Miss Anna Swan" with material on Chang and Eng and Zoebida Luti, in J. J. F.1, 29–30.

52. Frederick Treves, "The Elephant Man," in Howell and Ford, 242.

53. Ibid., 241–42. Why Treves infantilized Merrick is another interesting question. A complex set of beliefs certainly played a part in his condescension, including his own professional struggles and medical identity, his class prejudices, and his exposure to Victorian theories about human development and atavism.

54. "The moral revolution was the imposition on the whole society . . . of the traditional puritanism of the English middle ranks." See Harold Perkin, *Origins of Modern English Society* (London: Ark Paperbacks, 1985), 281, and also 280–90 and 444.

2

FREAKLORE

*The Dissemination, Fragmentation, and
Reinvention of the Legend of Daniel Lambert,
King of Fat Men*

JOYCE L. HUFF

THE VICTORIANS evinced what may be called an obsession with the
limits of human proportion. This fascination with body size had its
roots in the eighteenth century, when technologies for weighing and
measuring objects became more reliable and inventors such as John
Merlin and Thomas Weeks created machines for weighing individual
bodies. According to Pat Rogers, at the turn of the nineteenth century
Londoners could visit Merlin's Museum and Berry's Wineshop to be publicly weighed.[1] A certain amount of curiosity about body size is evinced
by the fact that the Prince of Wales, Beau Brummel, and James Boswell
all weighed themselves and kept records of the results, while some, like
Sir John Dashwood, even competed with others to determine who could
gain the most weight.[2]

By the mid-nineteenth century, with the consolidation of medical
authority and the rise of arithmetical ways of knowing in the sciences,
this curiosity had developed into a perceived need to determine the
relative sizes of individual bodies in relation to emerging statistical
norms.[3] The fact that statistics were considered valuable as a way of
knowing a population can be seen when one looks at the writings of
African explorer John Hanning Speke, who measured the bodies of
native women and recorded their measurements in his journal next

to statistics about the sizes of mountains and lakes.[4] Lennard J. Davis has noted that there was a burgeoning of interest in statistics in the nineteenth century, evidenced by the founding of institutions such as the General Register Office. He points out that early British statisticians were also often eugenicists and that they regarded differences as deviations.[5] Indeed, in the 1860s Poor Law Board inspector Edward Smith studied the weight of individual paupers in relation to statistical norms and used his results to adjust workhouse diet in order to reduce deviations from those norms, while Sir William Guy conducted similar studies on prison inmates.[6]

The first English actuarial tables for determining ideal body weight in relation to height were formulated by insurance companies at the turn of the nineteenth century, and they influenced nineteenth-century individuals to strive for the "happy medium" where weight was concerned.[7] Both corpulent and slender bodies fell outside of the limits that these tables constructed. The attention paid to those whose bodies did not conform to cultural norms is clear from the well-documented Victorian infatuation with the American sideshow performer General Tom Thumb.[8] But the Victorians did not neglect the other side of the scale, either; for example, in the 1860s two articles on human "curiosities" famed for their large dimensions and appetites appeared in Dickens's *All the Year Round*.[9]

At the time that statistics came into vogue, Britain was developing a consumer culture. Bryan S. Turner places the start of a mass consumer culture in the 1880s.[10] Thomas Richards, however, argues convincingly that the "cultural forms of consumerism" were in place before the full development of a mass consumer economy was complete.[11] The Great Exhibition of 1851, for instance, contributed to the ongoing formation of "a phenomenology and a psychology for a new kind of being, the consumer, and a new strain of ideology, consumerism,"[12] and that exhibition had its roots in even earlier commodity spectacles. It is not surprising, then, that the Victorians, as Gail Turley Houston has noted, "had to deal in complex ways with the meaning of their material production and consumption"[13] and that much of their literature reflects "an attempt to define and account for the practice of consumption" in all its various guises.[14]

As Houston argues, nineteenth-century writings tend to collapse economic and alimentary consumption. Indeed, the logic of early capitalism was interwoven with metaphors relating to digestion and nutrition. The need to consume food was often made to serve as the quintessential representative of all forms of consumption; in Victorian writings, it is hunger that drives the marketplace. For example, according to an 1861 article in *Cornhill Magazine*, the stomach is man's "task-master"; it makes him a "working animal" in "spite of his laziness."[15] As the Victorians extended their association of fat with aberrant consumption to include economic as well as alimentary consumption, it is not surprising that their interest in discovering and documenting the dimensions of the human body should be intertwined with concerns about not simply bodily control but also the management of economic, and specifically consumer, desires.

These concerns are evident in the Victorians' continuing attempts to account for the body of Daniel Lambert, a seven-hundred-pound man who exhibited himself in England at the turn of the nineteenth century (figure 2.1).[16] Although Lambert died in 1809, his legend was preserved and transmitted throughout the nineteenth century, and, in the process, it was fragmented, revised, and made to serve a multiplicity of purposes. Posthumously, Lambert took on many roles, some of which bore conflicting connotations. For example, when, in 1846, General Tom Thumb performed with a suit of Lambert's clothing, walking through the arm of Lambert's jacket, the spectacle emphasized both men's difference from an implied norm.[17] Furthermore, as viewers were invited to marvel at the amount of cloth needed to make his suit, Lambert's difference from the normative middle-class consumer was highlighted as well. Yet when his image was emblazoned on the sign of a public house bearing his name, Lambert was transformed into the representative of the normative middle-class consumer's appetite for premium goods.[18]

References to Lambert in Victorian writings provide a focal point for readers' fears about the ability to manage consumer desires in a developing commodity culture. Because Lambert's fat was associated by the Victorians with the consumption of resources—not simply space, but also food and other goods such as the cloth for his suits—the tension between Lambert's roles as freak and as typical Englishman reflects conflicts within the self-definition of the British middle-class consumer, and Lambert's continuing popularity can, at least in part, be explained by the centrality of the consumer dilemmas that plagued the Victorian British middle classes.

"The Life of That Wonderful and Extraordinary Heavy Man"

In the summer of 1806, London tourists flocked to visit Daniel Lambert, "The Jolly Gaoler of Leister," at his apartments in Piccadilly.[19] For the

Figure 2.1
Daniel Lambert. Photo courtesy of Stamford Town Council.

price of a shilling, spectators could call upon and visit with Mr. Lambert, whose handbills advertised him as "the heaviest man that ever lived."[20] Lambert would only exhibit himself in Piccadilly for five months before returning home to his native Leicester, where he had served most of his life as custodian of the local prison. Over the course of the following three years, he could occasionally be seen on display at fairs and races across the country, though he did make two more brief visits to London for repeat performances before his death in 1809, by which time he had attained the weight of 739 pounds. Although his career as a freak was short, it was highly successful. In fact, one man claimed to have visited Lambert so many times and paid so many shillings to see him that he had "fairly had a pound's worth" of him, while spectators came from as far as Guernsey to view him.[21]

Lambert's posthumous career, however, lasted considerably longer. His spectacular afterlife began with his funeral. He had gone to Stamford to exhibit himself at the races and had died in his sleep, presumably of heart failure, on the night before his scheduled performance. The local paper and at least one spectator reported that hundreds of people, not wanting to be deprived of the promised spectacle, attended his burial to see the enormous coffin and to marvel at the probable dimensions of the body it held.[22] Not long afterward, objects associated with Lambert began to circulate, particularly his clothes and other items that—like his coffin—denoted the proportions of his body. Lambert's specially built coach and his clothing were auctioned, after which his tailor made additional suits of clothes to Lambert's dimensions for sale to collectors. Lithographs and prints were made from the four portraits that had been taken of him during his life. Wax models of his body were constructed, one of which was exhibited as far away as America and resided until recently in the American Dime Museum in Baltimore, Maryland. There were even Lambert collectibles, such as whisky crocks fashioned in his image. This interest in Lambert continued well into the mid-century. In 1842, for example, an innkeeper in Stamford was able to purchase a suit of Lambert's clothes from an American dealer and displayed them at his public house, rechristened the Daniel Lambert in honor of the clothing's original owner, along with a suit donated by General Tom Thumb (figure 2.2).

While objects associated with Lambert continued to be disseminated throughout the nineteenth century, legends about him also spread. These began to appear in print soon after his death, and some of them seem likely to have been used originally to promote his performances. According to the tales, Lambert defied all of the stereotypes normally associated with corpulence in the nineteenth century: he was "very partial to the female sex,"[23] enjoyed "perfect and uninterrupted" health, displayed uncommon intelligence and quick wit, and showed a remarkable amount of temperance and restraint at meals. He also exhibited a "truly extraordinary" degree of energy and activity, and as a young man, he was "passionately fond" of "sports of the field."[24]

Little is known about his childhood, except for the (alleged) fact

EVERY VISITOR TO STAMFORD

SHOULD CALL AT

THE "LONDON" INN,

ST. JOHN'S STREET,

And see the wonderful Clothing of the celebrated Human Mammoth.

ROUND THE BODY 112 INCHES.
ROUND THE LEG 37 INCHES.

WEIGHING 52 STONES 11 POUNDS

(14lbs. to the Stone.)

DANIEL LAMBERT

Who died and was buried at Stamford in June, 1809.

Also the MINIATURE CLOTHING presented by the Original

GENERAL TOM THUMB,

When only 15lbs. in weight,

To be shown with the above as the greatest contrast ever witnessed.

Photographs of Lambert and his Gravestone 6d. each. History of his Life, 3d. each.

Wines, Spirits, Ales, Stout, Cigars, &c.

YE "OLD LONDON" TAVERN,

St. John's Street, Stamford.

T. T. WELLS, Proprietor.

Late 19th century handbill from original printing block in Stamford Museum

Daniel Lamberts clothes are presently displayed on a lifesize model in Stamford Museum, together with those of Tom Thumb

Lincolnshire Recreational Services Stamford Museum
1985

Figure 2.2

Daniel Lambert's clothing. Photo courtesy of Lincolnshire County Council: Stamford Museum.

that Lambert was not particularly fat as a boy. At fourteen, he was apprenticed to a button and buckle engraver, but changes in fashion displaced many engravers at that period and, after four years, Lambert was forced to seek other employment as keeper of the Leicester jail. If the tales be true, all of the prisoners testified to his benevolence, and some even wept upon being released. It was at about this time, by all accounts, that he began to gain weight and, not surprisingly, to show signs of extraordinary ability. He could, for example, reportedly lift five hundred pounds with ease and was supposedly able to stand on one leg and kick the other leg seven feet in the air. In addition, he was reputed to have performed amazing feats at this stage in his life. Once a troupe of traveling entertainers brought some bears to Leicester, one of which escaped to attack a local dog. Lambert is said to have wrestled with this bear in an attempt to rescue the dog. In some versions of this tale, Lambert is defeated because he falls and, encumbered by his weight, cannot rise again.[25] In a more fanciful account, however, Lambert arises to triumph over the bear, while another bear performer tips its hat to Lambert in recognition of his superior prowess.[26] Another tale has Lambert courageously escaping a burning building and, in some reports, returning to save seven children. Yet another anecdote casts him as the local swimming instructor, because his fat gives him extraordinary buoyancy. In this story, he saves children from drowning by allowing them to ride on his belly as he floats. It is said that as rumors of his marvelous exploits spread throughout the land, this normally shy and retiring man was called forth by the public to exhibit himself. More creditable, however, is the story that Lambert became a freak because he experienced pressing financial need, due to the expense of obtaining special accommodations in a culture adapted to meet the needs of much smaller men.

As the century continued, images of Lambert, both pictorial and literary, proliferated as the legends were passed down in both oral and written form. Lambert appeared not simply as an object of study and wonder in books and articles on scientific and medical curiosities but also as a carnivalesque Bacchus figure in a broadsheet ballad, a role model in a Christian tract, and a British national icon, in the style of John Bull, in at least five political cartoons. By the mid-nineteenth century, Lambert's name had passed into slang discourse as a descriptor for a corpulent man and had become a household word. This is demonstrated in the numerous casual allusions to Lambert that appear in literary works such as Dickens's *The Pickwick Papers* and *Nicholas*

Nickleby and Thackeray's *Vanity Fair* and *Men's Wives*. References to Lambert even turn up in texts by American authors such as Elizabeth Cady Stanton and humorist Charles F. M. Noland.[27] Lambert's name and image were associated not merely with corpulence but also with feasting and drink. Despite the fact that Lambert himself had reportedly been a teetotaler who ate sparingly, "The Jolly Gaoler" and "The Daniel Lambert" became popular names for public houses, and his likeness was used to decorate their signs.

To begin to understand the cultural work that Lambert's image accomplished in the Victorian era, one must examine the contexts in which his image appeared and the uses to which it was put by the Victorians. It is not surprising that the figure of Lambert is frequently invoked as an example of what Rosemarie Garland-Thomson has called an "extraordinary body,"[28] though it may be unexpected that Lambert's physical difference is cast as both freakish and heroic. More surprisingly, however, Lambert's body sometimes appears as the representative English body. As Lambert's size was associated not simply with the consumption of space but also with the consumption of resources, it will be seen that these opposing modes for representing Lambert reflected tensions in British self-definition regarding consumerism.

Consumer Anxiety

One mode of representation continued to depict Lambert as a freak, a signifier of aberrant consumption that both warned consumers to control their own appetites and reassured them that their lesser consumer desires were "normal." As Garland-Thomson has asserted, with the emergence of the "unmarked norm" as "reference point" in the nineteenth century, the body marked by its physical difference from that norm was stigmatized, or "freakified," to delineate the boundaries of the normal.[29] Garland-Thomson calls the process of stigmatization "enfreakment."[30] She argues that, since the nineteenth century, the freak's body has functioned as a site upon which an audience could "projec[t] cultural characteristics they themselves disavowed."[31] In human exhibits, freakified bodies mark the boundaries that define the normal, serving to warn individuals to stay within those boundaries. But Garland-Thomson notes that freaks also serve a more reassuring function. Freakified bodies are represented as existing in a binary relationship to the norm. The logic upon which this binary is constructed aligns nonstigmatized bodies with the cultural ideal. What this opposition offers to subjects whose bodies are thus defined as normal is the illusion of freedom from the uncertainties, flux, and grotesqueries of bodily existence. This fiction can only be maintained, however, by the continued and systematic devaluation of the freakified body, for it is only by comparison with stigmatized subjects that "normal" ones appear free.

Thus, the continuing enfreakment of Daniel Lambert in the Victorian era, through the display of his coach, chair, clothing, and other personal items signifying his size, was a part of the process by which the Victorians created a composite picture of the "normal body," of which bodily proportion was a major component. In such an atmosphere, someone like Lambert is reduced to his dimensions and transformed into a representative of the limits of the human. For example, writing in 1884, G. H. Wilson describes Lambert's audiences as eager "to behold to what an immense magnitude the human figure is capable of attaining."[32] Similarly, an 1864 article from Dickens's *All the Year Round* introduces Lambert, the "king" of fat men, by addressing a reader hungry for statistical knowledge of the human condition: "What is the average weight of a man? At what age does he attain his greatest weight? How much heavier are men than women? What would be the weight of fat people; and what of *very* fat people?"[33] Tellingly, the essay contains little biographical information about Lambert's fat subjects, beyond statistics regarding the weight of each fat person and the dimensions of his or her coffin. Such accounts appear to have provided a touchstone grounding readers' anxieties with regard to the relationship between individual bodies and the supposedly universal corporeal standards developed in the nineteenth century.

Capitalism played a large part in the defining these standards for the Victorians. Mass production assumes a consumer who possesses an adaptable body, a body that can and will adapt to fit into preconstructed spaces.[34] As the century progressed, the public sphere was slowly standardized and, increasingly, those with bodies that did not fit the norms found themselves out of place in an environment built to meet the needs of the "average" body. In 1863 William Banting, self-proclaimed expert on obesity, complained that the corpulent man daily faced "the annoyance of finding no adequate space in the public assembly if he should seek amusement or need refreshment."[35]

It is not surprising, then, that Lambert's difference from the emerging norms of the time was specifically expressed through the display of his clothing. The rise of the ready-made clothing industry exemplified the standardization trend. With ready-made clothing, the individual body does not serve as a reference point, as the immobile absolute to which the environment must be adapted; rather, the body itself is perceived as adaptable, conforming to the clothing manufacturers' standards. In the practice of auctioning and displaying Lambert's clothing, Lambert's dimensions were preserved while the social interaction that was integral to his original performance was lost. Lambert's clothes could continue to draw crowds without him, and if the actual clothing were not available, suits made to his measurements would do just as well.

This last example highlights the way in which anxieties over bodily proportion and body management were read through and against anxieties about consumerism. For it was not merely Lambert's proportions that fascinated the Victorians. They wanted to learn how much a person of Lambert's size would consume, in terms of space, food, clothing, and other resources, and, through doing so, construct limits on consumer desire. If Garland-Thomson is correct that the Victorians projected the characteristics that they themselves disavowed onto the bodies of freaks, then the specific "disavowed characteristic" that the British population projected onto the body of Daniel Lambert was consumer desire, especially anxieties about the management of consumer desire. The management of consumer desire is a continuing problem in a capitalist society. As Susan Bordo has noted, capitalist cultures make conflicting demands on consumers: "On the one hand, as producers of consumer goods and services we must sublimate, delay, repress desires for immediate gratification; we must cultivate the work ethic. On the other hand, as consumers we must display a boundless capacity to capitulate to desire and indulge in impulse; we must hunger for constant and immediate satisfaction. The regulation of desire thus becomes an ongoing problem, as we find ourselves continually besieged by temptation, while socially condemned for overindulgence."[36]

For the Victorians, the image of Lambert provided a focal point through which they could fashion consuming bodies; he placed their own consuming practices in context. The stigma of corpulence was the stigma of unchecked appetite; corpulent people, it was assumed, could not manage their desires effectively. When, in the mid-century, doctors such as Thomas King Chambers proclaimed that the etiology of obesity was unknown or that it proceeded from multiple causes,[37] the public responded, "The grand cause of obesity is our eating and drinking more than enough."[38] Fat bodies thus bore a metonymic association with consumables in the Victorian mind, and Lambert was associated with literary characters that failed to regulate their appetites, not simply for food and drink but also for goods.

In *Vanity Fair*, for example, William Makepeace Thackeray associates Lambert with the ultimate unregulated consumer, Joseph Sedley. *Vanity Fair* is a novel about consuming. According to Barbara Hardy, successful consumers in *Vanity Fair* are those like Becky Sharp, who can remain "coolly acquisitive," as opposed to those like Joseph, who fetishize commodities and become entrapped within their roles as consumers.[39] Joseph invests objects with far too much desire and is thus held prisoner by his appetites. His interaction with the world is limited to meaningless consumer display. He spends hours each day adorning himself with numerous weskits and neckcloths in order to display himself by riding around the town in his expensive carriage, and then he returns home to eat a solitary meal and retire alone. The few social interactions in which he does engage are mediated by goods and particularly by food; he even finds conversation "delicious."[40] When Amelia is pining for her husband who is at war, for example, Joseph "show[s] his sympathy, by pouring her out a large cup of tea."[41] Furthermore, when the family loses their fortune, Joseph responds to the material loss by sending money but neglects the human loss by refusing to visit and to help restore his father's sense of self-respect.[42]

Like Lambert's, Joseph's body is large enough that it calls attention to him whenever he enters the public sphere. And, also like Lambert's, Joseph's body is not merely a spectacle but rather a spectacle of consumer desire unleashed. When Joseph drinks "the whole contents of the bowl" of rack punch at Vauxhall, Thackeray explicitly evokes Lambert to emphasize the spectacle of Joseph's consuming feat. His drunken antics draw a crowd, who taunt him about his size by calling out, "Angcore, Daniel Lambert!"[43] For the rabble of pleasure seekers at Vauxhall, the spectacle of Joseph's enormous body, coupled as it is with Lambert's freakified image, provides comforting, if false, reassurance that their own desires are under their control.

Capitalist Nostalgia

Legends presenting Lambert as extraordinary were not, as one might imagine, entirely negative. In the folk tales that flourished after Lambert's death, he is frequently depicted as a rescuer, saving animals and children. In 1815 Lambert even appeared in a Christian tract extolling the "humanity, temperance and liberality of sentiment" that made him "a model worthy of general imitation."[44] This pamphlet was reprinted and plagiarized throughout the nineteenth century, until at least the 1880s. Given the association of fat with aberrant consumerism, how does one explain the continuing popularity of legends that present Lambert as heroic?

Heroic tales depict Lambert in a mode that Robert Bogdan has characterized as the "aggrandized mode" of presentation, a technique of freak show performance that draws attention to a human exhibit by making claims that enhance his or her status.[45] The politics of aggrandized performance, in my opinion, depend upon context. In this case, the very norms that forced actual bodies like Lambert's out of the public sphere, abjected them, and labeled them freakish also enabled the symbolic portrayal of these bodies as heroic. I will label the process by which the deceased Lambert is idealized, at the very point in time when capitalism is creating an environment hostile to those of Lambert's size, "capitalist nostalgia."

In a chapter titled "Imperialist Nostalgia" in *Culture and Truth*, Renato Rosaldo remarks that nostalgia frees individuals of guilt by allowing them to "mourn the passing of what they themselves have transformed."[46] Capitalist nostalgia enabled the Victorian public to enjoy wonder tales that celebrated Lambert's difference while simultaneously participating in the creation of an increasingly standardized environment that devalued actual fat people. The more fantastical the tale, the more Lambert seemed to be removed from the socioeconomic milieu that placed increasingly restrictive limits on the lives of fat people and forced Lambert himself to become a human exhibit in order to pay for specially made chairs, coaches, and clothing. Such stories also often stressed Lambert's difference from other fat people, facilitating identification with Lambert while distancing the audience from the majority of fat individuals.[47] Furthermore, by highlighting Lambert's extraordinariness, even in a positive light, these legends simply reified the idea that Lambert was different from the "average man" and thus worked to reinforce the norms that stigmatized fat people.

But, more interestingly, such narratives functioned to relieve any guilt the Victorians felt over their own roles as consumers of the Lambert phenomenon. This is particularly true of tales that celebrate Lambert's extraordinary wit, in which Lambert is frequently portrayed in the act of resisting objectification through direct verbal confrontation. In these stories Lambert defies the objectifying gaze—or "stare," as

Garland-Thomson has called it[48]—by making his audience aware that he is looking back at them. According to Wilson, Lambert's "apartments [in Piccadilly] had more the air of a place of fashionable resort, than of exhibition," and his guests are described as "not merely gazing at him as a spectacle, but treating him in the most friendly and soothing manner."[49] Wilson recounts several surviving anecdotes regarding Lambert's wit at the expense of those few impertinent viewers who insisted on objectifying him through their interactions by neglecting to observe the everyday social rituals through which one acknowledges another's humanity. For example, on one occasion Lambert supposedly told a woman who inquired about the price of one of his enormous coats, "If you think it proper to make me a present of a new coat, you will then know exactly what it costs." Another time, he refused to answer the same question and when the inquisitor replied that he had a right to know, having paid a shilling to view Lambert, Lambert retorted, "If I knew what part of my next coat your shilling would pay for, I can assure you I would cut out the piece."[50]

Such stories evoke Victorian guilt over the consumption of Lambert's image, only to allay it by distancing the "normal" consumer from the impertinent one. The continuing popularity of these stories, even seventy-five years after Lambert's death, highlights the Victorians' discomfort with their own roles as consumers of spectacles such as Lambert's. These tales allow the Victorians to condemn the crass consumerism of certain members of Lambert's original audience, even as they themselves marveled openly at representations of him.

The concept of capitalist nostalgia can also serve to explain, at least in part, representations of Lambert as a sort of everyman. When Lambert appears in advertisements for pubs and eating houses, it is as a signifier of the satisfied customer, whose appetite for plentiful and high-quality goods is coded as normal. In such images, Lambert may actually serve as the vehicle for the carnivalesque fantasies of unregulated consumption and continually fulfilled desire that are produced within an atmosphere that stresses the need to regulate consumer desire. The fact that Lambert is recalled from the past to serve as the tabula rasa onto which such fantasies could be projected demonstrates the nostalgic nature of these fancies; they represent a longing for an imagined past in which consumption was supposedly unregulated. And Lambert's fat enhances the carnivalesque nature of these fictions. Fat, as M. M. Bakhtin has pointed out, is one of the principal symbols of the carnivalesque tradition.[51] That Lambert's fat could be read as carnivalesque in the nineteenth century is apparent from his appearance in works such as a broadsheet ballad with the title "The World Turned Upside Down." According to Bakhtin, in the nineteenth century the grotesque aesthetic associated with carnival was sanitized to such an extent that in Victorian writings fat displaced all other aspects of the grotesque body, especially those that were scatological or sexual in nature, and the carnivalesque aesthetic was reduced to symbols of feasting and fat, such as Mr. Pickwick's "fat little paunch."[52] Bakhtin mourned this change, as he felt that the all-inclusive, communal values of the "people" were lost when the eminently middle-class Pickwick became the representative of carnival.[53]

Dickens actually invokes Lambert in *The Pickwick Papers*, in association not with Mr. Pickwick but with a more carnivalesque consumer, the working-class Joe, known familiarly as the Fat Boy. Following carnivalesque tradition, Joe's body is continually expanding; each time the Pickwickians encounter him, he is "fatter than ever."[54] When Sam Weller warns him to "take care you don't get too fat," the caution does not seem appropriate, for, although at first Joe appears "much affected" by Sam's warning, immediately afterward he takes "the opportunity of appropriating to his own use, and summarily devouring, a particularly fine mince-pie."[55] The Fat Boy's expansion is almost always associated with his prodigious consuming practices, and all who see him acknowledge him to be a consuming phenomenon. Sam, for instance, remarks, "Vell, young twenty stun [stone] . . . you're a nice specimen of a prize boy, you are!"—as if the Fat Boy, like Lambert, were on exhibit at a fair,[56] while Joe's employer Mr. Wardle boasts, "I'm proud of that boy— wouldn't part with him on any account—he's a natural curiosity."[57] It is not without reason that Dickens dubs him "the infant Lambert."[58]

Yet Joe's astonishing ability to consume is not constructed as negative, for, as James R. Kincaid has pointed out, in the nostalgic economy of *The Pickwick Papers*, nothing is ever used up. Indeed, it seems that the more the Fat Boy eats, the more he has to share with others and thus "no speculative observer could have regarded [him] for an instant without setting down as the official dispenser of the contents of the . . . [picnic] hamper," the giver of food to others.[59] Kincaid cites Joe as the ultimate representative of the carnivalesque economy of the novel, an economy in which the body is "infinitely expandable, as well as insatiable" and the resources on which it feeds are "endless." Kincaid also associates the novel's vision of unrestricted yet always satisfied appetite with nostalgia, as I do, although he reads it as nostalgia for "the oral-erotic fantasies of childhood" rather than historicizing it in relation to Victorian consumer dilemmas.[60]

English Identity

Lambert, however, is not always merely a generic consumer figure. He is often depicted as quintessentially English. It may seem surprising that the English would choose one whom they regarded as a freak to represent their national character. But human curiosities were often referred to in the nineteenth century as "eccentrics," as the title of Wilson's *The Eccentric Mirror* demonstrates, and eccentricity had deep moral and philosophical connotations for the Victorians. John Stuart Mill, for example, points to the moral ramifications of eccentricity in *On Liberty:* "Precisely because the tyranny of opinion is such as to make eccentricity a reproach, it is desirable, in order to break through that tyranny, that people should be eccentric. . . . That so few dare to be eccentric marks the chief danger of our time."[61] But while Mill characterized England as a land in which few dared to be true eccentrics, Julia F. Saville argues convincingly that the English saw eccentricity as a defining national characteristic and the need to balance the tension between conformity and individualism as a pressing social tension.[62] Indeed, Mill himself feels that it is their defiance of the "despotism of Custom" that makes the English more "progressive" than the rest of the world.[63] When eccentricity becomes a defining national trait, however, it loses much of the ability to signify the sort of nonconformity that Mill advocated.

According to Saville, the Victorians defined eccentricity as "an assertion of individual liberty that will not capitulate to containment but instead celebrates excess."[64] That Lambert's corporeal excess was viewed as a positive symbol of English eccentricity is clear from the period's penchant for associating him with that icon of Britishness, John Bull. For example, there is a tale in which a Frenchman and a Jew offer to manage Lambert and to exhibit him on the continent, at which Lambert, "in the emphatic style of a true son of John Bull," refuses to leave England.[65] Lambert also appears as a representative of Englishness in Napoleonic-era political cartoons. In "Two Wonders of the World, or A Specimen of a New Troop of Leicestershire Lighthorse," Lambert, in military dress, charges a scrawny Napoleon, who remarks in an exaggerated French accent, "Parbleu!! if dis be de specimen of de English

Figure 2.3

Lambert and Napoleon cartoon. Photo © Copyright the Trustees of The British Museum.

light Horse, Vat vill de Heavy Horse be!! Oh by Gar I vill put off de Invasion for an oder time!"[66] (figure 2.3). In another cartoon, Napoleon says to Lambert, "I contemplate this wonder of the world and regret that all my conquered domains cannot match this man, pray sir, are you not a descendant from the great joss of China?" to which Lambert replies, "No, sir, I am a true born Englishman from the county of Leicester, a quiet mind and good constitution nourished by the free air of Great Britain makes every Englishman thrive." Yet another shows a robust Lambert feasting next to a weak and undernourished Napoleon, who is sipping broth. The caption reads, "The English Lamb and the French Tiger. Roast Beef and French Soup."[67] These cartoons may serve to mock Napoleon's famed appetite for land by making his desires appear inconsequential and thus soothing anxieties regarding the threat that he posed to the English. But they also objectify Englishness and present it as something to be consumed, whether in the form of roast beef or free air.

Of course, corpulence was quite literally associated with Englishness in the nineteenth century. Physician Thomas King Chambers, the leading authority on obesity in the 1850s, believed fatness to be a hereditary English trait. He writes, "Erasmus says, that in his day for one stout person to be seen on the Continent there were four in England. Among the Celts who live in the same climate we do, it is less frequent. It has been diminished in our Transatlantic brethren, probably from the more general mixture of blood through intermarriage."[68] But the linking of corpulence with Englishness also provided a naturalizing corporeal anchor for certain personality traits to which the English laid claim. In *Reflections on the Revolution in France*, for example, Edmund Burke compares the British favorably to "great cattle" chewing their cud under "the shadow of the British oak," arguing that, like cattle, the British possess a "sullen resistance to innovation." It is the "cold sluggishness" of their "national character," symbolized by fat and sedentary cattle, that in Burke's opinion allows the British to reject the revolutionary ideas of the more incendiary French.[69] Burke extends the metaphor that associates the British citizen with the consumption of British products, such as beef, making the beef itself stand for the citizen. This, like the cartoons above, highlights the fact that, in many ways, the British began to define themselves, not simply as a nation of eccentrics but also as one of consumers.

The association of fatness with positive English traits, however, did not lead the English to view foreign fatness in a positive light. In fact, fatness could provide the scientific grounding for the stigmatization of whole races of people. To the Chinese, for example, Chambers attributes an unusual propensity to corpulence. But he views this tendency as a punishment for inbreeding: "It is an evil which the exclusiveness of that singular people has entailed upon them."[70] This seems ironic, given Chambers's remarks about the diminishment of the English waistline through continental intermarriage, quoted above, which appear as a warning against miscegenation and loss of national identity; what in the Chinese is seen as a punishment for cultural isolation becomes for the English a reward for maintaining cultural purity.

The stigmatization of foreign fat and, by extension, foreign consumer practices also worked to allay British consumer anxiety. British scientists, in general, tended to view cultural differences in eating practices as deviations from a Western norm. The inherent racism of this view becomes clear when physician William Wadd compares abnormalities of English diet to the supposed diets of those in foreign lands. In 1829 Wadd documented what he considered the "morbid or extravagant propensities of English stomachs" as models for understanding why "an Esquimaux may dine very daintily on a slice of whale" or "African gentlemen should eat one another."[71] In so doing, Wadd casts natives of exotic lands as morbid versions of Englishmen, which reinforces the normalcy of the average Englishman's consuming practices.

Conclusion: Lambert Today

In the early twenty-first century, a traveler visiting the town of Stamford, where Daniel Lambert met his end, could view not only a replica of Lambert's famous suit of clothing alongside which Tom Thumb performed in 1846 but also his hat, his walking stick, a life-sized model of his body, a porcelain collectible statue emblazoned with a Union Jack, two portraits, his grave, and the inn where he died. At the Stamford Museum, one could even play a Lambert-themed game, in which tourists compare their own bodies to Lambert's silhouette and attempt to guess how many of them can fit into a space the size of Lambert's waistline (figure 2.4). Proceeding to the Newarke Houses Museum in Lambert's hometown of Leicester, one could view more of Lambert's clothing and personal effects, another portrait, another life-sized model, and his specially made chair. Between the two towns, one could purchase Lambert jigsaw puzzles, greeting cards, postcards, refrigerator magnets, bookmarks,

Figure 2.4
Lambert game at Stamford Museum. Photo courtesy of Lincoln-shire County Council: Stamford Museum.

coloring pages, pins, and badges.[72] One could even have a drink at a Stamford pub that was rechristened the Daniel Lambert in 1984.[73]

The popularity of such exhibits leads one to question how invested the spectators of Lambert's image are in maintaining the ways of see-ing and knowing that stigmatized Lambert in the first place. In fact, the Stamford Museum is actively engaging in this sort of questioning, as they renovate their Lambert exhibit as part of the "Rethinking Dis-ability Representation in Museums" project.[74] In twenty-first-century Britain and America, our consumer disorders have intensified with the development of a full-blown culture of mass consumption and the consolidation of the ideologies and institutions of capitalism. Corpulent bodies continue to serve as the abjected forms onto which new consumer dilemmas are displaced. As readers approaching nineteenth-century texts, we must ask ourselves how much our readings of corpulent bodies participate in their stigmatization and the furthered devaluation of corpulence in our own cultures.

Notes

1. Pat Rogers, "Fat Is a Fictional Issue: The Novel and the Rise of Weight-Watching," in *Literature and Medicine During the Eighteenth Century*, ed. Marie Mulvey Roberts and Roy Porter (New York: Routledge, 1993), 174. Rogers gives an excellence discussion of these early "self-weighers."

2. Ibid., 176.

3. For extended discussions of these phenomena, see Roy Porter, "Consumerism," in *An Oxford Companion to the Romantic Age: British Culture, 1776–1832*, ed. Iain McCalman et al. (Oxford: Oxford University Press, 2001), 181–86, and Michel Foucault, "The Politics of Health in the Eighteenth Century," in *Power/Knowledge*, ed. and trans. Colin Gordon (New York: Pantheon, 1977), 166–82.

4. John Hanning Speke, *Journal of the Discovery of the Source of the Nile* (1863, reprint, London: Dent, 1908).

5. Lennard J. Davis, "Constructing Normalcy: The Bell Curve, the Novel, and the Invention of the Disabled Body in the Nineteenth Century," in *The Disability Studies Reader*, ed. Lennard J. Davis (New York: Routledge, 1997), 14.

6. Edward Smith, *Dietaries for the Inmates of Workhouses: A Report to the President of the Poor Law Board* (London: Eyre and Spottiswoode, 1866); idem, *The Present State of the Dietary Question* (London: Walton and Maberly, 1864); and William Augustus Guy, *On Sufficient and Insufficient Dietaries with Special Reference to the Dietaries of Prisoners* (London: Harrison, 1863).

7. William Banting, *A Letter on Corpulence*, 3rd American ed. (New York: Harper, 1864), 21.

8. For more information about the Victorian love of the miniature, see Susan Stewart, *On Longing: Narratives of the Miniature, the Gigantic, the Souvenir, the Collection* (Baltimore, MD: Johns Hopkins University Press, 1984).

9. "Fat People," *All the Year Round* (October 9, 1869): 442–44; and "Great Eaters," ibid. (March 12, 1870): 343–45.

10. Bryan S. Turner, *The Body and Society*, 2nd ed. (London: Sage, 1996), 116.

11. Thomas Richards, *The Commodity Culture of Victorian England: Advertising and Spectacle, 1851–1914* (Stanford, CA: Stanford University Press, 1990), 8.

12. Ibid., 5.

13. Gail Turley Houston, *Consuming Fictions: Gender, Class, and Hunger in Dickens's Novels* (Carbondale: Southern Illinois University Press, 1994), xi.

14. Ibid., 5.

15. James Hinton, "Food—What It Is," *Cornhill Magazine* (April 1861): 460.

See also William Wadd, *Comments on Corpulency and Lineaments of Leanness* (London: Ebers, 1829), 13–14.

16. Many thanks to the staff and curators at the Stamford Museum, especially Philippa Massey, for allowing me access to their collections and to the staff and curators at the Newarke Houses Museum, Leicester, especially Philip French, Helene Kelly, Mary Hider, and Lee Richard, for providing information and literature regarding Lambert.

17. Ashley Phillipson, *Heritage Information Sheet, Stamford Museum: Daniel Lambert and Tom Thumb* (Stamford: Lincolnshire County Council, 1994), 2.

18. For an alternate reading of Lambert's body, see Paul Youngquist, *Monstrosities: Bodies and British Romanticism* (Minneapolis: University of Minnesota Press, 2003).

19. The information presented here is repeated in multiple sources. Because it includes the longest and most complete summary of Lambert legends I have yet to find, I rely primarily on the version given in G. H. Wilson, *The Eccentric Mirror: Reflecting a Faithful and Interesting Delineation of Male and Female Characters, Ancient and Modern, Who Have Been Particularly Distinguished by Extraordinary Qualifications, Talents, and Propensities, Natural and Acquired*, 4 vols. (London: J. Cundee, 1884). Other sources include Elizabeth Batt, *Daniel Lambert*, June 25, 1999, http://www.suite101.com/article.cfm/leicestershire/18072 (accessed September 1, 2000); *The Child's Magazine*, 2 vols. (New York: Samuel Wood, 1815); David T. D. Clarke, *Daniel Lambert* (1950, reprint, Leicester: Leicester Museums and Art Gallery, 1973); *Daniel Lambert* (Leicester: Leicestershire Museums, 1993); "Fat People"; *Leicester City Museums*, http://www.leicestermuseums.ac.uk/events/evenframe.html (accessed June 12, 2003), Leicester City Council; *The Life of That Wonderful and Extraordinary Heavy Man, Daniel Lambert, from His Birth to the Moment of His Dissolution* (Stamford, UK: J. Drakard, 1809; New York: Samuel Wood, 1815); Daniel Macfie, *Stamford: History in Evidence*, http://www.dmacfie.freeserve. co.uk/aboutstamford.html (accessed September 1, 2000); Phillipson; *Stamford Museum*, 2003, http://www.stamford.co.uk/tourism/museum.htm (accessed June 12, 2003); and Stamford Museum Collections and Exhibits, Stamford, Lincolnshire (June 2001).

20. "Fat People," 355.

21. Wilson, 14.

22. Elizabeth Gilbert, letter to her sister Ann, June 29, 1809 (Stamford Museum, Stamford, UK, photocopy), and extract from *The Lincoln, Rutland and Stamford Mercury*, June 30, 1809 (Stamford Museum, Stamford, UK, photocopy), 1.

23. Clarke, 5.

24. Wilson, 2–4.

25. Phillipson, 2.

26. Wilson, 6–7.

27. Charles Dickens, *Nicholas Nickleby* (1838–39, reprint, New York: Penguin, 1982); idem, *The Pickwick Papers* (1836–37, reprint, New York: Bantam, 1983); William Makepeace Thackeray, "Men's Wives," in *Project Gutenberg*, 1857, reprint, December 1999, http://onlinebooks.library.upenn.edu/webbin/gutbook/lookup? num=1985 (accessed June 12, 2003), University of Pennsylvania; idem, *Vanity Fair*

(1847–48, reprint, Oxford: Oxford University Press, 1992); Elizabeth Cady Stanton, "Address by Elizabeth Cady Stanton on Woman's Rights" 1848, in *Stanton and Anthony Papers Project Online*, ed. Kimberly J. Banks, July 12, 2001, http://ecssba.rutgers.edu/docs/ecswoman1.html (accessed June 12, 2003), Rutgers University; Charles F. M. Noland, "Pete Whetstone's Last Frolic," 1859, reprint, February 22, 1998, http://xroads.virginia.edu/~HYPER/DETOC/sw/pw2.html (accessed December 1, 2000).

28. For more on extraordinary bodies, see Rosemarie Garland-Thomson, *Extraordinary Bodies: Figuring Physical Disability in American Literature and Culture* (New York: Columbia University Press, 1997).

29. Ibid., 40.

30. Ibid., 59.

31. Ibid., 55–56.

32. Wilson, 14.

33. "Fat People," 352.

34. For more on bodies that are adaptable and their subjection to regimes of power/knowledge, see Michel Foucault, *Discipline and Punish: The Birth of the Prison*, trans. Alan Sheridan (New York: Vintage, 1979).

35. Banting, *A Letter on Corpulence*, 9.

36. Susan Bordo, *Unbearable Weight: Feminism, Western Culture, and the Body* (Berkeley: University of California Press, 1993), 199.

37. Thomas King Chambers, "On Corpulence," *The Lancet*, May 4, 1850, 523–25; May 11, 1850, 557–60; May 18, 1850, 581–83; June 1, 1850, 651–54; June 8, 1850, 687–90; June 22, 1850, 747–49.

38. "The Art of Unfattening," *Chambers' Journal* (1857), reprint, *Littell's Living Age* (July 11, 1857): 71.

39. Barbara Hardy, *The Exposure of Luxury: Radical Themes in Thackeray* (Pittsburgh, PA: University of Pittsburgh Press, 1972), 103.

40. Thackeray, *Vanity Fair*, 862.

41. Ibid., 374.

42. Ibid., 206.

43. Ibid., 66.

44. *Child's Magazine*, 46.

45. Robert Bogdan, *Freak Show: Presenting Human Oddities for Amusement and Profit* (Chicago: University of Chicago Press, 1990), 108.

46. Renato Rosaldo, *Culture and Truth* (Boston: Beacon Press, 1989), 69.

47. These tales function in much the same manner as current myths of the "supercrip."

48. Garland-Thomson, 26.

49. Wilson, 13.

50. Ibid., 17–18.

51. M. M. Bakhtin, *Rabelais and His World*, trans. Helene Iswolsky (1965, reprint, Bloomington: Indiana University Press, 1984).

52. As Peter Stallybrass has pointed out, for example, the grotesque aesthetic was used to demonize the lumpenproleteriat as dirty, diseased, and dangerously reproductive, constantly threatening to escape the slums and spread contagion among

the "decent" classes. See Peter Stallybrass, "Marx and Heterogeneity: Thinking the Lumpenproletariat," *Representations* 31 (1990): 69–95.

53. Bakhtin, 292.

54. Dickens, *Pickwick Papers*, 355.

55. Ibid., 368.

56. Ibid., 356.

57. Ibid., 52–53.

58. Ibid., 80.

59. Ibid., 48.

60. James R. Kincaid, *Annoying the Victorians* (New York: Routledge, 1995), 28.

61. John Stuart Mill, *On Liberty*, 1859, in *The Longman Anthology of British Literature*, vol. 2B, ed. David Damrosch et al. (New York: Longman, 1999), 1130–31.

62. Julia F. Saville, "Eccentricity as Englishness in *David Copperfield*," *SEL* 42, no. 4 (2002), 781–97.

63. Mill, 1131.

64. Saville, 782.

65. Wilson, 17.

66. Clarke, 7.

67. Ibid., 16.

68. Chambers, 689.

69. Edmund Burke, *Reflections on the Revolution in France* (1790, reprint, New York: Doubleday, 1961), 99.

70. Chambers, 689.

71. Wadd, 19.

72. This information was gathered from a visit to Stamford and phone and e-mail interviews with the staff at the Newarke Houses Museum (see note 16).

73. "The Signs They Are a Changin'," in *Campaign for Real Ale Peterborough Pub History Journal*, August 1996, http://www.pcamra.demon.co.uk/phj/1/phj0108.htm (accessed September 1, 2000).

74. According to a private e-mail communication from Philippa Massey, dated April 17, 2007.

3

WHITE WINGS AND SIX-LEGGED MUTTONS

The Freakish Animal

TIMOTHY NEIL

IN THE SIXTEENTH and seventeenth centuries, consideration of freaks, monsters, and prodigies confounded human and animal categories.[1] The nineteenth century saw these categorizations find their "natural" places as the developing sciences and the influence of Darwin reduced the controversies to questions of taxonomy. In spite of the seemingly clear demarcations in the system and the interest in categorization, the presentation of animals on stage still often blurred the boundaries between animal and human. Though the nineteenth century was awash with curious creatures both exhibited and performing—the volume of animal exhibitions, as well as the exhibition of the ethnographic freak[2] in association with animals[3] is well documented—contemporary criticism regarding the freak has sidelined the animal almost entirely. In the place of careful study, the presence of humans on the same stage as animals is often simply understood as *a priori* condemning the human to the realm of the beast. Moreover, little attention has been paid to the fact that the beasts in question were not simply six-legged sheep or other "abnormal" births but also healthy, "normal" animals. There are many ways in which animal enfreakment played a role in notions of human normalcy—the presence of the animal in the human, prominent in the exhibition practices of Barnum[4] and most famously the Elephant Man,[5] for example. In this essay I will concentrate on the animal itself in the human context and consequences of its exhibition. I argue that the exhibition of animals in the nineteenth century revealed aspects of the process of enfreakment and norming and provided a context conducive to the exhibition of human freaks, due to the enfreakment of animal exhibition and performance itself.[6]

In the first part of this essay I provide a brief overview of the development of nineteenth-century animal entertainments. This is followed by a discussion of a variety of these events, with an analysis of the often blurry boundary between the human and the animal and the implications of such slippage. The final section develops the discussion through a more detailed analysis of both the mechanics and the ethics of animal exhibition and enfreakment and its relationship to freakery overall.

Performing and Exhibited: Deciphering the Animal, Locating the Human

The presentation of animals in both the public and private sphere was a result of historical practice, changing technologies, and increasing leisure opportunities. There is a long relationship between humans and animals. Animals were central to all human activity, not just in agricultural practices. Even as the urban centers grew, animals played an important role—in spite of the increasing success at harnessing water power and eventually steam power—and animal traction for freight continued to increase well into the twentieth century.[7] Throughout the Victorian period, people were intimately connected to animals.

This intimacy continued in animal exhibitions for entertainment. During the late eighteenth century, the practice of visiting static menageries such as the Tower Menagerie in London combined with existing traditions of animal exhibition on the fairground and in various temporary locales and found expression in the traveling menageries. These popular, itinerant exhibitions of animals moved around the country either as part of the fair or independently. Traveling menageries drew wagons into a rectangle with a single entrance point, often very ornate, on one side. The exhibition space was a semipermeable arrangement that invited audience participation—something enhanced by the noisy arrival of the menageries in town, itself an aspect of their performance. Contemporaneously with the opening of Astley's Amphitheatre in London in 1768, the circus developed a mixture of skilled horsemanship and clowning, making humans a part of the animal show, as well as the audience. From the 1830s onward, imitating the successes of American animal trainer Van Amburgh,[8] animal tamers entered the arena, forming the triple axis characteristic of nineteenth- and twentieth-century circus: trained and tamed animals, human acrobatics, and clowning. Although the circus originally referred to the building, it came metonymically to refer to the show itself.

Itinerant circuses developed throughout the nineteenth century, distinguished from the menageries principally through the inclusion of human performances without animals, although this separation of the two spectacles was not consistent, with many menagerie owners turning to the circus and later the zoo. Many traveling circuses included a "circus menagerie" as well, implying a static display of animals, while traveling menageries often used performance as a central part of their presentation. The growth of the circus[9] as a permanent popular entertainment venue through the efforts of entrepreneurs such as Frederick "Charles" Hengler[10] saw a process through which performing animals entered the "human" spaces that would become the music hall circuit and later vaudeville. The period also saw the growth in popularity of the Zoological Garden as a venue for exhibition and in some cases performance, with, as a result of the 1851 Great Exhibition in London, the appearance of world's fairs as exhibition centers. Animal exhibition in the Victorian period saw continual growth and development, and it regularly connected humans and animals in a multitude of ways.

The traveling menageries are perhaps the most appropriate focus in the study of Victorian animal exhibition, as they combined elements of the static menageries with itinerant fairground traditions (which by the early twentieth century had developed a structure that had much in common with zoos and the circus), so my discussion focuses primarily on these, though I do attend to the other forms of exhibition as well. Several examples come from Wombwell's Menagerie (later Bostock and Wombwell), the traveling menagerie that came to epitomize itinerant displays of animals in the Victorian period.[11] By the time of his death, its founder, George Wombwell, had become a household name the length and breadth of Britain.[12] Indeed, his popularity gives some sense of the significant social presence of animal exhibition. Other examples come from the variety theater where performing animals were hugely popular, forming part of practically every program. These latter acts grew more numerous toward the end of the 1800s as the density of entertainment rapidly developed.

The enormous popularity of these acts is striking in itself, and in the way they parallel the growth of the human freak show. In both, the attempt to establish clear boundaries between the freak and the human is disrupted, and this disruption is often embodied in the blurring of the human and animal. As one commentator wrote of an animal performance: "It is a peculiar happiness to me . . . as an Adventurer, that I sally forth in an age which emulates those heroick times of old, when nothing was pleasing but what was unnatural. . . . That the intellectual faculties of brutes may be exerted beyond the narrow limits which we have hitherto assigned to their capacities, I saw sufficient proof in Mrs Midnight's dogs and monkies. Man differs less from beasts in general, than these seem to approach man in rationality."[13] Written in 1751 upon seeing a company of performing dogs and monkeys, this piece displays an irony typical of writing about performing animals. The butt of the humor is the human to whom the animal corresponds briefly during performance and to whom the commentator makes reference after the performance. This same blurring of boundaries is offered in a multitude of ways in the following extract, published some 150 years later:

> Impelled, perhaps, primarily by the undesirable but unavoidable necessity of providing himself with one or more meals a day, and after that by a genuine interest in a most fascinating pursuit, man has discovered that certain members of that section of animate society which he is pleased to call the lower animals may be successfully taught by his superior intellect to emulate the pursuits of his lighter fancy. And not only this—he has found that some of them actually take an interest, nay more, a positive pleasure in forsaking, under his tuition both the traditions and the postures of their race, and that, too, for the sake of making, or at any rate enlivening, a human holiday.[14]

Here we see what might be called the "animal" needs of man mentioned first, in his requirements for food, and even when these bodily interests are satisfied, man turns again to the animal for his entertainment, drawing close to animals in his leisure time. This is not the only way in which the line between them is blurred. These animals themselves cross the boundaries of human/animal when they are taught to take on the postures of humans. When the animal undermined "natural" animal states and became more "human," it softened the line between the human and the animal, and between the normative and nonnormative as well.

Performance by animals also acted metaphorically to connect the human and animal. As one contemporary critic noted, "Throughout history there have been animal performances. Elephants were made to dance in the train of Roman victors. The study of our popular entertainments here at home leads one to the very church door. Wild beasts were first employed, in the way of amusement, in the mystery plays, illustrating the creation of the world."[15] Always a part of the human drama, the animal comes to seem an indispensable part of human life—and even the social issues that humans perceive as being solely their province. Composed by a longtime aficionado of lion taming, the piece continues with references to "Hanno, the Carthaginian general" and later "Mark Anthony [driving] a pair of lions round the arena." These pieces demonstrate the role animals played in dramatizing and speaking to imperial projects.

Animal performance was frequently directly mimetic of human dramas, most clearly when animals were used to stage productions such as *The Brute Tamer of Pompeii.*[16] In this way they provided an acting out of social concerns and drew humans and animals together again. Representing, picturing, or presenting the human world was a quality also evident in the traveling menageries as with the performing Elephant advertised at Wombwell's Menagerie in Bristol:

MUSICAL PRODIGY

Of all Modern Prodigies certainly the most prodigious is the Royal Modern Musical Elephant at Wombwell's which plays several popular airs and polkas, by Handel, not known to be by that immortal composer, a fact which beats "Creation" or any other Oratorio—or Menagerie—Glasgow Citizen[17]

The elephant/prodigy/musician indicates the way in which such performances crossed and recrossed the lines between the human and animal. Elements of narrative, like the one above, often informed the more static exhibitions, typically anthropomorphizing the animals and blurring the boundaries again, as is seen in menagerie catalogues where detailed natural histories of each animal are presented and structure the context.[18] Advertisements also hinted at this phenomenon, as when the "Veteran Lion 'WALLACE'" appeared at Halifax Fairground in 1902, some seventy-five years after Wallace had a mythical fight with bulldogs at Warwick.[19] Not only is the lion a "veteran," a characterization that makes little sense with an animal unless we think of it anthropomorphically, but the name "Wallace" was enough to evoke a recognizable narrative that demonstrates the social significance of such performances to Victorians and their relationship to the mainstream.

Another common practice in animal performance was the presentation of tableaux, which were also likely to integrate humans and animals in disruptive ways. The Royal Italian Circus used trained animals to enact scenes from a military tribunal including the eventual simulated execution.[20] The human performer, too, realized tableaux, often illustrating contemporary or historical events and personalities, while in the fairground shows the performer's immobility invited spectators to gaze at a display of human flesh, much like a freak show. The animal tableau is typically represented by Van Amburgh as he is seen through the palette of Landseer, the lion lying down with the lamb. Scenes such as this were recreated many times in which beasts overcame their "natural" state—in this way creating an "unnatural" or "freakish" union, much like the marriage of the thin man and the fat lady. While the lion and lamb tableau was freakish,[21] it critiqued the naturalness of social norms that said such commingling was impossible. Perhaps it was inevitable that freak animals functioned in this way, calling into question the social norms.

Lions and other felines feature large in Victorian entertainment, and their displays often disrupted the expected hierarchy of human over animal, calling into question the taxonomies in which they were placed. These animals took their places on stage creating the illusion of a pyramid and lay with mouths open as the trainer laid his or her head inside and paused momentarily. The barber shaved the keeper of the animals inside the lion's cage and was applauded loudly upon his exit.[22] These performances, however, were fraught with danger and disruption. For instance, at Wombwell's Menagerie Wallace the lion attacked and ate the hand of the drunken Mr. Johnston, a night watchman, who tried to show Wallace to friends.[23] Onstage, the cowed participants when "The Lion Queen Performs"[24] were the overpowering victors in her eventual demise. While the animals were unconscious of social narrative in each instance, these stories commented on the instability of the power hierarchies: human/animal, "normative"/freak.

In another example, the trained dog, swinging freely on a trapeze, briefly assumes the postures of our race. *Place aux dames!*—I ought to have introduced the ladies first. . . . The damsel on the trapeze is Mademoiselle Blanche, and she, by the way, if you take another look at her portrait, appears also to have mastered the art of performing the elevated kick with her tail in a style worthy of exciting the envy even of a skirt dancer without a tail. It took her nearly a year to learn this, and a glance at the illustration on page 410 will show you how, clothed in her native charms, she began to acquire the really difficult art of which she is now a past mistress."[25] Mademoiselle Blanche was a poodle, yet redolent of humanity. What was being recognized and gazed upon was human occupation of space through the body of the Other, disrupting the line between the human and poodle, the normative and enfreaked. Animals performed such human feats in more ways than one. A war hero, "the genuine bell ringing ape from Mafeking, who so ably assisted the gallant 'B. P.' in his famous 200 days-defence," appeared regularly on Bostock and Wombwell's Menagerie.[26] The lions appear as ominous extras who refrain from slaughter in the novelty feat of the barber Mr. G. R. Parry, winning a wager by undertaking to "enter the lion's cage and shave the keeper of the beasts."[27] Each of these instances suggests the tenuousness of human superiority and of the stability of the human/animal binary.

There was often an emphasis on the exotic animal whose origins confounded the emergent taxonomist, like the racial others encountered in colonization. The categories offered were frequently disruptive—just as unstable as those employed in descriptions of the colonized subject. The advertisement that read, "Also, just added, a fine specimen of the CHACMA, or 'New Man Monkey'"[28] indicates this confounding of terms. As other essays in this collection indicate, these strained categories participated in larger social shifts. In the later years a more general dissemination of categories of natural science nurtured an exhibition practice based on exceptions to recognized normality, and these "animal freaks" accentuated this phenomenon: "[Wombwell's exhibited] many novelties of 'animal nature' absolutely unique of their kind. Firstly, there is the handsome pure milk-white 'Yankee' horse, possessing mane and tail of the actual combined length of 40 feet, the posters are said to give a true idea of this striking animal curiosity, which alone will attract many to the show. Then comes a giant cart horse, 21 hands (84 inches high), miniature horse, 6 hands, or 24 inches high, giant mule, 19 hands, and a miniature mule 24 inches high, a hairless, or India rubber skinned mare from Kruger Land."[29] Animals whose bodies did not equate with the norm, for example, sheep with six legs,[30] could be exhibited as novelties in sideshows at fairs either dead or alive. In fact, so frequent was the former that showmen would advertise their novelties as "alive" in order to overcome suspicion. All of these exhibits undermined the clean categories that seemed to be offered by science, calling both the taxonomy and its creators into question.

The exhibited animal, whether freak or not, was removed from the wild and lodged into a context of human concerns. Medieval and Renaissance theology and philosophy, with their roots in the Bible and Aristotle, were anthropocentric, but the modern period can be characterized as anthropomorphic,[31] attributing human personality to the impersonal, irrational, and even animal. While this does not mean the human has been replaced as the central fact of the universe, this concept is at the center of Lévi-Strauss's proposal that "animals are good to think with." In this sense animals provide a ready technology with which we may discuss our ideas about far more than sentience itself. The animal, in these moments, invokes disparate responses. The resonance of the animal, the profundity of the echo, makes it malleable. Animals are what we make of them: idealized, they may be conducive to an ethical humanism or, as brute beast of creation, a "model of disorder."[32] This flexibility has made them even more available as a means of speaking to human social concerns.[33]

Both performance and exhibition are understood as passive as far as the animal is concerned—in other words, the critical debate over the performer's willingness to take the stage drawn out by Robert Bogdan and David Gerber[34] does not apply in the same way to animals as human subjects, nor does it allow us to view animals as active participants. This construction, however, does not account for the complex relationship between humans and animals. Nor does it attend to the precarious nature of many of the acts—the possibility, the inevitability even, that the animal would behave outside the script and disrupt the display. In this way, the animal retained a kind of "agency" in the process and served the social function of drawing in an audience and engaging the public in dialogue about the animal/freak. Bostock, for example, admitted that an attack on the trainer provided good publicity, echoing P. T. Barnum's attempts to create controversy surrounding the human freaks in his shows to draw in an audience.[35] The role of the animal, the parallels to the human freak show, and the relationship between the animal and human suggest to us that we may need to reexamine the use of the concept of freakery with regard to animals.

The Animal as Freak

The other essays in this collection demonstrate how catholic the use of the term "freak" is. However, unless they display marked variation from their type, animals are not generally classed as freaks. It would perhaps be seen as pejorative or unsympathetic, in part because animals are implicitly understood to be present solely through the intervention of human agency. Here I have suggested, foremost, that the categories of human and animal are not clear, that the system of taxonomy in the natural sciences[36] establishes the fluidity of the animal/human category. Second, animals were often situated in very human contexts. When elephants performed and boa constrictors behaved, both were far removed from the environment in which they originated and were physically and socially installed in a human environment. Moreover, they required other kinds of human intervention, like narrative explanation. In ever greater detail, as the old narratives became familiar and the exotic became commonplace, animals were enfreaked for their show value. More and more, animals became freaks, invoking "amazement and moments of a particular gaze . . . [a] momentary dreaming."[37]

We might resist such a characterization, believing that our contemporary taxonomy, which separates animals and humans and marks out our species as discrete, is the recognition of a natural law. Indeed, the contrary position, that biological species are not natural kinds, seems to deny scientific rationalism. However, it is faithful to the precepts of Darwinism, which suggests that "since species evolve . . . they should be treated not as classes whose members satisfy some fixed set of conditions—not even a vague cluster of them—but as lineages, lines of descent, strings of imperfect copies of predecessors."[38] The sense that we as humans are wholly separated from the other animals, as well as from the inanimate, is a convenience contrived to account for the complexity and perhaps the implausibility of thinking in Darwinian epochs. Where the moral and political effects of thinking that any biological human population is less than "human" have been catastrophic,[39] the corollary has been that it is equally unthinkable that a nonbiologically human population be considered human. Still, the undeniable fluidity of the taxonomic process and the slipperiness of the human/animal categories have allowed this to occur. The enormous cultural variation in the construction of the animal both underscores and reveals the instability of the categories. Another corroborating fact is the way in which human groups have often regraded new groups they have encountered, labeling them (both human and nonhuman) as nonhuman and "other." What this suggests, however, is that "human" may more usefully function as a folk taxonomy than a scientific class.

In spite of this slipperiness, the role of animals has not been recognized in critical studies of culture and freakery. Placing animals in the category of "freaks" allows us to acknowledge the complex position they take in the process of enfreakment and to flesh out their significance. The animal in the cage or ring could be none other than a freak—the figure of fear, indifference, amusement, ridicule, cruelty, admiration, or pity, but also a figure of potential social power. Animals can be given life beyond their cages and a role beyond suffering; their significance can be interrogated. Studying animals can aid us in our ability to imagine ourselves "in forms other than this [one in which we currently exist, and which] seems to require that [we are] not quite identical with this bodily organism."[40] This power to imagine ourselves differently made the animal particularly significant. We can begin to understand how when we look at the way in which the animal was positioned in the nineteenth century. The animal had always been close to humans, and the Victorian period saw this proximity taken out of the workplace and given a spectacular role: entertainment. As freaks of nature, animals were exhibited for their exotic or rare qualities; as freaks of culture, they dramatized the slippery line between human and animal, a phenomenon with social effects.

The Spectacle of Animal Performance

The animal performs with the human literally in the background—when absent, there can be no performance. The leopard cowers, but only from the trainer, and the lioness can only escape from the show when there is a person from whom to escape. Performance and exhibition create possibility that the zebra, in flesh and blood, takes part in the social, its agency choreographed but not completely controlled. The show was not simply a cage, but an arena intimate to human concerns.

> For there was Polito, with condors from Quito,
> And serpents from Ceylon, and apes from Japan,
> Whose sly-demure faces, as often the case is,
> Is like, very like, the arch hypocrite man;
> . . .
> And six legged muttons [sheep] hear this, you gluttons,
> And calves, double headed, and ducks, with one leg,
> And the learned dog Toby, who gave me the go by,
> So well could the creature tell fortunes and beg.[41]

In this poem celebrating the visit to Bristol of Polito's traveling menagerie in 1845, the themes of this essay emerge: the animal's "humanity"
is recognized and partially mediated through humor; we are urged to
recognize our normality in contrast to the animal freaks, but also to call
it into question when we hear of the human agency of Toby. Human
narrative, here, was the key to comprehension. Performance and exhibition, like the moon, pulled an inevitable narrative tide. The animals
stood before the trainer, the tamer, or the lecturer and were gazed upon
by the spectator on the shore. This spectacle is the spectacle of the
freak—the observed, the one defying category, the one that narrative
alone will reveal, the one that demands the attention of the spectator,
the prop to the storyteller. The images and stories of exhibited and
performing nonhuman animals are washed up by this tide, left high and
dry by most critical narratives.

The freak is not born freak[42] but made freak by a particular gaze; the
exhibited animal was the receptor of that gaze, as a novelty or performed
as such, with the human always in the foreground, capturing, revealing,
cajoling, and laughing, present in a passive imperative. Imperfect in
their humanity, yet resonant with human traits—including their lack
of power—the animals were mired in their species. They both invited
rapprochement and denied its possibility. We assume the animal has
no say in the matter of performance. The human, even when offered
no choice, is, like the gladiator or the courtesan, honored with a voice.
The animal has no such option. The modern usage of the term "freak"
and its assumption of alternative seeing and its honoring of difference
must be extended to exhibited animals and their performances.

In the context of modern performances by trained elephants, attention has been drawn to the way in which compelling circus animals to
"perform human" makes them into freak animals.[43] In his discussion of
performing elephants in Cottle's Circus, Carmeli notes that human presence is implied in the elephants' bodies' movement and display. This
anthropomorphism is one aspect of the play; another is the importance
of the similarity of all circus acts: "What the spectators expect in the
circus animals acts are not the routines' particularities, but the human
presence betrayed in them all."[44] It is this human presence, seen through
the body of the animal, that is central to the idea of the freakish animal.
As with the human freak, it is through the context of exhibition and
presentation itself that the freak is made. Seen in this light, both exhibition of and performance by animals can be understood as constructing
them as freaks, and studying the particular contexts of freakery in the
nineteenth century will give us more insight into the period overall.

Conclusion

In the Italian folktale "The King of the Animals," a young girl, Stellina, is tempted by a handsome youth who persuades her to live in a mysterious castle surrounded by a beautiful park stocked with all sorts of animals, including dogs, cats, donkeys, hens, and giant toads. They sound like a group of people all talking at once. For several months she lives in the castle waited upon by invisible servants until one fateful day she learns that her young man, whom she only sees briefly each morning, is none other than the King of the Animals, and he intends to devour her. She plots her escape but is obliged to bring about his death. No sooner has he fallen than all the animals change back to their true form: kings, queens, and princes alike.[45]

Many will wish that such could be the destiny of the exhibited and performing animals whose lives in the beautiful park of Victorian entertainment were so rudely constrained. That they should find their liberation as human beings would be particularly appropriate, destined as they were to embody particular human attributes, attitudes, and postures in their working life. The spectacle of a performing dog pushing a pram containing a dressed cat is perhaps an unpalatable icon. In spite of this, our modern sensibility of the nonhuman, our assumption of the entire natural world as our totemic right, is imperial and self-aggrandizing.

In this essay I argue that we see the "freakish animal" based, in part, upon the centrality of human narrative in animal performance and exhibition in the Victorian period. Is it thus to be understood as a category of the animal itself or of the exhibitor and the audience? Drawing an analogy between zoo visitors in front of the primate enclosures, archaeologist Cornelius Holtorf recognizes the struggle to define "precisely what it means to be human and where the human-animal boundary can be drawn in time and space." The limits of the cage materialize the human-animal boundary with the Victorian zoo displaying "animals [that] were visually near but physically separate." Moreover, Darwin's revelation of common ancestry and an increased understanding of the complex social organization of both the higher and lower animals left the nineteenth century "coming to terms with this new, and sometimes threatening, proximity of animals."[46]

A paradox of the modern condition is that we no longer wish to see animals behind bars, as performers or exhibits—unless they act out the modern condition as is the case with wildlife documentaries and wildlife parks and in the documenting of cruelty. The bounded animal in an exhibition booth, upon a stage, in a ring, or behind bars plays an ontology in flux. Human physical supremacy seems ascendant in this case, but the animal, too, was gaining ground through this very knowledge. The spectacle, the playing of life in remove, was to bring the animal to the forefront of consciousness.

In a recent article, "The Animal Other,"[47] Donald Turner proposes that notions of civility be extended to animals—not on account of human-generated empathy but rather because ethical imperatives can be seen as emanating from the beings themselves. Both nonhuman animals and humans have ethics. The "structural asymmetry" that exists between humans and animals should be respected, not abused. The willingness to consider that animals, both exhibited and performing, partake of the very human category of freaks is to acknowledge that there is a genuine continuum from the human to the nonhuman animal, and to see the stability of all those categories upset. We need to recognize freaks in the past and heed freaks in the present. The human capacity to make worlds, to create physical structure and rules that affect others, is the capacity that produces freaks. If we fail to acknowledge their place as freaks, we fail also to acknowledge the social politics of their enfreakment and the corollaries it provides to human enfreakment.

Sheep with six legs or calves with two heads were not common and were pronounced novel; they were recognized as freaks. However, it is as freaks of culture, not of nature, that they should be understood. They were not evidence of natural or holy error but rather were floated in preserving jars as proof of normality and an assurance of social norms. The exception proves the rule. White Wings, a horse that traveled widely with Bostock and Wombwell's Menagerie sporting an exceptionally long mane and tail,[48] was not advertised as a freak but rather a novelty of animal nature. It is the contention of this essay that, like the hirsute Lionel,[49] performing and exhibited animals such as White Wings were, regardless of their objective condition, freaks. Moreover, the slipperiness between the animal and human, between the freak and the norm, and the very process of enfreakment are evidenced in the condition of animal performer.

Contemporary critical studies are often concerned with freak as a social category that can be used subversively and can disrupt the sense of normativity. The animal freak, indeed the "normed" animal, deserves consideration in this conversation. There is no value in continuing the very categorizations of the Victorian epoch and refusing humans and nonhuman animals space in the same stable. Any discussion of exhibited and performing animals must avoid above all repeating this trope, and any discussion of freakery in the nineteenth century must open the doors to discuss animal freaks as well as humans.

Notes

1. Katharine Park and Lorraine Daston, "Unnatural Conceptions: The Study of Monsters in Sixteenth- and Seventeenth- Century France and England," *Past and Present*, no. 92 (August 1981): 20–54.

2. Vaughan Christopher, "Ogling Igorots: The Politics and Commerce of Exhibiting Cultural Otherness, 1898–1913," in *Freakery: Cultural Spectacles of the Extraordinary Body*, ed. Rosemarie Garland-Thomson (New York: New York University Press, 1993), 219–33.

3. Vanessa Toulmin, "Abnormitäten und Exotik: Ein Überblick über die Präsenz von Völkerschauen im Europa und Amerika des 19.Jahrhunderts" [Abnormalities and the Exotic: An Overview of the Presence of Native Shows in Europe and America in the Nineteenth Century], *Grüsse aus Viktoria: Film-Ansichten aus der Ferne*, Kintop Schriften 7 (Autumn 2002): 43–60.

4. Jan Bondeson, *The Feejee Mermaid and Other Essays in Natural and Unnatural History* (Ithaca, NY: Cornell University Press, 1999).

5. Ashley Montagu, *The Elephant Man: A Study in Human Dignity* (London: Allison and Busby Ltd., 1972).

6. The scope of this essay does not allow the history of animal and human relations to be examined in detail but rather concentrates on the exhibition and performance. For the purposes of this essay these terms are used almost interchangeably, it being a central contention that the exhibited animal performed and the performing animal exhibited.

7. Theo Barker and Dorian Gerhold, *The Rise and Rise of Road Transport, 1700–1990* (Cambridge: Cambridge University Press for the Economic History Society, 1993), 51, 60.

8. He was famously credited with introducing lion taming onto the stage.

9. For a good account of the development of the circus see George Speaight, *A History of the Circus* (London: Tantivy Press, 1980).

10. John M. Turner, *Victorian Arena: The Performers: A Dictionary of British Circus Biography* (Formby: Lingdales Press, 1995).

11. John M. Turner, *Wombwell's Travelling Menagerie* [UK]: [n.p.], 1995.

12. *Banbury Guardian*, November 28, 1850. No one has done "so much to forward practically the study of natural history amongst the masses, for his menageries visited every fair and every town in the kingdom, and was everywhere popular."

13. Thomas Frost, *The Old Showmen, and the Old London Fairs*, 2nd ed. (London: Tinsley Brothers), 169. The animals were brought by Ballard from Italy and exhibited on the Haymarket in Mrs. Midnight's Oratory.

14. H. J. Milton, "Animal Actors," *Pearson's Magazine* 1 (January–June 1896): 407–12.

15. Harry Wilding, *Lion Tamers and Lion Taming* (The World's Fair), March 28, 1925, 10.

16. William Johnson, *The Rose-Tinted Menagerie* (London: Heretic, 1990).

17. *Clifton Chronicle and Directory* (June 3, 1868).

18. *Bostock and Wombwell's Menagerie.—Visitors' Guide and Illustrated Catalogue of Bostock Late Wombwell's Grand. . . .* 5th ed. ([n.p.], 1888).

19. *Halifax Evening Courier*, September 13, 1902, 1.

20. *Hull News* (April 6, 1901), 6.

21. *The Blackpool Times* and *Fylde Observer* (June 24, 1905). Bostock's animals at Blackpool appear in a show where no expense was "spared in making the animal arena one of the best extant for animal exhibition and performance."

22. *Liverpool Daily Post* (April 8, 1901), 9, c. 3–4: "DARING FEAT OF A BARBER. SHAVING IN A CAGE OF LIONS. Mr G. R. Parry, a barber, carrying on business at Church Street, Flint, has just performed a daring feat and thereby won a wager. A menagerie is at present on exhibition in the town, and the intrepid barber undertook to enter the lion's cage and shave the keeper of the beasts. A great crowd of spectators assembled to witness the operation, which was successfully performed on Thursday night, the barber plying his razor in a cool and businesslike way, amid the intense excitement of the onlookers. On emerging from the cage, he was loudly cheered."

23. *Bristol Mercury* (September 13, 1831).

24. *The Coventry Herald and Observer* (June 8, 1849), 1. The Lion Queen, performing in Wombwell's Menagerie, was to die mauled by her lions soon after.

25. Milton, 408.

26. *Doncaster Chronicle* (December 4, 1901), 5.

27. *Liverpool Daily Post* (April 8, 1901), 9, c. 3–4.

28. *The Coventry Herald and Observer* (May 31, 1861), 1.

29. *Doncaster Chronicle* (December 4, 1901), 5.

30. *World's Fair*, June 15, 1907, 1

31. Thomas, 19.

32. Tapper, 51.

33. Editor's note: see the introduction, the section titled "Dislocating the Freak: Social Ambiguity."

34. See Bogdan and Gerber's essay on the subject in Rosemarie Garland-Thomson's *Freakery: Cultural Spectacles of the Extraordinary Body* (New York: New York University Press, 1996), 23–37 and 38–54.

35. E. H. (Edward Henry) Bostock, *Menageries, Circuses and Theatres* (London: Chapman and Hall, 1927), 101.

36. Tim Ingold, *What Is an Animal?* (London: Unwin Hyman, 1981).

37. Yoram S. Carmeli, "The Sight of Cruelty: The Case of Circus Animal Acts," *Visual Anthropology* 10 (1997): 9, 5, 10.

38. A. Rosenberg, *Sociology and the Perception of Social Science* (Baltimore: Johns Hopkins University Press, 1980), 25.

39. Ibid., 27.

40. Ibid., 33.

41. "St James's Fair: A Reminiscence," poem by Inconnu, Bristol (September 1, 1845), Bristol Reference Library Collections.

42. Bogdan, 24.

43. Carmeli, "Sight of Cruelty," 9.

44. Ibid., 9.

45. Italo Calvino, ed., "The King of the Animals," in *Italian Folktales* (London: Penguin, 2000), 163–66.

46. Cornelius Holtorf and David Van Reybrouck, "Towards an Archaeology of Zoos," *International Zoo News* 50 (2003): 207–15.

47. Donald L. Turner, "The Animal Other: Civility and Animality in and Beyond Heidegger, Levinas, and Derrida," in *DisClosure* 12 (2003): 169–93.

48. *Doncaster Chronicle* (December 4, 1901), 5: "VISIT TO DONCASTER OF THE ONLY AND ORIGINAL WOMBWELLS. This mammoth travelling 'Zoo' will visit Doncaster for one day, Monday, Oct 7, exhibiting in the Magdelene Square. Many changes have been added, and many novelties of 'animal nature' absolutely unique of their kind."

49. Lionel the Lion Man traveled widely in the late 1800s.

PART II

Science, Medicine, and the Social

WHILE THERE is significant thematic overlap between the four sections of this book, this section attempts to plumb in greater depth what the previous section identifies as a preeminent discourse in the creation of freakery: science and medicine. Each of these essays, however, fleshes out these questions in relation to another British social tension as well. Meegan Kennedy's essay provides an English Victorian inquiry that complements work like Tchen's on Asians in the United States. She examines the social understanding of "monstrous or uncontrollable growth at the borders of British empire," situating the "Oriental" in Britain, with regard to the medical management of Hoo Loo, a man with a massive testicular tumor. Christine Ferguson looks at physician Frederick Treves's discursive manipulation of the famous Joseph Merrick as he "toured" London social circles. While it offers a particular focus on the famous "Elephant Man," this argument opens up questions about the linguistic/textual production of freakery in general. Finally, Nadja Durbach looks at scientific discourses about evolution, ideologies of imperialism, and their relationship to Krao Farini, a Laotian woman who opened her career at the London Aquarium in 1883 exhibiting as the "missing link." Durbach's essay not only tackles science but also forms a link to the next section of the book, which addresses the role of empire and social perception of race in shaping—and understanding—freakery.

"POOR HOO LOO"

Sentiment, Stoicism, and the
Grotesque in British Imperial Medicine

MEEGAN KENNEDY

MEDICAL NARRATIVES of extraordinary bodies must negotiate a long
tradition of "the curious" in British culture. Lorraine Daston and
Katharine Park, for example, argue that the unknown and the wondrous
were precisely what early modern science was charged with examining.[1]
However, that long tradition began to shift its ground during the nineteenth century. Curious cases were no longer as welcome in medicine
and the sciences, as workers in these fields struggled to define and to
attain a new ideal of professionalism. Medical texts began to demonstrate an increased anxiety of genre, in an effort to distinguish their
narratives from those such as R. S. Kirby's six-volume *The Wonderful and
Scientific Museum; or, Magazine of Remarkable Characters* (1803–20), for
example, which combined spectacle and entertainment with the claim
of educational content and offered copious illustrations to lure readers
(figure 4.1).[2]

In fact, even Kirby's text registers that cultural shift: the first volume
of his compendium was titled *The Wonderful and Scientific Museum*; the
third, *Kirby's Wonderful and Eccentric Museum*.[3] That shift in title—to
"eccentric" museum—anticipates the changes in what "science" could
comprehend during the 1830s and 1840s, with the intensification of
debates over the borders of appropriate medical practice.[4] As part of

Figure 4.1
"Mr. Matthew Buchinger . . . the Wonderful Little Man of Nuremberg, in Germany." From *Kirby's Wonderful and Eccentric Museum*, 1804, Rare Book Collection, Department of Special and Area Studies Collections, George A. Smathers Libraries, University of Florida.

the vexed process of professionalization, which included an increased interest in studying normative disease experience, curious phenomena fell out of favor as the proper matter for medical science.[5] This suspicion of the curious was well established even in popular discussions of medicine by 1859, when George Henry Lewes commented, in the course of a discussion of fantastic cases of fasting, "It is rather startling to find so learned a physiologist as M. Bérard recording such cases, and trying to explain them. The possibility of deception and exaggeration is so great, that we are tempted to reject almost every one of these cases rather than reject all physiological teaching."[6] Physicians began to consider the curious case as improper—inappropriate for a medical or scientific narrative—due to its generic markers: a singular patient or unexplainable event, a rhetoric of extremity, and an explicit appeal to the emotions. As a result, although curious cases do not disappear, most medical authors begin to shroud the profile of the curious in their unusual cases, instead emphasizing their use of clinical protocol, permitting a curious discourse only intermittently, and turning to euphemisms such as "interesting" to replace "curious" or "singular."[7]

The author of the medical report from Guy's Hospital in the *Lancet* of April 16, 1831, however, makes it clear that the case he records here *is* a curious case.[8] It is a remarkable case, in fact, bringing together a number of significant topics in British medicine: a disease of remarkable or unstoppable growth, a patient of an exotic race, a medical error, and the properly objective stance of a medical practitioner. The proceedings of the case testify to the British faith in, and the limits of, nineteenth-century clinical medical knowledge and recall the most spectacular aspects of eighteenth-century medicine, while the rhetorical and visual choices made in the text and illustrations, typical of the period, demonstrate a timely anxiety over problems of monstrous or uncontrollable growth at the borders of the British empire.

In this case, Hoo Loo, a thirty-two-year-old "Chinese labourer," journeys from Canton to England seeking treatment for "an extraordinary tumour [in his scrotum] . . . of a nature and extent hitherto unseen in this country" (86). Chinese surgeons would have had more experience with scrotal tumors, which were more common in Asia. Scrotal swelling can be caused by tuberculosis, syphilis, and hydrocele (a sac of fluid in the scrotum), among other diagnoses, but in Asia, Africa, and South America this condition is especially associated with scrotal elephantiasis.[9] John Esdaile, in *Mesmerism in India* (1846), reports on cases of elephantiasis, hydrocele, and syphilis in this context.[10] Elephantiasis probably accounted for Hoo Loo's fifty-six-pound tumor, based on the postmortem discussion.[11] Immense ("mature") tumors of every sort, ranging from five to eighty pounds, were also more common in China, in part because practitioners there only rarely performed surgeries at this time.[12]

Thus, despite their relative familiarity with afflictions like Hoo Loo's,

Chinese surgeons (and the English eye surgeon Thomas Colledge, who sent him to Britain) had declined to operate on him—prudently, as it turns out.[13] The famed Sir Astley Cooper, however, and his protégé, Charles Aston Key, accepted the challenge and proceeded to surgery on April 9, 1831.[14] Because of the complex anatomy of the area, Aston Key, the "operator," took longer than expected—this in the pre-anesthetic era, when speed was crucial in allowing the patient to withstand the rigors of surgery. Cooper decided to simplify the procedure by simply cutting off the penis and testes to save time, rather than attempting to preserve them, but the operation still lasted an hour and forty-four minutes, a "tremendous protraction" due to the occasional pauses to allow the patient to recover when he fainted from the pain. The various reports of the surgery differ on the amount of blood lost, agreeing that an emergency transfusion did take place, but "he sunk" anyway, from either shock or loss of blood.[15]

In its role as a spectacular failure of British medical superiority, the case of Hoo Loo triggered debate over surgical standards. The *Lancet*, the dominant reformist medical journal in Britain and a powerful voice in the struggle to professionalize medicine, loudly voiced the opinions of its editor, Thomas Wakley, on the sometimes egregious gaps in medical competence. Wakley printed the Hoo Loo case as the regular report from Guy's Hospital, probably written by one of the surgeons there, but he prefaced it with a scathing editorial that, while acknowledging "the manual skill of the operator," thundered against the "very serious errors" of judgment that doomed the case. He concluded that the length of the surgery, combined with "the time and place selected for the operation[,] showed an extraordinary, if not a fatal, want of professional discrimination."[16] The *Lancet*'s position is delicate. On the one hand, its editorial embraces the role of reformer. On the other hand, there is no indication that Wakley, as editor, called for revisions in the report from Guy's Hospital; and by printing it, the *Lancet* implicitly endorsed the report's version of events—a version that calls into question the professionalism of not only the operator but also his scribe.

That version of Hoo Loo's case stages the patient as a curious case; it also embraces sentiment in its portrayal of an exotic protagonist and his tragic, stoic death in extreme circumstances. And it triggered an equally impassioned discussion of medical standards, in and out of the professional press. Most interesting, perhaps, the striking full-length portrait of the patient, captioned "Poor Hoo Loo and His Tumour," raises questions about the relation of professional knowledge and medical representation to British beliefs about race, nationalism, and imperial ambition. In particular, Hoo Loo's case, like others in the *Lancet* during these crucial years of professionalization, suggests that the discourse of nineteenth-century case histories enabled the exoticization of "grotesque" diseases, such as elephantiasis, genital tumors, and morbid obesity. Diseases like these locate British concerns over excessive growth and the security of national borders. Because the bodies most frequently depicted as portraits in the mid-century *Lancet* depict illnesses of grotesquerie, in particular uncontrolled physical growth, they carry the potential of signifying monstrous, unsustainable appetite and expansion beyond "natural" bounds of the body. Because they are often associated with problems of generation, they offer a venue for the expression of anxieties over the reproduction of the British nation abroad. And because these bodies are also almost always exoticized, with their usually Asian or Southeast Asian features clearly marked, the sickness of monstrous growth coincides, here, with some of the global locations where the British empire was most rapidly expanding. The conjunction of sentimental discourses with curious and spectacular representations of these patients may represent one way of textually fixing onto the "other" the mid-century anxieties over the viability of British imperial appetite.

The Curious Case of Hoo Loo and His Fortitude

The report of Hoo Loo and his tumor displays a number of rhetorical characteristics typical of a singular genre of medical narrative: the curious case, which flourished in the eighteenth century and persisted into the nineteenth century, in the teeth of increasing pressure toward objectivity and normative cases. Such survivals are more common than might be expected, even late in the century, but the curious discourse in these cases is typically tempered with more careful scientific detail. By 1896, for example, with the publication of a collection of *Anomalies and Curiosities of Medicine,* the American editor carefully framed the encyclopedic but eccentric text as itself a curiosity in the era of clinical medicine.[17]

The rarity and difficulty of Hoo Loo's case immediately tags it as curious. Certainly mature tumors like his were rare in Britain, and his was enormous even compared to other mature tumors in the medical literature. Nonmedical reports on the case not surprisingly exhibit the rhetoric of extremity and emotion that marks curious discourse. The *Times*, for example, concludes its article on the case with the exclamation, "[The tumor's] circumference, when detached from the body, was exactly four feet!"[18] Even the Guy's Hospital report in the *Lancet* did little to diminish the curious aspects of the case, however, instead emphasizing them through its narrative choices. A curious discourse recurs in the report, conveying extremity ("an extraordinary tumour . . . hitherto unseen"), exoticism (Hoo Loo's Chinese ethnicity), and sexuality (the location of the tumor). Other cases of sizable genital tumors in the *Lancet* during the first half of the nineteenth century also often signal the status of their case as curious in phrases such as "most interesting," "an enormous size," and the like.[19] Like these, Hoo Loo's case history registers the uneven progress of the shift from a more curious and sentimental medicine to the more clinical and scientific medicine of the nineteenth century.

Another rhetorical hallmark of a curious case is its oscillation between sometimes discordant discourses and genres, as the author draws from different, even conflicting, narrative norms. Hoo Loo's case includes significant shifts in tone of this sort, recording the author's complicated response to the rapidly changing situation. The author of the Guy's Hospital report, probably a surgeon associated with the case, at first makes the most of the curious aspects of Hoo Loo's story. We hear that "the case excited considerable interest, both in and out of the profession," and in fact, on the day set for the excision of the tumor, "an assemblage, unprecedented in numbers on such an occasion, presented themselves for admission at the operating theatre, which was instantly filled in every part." Due to the crowd, Cooper moved the operation to the "great anatomical theatre . . . where accommodation was afforded to 680 persons" (86). Although the placement of the operation in the "great anatomical theatre" suggests that Hoo Loo's case is of educational value, it also proleptically figures him as a cadaver being dissected, while the "considerable interest" and great size of the audience unhappily recalls some of the great spectacles of early medicine, by this time considered inappropriate to professional decorum.[20]

While the hospital report sets the scene by soliciting attention through a discourse of the spectacular, it assumes a brisk clinical tone in order to chronicle and explain the complex surgery. Unfortunately, the procedure itself was not as brisk, ultimately causing Hoo Loo's death. It is at this point, when the narrative must detail how the powers of medicine begin to fail the patient (and his surgeons), that the consistency of the clinical narrative begins to falter as well. As if to fill this gap of clinical knowledge, a sentimental discourse emerges instead in statements such as this one: "Immediately after the removal of the tumour, another fit of syncope—if syncope could be said to be at all incomplete for the last half hour—came on, from which the poor fellow did not for a moment rally." The desperation of the operators becomes evident in the phrasing of the last moments of the procedure: despite the frantic blood transfusion "from the arm of a student" (one of "several" who volunteered), the narrator reports, "The patient did breathe after the operation, but that is as much as can be said. Artificial respiration was subsequently, but vainly attempted" (87). The image of the narrator here shifts from that of an expert observer or even participant to that of a sympathetic, even despairing spectator.

Hoo Loo's death, once it is established, prompts the narrator to launch into a eulogy that rehearses the operation from another, even more sentimental, perspective, and not inconsequently revises the image of British medicine in the process. This view emphasizes what is most curious about the patient: not his remarkable tumor, as it turns out, but his extraordinary stoicism in the face of unthinkable pain.

> The fortitude with which this great operation was approached, and throughout undergone, by Hoo Loo, was, if not unexampled, at all events never exceeded in the annals of surgery. A groan now and then escaped him, and now and then a slight exclamation, and we thought we could trace in his tones a plaintive acknowledgment of the hopelessness of his case. Expressions of regret, too, that he had not rather borne with his affliction than suffered the operation, seemed softly but rapidly to vibrate from his lips as he closed his eyes, firmly set his teeth, and resignedly strung every nerve in obedience to the determination with which he had first submitted to the knife. (87)

Here the language of extremity, typical of curious discourse—"fortitude . . . never exceeded"—pairs with a sentimental identification with the patient, in which the spectators "thought we could trace" his thoughts, his regret, and his resolve. Hoo Loo's body, too, is transformed here from a clinical object (originally evident in the title, which details the borders of the tumor as "extending from beneath the umbilicus to the anterior border of the anus" [86]) to a sentimental type, figured only in clichés evoked through the process of identification. That this process is an imaginative rather than an empirical one is evident from the narrator's claimed knowledge, despite the cloth obscuring the patient's face, that Hoo Loo's regret vibrated from his lips, as he closed his eyes, set his teeth, and strung his nerves up to the ordeal. In juxtaposing Hoo Loo's stoic demeanor during surgery to the medical narrator's more agitated, melodramatic apprehension of the event, this case reverses the doctor-patient hierarchy of objectivity over subjectivity that nineteenth-century British medicine would set itself to achieve.[21]

Reading the Event: Spectacle, Stoicism, and Race

The record of the surgery provided by the Guy's Hospital report is thus evidently a shaped narrative, pointing toward a particular reading of the situation. This becomes especially clear in comparing the report with other published versions of events. The *Times* article describes the scene as more chaotic than the *Lancet's* merely factual record of a massive audience. Indeed, the *Times* reports that the hospital was "absolutely besieged" by "the most celebrated medical men" and that "a rush was immediately made by those assembled" to the theater, which "was crammed in every part within two minutes of the doors being opened." Although the *Times* noted the presence of at least fourteen "celebrated medical men" by name, descriptions such as the one above suggest not a professional demonstration but a mob scene. Similarly, an article in *Bell's Weekly Messenger*, a conservative newspaper, provides details that only exacerbate the suggestion that the operation had become a spectacle: audience members were offering money to obtain Hoo Loo's "Chinese hat" or queue as "some memento" of the occasion. The hospital's report, not surprisingly, does not mention this rush for souvenirs.

Bell's also presents an image of Hoo Loo that is not nearly as stoic as that in the *Lancet*. In *Bell's* the author reports that hospital "authorities" very much regretted not having provided "persons . . . who could act as interpreters to the unfortunate foreigner; and who would, at the same time, by soothing the poor fellow in his own language, keep up his spirits, and render him that explanation and assistance . . . of which the poor fellow appeared so much in need." *Bell's* even dwells on Hoo Loo's agitation during the surgery, reporting (from a spectator familiar with Hoo Loo's language) that he called out, "Unloose me! Unloose me!" "Water! help! water! let me go!" and, finally, "Let it be—let it remain—I can bear no more!—Unloose me!"[22] There is little evidence in this horrific scene of the extraordinary stoicism that the Guy's Hospital report insists on seeing in Hoo Loo.

These lay periodicals attribute Hoo Loo's death to an unforeseen complication of his racial identity. *Bell's* comments that Hoo Loo "appeared to suffer greatly from the loss of [about sixteen ounces of blood], which would not have dangerously affected a European." Similarly, the *Times* concludes that Aston Key's delays throughout the procedure were prudent and responsible, and that Hoo Loo's death was due to "the shock inflicted on his nervous system by the operation, and to the loss of a quantity of venous blood, which an ordinarily healthy European would have borne without any dangerous effects."

The experiences of the surgeons Peter Parker and John Esdaile prove that this is not necessarily the case. Esdaile reported many successful resections of elephantiasis of the scrotum, and Parker excised many mature tumors. But while Aston Key was poised at the epicenter of British surgery and operating under the scrutiny of the assembled London medical community, Parker and Esdaile were clearly positioned at the margins of British surgery, in China and India. Ironically, however, their residence, far from the metropole but in the path of tropical disease, probably also accounted for the relative facility with which they performed operations like that on Hoo Loo, as they encountered such tumors far more frequently. The American missionary surgeon Peter Parker, whose Ophthalmic Hospital at Canton provides some of the best, and first, documentation of the practice of Western medicine in China, achieved remarkable success in his overcrowded hospital in the factory district of Canton. He successfully removed dozens of mature (immense) tumors, of a difficulty analogous to the case of Hoo Loo and involving major blood loss, such as a well-vascularized tumor two feet long and three feet in circumference, on the clavicle of a forty-nine-year-old man. Although that surgery was unexpectedly severe, so that Woo Kinshing convulsed and fainted, having lost "about *two pounds of blood*" (Parker's emphasis), he recovered completely.[23] In an 1846 treatise Esdaile reports having successfully removed twenty-eight large scrotal tumors over the course of eight months, without a single fatality (137). He represented an especially marginal voice in the medical conversation due to his promotion of mesmerism as an anesthetic. However, he attributed his success to that very technique. In the case of Gooroochuan Shah, who suffered from a "monster tumor" of eighty pounds that he "used . . . as a writing-desk," Esdaile comments that the mesmerized patient's freedom from "pain and struggling" or "bodily and mental anguish" allowed his body to withstand the blood loss, which was "great" (140). Notably, the case histories written by these physicians do not carry the sentimental charge that so inflects Hoo Loo's operative report.

Sentimental Medicine and Its Failures

Hoo Loo died, then, despite—or perhaps because of—his apparent advantage in being in London, under the knife of one of Britain's foremost surgical authorities. In fatal cases such as his, sentimental discourse regularly appears to compensate for, and (ironically) point up, surgical failure. Some of the common tropes of these fatal cases, as well as the singularity of Hoo Loo's case, become clear with comparison to another case of scrotal swelling. The *Lancet*, in an editorial on an inquiry into an 1825 case of hernia, promises to "recapitulate the facts of the case."[24] John Moore's case begins tersely enough:

> 1st. John Moore, aet. 32, admitted Wednesday, Feb. 23d, at half-past five in the morning, having an irreducible Hernia since the preceding day at two o'clock in the afternoon.[25] Taxis first . . . immediately on his admission.[26]
>
> 2dly Taxis by Joberns at nine o'clock—unsuccessful—urgent state of the symptoms at this period. (29)

But as the *Lancet* reviews Moore's situation, which was worsening while Joberns delayed operating, its tone becomes more and more extreme.

> 4thly. One o'clock, P.M. Arrival of Mr. BELL, who, with Mr. JOBERNS, again employed the taxis—symptoms deplorable—scrotum black and blue—operation deferred!!!
>
> 5thly. Half-past four, P.M. CONSULTATION!!! at which all the Surgeons were present. . . .
>
> 6thly . . . Proposal to postpone the operation till the following day!!!— Dreadful state of the patient at this period, and his solicitude for an immediate operation. . . .
>
> 7thly. About half-past five!!! The OPERATION performed . . . humiliating spectacle!!!
>
> 8thly. Subsequent treatment—DEATH of the patient, and its probable cause!!!—REFLECTIONS.

Such is a brief recapitulation of the outlines of this melancholy case, and it has never fallen to our lot to describe a scene so truly humiliating—so unequivocally demonstrative of the fatal effects of delay—or of the dreadful results of INDECISION!!! (29)

While the case of John Moore differs from that of Hoo Loo in several respects, most importantly Moore's Caucasian identity and his diagnosis of the more familiar British or garden-variety hernia rather than Hoo Loo's exotic scrotal elephantiasis, its similarities allow us to recognize an important aspect of how medical narrative used different kinds of discourse to construct and manage the beginnings of professional authority. Sentimental and clinical discourse, in particular, become tools in the case history of Hoo Loo, with which the author attempts to direct and restrict possible readings of this unhappy episode in the annals of surgery.

Many kinds of medical cases exhibit the physical necessity for swift decision and swifter action; why would the cases of Hoo Loo and John Moore in particular prompt this heightened rhetoric? We may compare these briefly to a similar narrative of delay and sorrow in the *Lancet's* report of the 1825 trial on the case of James Wheeler, who suffered from "inflammation of the lungs," for which he was bled from the arm (a common procedure at the time for inflammatory ailments). However, an artery was nicked during the bleeding, and in an effort to stem the hemorrhage, his arm was bound up tightly for three days, after which "mortification" set in and Wheeler died.[27] While Wheeler's case does include some sentimental passages, it significantly declines to indulge in much of the exaggerated rhetoric that characterizes Hoo Loo's and Moore's cases. Wheeler "died from the accidentally opening an artery in the arm, and from the want of proper attention," but here the sentimental editorializing of the *Lancet* is almost entirely unmixed with the horror and outrage (marked by capital letters and multiple exclamation points) evident in Moore's case in particular. The *Lancet* follows its generally sober discussion of Wheeler's fatal arm procedure with a recapitulation of Moore's mistreated hernia, wherein the more excitable rhetoric reappears.

Similarly, no sentimental discourse appears in another seemingly curious case, that of Nicholas Pearson, whose thirty-seven-pound adipose (fatty) tumor of the abdomen was successfully removed by Astley Cooper (Hoo Loo's surgeon). In Cooper's five-page report of the case, published in 1821 in *Medico-Chirurgical Transactions* with a plate depicting the patient, the only hint of curious discourse is in one word, his description of the tumor's size as "prodigious."[28]

Hoo Loo's and John Moore's cases, unlike Wheeler's or Pearson's, combine two situations in which curious or sentimental discourse seems more likely to be mixed with the emerging norm of clinical discourse: medical error and disease at the site of reproduction. In all these cases, the patient has died due to the failure of medical knowledge or treatment. Iatrogenic illness or injury (caused by medical treatment) and medical incompetence, although deplored for centuries, was only beginning to be considered a problem that could be ameliorated by organized effort, such as the *Lancet*'s reformist editorials. Evident in the editorial on John Moore is the author's (probably Wakley's) frustration at continued incompetence and the inability of medical prowess to save the patient once delay had occurred. In such a case, the sentimental discourse serves to signal outrage and the determination to improve standards of care, thus rhetorically standing in for the desired, professional action, even though the sentimental stance seems incompatible with the ideal detachment of an emerging professional identity. Ironically, in this familiar narrative, replete with tragic irony ("they could have saved him if only . . ."), the patient's death actually becomes rhetorically necessary to the editorial's narrative logic, to fulfill the implied trajectory of sorrow and dismay.

The *Lancet*'s editorial on Hoo Loo's case similarly employs sentimental and sensational discourse as a vehicle for a reprimand of medical ill judgment, terminating in the death of the patient, and sentiment serves a similarly vexed role in this case. Although declining to "call into question the manual skill of the operator," the editorial deplores several of Cooper's and Key's choices as "injudicious, nay, particularly unphilosophical" (84). These include, first, the decision to perform the operation before Hoo Loo's body could adjust to a foreign climate. "Medical geography" extensively influenced eighteenth- and early nineteenth-century medicine, so that one's constitution was thought to become habituated to a particular climate and to require particularly careful treatment upon travel, especially to an environment associated with disease.[29] Indeed, the Guy's Hospital report comments that during Hoo Loo's voyage, "the change of air had an effect on his constitution, as to occasion a material increase in the tumour" (86).

In a second failure to follow the dictates of medical geography, the editorial points out, the surgeons should have known not to perform the operation in an unventilated operating theater "rendered unfit for the purposes of respiration by the crowd," when Hoo Loo's body had been accustomed instead to the "pure and peculiarly invigorating breezes of the ocean" on his journey to England. The editorial reports that conditions in the operating theater were such that "many of the spectators were covered with perspiration, were pale as death, and closely approaching to a state of fainting," and rhetorically asks, "What then must have been the condition of Hoo Loo, who with bound limbs was compelled to breathe in such a place for a period of two hours, during one hour and forty-four minutes of which he was under the infliction of the knife?" (84). This concern for the ill effects of spectacularity and the curious crowd appears in cases as early as the seventeenth century, associated with the impulse toward objectivity, but here it appears in the guise of pathos.

Most of all, the surgeons were at fault for "the length of time which poor Hoo Loo was under the tortures of the knife" due to Key's decision to "discontinue the use of the knife, while the patient was in state of syncope" (fainting), since "the vital energy is unable to contend against the long continuance of such unusually severe pain." Here as in Moore's case, delay contributes to the irrevocable decline of the patient. In sum, "the time and place selected for the operation showed an *extraordinary, if not a fatal, want of professional discrimination*" (84). Interestingly, neither the *Lancet* editorial nor the Guy's Hospital report mentions a damning fact that emerges in the *Times* article: Sir Astley Cooper actually left the room after the procedure, in a remarkable misreading of the patient's condition, assuming that Hoo Loo would "speedily rally from his faintness."

The discourse of "the curious" in the hospital report conveniently minimizes these medical mistakes in Hoo Loo's case: his extraordinary tumor was a risky and unfamiliar surgery to begin with; his Chinese origin rendered his body exotic and strange to these British doctors; his Chinese culture meant that the tumor had not been removed at an earlier, simpler stage; his long journey and his sudden immersion in a strange climate no doubt tired his body and rendered it less resilient to pain; and so on. The *Lancet*'s editorial itself is not free from sensational discourse and the staging of the case as a spectacle, citing details such as the "tortures of the knife" or the spectators "pale as death" and close to fainting, but it claims the high moral ground of good judgment and medical progress regardless (84).[30]

In such a case, heavy with the pathos of the patient who came so far seeking help, only to be tortured to his death on the table, sentiment can serve the crucial purpose of demonstrating the physician's good intentions and empathic connection with his patient. In fact, the

Lancet's editorial, which prefaces and thus also frames the case, begins by referencing Hoo Loo as "the unfortunate Chinese" and foregrounding the "deep and painful anxiety" of its readers (83). While indirectly acknowledging the failure of nineteenth-century medical science and in fact defying the crucial tenet of scientific status—objectivity—that would develop later in the century, sentimental medicine draws upon the sensibilities of an earlier century to heal Hoo Loo figuratively, by signifying the physician's humane purpose and identification with the patient. The sentimental passages in the case history also rhetorically invoke the personality and virtues of Hoo Loo, as if to call his image up from the dead (like a eulogy). Likewise, an engraving in the *Lancet* depicting the final sutures must have been drawn from his dead body, but it also proleptically cures Hoo Loo's tumor and restores him to health.

In this way the sentimental passages in Hoo Loo's case act as rhetorical strategies similar in function to those common in eighteenth-century case histories—as an acknowledgment of the limitations of medicine, and as a means of symbolically recovering the patient through an empathic relationship expressed by the physician and shared by his readers.[31] Rather than permit the case to remain a truncated, failed surgical report, the excursion into sentimental narrative reorients the text, and this exotic case, around a familiar narrative that presumes death and certifies the narrator's virtuous concern.

But sentiment, ironically, is what kills Hoo Loo. The surgeons' sympathy for the patient contravened established medical practice by "allow[ing] [him time] for recovery from the fits of exhaustion which supervened" ("Guy's Hospital," 87). While his medical team humanely paused in the surgery, Hoo Loo continued to lose blood and eventually died, in the judgment of Mr. Key the surgeon, of "haemorrhage."

Sentimental Generation and the Orient

If iatrogenic injury often inspires case histories to veer toward curious or sentimental discourse, another trigger is a focus on diseases of the organs of generation—especially breast or uterine cancers, puerperal fever, or genital tumor. One also encounters sentimental moments in some cases involving children with severe illness, perhaps because these represent reproductive possibility. Around this time the *Lancet* published cases such as that of Wangke, a little slave girl with a large encysted tumor on her sacrum, whose mistress "felt for her the affection of a mother"; or Lew Akin, "the only child of her affectionate parents," with a ste-atomatous tumor on her right hip that was larger than her body itself, and whose father seemed more troubled by the surgery than she was.[32]

Unlike James Wheeler or Nicholas Pearson, both John Moore and Hoo Loo suffered from swollen genitalia. Although hernia and scro-tal elephantiasis develop from very different causes, the readiness with which the narrative turns to sentimental discourse in each of these cases suggests that there may be a symbolic, cultural resonance at work here, where excessive growth in the generative parts is conjoined with the inability to reproduce healthily and culminates in the death of the organism.

Two important differences between the cases of John Moore and Hoo Loo, however, suggest that the swollen genitalia of Hoo Loo carry a particular symbolic, cultural resonance as well as a professional reproof. The most obvious is perhaps Hoo Loo's visibility in the text, in engraved illustrations. The several renditions of John Moore's case do not offer any visual representation of his body, despite the surgeon's defense that "the tumour on the scrotum [was] of very unusual form and alarming appearance," which led him to postpone the diagnosis of hernia.[33] Hoo Loo's case, on the contrary, concludes with four illustrations: a full fron-tal view of Hoo Loo in Chinese robes displaying his tumor (figure 4.2); a view of the lower torso of Hoo Loo after the surgery; and two illustra-tions of the tumor itself, though without a depiction of the tissue upon microscopic analysis, a view that would become more common later in the century. The figures are captioned "Poor Hoo Loo and His Tumour," in an echo of the sentiment that distinguished the central section of the case.

"Poor Hoo Loo and His Tumour," as a caption, conventionally sug-gests a double subject for the illustration, or the presence of a pet (a dog or horse) with the subject, as was common in portraiture of the period. Stephen Rachman has noticed a similar illusion in Lam Qua's portraits of patients such as Woo Kinshing, wherein "the tumor often appears as the patient's prop."[34] Indeed, Parker and Esdaile note other instances in which a patient comes to treat his tumor as a prop—a cushion, a seat, or a desk, as in the case of Gooroochuan Shah.

But such a locution also suggests Hoo Loo's alienation from his own body, such that the tumor becomes his burden rather than flesh of his flesh. The full-length image, showing the tumor outside his robes, visu-ally corroborates this impression. If, as Susan Stewart suggests, the body

Figure 4.2
"Poor Hoo Loo." From "Guy's Hospital [Report]:
Removal of a Tumour Fifty-Six Pounds in Weight,
Extending from Beneath the Umbilicus to the
Anterior Border of the Anus," *Lancet* 16, no. 398
(April 16, 1831): 89.

is both "contained and container at once," here what should remain
internal and hidden becomes external, as if independent, and all too
evident.[35] In fact, Hoo Loo's tumor is his master, constraining his mobility and coloring his existence.

This unusual circumstance further differentiates and exoticizes Hoo
Loo, who is indeed not like any of the other 680 men in that sweltering
theater. The only one in thrall to such an imperious companion, his
loss of this alter ego on the table would entail a further loss of identity.

The *Lancet's* illustration of the postsurgical repair demonstrates Hoo Loo's potential loss through the comparative simplicity of this image. It depicts the corpse from abdomen to thighs only, utterly unremarkable, naked and with no identifying markings apart from the repair. Only, perhaps, the clenched hands suggest the memorable story of Hoo Loo. Clearly, this case would lose much of its curious and sentimental appeal were such a repair to have been successful.

It is perhaps not unusual to find illustration of Hoo Loo's case, given his diagnosis; curious cases like those of elephantiasis or hydrocele do tend to offer illustrations of these striking ailments more often than cases involving more mundane tumors. But it is remarkable to find multiple images of the patient, including a full-length portrait showing his face, especially given that images of patients were already rare in British medical journals of this period. Full-length portraits are extremely rare and occur almost always in "curious" cases.[36] Images of tumor are by no means standard, and when one is offered, the image is usually confined to a focused view of the tumor itself (figure 4.3). The illustration of the scrotal tumor of a "servant man Keogh" in 1836, for example, shows only the immediate area of the tumor, with cloths draped around the abdomen and thighs as if to obscure the rest of the body.[37] In fact, even when a tumor is on the patient's neck, an effort is generally made to exclude or play down the face in any illustration (figure 4.4).[38]

Perhaps we can account for Hoo Loo's full-length portrait by the need to depict the scale of his extraordinary tumor, but the image is still remarkable for what it displays and what it hides. Four other images in the *Lancet* between 1820 and 1870 also represent an immense scrotal tumor. In all these cases the patient was shown full-length and entirely unclothed, presumably so that the scale of the tumor could be ascertained in relation to the individual anatomy of the patient, and its size foregrounded against the background of the thin body that supports it. However, the clothing depicted on Hoo Loo obscures these important pieces of information. It can serve little purpose other than to register his cultural and ethnic derivation.

An examination of these other cases bears out this thesis. Only the earliest, an 1829 case, represents a European.[39] This soldier is depicted with an almost heroic physique and stance despite his sizable tumor (figure 4.5). The artist's attention to the patient's musculature and the care in posing this patient so as best to display the tumor result in a self-confident figure that seems to imitate some classical nude (were it not for the tumor), and stands in sharp contrast to Hoo Loo's hunched

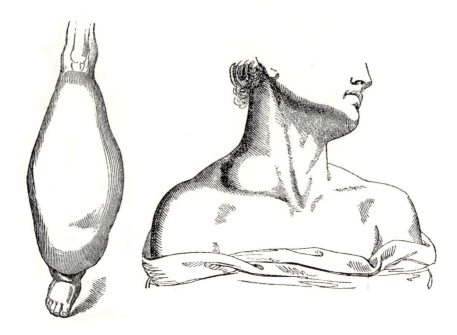

Figure 4.3
View of leg, with elephantiasis. From F. Harington Brett, "On Sarcomatous Tumours (Hypertrophy) Affecting the Male, and Sometimes the Female Organs of Generation," *Lancet* 47, no. 1174 (February 28, 1846): 244.

Figure 4.4
View of tumor on neck. From Robert Liston, "A Course of Lectures on the Operations of Surgery and on Disease and Accidents Requiring Operations, Delivered at University College, London, in the Session of 1844: Part II," *Lancet* 44, no. 1110 (December 7, 1844): 307.

stance. In the other cases, in an 1846 article on sarcomatous tumors, the patients represented are Indian, and the artist carefully depicts their "native" features and (in one case) long hair.[40] This convention of marking ethnicity is typical of the period; a similar full-length illustration of a nearly naked tumor patient with ethnic markers occurs as early as 1796 in another journal (figure 4.6).[41] The illustration of Paunchoo marks his ethnicity through his cap, the cord around his waist, and the long bamboo staff in his hand.[42] Again, the illustration seems to be due to the spectacular nature of the case, since the author, John Corse, describes the case as "very extraordinary," with an "amazingly large tumour." But because these other examples of scrotal tumor are depicted naked or nearly so, Hoo Loo's clothing represents a departure from the norm

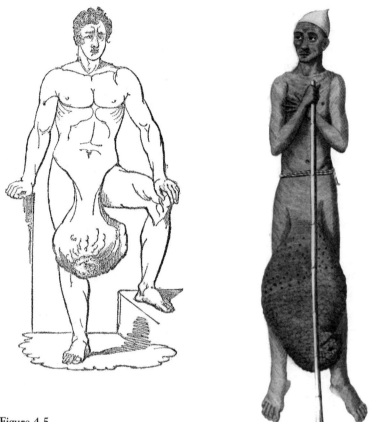

Figure 4.5
European with scrotal tumor. Review of *Chirurgie Clinique de Montpellier*. *Lancet* 13, no. 324 (November 14, 1829): 258.

Figure 4.6
Paunchoo. From John Corse, "The Case of Paunchoo, an Inhabitant of the Village of Gundassee, in Pergunnah Humnabad, and Province of Tiperah, Bengal," in *Transactions of a Society for the Improvement of Medical and Chirurgical Knowledge* 2 (1800): 262. Courtesy, Library of the College of Physicians of Philadelpia.

of illustration in medical periodicals and may well serve primarily as a marker of his "exotic" Chinese identity.

Many of these cases, although not the Guy's Hospital report, register concern over the accuracy of the illustrations. Corse boasts that his illustration is "justly esteemed a very true and striking likeness of the patient, as well as of the parts diseased, by all, and those not a few, who have seen him" (262–63). Wallace comments, "Here is a drawing of the disease, well executed, and by an admirable artist, Mr. O'Neil, yet it affords but a very inadequate idea of the disease."[43] In contrast, the Guy's Hospital report describes what is visible in its four engravings, but it does not address their accuracy as representations, another indication that the primary purpose of the illustration of "Poor Hoo Loo and His Tumour" may not be to educate.

One other unusual case in the *Lancet* also uniquely features a full-length patient portrait that offers little information other than ethnic marking. Strikingly, it also combines the attributes of extraordinary growth, exotic racial identity, spectacular status, and a disorder of generation. A "Remarkable Case of Obesity in a Hindoo Boy Aged Twelve Years" (1859) includes an etching of Shakarm, a Mahratta, "known in the streets of Bombay under the *soubriquet* of the 'Fat Boy.'"[44] The illustration of Shakarm (figure 4.7) does not offer much in the way of medical information, which is provided by the table of his measurements in the text, and no treatment for his condition is offered—or, indeed, even considered. Like Hoo Loo and his kin, Shakarm combines a body growing beyond its bounds with a peculiar inability to reproduce; his "genital organs . . . are not larger than those of an infant, while the testes are very small, and seem either to be undeveloped or to have become atrophied." His image does, however, offer a spectacle like the grotesqueries on display in the London streets and at Bartholomew Fair—a boy entirely "encased in an immense mass of solid adipose tissue"! The image complements Shakarm's stagy *soubriquet* of "The Fat Boy" of Bombay, given that he is portrayed wearing only his cap, which marks him even more definitively as "other."

These characteristics—the portrait-style posing and the inclusion of ethnically marked clothing—also characterize a series of oil paintings of Peter Parker's most striking cases, painted by the artist Lam Qua from 1836 to 1852. However, it is difficult to compare Lam Qua's paintings directly to medical illustrations in the *Lancet*, due to the many differences in context: Lam Qua's unique situation as a Western-trained Chinese painter, the status of his paintings as a possible gift instead of as part of a medical record intended for publication,[45] the uncertainty over how each patient was chosen to be a subject of portraiture, and the apparent intent of portraying a range of cases of mature (immense) tumors. However, these portraits do demonstrate some qualities familiar from the case of Hoo Loo: the impulse to represent the extraordinary; the practice of portraying Chinese patients with clothing or, if naked, other markers of ethnicity; and the fascination with diseases of extraordinary growth. The paradoxical effect of Lam Qua's portraits is in fact

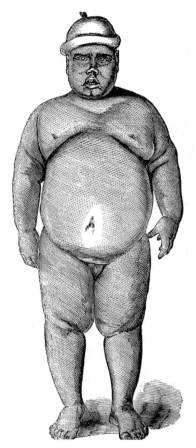

Figure 4.7
Shakarm, the "Fat Boy" of Bombay. From W. G.
Don, "Remarkable Case of Obesity in a Hindoo
Boy Aged Twelve Years," *Lancet* 73, no. 1858
(April 9, 1859): 363.

to normalize such diseases, since almost all of his 114 known paintings
depict a patient with a monstrous tumor.

The image of Hoo Loo, however, appears remarkable in the context
of the *Lancet,* where mature tumors are rare; and it is made more unusual
by this portrayal of the patient with clearly Asian features and dress: as
a racial rather than a merely physiological specimen. In this particular
case, then, the portrait of Hoo Loo stands in for the more detailed image
of the tumor itself that might have been most useful from a medical
standpoint. What it accomplishes instead is primarily—and even more

effectively than the long hair and foreign features of the Indian patients in 1846—to mark Hoo Loo's Chinese ethnicity clearly and unambiguously.

A second important distinction in Hoo Loo's case, made more visible by comparison to John Moore's, is the author's striking emphasis on Hoo Loo's stoical suffering. While John Moore pleads with his surgeons (note "his solicitude for an immediate operation"), Hoo Loo, as represented in the hospital report, exhibits a fortitude "never exceeded in the annals of surgery." Given the author's visual and rhetorical emphasis on Hoo Loo's ethnicity, his stoicism then registers as another accoutrement, albeit a physiological one, associated with the Chinese.

This is borne out by other cases published in the *Lancet* featuring stoic Chinese. In an 1840 article surveying tumors in Chinese patients, G. T. Lay relates how Akae, a thirteen-year-old girl with a sarcomatous tumor the size of her head projecting from her right temple, "cheerfully submitted to be blindfolded, and to have her hands and feet confined [for the excision]. . . . She vomited, but did not faint . . . [and] after a nap, the child awoke cheerful as usual." Similarly, Leäng Yen, a thirty-four-year-old woman with an immense tumor surrounding her right wrist, "bore" the operation "with uncommon magnanimity, and showed no uneasiness, save at not being allowed to follow the knife and the saw with her eye. She had always sneered at the idea of pain, and her practice was a full verification of her theory."[46] Parker frequently commented on the stoicism of his Chinese patients. In contrast, although Peter Stanley points to examples of fortitude among English patients as well, most English patients were considered to suffer greatly from pain during surgery before anesthesia.[47] Indeed, most surgeons even after the advent of anesthesia applied it selectively based on an array of factors, including the perceived sensibility of any particular body to pain, along a hierarchy in which patients who were (for example) female, wealthy, or white were thought to be more sensitive to pain than those who were male, poor, or nonwhite.[48] The need for the surgeon to complete his operation swiftly, before the utter collapse of the patient, meant, as Alison Winter shows, that he required utter dominance over that patient's writhing body.[49]

Stoicism may be an accepted characteristic of the Chinese, but Hoo Loo is not, in fact, stoic—certainly not in comparison with Parker's remarkable patients, given his anguished exclamations as the surgery progressed. His portrayal as stoic does not, then, accord with the facts of the case; it apparently serves discursive and rhetorical aims instead.

It helps fulfill the author's need for a hero worthy of a sentimental narrative. But it also, especially in the context of the illustration, marks Hoo Loo conclusively as racially "other."

What does it mean to present Hoo Loo's heroic determination as Oriental, to render it a cultural phenomenon instead of an individual virtue? In the context of Hoo Loo's sad tale, his "fortitude" presents an unacknowledged threat to the medical narrative by pointing up the contrast between the stoic patient, centered on his task of endurance, and his anxious physicians, changing their plan from moment to moment in reaction to a series of unforeseen crises.

However, the publication of this unusual illustration of Hoo Loo, by helping exoticize his stoicism as uniquely Chinese, regularizes the author's (and the surgeons') emotion, rendering their panic and dismay as an index of sensibility in the civilized English. The author's sentimental discourse manages the eruption of the grotesque into the clinical case by normalizing Hoo Loo as "poor Hoo Loo" (84), establishing a familiar narrative in which the surgeons' medical errors and emotional dissolution, in contrast to Hoo Loo's supreme self-command, register not as incompetence or lack of self-control but as sensitivity and the pity of a superior culture desiring to help a suffering creature. Hoo Loo's portrait, with its emphasis on traits "peculiar" to the Chinese, thus illuminates the importance of sentimental rhetoric in the case and its function as a rhetorical strategy. Clearly this text demonstrates not a failure to acknowledge medical reality but a strategic deployment of curious, clinical, and sentimental discourses as demanded by the exigencies of the text and its audience.

Anne Secord argues that, for many scientists, "visual pleasure could be tied to reason and lead to objective observation" via images, even (or especially) spectacular ones.[50] That said, scientists also recognized the disturbing power of the sometimes spectacular images of scrotal tumor. When David Esdaile put together a popular (1847) edition of his brother's treatise, *Mesmerism in India,* in which nearly thirty of the seventy-three surgeries discussed involved tumors or other problems with the genitalia, he chose not to publish the "nine beautifully executed drawings" (some of which were of scrotal tumor) but to allow the publisher, Longman, to retain them "for the inspection of the scientific, and the curious."[51] The images "are very striking," comments David Esdaile, "but, unfortunately, their very fidelity is a reason for their non-publication, for, assuredly, they are fitted to shock the delicate, who are unaccustomed to witness the fearful ravages of disease on the human frame."

Esdaile's nice distinction between the "scientific" and the "curious" acknowledges that there may be more than one way to observe these medical illustrations and carefully distinguishes "scientific" observation from mere "curious" gaping. His comments, with his care in restricting the circulation of the drawings, point to the continued importance of establishing and maintaining the generic identity of curious cases as science rather than spectacle—an issue I have also had to confront in choosing to reproduce similar images for the purposes of this discussion.

The Illustration of Empire

It is of course to be expected that the patients in cases of scrotal tumor would be largely Asian or Southeast Asian in ethnicity, since hydrocele and elephantiasis, the two most common causes of tumor in the groin, were known to be tropical diseases, and tuberculosis and syphilis, other common causes of tumor, were also prevalent in the area. Indeed, John Esdaile devoted an entire chapter of *Mesmerism in India* to hypertrophy of the scrotum because "it is so common in Bengal" (210). But why are elephantiasis, hydrocele, and other cases of excessive growth so commonly portrayed in illustrations, especially full-length ones, through the first half of the century in the *Lancet*, when other cancers, wounds, and dislocations are less so?

In part, these cases develop out of a newly awakened interest in tropical diseases. Textbooks on the subject appeared, from James Lind's *Essay on Diseases Incidental to Europeans in Hot Climates* (1768) and John Clark's *Observations on the Diseases in Long Voyages to Hot Countries* (1773), to James Johnson's *The Influence of Tropical Climates, More Especially the Climate of India, on European Constitutions* (1815) and James Annesley's *Sketches of the Most Prevalent Diseases of India* (1825). New professional organs such as the *Transactions of the Medical and Physical Society of Calcutta* (founded 1825) soon followed. Indeed, the surge in number and variety of tropical medical texts eventually led to a diverse array of resources including medical surveys, medical topographies, and imperial gazeteers.[52] Partially, then, the likelihood of illustration in cases of scrotal tumor and similar tropical disease indicated an awareness that these diseases represented a hot spot in medical knowledge, a site of increased interest and concern, reflective of the increased activity and engagement of Britain in the government of its interests overseas and its increased need for adequate medical knowledge in the management of its dominions.

But the prevalence of illustration in cases of scrotal tumor and other growths of the reproductive system, combined with their use of senti- mental and curious discourse, signals a further possible import to these cases, concentrated as they are among an Asian and Southeast Asian population. Despite the rise of medical professionalism and the gradual valorization of a circumspect, detached perspective in medical narrative, curious portraits in general continue to appear in medical illustration through about 1875. This indicates a fascination in medical culture, as in Victorian culture more generally, with the cultural other. As Sander Gilman has pointed out, images of the cultural other often conflate the foreign qualities of racial, sexual, and pathological difference. In fact, in a survey of the *Lancet* between 1820 and 1870, while the number of full-length or full-face illustrations of patients diminishes markedly, those that remain are—like Hoo Loo or Shakarm—disproportionately Asian or Southeast Asian patients, marked with their ethnic identity, and exhibiting disorders of extraordinary growth.[53] While these images do point to their subjects' ethnic identity, they offer a curious portrait of individual exoticism, rather than the anthropomorphic "type" that became popular in ethnological photographs of the 1860s and later.[54] They appear far in excess of their representation among the patient population of British physicians, and also in excess of their represen- tation within the collection of cases published in the *Lancet* during this period. These patients, then, may be considered Orientalized cases, their meaning overdetermined by spectacle and discourse. The attention paid to the bodies of these particular patients signals that these bodies, and their disorders, carry additional cultural import and resonance in their status as representatives of "the East." Even scientific narratives on China or Bombay could not avoid being freighted with some of the cultural meaning that collected around those particular prospective nodes of empire.

Rosemarie Garland-Thomson argues that "because [curious] bodies are rare, unique, material, and confounding of cultural categories, they function as magnets to which culture secures its anxieties, questions, and needs at any given moment. . . . Thus, singular bodies become politicized." In such a context, it is notable that the interest in these Orientalized cases arises in the same historical moment that "the anom- alous body" moves from "a narrative of the marvelous to a narrative of the deviant."[55] Unlike many of the "freaks" discussed in Thomson's book, however, Hoo Loo and his kin do not exhibit ambiguous bodies; they do not challenge cultural categories in the same way that a hermaphrodite or a porcupine man might. Instead, their visibility—which, like their bodies, was out of proportion to their number among patients of British physicians—serves as a kind of visual hyperbole, signaling the intensification of cultural interest around swollen "native" bodies. Reading these cases in conjunction with one another helps us recognize the significance in the publishing decisions of mid-century medical authors and of the *Lancet*, including their inclination to illustrate in particular these cases combining Oriental ethnicity with a body growing out of control, metaphorically consumed, apparently by its own overweening appetite.

Significantly, given the long tradition of considering the nation as a body, these Orientalized cases appear as metaphors of inflation located specifically in the site of reproduction. They are swollen bodies from the places where Britain might be most swiftly reproducing and regenerating itself: at the eastern borders of empire. The conclusion of the Napoleonic Wars in 1815 permitted a remarkable British expansion; one historian comments that "in the thirty or forty years after Waterloo the empire grew so rapidly and yet with so little sense of strain or effort that it looked as if there was some dynamic force which, once set in motion, carried its boundaries forward until they were stopped by mountains or oceans."[56] Another notes that the "massive expansion of British Imperial power" took place "especially in Asia [between 1786 and the late 1820s]."[57] In a century beginning with the Act of Union with Ireland in 1800, the political and cultural work of empire had continued at an increasing pace in multiple sites, including—just in the years preceding the case of Hoo Loo—Wellesley's unprecedented expansion of the powers of the East India Company (1798–1805); debates over Elgin's importation of the Parthenon marbles (beginning in 1801); the abolishment of the slave trade, part of a long debate on British responsibility in matters of international morality as well as economics (1807); the opening of the plains beyond the Blue Mountains in Australia (1812); the addition of the Cape Colony and Ceylon to British official holdings (1815); the unsanctioned founding of Singapore by the expansionist Sir Thomas Raffles (1819); the creation of British West Africa (1821); the first Anglo-Burmese war (1823); the establishment of the Straits Settlements, a Crown colony (1826); the British and French defeat of the Turks at Navarino (1827); and the first cholera epidemic, signaling the dangers of this more rapid pace of intercourse between lands (1831).

Even more important, physicians during this period were struggling to establish British medicine as an imperial force, attaining an "evangelizing zeal" by the 1830s and 1840s, and leading to both the expansion of medical facilities in India and a sharp rise in domestic medical awareness of empire and its issues.[58] It is not unlikely that, in such a context, British medicine might well evince an increased interest in the excessive growth of foreign bodies.

How does colonialism make meaning of these bodies? David Arnold argues that "colonialism used . . . the body as a site for the construction of its own authority, legitimacy, and control," and that "over the long period of British rule in India, the accumulation of medical knowledge about the body contributed to the political evolution and ideological articulation of the colonial system."[59] He focuses on the construction of a network of British medicine in India, but the process he describes also occurs, perhaps even more importantly, within British borders, in British periodicals and other media. The pattern I have noted in the cases above facilitates a particular view of the Indian and Chinese borders of empire as overgrown, inflamed, metaphorically rapacious, and—paradoxically—suggestive of a British impotence displaced onto the swollen figure of the "other."

According to Thomas Richards's figuration of the "imperial archive," the knowledge-making project of Victorian morphology attempts to eradicate monstrosity by providing a taxonomy within which to accommodate every variety of being. Richards argues, however, that by the end of the century a new kind of monster had emerged, "beings capable of sudden changes of form" that "do not follow, and cannot be understood by, the ordinal system of morphological development," threatening the disruption and downfall of a British empire built on knowledge.[60] And Georges Canguilhem argues that the appearance of Darwin's *Origin of Species* in 1859 revises the construct of the biological "normality of a living thing" so that it comes to represent "that quality of its relation to the environment that enables it to generate descendants exhibiting a range of variations and standing in a new relation to their respective environments."[61]

However, the attention paid to Hoo Loo, Shakarm, and other Orientalized cases of swollen bodies within the pages of the *Lancet* does not signal the presence either of the monstrosity that Richards sees in late-century Gothic texts or of the "abnormal," in the sense of an unreproductive relation to the environment, that Canguilhem identifies in post-Darwinian biology.[62] Rather, these cases represent another category entirely, that of the grotesque, which suffuses mid-century fiction and, despite physicians' valorization of detached rationality, persists in curious cases throughout the century. Stewart argues that the grotesque body is "inextricably tied" to the cultural other and represents "the assurance that the wilderness, the outside, is now territory."[63] If this is so, then since the grotesque is typically a disorder of size and proportion, as in Dickens's dwarves and giants, it thus presents an ideal site at which to represent an anxious fascination with rapid, perhaps disastrous growth where British "inside" touches or even everts out into exotic "outside."

Although these insoluble cases may not stand as empire-destroying monsters, they do signal a failure within the orderly production of imperial knowledge and a fascination for the places where the body may escape its bounds. Hoo Loo's doctors may be able to identify the cause of his tumor, but they cannot force his body to obey their dictates. In fact, Hoo Loo's vaunted stoicism, juxtaposed with the author's sentimental regret, advertises that the Chinese patient is in more control of his unlikely body than the doctors are of either themselves or of him. As Arnold shows of British medicine in India, "the body formed a site of contestation and not simply of colonial appropriation."[64] The *Lancet*'s fascination with Orientalized cases of "swelling" during a remarkable period of imperial expansion clearly locates at the borders of the empire—the site of cultural reproduction—the need to consider narratives of moderation, control, and knowledge; or, conversely, the unruly narratives that reveal unrestrained growth, lack of control, and the limits to medical knowledge.

Notes

This essay was completed with the aid of a Wood Fellowship from the College of Physicians of Philadelphia, and a Research and Creative Activities Grant from the Florida State University English Department, and with the kind assistance of the staff at the John Hay Library at Brown University, the Historical Library at the College of Physicians of Philadelphia, the Health Science Center Library at the University of Florida, the Countway Medical Library at Harvard University, the Watkinson Library at Trinity College, and the Medical Historical Library at the Harvey Cushing/John Hay Whitney Library of Yale University.

    1. Lorraine Daston and Katharine Park, *Wonders and the Order of Nature, 1150–1750* (New York: Zone Books, 1998).

2. R. S. Kirby, *The Wonderful and Scientific Museum; or, Magazine of Remarkable Characters*, vol. 1 (London: R. S. Kirby, 1803).

3. R. S. Kirby, *Kirby's Wonderful and Eccentric Museum; or, Magazine of Remarkable Characters*, vol. 3 (London: R. S. Kirby, 1805).

4. See Roger French and Andrew Wear, eds., *British Medicine in an Age of Reform* (London: Routledge, 1991); W. F. Bynum and Roy Porter, eds., *Medical Fringe and Medical Orthodoxy, 1750–1850* (London: Croom Helm, 1987); and Alison Winter, "The Construction of Orthodoxies and Heterodoxies in the Early Victorian Life Sciences," in *Victorian Science in Context*, ed. Bernard Lightman (Chicago: University of Chicago Press, 1997), 24–50.

5. For the norming of medical and scientific inquiry, see Georges Canguilhem, *On the Normal and the Pathological*, trans. Carolyn Fawcett, ed. Robert S. Cohen (London: D. Reidel, 1978); and Alice Domurat Dreger, *Hermaphrodites and the Medical Invention of Sex* (Cambridge, MA: Harvard University Press, 1998).

6. George Henry Lewes, *The Physiology of Common Life*, vol. 1 (Edinburgh: Blackwood, 1859). Lewes cites Bérard's "*Cours de Physiologie*, 1848, i.538." Lewes's chapter "Hunger and Thirst" had been first published in *Blackwood's Edinburgh Magazine* in 1859.

7. See Meegan Kennedy, "The Ghost in the Clinic: Gothic Medicine and Curious Fiction in Samuel Warren's *Diary of a Late Physician*," *Victorian Literature and Culture* 32, no. 2 (2004): 327–51.

8. "Guy's Hospital [Report]: Removal of a Tumour Fifty-Six Pounds in Weight, Extending from Beneath the Umbilicus to the Anterior Border of the Anus," *Lancet* 16, no. 398 (1831): 86–89 (hereafter cited parenthetically). This report was reprinted, without the images, in "Guy's Hospital.—Removal of a Tumour fifty-six pounds in weight . . . ," *Glasgow Medical Journal* 4 (1831): 209–13.

9. Elephantiasis is caused by lymphatic filariasis, a parasitic disease endemic in tropical climates but extremely rare in England. Jerome Goddard explains, "Bancroftian filariasis, caused by *Wuchereria bancrofti*, is widely distributed through much of central Africa, Madagascar, the Nile Delta, the Arabian seacoast, Turkey, India, Pakistan, Sri Lanka, Burma, Thailand, Southeast Asia, many Pacific islands, Malaysia, the Philippines, and the southern parts of China, Korea, and Japan. In the Western Hemisphere, it is found in the Caribbean and in Central and South America, including Haiti, the Dominican Republic, Costa Rica, Honduras, Guatemala, Guyana, Surinam, French Guiana, and parts of Brazil. There was at one time a small endemic center of the disease near Charleston, South Carolina, which has apparently disappeared. . . . Malayan filariasis [is] mostly confined to Malaysia and areas from the Indian subcontinent through Asia to Japan." See "Mosquitos and Lymphatic Filariasis," *Infections in Medicine* 15, no. 9 (1998): 607–9.

It is likely that tuberculosis (consumption), another cause of scrotal swelling, was more common in China as well, given that early twentieth-century figures show China with the highest tuberculosis rate in the world, at least four times that in Britain. See Bridie J. Andrews, "Tuberculosis and the Assimilation of Germ Theory in China, 1895–1937," *Journal of the History of Medicine and Allied Sciences* 52, no. 1 (1997): 114–57.

Elephantiasis, which is a lymphedema, should not be confused with other diagnoses such as neurofibromatosis or Proteus syndrome, both of which have been suggested to explain the symptoms of Joseph Merrick, the Elephant Man. Merrick did not suffer from elephantiasis.

10. James Esdaile, *Mesmerism in India: Its Practical Application in Surgery and Medicine* (1846; reprint, Honolulu: University Press of the Pacific, 2003), 134 (hereafter cited parenthetically).

11. The "mass of tubercules" on the surface of Hoo Loo's tumor are typical of scrotal elephantiasis (88).

12. An article in *Bell's Weekly Messenger* explains, "The Chinese surgeons at Canton declined to attempt the removal of the tumour; and the English surgeon there, attached to the Company [Thomas Colledge], absolutely refused to undergo the fearful responsibility of the loss of life in the event of the Chinese, during the operation, losing *his*; as it is a maxim with the Chinese, which they never fail to put into practice (and more particularly where the English are concerned), to take 'the blood of life from him by whom the blood of life is shed.'" See "Hoo Loo, the Unfortunate Chinese," *Bell's Weekly Messenger*, no. 1829 (April 17, 1831).

13. Colledge's pamphlet on "the heroic Hoo Loo" comments that Hoo Loo's tumor "bid defiance to all remedies" but that Colledge was "of opinion that it might be removed" (excerpted in A Philanthropist, "A Brief Account of an Ophthalmic Hospital at Macao, During the Years 1827 to 1832, Inclusive," *Chinese Repository* 3 [December 1834]: 365).

14. Charles Aston Key (1798–1849) was a respected surgeon and cardiologist, who, like John Keats, had been trained by Sir Astley Cooper (1768–1841). Cooper had been a pupil of the famous anatomist John Hunter.

15. "An Eye-Witness," "Operation Upon Hoo Loo, the Chinese, for a Tumour, in Guy's Hospital," *Times* (April 11, 1831): 2f.

16. "[Editorial on Hoo Loo]," *Lancet* 16, no. 398 (1831): 84 (hereafter cited parenthetically).

17. George M. Gould and Walter M. Pyle, *Anomalies and Curiosities of Medicine* (Philadelphia: W. B. Saunders, 1897). This self-consciousness increased over the century. J. G. Millingen's *Curiosities of Medical Experience* (Philadelphia: Haswell, Barrington, and Haswell, 1838), in contrast, is less anxious about its reception.

18. "Eye-Witness," 2f.

19. See, for example, F. Harington Brett, "On Sarcomatous Tumours (Hypertrophy) Affecting the Male, and Sometimes the Female Organs of Generation," *Lancet* 47, no. 1174 (1846): 241–44; and "[Review of *Chirurgie Clinique De Montpellier*]," *Lancet* 13, no. 324 (1829): 258–61.

20. For example, the *Philosophical Transactions* of 1668 tell of a blood transfusion from a calf to a madman, in which "the croud of spectators interrupted very much this operation" (620). J. Denis, "Extract of a Letter Written by Dr. J. Denis, of Paris, Touching a Late Cure of an Inveterate Phrensy by the Transfusion of Blood," *Philosophical Transactions of the Royal Society* II, no. 32 (1668): 617–24.

21. These discursive shifts continue through the rest of the case history. After this encomium, remarkable in itself, the narrator passes to an affectionate remembrance of Hoo Loo's "amiable" temperament and the "very cheerful and good-tempered expression" that endeared him to the nurses (87)—and then retrieves the

impersonal language of clinical medicine to detail Hoo Loo's physical appearance and his postmortem results, with the dissection of his tumor.

22. "Hoo Loo," *Bell's*. An excerpt from this article is reprinted in "Hoo Loo, the Unfortunate Chinese," *Times* (April 19, 1831): 3e.

23. For the case history of Woo Kinshing, see Peter Parker, "Ophthalmic Hospital at Canton: The Seventh Quarterly Report, Being That for the Term Ending on the 31st of December, 1837," *Chinese Repository* 7 (1838): 92–106, quotation on 101.

24. "Middlesex Hospital. The Case of Hernia, Vol. 6, No. 10, p. 317," *Lancet* 4, no. 80 (1825): 29 (hereafter cited parenthetically).

25. Emphasis in all quoted passages is in the original.

26. Taxis is the attempt to reduce the hernia manually, by physical manipulation. If unsuccessful, surgery is necessary to prevent potentially fatal infection.

27. "More 'Hole and Corner' Doings," *Lancet* 4, no. 87 (1825): 228.

28. Astley Cooper, "Case of a Large Adipose Tumor Successfully Extirpated," *Medico-Chirurgical Transactions* XI, part II (1821): 440–44, quotation on 443.

29. See, for example, Alan Bewell, *Romanticism and Colonial Disease* (Baltimore, MD: Johns Hopkins University Press, 2000), 27–65.

30. Remarkably, one version of the report comments, "Mr Key was the operator and is said to have distinguished himself." This is from the version carried in the *London Medical and Physical Journal*, reprinted in "Quarterly Summary of Medical Intelligence," *North American Medical and Surgical Journal* 12, no. 24 (October 1831): 482.

31. For example, in an eighteenth-century case of a little girl who drowned after being pulled under a mill wheel, once it is clear that she will not recover, the narrative shifts from chronicling the efforts to save her to imagining her, sentimentally, as she might have been had she grown to maturity, proleptically reviving her rhetorically when medicine fails to do so physically. See John Green, "Part of a Letter from John Green, M.D. Secretary of the Gentlemens Society at Spalding in Lincolnshire, to C. Mortimer, M.D. Sec. R. S. Serving to Inclose a Relation of a Girl Three Years Old, Who Remained a Quarter of an Hour under Water without Drowning," *Philosophical Transactions of the Royal Society* 41, no. 454 (July–October 1739): 166–68.

32. G. T. Lay, "Diseases Among the Chinese. Tumours," *Lancet* 34, no. 888 (1840): 851. These cases in the *Lancet* are actually reprinted from the records of Peter Parker, the missionary surgeon. His reports on his ophthalmic hospital, published in the *Chinese Repository* (*CR*), offer further details on such cases. For Wangke, see Parker's sixth quarterly report, *CR* 6 (May 1837): 36; for Lew Akin in the same report, see 38–39. The paragraph detailing Lew Akin's father's vigilance by her side and "the force" of his "natural affections" suggests that the stoicism elsewhere attributed to Asian patients may be limited to physical pain.

33. "More 'Hole and Corner' Doings," 228. Nicholas Pearson's case report does include a full-length image of Pearson, seated, drawing back his clothing to reveal his abdominal tumor, probably due to the unusual nature of the case, its relatively early (1821) publication date, and perhaps its publication in a periodical other than the *Lancet*, known for its drive to professionalize medicine. Even

so, the image is not exoticized or sentimentalized, and (unlike the image of Hoo Loo) enough of Pearson's body is disclosed to afford a sense of the placement of the tumor. The plate is captioned, "Represents the appearance of the patient having the large adipose tumor which was successfully removed by Mr. A. Cooper, as described in his paper, p. 440." At the foot of the plate itself, the tumor's dimensions are inscribed.

34. Stephen Rachman, "Memento Morbi: Lam Qua's Paintings, Peter Parker's Patients," *Literature and Medicine* 23, no. 1 (2004): 146.

35. Susan Stewart, *On Longing: Narratives of the Miniature, the Gigantic, the Souvenir, the Collection* (Durham, NC: Duke University Press, 1993), 104.

36. See, for example, W. C. Maclean, "Report of a Case of Lateral Transposition of the Heart and Liver in a Soldier," *Lancet* 82, no. 2084 (1863): 159. Here the image of the soldier from the knees up, including the head, illustrates (by outline on the body) where his transposed organs reside.

37. William Wallace, "Influence of the Hydriodate of Potash in Malignant Fungous and Cancerous Diseases," *Lancet* 25, no. 653 (1836): 894–901. Ironically, the close focus on the tumor has the effect of making the illustration much more explicit about its interest in the male anatomy.

The decision to illustrate Keogh's tumor at all is probably prompted by its status in a curious, sentimental case. The tumor is not large compared to Hoo Loo's, but Wallace notes its peculiar shape and the critical condition of "this poor man," celebrates the miraculous regression of the tumor under his experimental medical treatment, and concludes that "the progress of his dissolution was so tranquil, that he seemed to have gradually passed from sleep into eternity" (894, 898).

38. One exception occurs in a case of advanced breast cancer in an older woman, published in the same article as the neck tumor illustrated here (Robert Liston, "A Course of Lectures on the Operations of Surgery and on Disease and Accidents Requiring Operations, Delivered at University College, London, in the Session of 1844: Part II," *Lancet* 44, no. 1110 [1844]: 309). The illustration of the breast cancer depicts the patient to the torso, lying in bed, staring straight ahead with an expression of resignation, with a cabbage-sized cancer crouched darkly on her chest. As in some other images of women patients at this time, she is otherwise clothed even to her cap, perhaps in a gesture of modesty to counteract the exposure of her chest. Despite this remarkable image, Liston maintains a strictly scientific tone, not even referencing the woman's case in particular, but using the illustration merely to illustrate "the appearance of the swelling [in advanced cancer], the discoloration of the skin, the adhesion of the tubercules to it, and the retraction of the nipple" (309). It is possible that the half-length image was thought advisable to provide scale and perspective on this large, amorphous tumor, as with a closer focus, the tumor would be difficult to orient relative to the anatomy, due to the tumor's having devoured the surrounding area. Even with Liston's guidance, it is impossible to recognize the structure as a human breast.

39. "[Review]."

40. See Brett.

41. John Corse, "The Case of Paunchoo, an Inhabitant of the Village of Gundassee, in Pergunnah Humnabad, and Province of Tiperah, Bengal," *Transactions of*

a Society for the Improvement of Medical and Chirurgical Knowledge 2 (1800): 257–63 (hereafter cited parenthetically).

42. The native illustrator drew the figure apparently just as it stood, with the staff obscuring part of the front of the tumor. Many times practitioners might employ a local artist, who might not be aware of the norms of medical portraiture. This becomes evident in an incident preceding Hoo Loo's voyage to England. According to *Bell's*, Colledge commissioned "a full-length cast of Hoo Loo" to be sent to England. Unfortunately, the finished product entirely omitted the tumor. Practitioners retained the right to dictate how an artist proceeded, however, if they could but secure an artist. Colledge rejected that cast and continued seeking an acceptable one, but he could not find a sculptor willing to risk cursing himself by reproducing the tumor.

43. Wallace asks his readers to supplement the drawing by imagining "the head of an immense cauliflower seated in the right groin," among other details, to obtain "an ideal representation of the seat, extent, and form of the diseased parts" (895).

44. W. G. Don, "Remarkable Case of Obesity in a Hindoo Boy Aged Twelve Years," *Lancet* 73, no. 1858 (1859): 363.

45. There is evidence both that they were a gift (Lam Qua's nephew was Parker's first pupil) and that Parker paid for them; see Rachman, 141–42. To my knowledge, the paintings were not published during Parker's lifetime. Most of them are currently in storage at Yale University's Historical Medical Library; Parker donated others, possibly duplicates, to Guy's Hospital. See also Sander Gilman, "Lam Qua and the Development of a Westernized Medical Iconography in China," *Medical History* 30, no. 1 (1986): 57–69.

46. Lay, 852, 853. These cases are also reprinted from Parker's records, which repeatedly comment on the stoicism he perceived in his Chinese patients. He mused, for example, on "the fortitude of a heroine with which the child [Akae] endured the operation"; similarly, four-year-old Yat Akwang, who had a bleeding tumor on the eye, prompted the comment, "The little child endured the operation with much fortitude." This phenomenon becomes so familiar to Parker that when he removes a "large" tumor from the face of Lo Wanshun, he comments laconically, "The patient endured the operation with fortitude, characteristic of the Chinese." Parker's Chinese patients are portrayed as not just stoic but absolutely unruffled. Pang She did not even lay aside her needlework until the moment when Parker entered her room for her operation. Of Woo She, whose breast Parker removed, he remarked, "Her fortitude exceeded all that I have yet witnessed. She scarcely uttered a groan during the extirpation, and before she was removed from the table, clasped her hands, and, with an unaffected smile, cordially thanked the gentlemen who assisted on the occasion." And Leäng Yen, whose sarcoma of the right wrist required amputation of the arm, "contemned the idea of pain, and at the moment of sawing the bone inquired when that part of the process would take place" (578).

In some cases, the patient's composure triggered a question of whether his or her body was actually insensible to pain. Removing nasal polyps from the patient Tinqua, Parker reports, "The patient endured the operation as if insensible to pain." Of Yang She, a young women twenty years old and five months pregnant, from whose chin Parker removed a three-foot-long pendulous tumor, he remarked with wonder, "Seldom has there been less apparent suffering from so serious an operation, as there was manifested by the young woman." And Parker records that Leäng Ashing displayed a composure that the medical team found literally unbelievable. During the removal of an "enormous" tumor on his face, "he did not move a muscle, change a feature of his countenance, or draw one long breath, so that apprehensions were even entertained that he was insensible; but if spoken to he answered deliberately and correctly. Subsequently he informed me he was sensible of all that was done, but putting his arms across each other, he said, 'I determined not to move.'"

For the case of Akae, see Peter Parker, "Ophthalmic Hospital at Canton: First Quarterly Report, from the 4th of November 1835 to the 4th of February 1836," CR 4 (February 1836): 464–73, quotation on 438; for Yat Akwang, the third quarterly report, CR 5 (August 1836): 187; for Lo Wanshun, the fifth quarterly report, CR 5 (February 1837): 457; for Pang She, the first quarterly report, CR 4 (February 1836): 470–71; for Woo She, CR 6 (January 1838): 439–40, quotation on 439; for Tinqua, CR 5 (May 1836): 39; for Yang She, the seventh quarterly report, CR 6 (January 1838): 438–39, quotation on 439; for Leäng Ashing, the fourth quarterly report, CR 5 (November 1836): 32526; and for Leäng Yen, the ninth quarterly report, CR 7 (March 1839): 576–79, quotation on 578.

47. Peter Stanley, For Fear of Pain: British Surgery, 1790–1850 (Amsterdam: Rodopi, 2003), 264–65.

48. Martin S. Pernick, A Calculus of Suffering: Pain, Professionalism, and Anesthesia in Nineteenth-Century America (New York: Columbia University Press, 1985), 4–7.

49. Alison Winter, Mesmerized: Powers of Mind in Victorian Britain (Chicago: University of Chicago Press, 1998), 103, 163–86.

50. Anne Secord, "Botany on a Plate: Pleasure and the Power of Pictures in Promoting Early Nineteenth-Century Scientific Knowledge," Isis 93, no. 28–57 (2002): 45. Secord focuses on botany but acknowledges the usefulness of medical images of the body before the Anatomy Act of 1832 made cadavers more readily available for study. Illustrations would, of course, continue to be useful in curious (rare) cases even thereafter.

51. David Esdaile, "English Editor's Preface," in Mesmerism in India: Its Practical Application in Surgery and Medicine, by James Esdaile, 1846, 1902 (Honolulu: University Press of the Pacific, 2003), 5. I have not been able to locate copies of these images.

52. See David Arnold, Colonizing the Body: State Medicine and Epidemic Disease in Nineteenth-Century India (Berkeley: University of California Press, 1993), 23–28; and Bewell, 27–46, on the development of tropical medicine.

53. In fact, this pattern persists through the century. Nancy Leys Stepan notes the disproportionate, "almost obsessive" visual representation of elephantiasis in tropical medicine treatises late in the century (during another spurt of imperial growth) and attributes this phenomenon to the disease's role as "an iconic image of the diseased tropics" and its ability to encapsulate an imagined link between "blackness, sexuality and pathology" (Picturing Tropical Nature [Ithaca, NY: Cornell University Press, 2001], 173, 177). However, I would argue that the cases and images I analyze here counter Stepan's claim that "a special genre of tropical medi-

cal pictures did not develop" until the pocket camera enabled realist photographic representation of such patients from the 1880s on (171). In fact, the cultural constructs around what would become tropical or imperial medicine fostered particular perspectives and details in the engravings of such patients, many decades earlier.

54. See James R. Ryan, *Picturing Empire: Photography and the Visualization of the British Empire* (Chicago: University of Chicago Press, 1997), 140–82.

55. Rosemarie Garland-Thomson, "Introduction: From Wonder to Error—A Genealogy of Freak Discourse in Modernity," in *Freakery: Cultural Spectacles of the Extraordinary Body*, ed. Garland-Thomson (New York: New York University Press, 1996), 2, 3.

56. T. O. Lloyd, *The British Empire, 1558–1995*, 2nd ed. (Oxford: Oxford University Press, 1996), 134.

57. A. J. Stockwell, "British Expansion and Rule in South-East Asia," in *The Oxford History of the British Empire: The Nineteenth Century*, ed. Andrew Porter (Oxford: Oxford University Press, 1999), 376. See also C. A. Bayly, *Imperial Meridian: The British Empire and the World* (London: Longman, 1989).

58. Arnold, 58.

59. Ibid., 8.

60. Thomas Richards, *The Imperial Archive: Knowledge and the Fantasy of Empire* (New York: Verso, 1993), 49.

61. Georges Canguilhem, *Ideology and Rationality in the Life Sciences*, trans. Arthur Goldhammer (Cambridge, MA: MIT Press, 1988).

62. In fact, the case of Gooroochuan Shah, in Esdaile's *Mesmerism in India*, displays the adaptability of a subject with hydrocele. While Esdaile identifies Shah's eighty-pound growth as a "monster tumour," the patient offers an alternate, more quotidian (and suggestive) metaphor for the appendage: he has "used it for a writing-desk for many years" (221).

63. Stewart, 109–10.

64. Arnold, 10.

5

ELEPHANT TALK

Language and Enfranchisement in the Merrick Case

CHRISTINE C. FERGUSON

THE MASSIVELY DEFORMED "Elephant Man," Joseph Merrick,[1] found by Dr. Frederick Treves in a filthy Whitechapel shop room in 1884, remains one of the most iconic and best-known members of the Victorian freak pantheon. Merrick's great suffering, and equally great resilience of spirit in the face of constant physical privation, received its first extensive, and arguably most poignant, treatment in Treves's "The Elephant Man" (1923), a mythopoeic medical memoir that has inspired numerous creative works and forms a valuable contribution to the literature of metamorphosis.[2] While it has become critically commonplace, even clichéd, to comment on the archetypal resonances of Merrick's rhetorical transformation from animalized freak to noble hero, the precise cultural dimensions of Merrick's humanization in the course of Treves's prose remain underexamined.[3] Tales of human-brute transformation may be timeless, but the process by which metamorphosis is accomplished routinely corresponds to historically embedded concepts of human identity. In the essay that follows, I argue that Merrick's narrative movement from "elephant" to "man" is accomplished through Treves's manipulation of his patient's relationship to what had become at the end of the nineteenth century a particularly important and troubled emblem of human progress—language. I read Treves's narrative against contemporary discourses of language origin and silence, showing how Merrick's initially perceived speechlessness participated within larger cultural associations of inarticulacy with animality. In "The Elephant Man," Treves seems to enact a triumph of language, in which the deviance of the freak is (partially) abated through his adoption and refinement of those linguistic skills—speaking, reading, and writing—deemed essential to human subjectivity. Yet in this process, language itself loses its status as a transcendent marker of human progress and comes to denote the same kind of mythological atavism associated with Merrick's freak show presentation. As a freak show spectacle, Merrick's alterity was created through exaggerated reference to his physical deformity; as a character in Treves's medical memoir, his alienation from the realm of fully evolved masculinity is a product of his linguistic abilities.

By tracing the story's indebtedness to broader historical concerns about the relationship between language and civilization, my essay participates in the project of recent cultural model scholarship on disability.[4] This discourse has worked to denaturalize the meaning of disability, arguing that physical abnormality is more a construct of culture than of nature. As Lennard J. Davis writes, disability "is part of a historically constructed discourse, an ideology of thinking about the body under certain historical circumstances. Disability is not an object—a woman with a cane—but a social process that intimately involves everyone who has a body and lives in the world of the senses."[5] Physical normalcy and irregularity, rather than representing two permanently opposed and inherent states of being, are fluid concepts involved in a recurrent process of dialogue and mutual remaking. Such a claim, while by no means novel within the poststructuralist identity politics of race, class, and gender, has only relatively recently been applied to the category of disability, with the handicapped body still appearing to many as a last bastion of essential, irreducible difference.[6] To call for a reevaluation of the latter assumption is not to suggest that the chief impediments faced by people with disabilities are solely, or even primarily, socially imposed—to make such a claim about Joseph Merrick's condition would be to gratuitously underestimate the extent of his physical disability—but rather to mobilize a more politically and culturally nuanced approach to the history of physical aberration.

As we interrogate the literary and historical contexts through which the dehumanization of specific groups—the disabled,[7] women, racial minorities, and so on—has been produced, we also need to excavate the assumptions behind our favorite metaphors of liberation. In particular, it is time for a reevaluation of the ideological function of voice. It has long been common in the radical identity politics of the left to assume a rather simplistic connection between language, autonomy, and rights. The oppressed are the "silenced" whose liberation will ensue when credence is finally granted to their marginalized "voice." A perfect example of this trope can be found in the introduction to *The Body and Physical Difference: Discourses of Disability* (1997), in which editors David T. Mitchell and Sharon L. Snyder state, "As with most minority populations who have sought to break down the barriers of racial, class, and gendered discrimination, disability studies scholars define their political program as an effort to redress the social 'voicelessness' and institutional neglect of disabled people."[8] It is my contention that we need to rethink and perhaps abandon this rather exhausted formula of language as enfranchisement, particularly in the study of disability, for several reasons. The first is metaphoric: to anathematize speechlessness is to sustain what Lennard J. Davis calls the "foundational ableist myt[h] of our culture . . . that the norm for humans is to speak and hear, to engage in communication through speaking and hearing."[9] A scholarship that addresses, among other topics, the social history of the deaf and mute should perhaps seek another critical register. The second, and most compelling, reason lies in the unreflective ahistoricism of the critical equation of language, voice, and empowerment. Rather than simply assuming the connection between voice and autonomy to be a natural one, we need to interrogate the problematic social, historical, and political means by which speech became installed as guarantor of the kind of human sovereignty denied to "freak" subjects such as Joseph Merrick.

"The Elephant Man" was not Treves's first published account of the rare medical condition, now diagnosed as Proteus syndrome, that covered Joseph Merrick's body with disfiguring tumors.[10] His initial description of the case appeared more than thirty-five years previously, in the *Transactions of the Pathological Society* for March of 1885. His article, titled "A Case of Congenital Deformity," summarized the content of his presentation of Merrick to the society in December of 1884. Following a lengthy discussion of Merrick's physical abnormalities, the piece speculates on the patient's mental condition. "His intelligence," notes Treves, "was by no means of a low order."[11] This assessment was shared by London Hospital chairman F. C. Carr Gomm in a letter to the *Times* seeking subscriptions for Merrick's maintenance within the isolation ward. Gomm states that the patient is "superior in intelligence, can read and write, is quiet, gentle, not to say even refined in his mind."[12] Gomm's estimation, coming as it does six months after Merrick's deliverance from the freak show into the respite of the hospital, accords well with the teleological chronology of the familiar Elephant Man narrative; but Treves's passing comments are flatly astonishing in their contradiction of the later, canonical script of his relationship with Merrick published in "The Elephant Man." Here he insists that their initial encounters had left him with the impression that "Merrick was an imbecile from birth. The fact that his face was incapable of expression, that his speech was a mere spluttering and his attitude that of one whose mind was void of all emotions and concerns gave grounds for this belief."[13] How are we to account for the divergence of these two descriptions? Was Treves's subsequent downplaying of his initial impression of Merrick's intellect, perhaps like his inaccurate substitution of "John" for "Joseph," simply the result of lapsed memory? Or was it the product of deliberate artistic license? Rather than attempting to establish the intention behind the shift, I want to consider the narrative effect that it produces and, more importantly, the cultural rhetoric of silence and speech with which it engages. In order to understand the significance of Merrick's repositioning from intelligent yet deformed patient to mute imbecile whose mental powers become evident only *after* his institutionalization, we need to consider late-Victorian debates about the relationship of language to human evolution and progress.

The connection of language with human distinction, and more particularly, with reason, has long been part of the Western philosophical tradition. In the Genesis account of creation, language is given to Adam by God as a means of denoting his difference from, and power over, the other members of brute creation. Subsequent Enlightenment thinkers, while challenging the biblical script of the Adamic moment, nonetheless shared the assessment of language as both source and effect of hegemony. In the first volume of *On the Origin and Progress of Language* (1772), Lord Monboddo writes, "without reason and speech, we have no pretensions to humanity, nor can we with propriety be called men; but must be contented to rank with the other animals here below, over whom we assume so much superiority, and exercise domination chiefly by means of the advantages that the use of language gives us."[14] Language thus becomes the *sine qua non* cause of human identity and power, the ineluctable signifier that, as Jean-Jacques Rousseau notes, separates humans both from animals and from each other. "Speech distinguishes man from the animals. Language distinguishes nations from each other; one does not know where a man is until after he is has spoken."[15] What is fascinating in both these passages is their effortless conflation of language with speech, the latter appearing not simply as an audible sign of the former but as the thing itself. The implications of such rhetoric for those who were organically deprived of the faculty of articulate speech—the deaf and mute, for example—were dire indeed, reducing them to the level of irrational brutes through their inability to enunciate language sounds in a conventional manner.[16]

These connections between language, speech, and human reason became the object of renewed scrutiny and feverish debate with the rise of Darwinian theory in the latter half of the nineteenth century. As Douglas Baynton notes, "The idea that speech separates humans from animals is by no means associated exclusively with evolutionary thought. . . . What a particular culture *emphasizes* at any one time is what is significant, however, and during the latter half of the nineteenth century the emphasis shifted in Anglo-American thought from the possession of an immortal soul to the possession of speech."[17] When the evolutionary hypothesis replaced the theory of separate species creation with one of gradual descent from a common ancestor, language emerged as the (seemingly) sole exclusive trait left to humans, one at which Darwin marveled without ever being able to satisfactorily explain. Deeming it "half-art and half-instinct,"[18] he claims in *The Descent of Man* (1870) that "through the power of intellect, articulate language has been evolved; and on this his [man's] wonderful advancement has mainly depended."[19] In the same work, however, he had previously traced a different arc for linguistic evolution, arguing that "the continued use and advancement of this power [of speech] would have reacted on the mind itself, by enabling and encouraging it to carry on long trains of thought."[20] Language is rendered arcane through its positioning as both aftereffect and catalyst of human progress and intellectual development. Evolutionary theory further destabilized the traditional status of language by presenting it as a vulnerable product of a random natural selection process that might just as easily lead to its eventual extinction. In its post-Darwinian incarnation, the assertion that "speech equals humanity," inherited from the theological and the rationalist tradition, became particularly fraught, straining under the weight of a new monogenetic paradigm that denied innate species difference.

It is perhaps as a result of these pressures that the relationship between speech and humanity became the focus of such heated debate in late-Victorian philological and scientific circles. Scholars continually

cited language in either their rejection or teleological appropriation of
Darwin's work, insisting that it stood as evidence of our total separation
from the animals or of the necessarily progressive (and human-centered)
course of evolution. The most vocal and exuberant participant in these
debates was German-born philologist F. Max Müller, whose famous
declaration in 1861 that "Language is our Rubicon, and no brute will
dare to cross it" posits language as supreme weapon in the contest for
species supremacy, one that animals simply lack the courage to claim.[21]
For Müller language and human thought were not simply connected
but synonymous, and thus implicitly any individual incapable of the
former must necessarily be devoid of reason.[22] Müller's "scientific" work,
seemingly anthropocentric in its insistence on the exclusivity of human
language, in fact creates a criterion whereby certain subjects (mutes,
aphasiacs, infants) may be disqualified from the category of the human.
To speak is to be human, and to be silent or inarticulate is to be something else entirely—an animal, a savage, an infant, or an evolutionary
throwback. Summing up this sentiment with particular clarity, Müller's
most famous disciple, Ludwig Noiré, notes in 1895 that "so long as the
child does not feel this instinct [language], so long as it contemplates,
touches, cries, asks for food, and so on, up to that time it represents the
period of speechless humanity—this time at which human nature has
not as yet separated from animal nature."[23] Humanity, far from being a
birthright to all those born of *Homo sapiens* parents, becomes a selective
status one earns through the acquisition of language.

Of course, the rather extreme Müllerian view of the necessity of
articulate language to reason was not accepted unanimously in late-
Victorian scientific and philological communities. Opponents such as
anthropologist E. B. Tylor, linguist W. D. Whitney, and Assyriologist
A. H. Sayce pointed to the existence of gesture and sign communication systems as evidence of the existence of language without audible
words.[24] "We must be careful to remember," cautions Sayce in *Introduction to the Science of Language* (1879), "that language includes any kind
of instrumentality whereby we communicate our thoughts and feelings
to others, and therefore that the deaf-mute who can converse only with
his fingers or the lips is as truly gifted with the power of speech as the
man who can articulate his words."[25] Sayce's theoretical move here is as
fascinating for what it leaves intact as for what it accomplishes—rather
than rejecting the dependence of language on conventional signification that underlies Müller's logic, he simply extends the definition
of signification to include sign language. Deaf-mutes may be said to

"speak" because they manifest thought through a recognizable physical performance. But what of those subjects who, by virtue of physical incapacity, are unable to engage in a similar performance, who are rendered doubly abject through their inability to speak or signify thought through other kinds of bodily movements? Speculating on the condition of such individuals, E. B. Tylor had written in *Researches into the Early History of Mankind and the Development of Civilization* (1865) that "though . . . the deaf-and-dumb prove clearly to us that a man may have a human thought without being able to speak, they by no means prove that he can think without any means of physical expression."[26] The physically inexpressive are here relegated to the same dehumanized and irrational status previously occupied by the deaf and dumb. Language, Tylor suggests, may exist without vocal support, but not without *some kind* of physical accompaniment. Reason, that highest and most exalted quality of the human, can be manifested only through the functioning body.

This equation of reason with speech allows us to better understand the commonly noted alliance of certain types of disability with animality in nineteenth-century culture.[27] The disabled body is deemed alien, not simply by virtue of irregular appearance or function but by the extent to which it is unable to perform the external cultural rituals associated with evolved humanity—the cojoining of thoughts to signs, for example. In his freak show appearances, Joseph Merrick's alterity seems to have been produced chiefly through the *visual* register, emphasized through tawdry handbills depicting the spectacular transformation of a man into an elephant. Far from being denied, Merrick's linguistic proficiency was incorporated into the show, exemplified in a (perhaps ghostwritten) autobiographical pamphlet that poignantly detailed his sufferings before receiving the "kindness" of showman Sam Torr.[28] In Treves's account, however, Merrick's initial animality is less a product of the physical deformities that receive diminishing attention throughout the narrative than of the verbal and expressive difficulties that result from his condition. Unable to cure his patient's physical body, Treves instead "humanizes" Merrick by equipping him with the language skills he (seemingly) hitherto lacked.

"The Elephant Man" opens with a scene of cartoonish physical metamorphosis. In tones of fascination and repugnance, Treves describes the canvas banner that first drew his attention to Merrick's exhibition in premises across from the London Hospital. Of particular horror to Treves is the manner in which the freak's hybridity is staged, suggestive not of grotesque fusion but of a steady evolutionary reversal.

Painted on the canvas in primitive colours was a life-size portrait of the Elephant Man. This very crude production depicted a frightful creature that could only have been possible in a nightmare. It was the figure of a man with the characteristics of an elephant. The transfiguration was not far advanced. There was still more of the man than of the beast. This fact—that it was still human—was the most repellent attribute of the creature. There was nothing about it of the pitiableness of the mis-shapen or the deformed, nothing of the grotesqueness of the freak, but merely the loathing insinuation of a man being changed into an animal. Some palm trees in the background of the picture suggested a jungle and might have led the imaginative to assume that it was in this wild that the perverted object has roamed.[29]

The image derives its potency from the contemporary obsessions with degeneration and racial decline. Treves is disgusted by what he recognizes as a specter of colonial and biological "backsliding."[30] His own project might be read as an attempt to restore evolutionary development to an anthropocentric course, presenting Merrick not as man-turning-into-animal but as animal-turning-into-man through the ministration of love, cleanliness, and conversation. In humanizing Merrick, Treves also recuperates the nineteenth-century logic of social and evolutionary progress that this initial iconography violates.

Treves responds to Merrick's real presence with as much uneasiness as he does to the show banner, yet for different reasons. In his pictorial depiction, the Elephant Man presents a spectacle of evolutionary recidivism; in the flesh, he is a figure of lack, a body devoid of mind. Ushered to the back of the showroom, Treves finds Merrick huddled alone over a tiny fire, appearing as "the embodiment of loneliness."[31] When Merrick stands up, the full extent of his malformation becomes apparent. "In the course of my profession," Treves writes with palpable discomfort, "I had come upon lamentable deformities of the face due to injury or disease, as well as mutilations and contortions of the body depending upon like causes; but at no time had I met with such a degraded or perverted version of a human being as this lone figure displayed."[32] The narrative then moves into a lengthy and almost ornate description of Merrick's specific abnormalities, intricately detailing the stumpish protuberance covering his mouth and the papillomas growing over his skin. In these descriptions, one has the sense of a human being reduced to pure matter. Merrick, at this stage, is all body, a physical specimen whose seeming lack of any transcendent, intellectual, or moral qualities is more unsettling than the deformities he presents.

What is the source of lack, the missing ingredient that allows Treves in his early description to present Merrick not as a human but as a ramshackle compendium of competing pathologies? It is linguistic expression. Unable to comprehend Merrick's speech or indeed recognize it as such, Treves the medical examiner simply cannot, as his prose playfully suggests, make the specimen into a man. He writes, "I made little of the man himself. He was shy, confused, not a little frightened and evidently much cowed. Moreover, his speech was unintelligible. The great bony mass that projected from his mouth blurred his utterance and made the articulation of certain words impossible."[33] Without the animating principle of articulate language, Merrick appears simply as a bundle of animal flesh, a "thing," a "panic-dazed dog," and an "object" not yet recognizable as a human being.[34] These perceptions were further augmented by the deformities of the head that rendered Merrick as unable to make facial expressions, as to utter his thoughts through intelligible words. Indeed, it is the combination of these two incapacities—to signify via speech or facial expression—that drives Treves's initial narrative assessment of Merrick's mental state. "I supposed that Merrick was imbecilic and had been imbecilic from birth. The fact that his face was incapable of expression, that his speech was a mere spluttering and his attitude that of one whose mind was void of all emotions and concerns gave grounds for this belief. The conviction was no doubt encouraged by the hope that his intellect was the blank I imagined it to be. That he could appreciate his condition was unthinkable."[35] Most interesting about this passage is its radical relocation of the source of Merrick's aberrance from the body to the expressive faculties. Merrick's deformities, compelling and substantial as they were, are not alone enough to account for his profound alterity: they only acquire their full pathos when supplemented by silence. Merrick's appearance is horrifying, but worse still, indeed, beyond the limits of Treves's imagination, is that this appearance thwarts the manifestation of an active and intelligent mind. Robert Bogdan's contention that the freak is a socially constructed rather than natural artifact finds eloquent confirmation in Treves's careful displacement of Merrick's tragedy from his physical to his linguistic condition.[36] While Treves's motivations in this presentation must remain to a certain extent unknowable, the emphasis on language allows him to retain a self-presentation as physician-hero. As would-be healer of Merrick's body, Treves was a failure; as restorer of Merrick's communicative abilities, Treves was an unqualified success.[37]

Yet the fact that, as we have seen, Treves almost certainly exaggerates the extent of Merrick's linguistic incapacities in "The Elephant Man" seems less indicative of a deliberate mendacity than of his engagement with a surrounding literary tradition that reproduced the philological equation of voice with agency. This scenario, in which the subject transforms from mute animal to fully realized human through the discovery or improvement of language skills, is one that had been played out repeatedly in Victorian realist and fantastic fiction. Wilkie Collins and Charles Dickens both work within this paradigm of linguistic humanization in their respective sentimental treatments of deaf-mutism, *Hide and Seek* (1854) and "Dr. Marigold" (1865). Each narrative features a beautiful and loving deaf-mute female protagonist who, after being exhibited as a freak in early childhood, gains dignity and freedom when rescued by a benevolent male protector (the role that Treves would assume toward Merrick) and admitted into a wider network of written or signed communication. Thus the ill-used Sophy in "Dr. Marigold," who, on first appearance, looks "as if she had escaped from a Wild Beast Show,"[38] grows into maturity and motherhood after her tutelage in a school for the deaf and dumb. The more she is able to, if only metaphorically, "voice" her thoughts through signs, the more autonomous and the more content she becomes. A similar process of humanization through language acquisition occurs in late-century imaginative fictions such as Rudyard Kipling's *The Jungle Book* (1894) and H. G. Wells's *The Island of Doctor Moreau* (1896). In the former, the feral child Mowgli gains ascendancy over the other animals through his expert acquisition not only of the Master Words of the Jungle but also of the speech of men. His linguistic proficiency is contrasted with the gibbering chatter of the monkey people who "have no speech of their own" and thus live in total anarchy.[39] In Wells's short horror novella, Moreau's animal subjects are transformed into quasi-humans through their surgical equipment with larynxes. While the transformation is never quite complete—the Beastfolk become terrible parodies of humans rather than idealized rational citizens—the logic of Moreau's perverted science is coextensive with that of these other literary metamorphoses. Language acquisition is the prime catalyst for the category collapse between the animal and the human, the "freak" and the normal. Treves, whose writing displays an affectionate familiarity with the conventions of popular romance, manipulates the events of Merrick's history to make them resonant with an eager public taste for tales of exotic metamorphosis and linguistic enfranchisement.[40]

Recast as a casualty of language rather than of disease, Joseph Merrick becomes curable in a way denied to him through the medical paradigm alone. Treves establishes the trajectory for this treatment almost immediately upon his installation of Merrick within the isolation ward at the London Hospital. His first task is to document Merrick's speech. "I at once began to make myself acquainted with him to endeavour to understand his mentality. It was a study of much interest. I very soon learnt his speech so that I could talk freely with him. This afforded him great satisfaction for, curiously enough, he had a passion for conversation, yet all his life no one had talked to him."[41] Merrick's "passion" for dialogue is perhaps not so curious after all, suggesting a canny complicity with Treves's plan of rehabilitation. Conversation afforded him the entrance into the social networks from which his malformed body had excluded him; it is for this reason that Merrick expressed the desire to be housed in an institute for the blind and continually displayed a preference for being heard rather than being seen, despite Treves's suggestions to the contrary.[42] Deprived of almost all other activities, Merrick reads, writes, and talks—to Mr. Carr Gomm, to the Princess of Wales, to the nurses and doctor who manage his care, to the various society members who visit and bring him books, to actress Mrs. Kendal, and, most of all, to Treves himself. And through this intercourse a magical type of transformation seems to ensue. The speech that "was so maimed that he might as well have spoken in Arabic" begins to change, to lose the character of random, phatic sound and morph into a legible and rich language, one through which Merrick is able to narrate the poignant and tragic events of his personal history.[43] The emergence of this self-narration is itself the most significant event in his history, signaling a resistance to, if not reversal of, the continual waves of deformity that had been gradually "animalizing" Merrick since birth. In the narrative, Merrick as individual is made to recapitulate the evolutionary history of the species, shedding the taint of a bestial past and ascending to human status as he attains control over speech.

Yet just as the text seems to epitomize the triumphant and familiar plot of language as humanizing agent, so does it foreground some of its failures and gaps. Imaginatively inspired by contemporary literary, anthropological, and philological accounts of speech origin, "The Elephant Man" inherits some of their uncertainties about the transcendent and empowering function of language. Merrick, does not, after all, actually "acquire" language after a period of mutism; he has had it all along and simply went unheard. His voice, when finally articulated, works not to grant him his own agency but to interpolate him into a master narrative created by someone else. Throughout his tenure in the London Hospital, Merrick remained dependent on Treves as translator, a task necessitated by the persistent ungainliness of his speech. Due to Merrick's irregular pronunciation, recounts Treves, "I had occasionally to act as an interpreter."[44] While Treves downplays the possibility of any interpretive license in these translations—noting, for example, that he allowed a letter from Merrick to the Princess Alexandra, which opened with the unorthodox salutation "My dear Princess,"[45] to pass unedited—his enduring confusion as to Merrick's Christian name points to the existence of misrepresentation, whether deliberate or unintentional. The much-vaunted voice acquired by Merrick is one, as numerous commentators have pointed out, subject to constant mediation. Far from denying this rupture between speaking and accurate self-representation, between language and autonomy, "The Elephant Man" foregrounds the necessity and vagaries of translation that attend every act of articulation.

Thus, while Merrick is humanized in and through language, the humanity thus conferred is hardly an independent, masterful, or, indeed, masculine one. His "voice," once recognized, remains generally incoherent and frequently invokes the same chain of associations—the deformed body as primitive, childish, and unmanly—present in Merrick's freak show exhibitions. Merrick's speech is routinely described as "chatter," not the eloquent expression of a long-suppressed intellect but the trivial and idle prattle of an incessant talker. Describing Merrick's early days in the isolation ward, Treves writes, "I—having then much leisure—saw him almost every day, and made a point of spending some two hours with him every Sunday morning when he would chatter almost without ceasing."[46] Speech here becomes a pleasurable activity rather than a vehicle of thought, a form of indulgent physical exchange between patient and physician. Treves infantilizes Merrick by reference to his mode of, and juvenile enjoyment in, conversation. The articulate Elephant Man, "amiable as a happy woman" in his new home, displays a verbal eloquence notable more for its "childlike simplicity" than its depth.[47] The narrative ascribes a similar childishness to Merrick's written communication. During a holiday in the country, Merrick writes to his patron repeatedly, documenting the banal daily events of his first-ever sojourn in nature. Treves declares these epistles to be "the letters of a delighted and enthusiastic child."[48] In contrasting the naïve and giddy femininity of Merrick's language to Treves's authoritative masculinity, such descriptions reinforce the conventional gender dynamics of the doctor-patient relationship. Figured as an amiable and compliant child-woman, Merrick becomes a suitable subject for penetration by a male medical gaze that constructs, defines, and controls his identity according to its own rules. The process is strikingly analogous to Said's account of nineteenth-century Orientalist philology—in either case, the language of the racial or physical deviant becomes evidence not of a disavowed equality but of that Other's essential passivity and infantile inferiority to the dominant mainstream culture on which it relies for explication.[49]

No linguistic practice more signifies Merrick's failure to attain complete civilized masculinity in "The Elephant Man" than reading. In one of the narrative's greatest (and perhaps least self-conscious) ironies, the same passionate literacy that initially testifies to his unsuspected intelligence comes to reinscribe Merrick in the paradigmatic savagery he seeks to abandon. Treves notes:

> I found Merrick, as I have said, remarkably intelligent. He had learnt to read and had become a voracious reader, I think he had been taught when he was in hospital with his diseased hip. His range of books was limited. The Bible and Prayer Book he knew intimately, but he had subsisted for the most part upon newspapers, or rather upon such fragments of old journals as he had chanced to pick up. He had read a few stories and some elementary lesson books, but the delight of his life was a romance, especially a love romance. These tales were very real to him, as real as any narrative in the Bible, so that he would tell them to me as incidents in the lives of people who had lived. In his outlook upon the world he was a child, yet a child with some of the tempestuous feelings of a man. He was an elemental being, so primitive that he might have spent the twenty-three years of his life immured in a cave.[50]

Merrick's passion for romance becomes here emblematic not of a love of literature but of a primitive mentality unable to distinguish the parameters between the real and the fabulous. Like the fetish-worshipping savage of Victorian anthropological literature, he cannot differentiate between the products of nature and those of the imagination.[51] Thus Merrick's enduring belief (never actually disproven) that his mother was beautiful is described as a "fiction . . . of his own making,"[52] his attitude toward women derived not from experience but from "the many romances he had read."[53] Just as he endows real individuals with idealized features drawn from sentimental fiction, so, too, does he reify the lives of invented characters. Following a memorable trip to the pantomime, Merrick develops what, for Treves, is a curious and endearing investment in the reality of the performance. "To him, as to a child with the faculty of make believe, everything was real: the palace was the home of kings, the princess was of royal blood, and fairies were as undoubted as the children in the street, while the dishes at the banquet were of unquestionable gold. He did not like to discuss it as a play but rather as a vision of some actual world."[54] Merrick's engagement with art, as with his practice of conversation, is intended to aid in his transformation from animal to man, but instead it again marks him as a child and primitive.

Treves's insistence on the quasi-atavistic nature of Merrick's reading practices indicates not only a paternalistic condescension toward his patient but also his own critical self-positioning as a writer. In juxtaposing the love of romance with savagery, he aligns himself with late-Victorian romancers such as Andrew Lang and H. Rider Haggard who defended their genre on the basis of its appeal to our submerged instinctual impulses. For Lang writing in 1886, the love of the romance constituted a "savage survival," one that Haggard claimed to be "coeval with the existence of humanity . . . it is like the passions, an innate quality of mankind."[55] But while Lang and Haggard put a decidedly positive spin on the "primitive" taste for romance, seeing in it a means of revitalizing or, more importantly, remasculinizing a literary climate exhausted by naturalism, Treves clearly reads it as a sign of cultural and personal immaturity. The troubling reality of Merrick's erotic desire for women is thus sublimated through the romanticized and thus infantile manner in which it manifests, his genre preference being used to negate both his sexuality and his maturity. Given Treves's clear identification of the romance with childishness, misrepresentation, and primitivism, it is curious that he should choose to imbue his own narrative with some of its elements. His conclusion borrows romantic techniques and tropes, presenting Merrick not as a terribly afflicted everyman but as a fantastical hero whose own life challenges the distinction between the real and the invented. Referencing Bunyan's *The Pilgrim's Progress*, Treves writes: "As a specimen of humanity, Merrick was ignoble and repulsive; but the spirit of Merrick, if it could be seen in the form of the living, would assume the figure of an upstanding and heroic man, smooth browed and clean of limb, and with eyes that flashed undaunted courage. . . . He had escaped the clutches of the Giant Despair, and at last had reached the 'Place of Deliverance' where 'his burden loosed from off his shoulders and fell off his back, so that he saw it no more.'"[56] Release comes at last to Joseph Merrick through the soothing power of metaphor.

As a tale of metamorphosis, "The Elephant Man" remains incomplete. Certainly, Merrick transforms over the course of the narrative—from filthy, mute animal into woman, child, noble savage, and, lastly, literary hero—but he never fully attains the latter part of his famous freak show epithet; while no longer "elephant," he is not quite fully developed "man," either. This failure is not a result of personal inadequacy but of the medium through which Treves attempts to change his patient's status. Language does not function here as the straightforward appendage to hegemonic human subjectivity. When silent, Merrick is little more than a beast, but when he speaks, he chatters like a woman; when he writes, he does so with the innocence and naïveté of a child; and when he reads, it is with the untutored wonder of a primitive savage. The very faculty that should elevate humanity above the lesser animals instead situates Merrick within other categories of subalternity.

In its depiction of this potential for language to depreciate as well as elevate the speakers in which it is installed, Treves's narrative underlines Alastair Pennycook's important critique of the discourses of (Anglo)-linguistic humanism. Rather than unreflectively celebrating the empowering function of language training, Pennycook writes, "we need to consider what language is all about, that language has to do with discourses and voice, that we cannot stop short by assuming that once someone has access to a language, they have access to doing what they need or want to do through language."[57] Simply put, to use a language (whether your first or second) is not necessarily to have control of it. Merrick's failure to attain through language an equivalent status to that of his benevolent and learned English male patron is not an exception to a strategy that worked for others, as the briefest survey of Victorian colonial and working-class education will show. Like Merrick, the Indian recipients of Thomas Babington Macaulay's infamous Anglicized educational policy and the British working-class beneficiaries of the 1870 Education Act never quite received the transcendent boon that English language and literacy was supposed to have conferred on them.[58] Without wishing to undermine the dire psychological consequences of colonial language imposition, it remains important to point out that the possibility for empowerment through language remains limited in *any* context, whether imperial or not. Language may have been vaunted by the Victorian philologists as sovereign key to human identity, but in practice it remained simply one trait among many, its humanizing significance easily trumped by other pathological, racial, class, or gender stigmata. This point continues to be overlooked in the contemporary politics of oppression that persistently equate voice with agency. Just as commentators such as Lennard J. Davis and Elaine Scarry have observed, "silencing" can be a politically repressive strategy, and so too can the installation or "discovery" of language within a hitherto silenced subject.[59] Treves's "The Elephant Man," itself a freakish narrative in its grotesque genre conflation of medical realism, Victorian sentimentalism, and sensational romance, might serve as a foundational text for a reevaluation of the terms and ideological premises through which we seek to liberate the socially abject.

Notes

1. Despite Treves's continual references to his patient as "John," Merrick's actual Christian name was Joseph. It remains unclear, as Peter Graham, Fritz Oehlschlaeger, Michael Howell, and Peter Ford point out, whether Treves's mistake was the result of memory lapse, mishearing, or deliberate renaming. See Peter W. Graham and Fritz Oehlschlaeger, *Articulating the Elephant Man: Joseph Merrick and His Interpreters* (Baltimore, MD: Johns Hopkins University Press, 1992), and Michael Howell and Peter Ford's *The True History of the Elephant Man* (New York: Penguin, 1980).

2. Graham and Oehlschlaeger's *Articulating the Elephant Man* provides a comprehensive survey of the most prominent retellings of the Merrick story, including Bernard Pomerance's play *The Elephant Man* (1979) and David Lynch's film of the same name and same year.

3. This tendency to view the freak as a psychological archetype is epitomized by Leslie Fiedler in *Freaks: Myths and Images of the Secret Self* (New York: Anchor Books, 1978), a groundbreaking work that helped catalyze the recent resurgence of academic interest in spectacular performances of disability. Like Fiedler, Graham and Oehlschlaeger trace the popularity of "freaks" to their evocation of timeless fears and desires about human identity. They claim that "Merrick's story has endured primarily because its depths are truly mythic. . . . As the epithet 'Elephant Man' suggests, Merrick's is a story of metamorphosis. Imprisoned in a body being continuously and grotesquely remade through a process he could neither understand nor control, Merrick faced what every human being who grows old or falls ill must endure: the sense of exclusion from the world of the healthy and normal, the dilemma of whether to accept a blighted body as an attribute of essential identity or to reject it as a misleading mask, the sufferer's painful questions about cause and effect, about personal guilt or cosmic cruelty" (3). Here, Merrick's story, like that of so many other so-called freaks, becomes depersonalized, moving from case history into abstract, universal metaphor for all humankind.

4. For more on the distinction between medical, cultural, and social models of disability, see Sharon L. Snyder and David T. Mitchell's *Cultural Locations of Disability* (Chicago: University of Chicago Press, 2006).

5. Lennard J. Davis, *Enforcing Normalcy: Disability, Deafness, and the Body* (New York: Verso, 1995), 2.

6. For a discussion of this point, see ibid., 4, and David T. Mitchell and Sharon L. Snyder, eds., *The Body and Physical Difference: Discourses of Disability* (Ann Arbor: University of Michigan Press, 1997), 2.

7. The term "disabled" has rightly been criticized for robbing individuals of their dignity by defining them wholly through their disability rather than recognizing them as complex agents whose physical differences form only one part of a complex identity. While recognizing the legitimacy of this protest, I preserve the term here for motives of historical accuracy. Victorian writings on the case unanimously essentialize Merrick through his pathology: he never emerges as simply "a person with disabilities" but constantly as a *disabled person*, whose every action and personality trait is interpreted through the lens of his physical aberration. We risk blurring the representational violence historically perpetrated against people like Merrick if we wish away the invidious terms used to define them and replace them with gentle anachronisms that were never used in the nineteenth century.

8. Mitchell and Snyder, 11.

9. Davis, 15.

10. Merrick's pathology, as Howell and Ford have pointed out, has been subject to a long series of misdiagnoses (141). His freak show name inadvertently promoted the false impression that he suffered from elephantiasis, and Merrick himself believed his condition to be the result of maternal impressions. Recent investigators have discarded the most common twentieth-century diagnosis of neurofibromatosis and named Proteus syndrome as the most likely source of Merrick's deformities. See Graham and Oehlschlaeger, 81.

11. Quoted in Graham and Oehlschlaeger, 17.

12. F. C. Carr Gomm, "The Elephant Man," *Times* (December 4, 1886): 6.

13. Frederick Treves, "The Elephant Man" (1923), in Howell and Ford, 194. All subsequent references from the text are taken from this edition.

14. Lord Monboddo (James Burnett), *On the Origin and Progress of Language* (1772; New York: AMS Press, 1972), 2.

15. Jean-Jacques Rousseau, "Essay on the Origin of Languages," in *Essay on the Origin of Languages and Writings Related to Music*, trans. and ed. John T. Scott (Hanover, NH: University Press of New England, 1998), 289.

16. Monboddo deliberately excludes inarticulate communication from the category of rational language, writing, "though we say, the language of looks, and of gestures, or signs, such as our dumb persons use; also the language of inarticulate cries, by which the brutes signify their appetites and desires; yet, in all those senses, the word [language] is used metaphorically, and not as it ought to be used in the style of science" (6). Thus discussions of the "language" of the dumb are deemed as unscientific as those of the language of animals.

17. Douglas C. Baynton, "Savages and Deaf-Mutes: Evolutionary Theory and the Campaign Against Sign-Language in the Nineteenth Century," in *Deaf History Unveiled: Interpretations from the New Scholarship*, ed. John Van Cleve (Washington, DC: Gallaudet University Press, 1993), 104.

18. Charles Darwin, *The Descent of Man*, in *On the Origin of Species*, ed. Joseph Carroll (Peterborough, ON: Broadview, 2003), 552.

19. Ibid., 534.

20. Ibid., 519.

21. F. Max Müller, *Lectures on the Science of Language, delivered at the Royal Institution of Great Britain in April, May, and June, 1861*, 2nd rev. ed. (London: Longman, Green, Longman, and Roberts, 1862), 356.

22. Müller declares in the preface to *The Science of Thought* (1887), "No reason without language, no language without reason" (Chicago: Open Court Publishing Co., 1909), iii.

23. Ludwig Noiré, *On the Origin of Language and the Logos Theory* (1895; Chicago: Open Court Publishing Company, 1899), 8.

24. For more on the distinction between speech as reason or as vehicle for thought, see W. D. Whitney's *The Life and Growth of Language* (London: Henry S. King & Co., 1875) and *Max Müller and the Science of Language: A Criticism* (New York: D. Appleton & Co., 1892), and A. H. Sayce's *Introduction to the Science of Language* (1879; London: Kegan Paul, Trench, Trubner & Co., 1900).

25. Sayce, 2.

26. E. B. Tylor, *Researches into the Early History of Mankind and the Development of Civilization* (1865; Chicago: University of Chicago Press, 1964), 57.

27. Davis, 40.

28. Howell and Ford, 183. The authors also write, "There is room for some debate as to whether he actually wrote it or whether it was written for him. On this point anyone who reads it must make their own judgement, but on balance the tone and content, the words and phrases chosen, have an authentic feeling. Joseph most probably was its author, even if he did write it under the expert tutelage of Mr Torr or his resident copywriter. The fact that he gets his own birth date wrong may itself be seen as a slight confirmation of his authorship since, as we know, he rarely got it right" (89–90).

29. Treves, 190.

30. It should be noted, of course, that there is no such thing as backsliding in evolution. The term itself, as H. G. Wells points out in "Zoological Retrogression," simply refers to adaptation through natural selection rather than progressive improvement. Nonetheless, the Victorian tendency to read evolution as a perfecting process allowed certain kinds of modifications to be read as reversals. See H. G. Wells, "Zoological Retrogression," *Gentleman's Magazine* 271 (1891): 246–53.

31. Treves, 191.

32. Ibid.

33. Ibid., 193.

34. Ibid., 191, 195.

35. Ibid., 194.

36. Robert Bogdan, *Freak Show: Presenting Human Oddities for Amusement and Profit* (Chicago: University of Chicago Press, 1988).

37. Treves is not, however, to be blamed for his inability to treat Merrick's physical ailments. The extremely rare condition from which Merrick is now commonly supposed to have suffered, Proteus syndrome, remains difficult to diagnose and treat today.

38. Charles Dickens, "Dr. Marigold" (1865), in *Christmas Stories* (Toronto: Oxford University Press, 1987), 448.

39. Rudyard Kipling, *The Jungle Books* (Toronto: Oxford World's Classics, 1996), 26.

40. While public taste is notoriously prolix and difficult to pin down at any given moment, romantic tales of exotic adventure and fantastic transformation came to constitute a significant portion of the publishing market at the end of the nineteenth century. Representative authors in this style include H. Rider Haggard, H. G. Wells, Rudyard Kipling, Grant Allen, Bram Stoker, and Robert Louis Stevenson. Also popular were naturalist accounts of working-class attempts to transform the protagonists' lives through either literacy or literary success, such as George Moore's *Esther Waters* (1894), George Gissing's *New Grub Street* (1891), and Thomas Hardy's *Jude the Obscure* (1895). The reading public's interest in such narratives may have derived from their own sense of the nation's linguistic transformation at the hands of recent educational reform. The 1870 Forster Education Act had mandated primary education for all, regardless of class, thus seemingly creating Britain's first mass reading (and writing) public. It is hardly surprising that the public might be interested in fantastic narratives about the humanization of their own fellow citizens through language.

41. Treves, 197.

42. In speaking of Merrick's wish to be housed amidst the blind or in a lighthouse, Treves claims, "I had no great difficulty in ridding Merrick's mind of these ideas. . . . He appeared day by day less frightened, less haunted looking, less anxious to hide, less alarmed when he saw his door opened" (200). He even suggests that this tolerance for other peoples' gaze grew into a marked fondness, stating, "He liked to see his door pushed upon and people look in" (202). While it certainly seems true that Merrick grew more accustomed to being seen while under Treves's care, his continual avoidance of unmediated public space indicates that Merrick's fear of visual exposure never entirely evaporated.

43. Ibid., 195.

44. Ibid., 197.

45. Ibid., 203.

46. Ibid., 197.

47. Ibid., 199.

48. Ibid., 209.

49. Nineteenth-century linguists imagined themselves, writes Said, as "surveying, as if from a particularly suited vantage point, the passive, seminal, feminine, and even silent and supine East, then going on to *articulate* the East, making the Orient deliver up its secrets under the learned authority of a philologist whose power derives from the ability to unlock secret, esoteric languages." See Edward Said, *Orientalism* (New York: Vintage Books, 1979), 137–38.

50. Treves, 197.

51. In his classic anthropological work *Prehistoric Times* (1865; London: Williams and Norgate, 1912), John Lubbock establishes the inability to distinguish between the external world of reality and the internal world of the imagination as a unifying characteristic of savage societies. "Savages very generally believe in witchcraft. Confusing together subjective and objective relations, he is a prey to constant fears" (557).

For more on late-Victorian representations of savage thought, see George Stocking's *Victorian Anthropology* (New York: Free Press, 1987) and Brian V. Street's *The Savage in Literature: Representations of "Primitive" Society in English Fiction, 1858–1920* (Boston: Routledge & Kegan Paul, 1975).

52. Treves, 198.

53. Ibid., 201.

54. Ibid., 207.

55. Andrew Lang, "Realism and Romance" (1886), in *The Fin de Siècle: A Reader in Cultural History, c. 1880–1900*, ed. Sally Ledger and Roger Luckhurst (Oxford: Oxford University Press, 2000), 103; H. Rider Haggard, "About Fiction," *Contemporary Review* 51 (February 1887): 172–80, quotation on 172.

56. Treves, 210.

57. Alastair Pennycook, "The Right to Language: Towards a Situated Ethics of Language Possibilities," *Language Sciences* 20, no. 1 (1998): 86.

58. Macauley's 1835 "Minute on Indian Education" claimed that English education in India would produce "a class of persons, Indian in blood and colour, but English in taste, in opinion, in morals, and in intellect." Qtd. in Benedict Anderson, *Imagined Communities: Reflections on the Origin and Spread of Nationalism* (New York: Verso, 2002), 91.

59. Davis, 109; Elaine Scarry, *The Body in Pain: Making and Unmaking the World* (New York: Oxford University Press, 1985), 14.

6

THE MISSING LINK AND THE HAIRY BELLE

*Krao and the Victorian Discourses of
Evolution, Imperialism, and Primitive Sexuality*

NADJA DURBACH

N 1883 G. A. Farini, the great Canadian impresario, unveiled his latest discovery, "Krao, the Missing Link," at the Westminster Aquarium in London.[1] Krao was a seven-year-old girl from what Victorians called Indochina[2] whose small dark-skinned body was covered in soft, brown hair. Farini exhibited her for seven months as "A Living Proof of Darwin's Theory of the Descent of Man," the missing link between man and monkey. She then appeared in France, Germany, and the United States. Indeed, Krao was a staple of the late nineteenth- and early twentieth-century international freak show circuit, performing with Barnum and Bailey, then Ringling Brothers, and later their combined circuses, until her death in 1926 from influenza. This paper argues that Krao's popularity as a sideshow exhibit, and thus her importance to the historical study of the Victorian freak show, stemmed from her relationship to late nineteenth-century preoccupations with Darwinism, imperialism, and the sexuality of the "primitive" body.

Krao made her first public appearance in January of 1883 at the Westminster Aquarium in London, although she had been shown to members of the press during the 1882 Christmas season. "The Aq," as it was affectionately known, had been built in 1876 as part of London's expanding entertainment industry. A pleasure palace within easy reach of Charing Cross, the Aquarium boasted a theater, concerts, variety shows, freak acts, temporary exhibits of extraordinary marine animals such as a whale, a walrus, and a manatee (which Farini advertised as a "mermaid"[3]), and of course fish. Despite the venue's name, the fish were an afterthought, as they were few in number and apparently far from the main attraction. According to one contemporary, the fish were "on view for some time; in fact, I think that one or two lingered on to the very end twenty-seven years later." "I have always wondered," he continued, "whether anyone went to look at them and if the water was ever changed!"[4] Despite the lack of fish, "the attractions of the place soon began to be very 'fishy' indeed," as the Aquarium became known as a promenade for prostitutes.[5] In 1889 the London County Council's Theatre and Music Hall Licensing Committee debated denying the venue an operating license precisely because of numerous complaints that it was little more than a convenient central location for the soliciting of sex.[6] The following year it was involved in a scandal over sexually provocative posters advertising the scantily clad gymnast Zaeo.[7] The Aquarium was thus a pleasure palace masquerading as a site of scientific and educational interest. It was, therefore, the perfect place for Krao, a sideshow freak whose appeal stemmed both from her claim to be "a perfect specimen of the step between man and monkey"[8] and from the erotics of her hairy, "primitive," body.

Throughout the latter half of the nineteenth century, popular understandings of evolutionary theory structured audiences' approach to the freak show, as the anomalous bodies on display were often interpreted as "steps on the evolutionary ladder" or "throwbacks" to earlier forms.[9] The liminal being that bridged the animal and human worlds was a trope of the display of human oddities in the eighteenth and nineteenth centuries as acts such as the Bear Lady, the Tiger Lady, and the Elephant Man make clear. After the publication of *Origin of Species* in 1859, these half-animal, half-human characters "became easily defined as 'missing links'" in an "increasingly fluid chain of being."[10] Farini's use of the scientific discourse of evolution to frame his exhibition of Krao was only the most explicit attempt by a variety of freak show entrepreneurs to capitalize on widespread interest in Darwinian theory. But significantly, it also served to legitimize Krao's exhibition and to attract audience members who might not otherwise attend this type of show.

The use of scientific language enabled both Farini and the popular press that reported on this attraction to distance themselves from what was toward the end of the nineteenth century increasingly coming to be seen, at least by middle-class morality mongers, as an indecent and prurient form of entertainment. In order to attract the widest audience, with the deepest pockets possible, Farini stressed that this was no "freak of nature" and encouraged the press to promote her as an educational exhibit in much the same way that "ethnological types" were advertised, particularly in the latter half of the nineteenth century.[11] "There are many who condemn, perhaps with justice, the taste which takes the form of looking upon 'freaks of nature,'" reported the *Morning Post*, but Krao "does not come within that unwholesome category, because her peculiarities are hereditary."[12] Indeed, the press and the showman repeatedly stressed that Krao was not "offensive" or "repulsive" but a "fascinating" "specimen" of interest to the "ethnologist" and "natural-ist" alike and thus not only an acceptable but also an edifying form of entertainment.

While a scientific discourse was strategically employed to circum-vent accusations of impropriety, this hirsute child did in fact serve as a focal point for public discussions of Darwinian theory, revealing that the freak show operated as an important space for the popularization of scientific debates. Whether Krao was more human than monkey, part of a separate race or a member of a transitional species, or merely a true "freak of nature" preoccupied accounts of her exhibition in the 1880s. Indeed, Farini structured the show as a scientific demonstra-tion, the "Living Proof of Darwin's Theory of the Descent of Man." Throughout the promotional pamphlet that accompanied her exhibi-tion, Farini upheld Krao as a scientific "specimen." Krao, Farini argued, "transcends in scientific importance and general interest any creature that has yet been seen in Europe."[13] He maintained, in fact, that the Siamese monarchy had eventually allowed her to leave the country in order to assist "Europeans in their researches in connection with the theory of the Descent of Man."[14] Krao, he claimed, was the "keystone to the arch" that the many builders of evolutionary theory had labored to construct, explicitly placing himself in the illustrious company of evolutionary theorists such as Ernst Haeckel, Alfred Russel Wallace, and Charles Darwin.[15] Many years later Farini told a reporter that he had "saturated" himself with Darwin in order to be able to "talk to the most learned scientist of them all."[16] The *Sporting and Dramatic News* further aggrandized Farini's self-proclaimed scientific achievements: "There stood the great Farini," it maintained, "he who had done with a Cook's tourist ticket and an agent, in a few months, more than poor Darwin had achieved with the aid of all the animal world in a lifetime."[17] Farini did not fail to capitalize on this quote, placing a version of it on the back of the pamphlet. He also issued a carte de visite that, borrowing from the conventions of spirit photography, featured an apparition of Darwin floating above an especially simian depiction of Krao. Darwin himself, this photographic souvenir implied, bore witness to this great discovery and marveled at Farini's scientific triumph even from beyond the grave.[18]

Darwin's *Origin of Species* merely alluded to the application of the principle of natural selection to the study of human evolution. However, "Darwin's Bulldog," Thomas Huxley, had by the 1860s fully expanded the theory to situate man's place in nature nearer the apes than the angels. By the time of the publication of *The Descent of Man* in 1871, Darwin's name was indelibly associated with "the ape theory."[19] Caricatures of Darwin-as-monkey proliferated in the popular press as scientific debates quickly found currency within the wider cultural milieu. One of the key ways in which Darwinian principles were more broadly understood was through the concept of the missing link. Critiques of Darwinian evolution had centered on the fact that no species between man and monkey had been identified. In the popular imagination this missing link would be proof of the theory of human evolution. In the second half of the nineteenth century the missing link began to appear as a character in popular fiction, although it was largely the subject of satire and was often discredited, as the man-monkey invariably turned out to be either entirely man, entirely monkey, or a monkey sitting on a man.[20] Beginning in the 1860s P. T. Barnum exhibited an African American man in a fur suit as the "missing link" or "Man Monkey." "Zip," as he was later known, however, received greatest fame not primarily as a missing link but as a "nondescript," as Barnum marketed this act under the title "What is It?"[21] In the 1870s a hairy fourteen-year-old microcephalic girl was also exhibited in France as "Darwin's Missing Link."[22] It was Farini, however, who most successfully capitalized on popular interpretations of Darwinian theory by promoting Krao as the missing link. Indeed, she continued to market herself as "the original missing link" throughout her career, suggesting both that she was the first widely popular act of this nature and that others had piggybacked on her success.[23]

Krao's pamphlet advertised her as the crucial, but heretofore elusive, piece of the evolutionary puzzle. It began: "The usual argument against the truth of the Darwinian theory, that Man and Monkey had a common origin, has always been that no animal has hitherto been discovered in the transition state between 'Monkey' and 'Man.' This 'Missing Link' is now supplied in the person of KRAO, a perfect specimen of the step between man and monkey."[24] In order to accentuate Krao's status as missing link, Farini underscored her simian characteristics: her nose was level with the rest of her face, her cheeks contained pouches in which she could store food, she shot out her lip like a chimpanzee when pouty, her joints were flexible, she turned the soles of her feet up when sitting down, she had the rudiments of a tail, and of course was covered in hair. Farini excerpted quotes from the popular press that stressed these monkeylike attributes, such as the *Standard*'s report that "she has a double row of teeth on the upper jaw; that she can, in the hollow of her cheeks, stow away food to be eaten when required as the monkey does in his 'pouches,' and that the fingers and toes bend backwards and forwards to the same extent and with equal ease."[25] Farini had clearly lectured to the press at a special viewing of Krao on her simian qualities. He then deliberately chose quotations for the front and back of Krao's promotional pamphlet that parroted his contention that Krao was half human, half monkey, although which half was which was clearly a matter of debate. "The lower portion of the body is more like that of a monkey," maintained the *Daily Chronicle*, while the *Evening News* reported that her "face presents an aspect singularly akin to that of the gorilla, but with a humanised expression."[26] Other reports drew attention to her resemblance to Pongo, a gorilla that Farini had previously exhibited at the Aquarium, and gestured to her similarities to the "lower order of animals whose pranks are a never failing source of delight to visitors at the Zoological Gardens."[27]

The images that accompanied Krao's 1883 exhibition stressed her simian characteristics. The illustration that adorned the cover of her souvenir pamphlet represented Krao as a small monkeylike child, naked except for copious amounts of body hair, indeed much more hair than contemporary photographs of her indicate that she actually possessed. Alternatively, she was seen in a promotional photograph clinging to her adoptive father, naked with hairy arms and legs wrapped around him in a simian embrace. A cartoon of this photograph was reproduced in the *Sporting News* with the caption "Linked Sweetness," stressing Krao's "winsome ways" but implying that she was as much animal as human. Beside this cartoon appeared another that depicted Krao in her "bib and tucker." Here the artist exaggerated her lips to stress her status as a "talking monkey," accentuating her racial otherness, which contrary to the "Linked Sweetness" image rendered Krao grotesque.[28] As Z. S.

Strother has argued in relationship to the representations of Sara Baart-man, the "Hottentot Venus," Krao's body clearly "did not speak for itself," and thus her souvenir pamphlet guided the eye to seek out her simian qualities.[29] The unofficial images that surrounded her appearance at the Aquarium thus also helped to structure the public's consumption of Krao as "the missing link."

Krao's reputation, like that of many other freaks, rested on her authenticity. It was, therefore, essential for Farini to engage with sci-entific "experts," although how much of their interest in her was purely scientific, and the precise nature of their expertise in the authentication of missing links, are open to question. Farini commenced Krao's souvenir pamphlet with a conversation between himself and Francis Buckland, a well-known naturalist, who was also a personal friend. Unabashedly interested in "curiosities of natural history," Buckland was nonetheless a respectable scientist.[30] His presence in the narrative helped position Krao as a legitimate subject of scientific study. During a visit to Dublin in 1883, Farini arranged for Krao to be exhibited at a private gather-ing of local intellectuals including Trinity College professors, doctors, veterinarians, members of the Royal Society, and select representatives of the press. She was presented in her undergarments and was exam-ined and touched by the audience, who were encouraged to verify her status as missing link. Well trained by Farini, she greeted each visitor with a "How d'you do, Sir?"[31] By conducting these private viewings for selected distinguished guests apart from her regular public exhibitions, Farini sought to construct Krao as "worthy of [both] public attention and careful scientific examination."[32]

Much of the "scientific" discussion of Krao focused on the proposi-tion that she came from a hairy family, and indeed a hairy species. She was not a freak, the press reported, no "*lusus naturae* such as bearded women, spotted dogs, or giantesses." Rather, argued *Bell's Life in Lon-don*, "she is a regular production in the regular order of Nature."[33] This was not merely an attempt to distance her from the freak show, which occupied the moral borderlands of popular entertainment, but also to emphasize her scientific importance. If she were a freak, a true anomaly, then she could not be considered a missing link, which by definition was a member of a transitional species. Accentuating her hairy family, therefore, was essential to protecting her status. Krao's pamphlet spent a great deal of time on her capture and on the hairiness of her parents, who did not accompany her to England. Krao's father had apparently died of cholera two weeks before they left, but as an accompanying woodcut revealed, his "whole body was completely covered with a thick hairy coat, exactly like that of the anthropoid apes."[34] By constructing Krao as the missing link, with a hereditary condition, common not only to her family but to a tribe, and indeed a species, Farini suggested that she was a subject not for pathologists and teratologists, who were concerned with diseases or congenital anomalies, but rather for the anthropologist.

In an article entitled "Krao, The 'Human Monkey,'" which appeared in the scientific journal *Nature* in January of 1883, A. H. Keane, the English traveler and anthropologist, reported on Farini's discovery. Without fully endorsing the showman's claims, Keane nevertheless underscored Krao's "prognathism," her protruding lips, and her other apparently apelike characteristics, proclaiming that "apart from her history" one might feel inclined to regard "this specimen merely as a 'sport' or *lusus naturae*, possessed rather of a pathological than of a strictly anthropological interest." But if the pamphlet about her is indeed true, he continued, then she is of "exceptional scientific importance."[35] A few months later, however, *Nature* published a letter from a resident of Bangkok shedding light on Krao's personal history. Krao, the author declared, was a Siamese child who came from ordinary parents. "Krao" was not the sound her parents made when calling her, as Farini had claimed, but rather meant "whiskers," her nickname. She was no more flexible than any other Siamese person, the letter writer maintained, and "beyond her abnormal hairiness presents no peculiarity." The child was looked upon at home "as even a greater natural curiosity than she is considered to be in England," declared the correspondent; in fact, her parents had also exhibited her to paying customers before selling her outright.[36]

While Keane corroborated these particulars, Farini of course ignored and suppressed them, continuing to quote Keane's original observations on the back of Krao's pamphlet. Indeed, as was to be expected, he only included quotes that emphasized her monkeylike nature, conveniently expunging material that clearly indicated that neither the scientific community nor the popular press was convinced of her authenticity. Both the *British Medical Journal* and *Scientific American* concluded that she was merely a case of "hypertrichopherosis (superabundance of hair)."[37] Indeed, the *BMJ* noted that all her physical peculiarities were common "amongst the yellow coloured races found inhabiting the eastern parts of India."[38] The *Daily News* maintained that "Anatomists and anthropologists must decide whether Krao is in any degree structurally allied to the ape. The ordinary observer is not likely to discover that she is."[39] She shows "far too much intelligence to please the out-and-out Darwinite," suggested the *London Figaro*, while the *Morning Advertiser* maintained that the true link that needed to be found was the one that connected Krao "with the monkey-world."[40] In fact, while Krao was certainly a curiosity, some were clearly disappointed with the exhibition. "I had steeled myself to behold something very Darwinian," reported *Land and Water*, "picturing a gorilla-like half-animal being" but instead finding "a bright little girl."[41]

Despite her dubious authenticity, Krao's exhibit was undoubtedly a popular and financial success. She was, according to another per-former, "immensely popular for years."[42] A contemporary showman recalled that Krao "was showing at the time when Darwin's theory was in the news so enormous crowds for a long time [were] the order of the day."[43] Whether or not freak show audiences were convinced of Farini's claims about Krao, they were clearly attracted by the link to Darwinian theory. Krao's exhibition was successful, therefore, because she literally embodied popular interpretations of evolutionary theory, reflecting back to the freak show audience its own understanding of the processes of human evolution and encouraging these spectators to participate in the advancement of scientific knowledge. At the same time, as we shall see, Krao reinforced British beliefs about the distance between their own civilized and evolved bodies, and primitive "others."

If the pamphlet sold at Krao's exhibition framed the show as scien-tific and educational, leading to a better understanding of evolutionary theory, it also situated Krao as part of a triumphant narrative of British imperialism. Evolutionary theory and imperialism were linked by what Anne McClintock has called "anachronistic space." Colonized people were, according to this trope, mired in "a permanently anterior time within the geographic space of the modern empire as anachronistic humans, atavistic . . . the living embodiment of the archaic 'primi-tive.'"[44] Colonial subjects thus represented lower branches of the mono-genetic family tree, both less physically and less culturally evolved. The imperial element of Krao's story enhanced the scientific positioning of her as an intermediary life form, for where else would the missing link be found but in the underexplored and undeveloped regions on the edges of the empire.

The dramatic tale of Krao's capture was part of a pervasive late nineteenth-century narrative that figured imperialism as an adventure that tested men's mettle. While this part of Southeast Asia was not yet part of the British empire, Krao's capture in Laos and the complex negotiations with the Laotian, Burmese, and Siamese monarchies over her removal reads like an imperial adventure novel, a genre that reached its apotheosis with H. Rider Haggard's *King Solomon's Mines* (1885) and *She* (1887).[45] While Krao was likely born in Siam, she was, according to her souvenir pamphlet, captured in Laos. Farini's freak hunters had been dispatched to Southeast Asia, for rumors abounded that tailed men could be found in the region. In addition, it was known that King Theebaw of Burma kept a "hairy family" at his court (who also hit the freak show circuit in the late 1880s, appearing in London in 1886 and in Paris the following year). Southeast Asia, or Indochina as it was commonly called in the late nineteenth century, sat at the edge of empire. The British, contesting French colonial expansion in the region, had been actively encroaching into this territory since the Anglo-Burmese war of 1826. Britain annexed the port of Rangoon in 1852, converted the Straits Settlement into a Crown colony in 1867, and formally absorbed Burma into the British empire in 1885. While India had been effectively domesticated by the 1880s, Indochina figured in the British imagination as a mysterious and savage outpost of empire that few could in fact locate on a map. Indeed, the press coverage of Krao suggests widespread confusion about where exactly Laos lay.[46] By 1883, a tense moment in British-Burmese relations over the balance of power in the region, the Victorian press had begun to depict the Burmese as uncivilized, corrupt, and barbaric.[47] Krao's pamphlet contributed to this rhetoric. It was into this "country of bribery and corruption" ruled by a "bloodthirsty and treacherous sovereign" home to "wild tribes" of "robbers and murderers" that Farini plunged his audience.[48]

The *Strand* magazine noted in 1897 that a "whole library of entertaining facts might be written about the romance of freak-hunting and curiosity-finding for the side-shows of the world." Farini's "costly expedition to Northern Siam in search of 'Krao, the Missing Link,'" it continued, "reads like one of Jules Vernes's wildest flights."[49] Even years after her debut, Krao was clearly still selling the same souvenir pamphlet at her shows. The narrative of her capture was so appealing to freak show audiences, and survived for at least two decades, because it tapped into late nineteenth-century taste for imperial adventures. Indeed, Farini had clearly modeled Krao's pamphlet not only on imperial fiction but also on the story of "The Wild Men of Borneo." From the 1850s the diminutive Barney and Hiram Davis toured the United States and Europe as Waino and Plutaino, "The Wild Men of Borneo."

When P. T. Barnum exhibited them in the 1870s, he sold a pamphlet at the show that detailed their exciting capture off the "rocky coast of the Island of Borneo." It theorized that these "savage" brothers came from Siam or Burma and were "hardly more elevated in social standing than ourang-outangs."[50] These freak show "true life histories" were thus highly formulaic and both borrowed from and informed not only each other but also fictional and nonfictional imperial adventure stories that circulated widely throughout Victorian culture.

Like Haggard's exotic tales, the story of Krao's capture is rife with adventure. Edward Sachs, the first of Farini's explorers, is bound hand and foot by his supposed guides and left hanging upside down from a tree to be "torn to pieces by wild beasts." He outwits the natives by "extending his powerful muscles to their fullest extent" before he is bound, so that the ropes loosen as his muscles relax. By the "superhuman effort of his powerful muscles" he escapes and returns to Mandalay to surprise his betrayers.[51] Sachs, however, like many an imperial explorer, contracts both smallpox and dysentery and is forced to give up the search. The quest for the missing link was then taken up by Carl Bock, who had already procured a walrus and a group of Laplanders for Farini in the Arctic, another site of nineteenth-century adventure stories. Bock was already engaged in an equally "onerous journey" through "some of the most difficult regions of Borneo, amid the 'head hunters,' and the cannibals" (which resulted in his sensational *The Head-Hunters of Borneo* [1881]) when he agreed to take up the search for the missing link.[52] The "dangerous journey" into Laos "surrounded by tigers and bears, by leopards and panthers, by elephants and rhinoceri, by snakes and crocodiles" results in the successful capture of Krao and her parents. But when he tries to leave Laos with his treasure, the king detains him. Bock is held as a "virtual prisoner" for months until he threatens the Laotian monarch with the wrath of the king of Siam, who had, apparently, sanctioned the search for the missing link.[53] The trials and tribulations of Sachs and Bock are typical of the imperial adventure genre. They penetrate the dark jungles of distant conquerable lands, survive the attacks of savage tribes, suffer tropical diseases, hunt for treasure, and outwit foreign rulers. Their superior physical strength and European intellect and rationality trump the weak and superstitious natives, and in the end their courage and persistence are rewarded. Krao's appeal was thus due in part to her pamphlet's success in catering to the desires of the audience for these tales from dark continents.

Not only did the story of her capture fit perfectly into the genre of imperial fiction, but Krao also served as a human trophy of imperial expansion, a synecdoche of Indochina, parts of which were on the verge of being absorbed into the British empire. Like the "Burmese Imperial State Carriage and Throne Studded with 20,000 precious stones Captured in the Present Indian War," which was exhibited at the Egyptian Hall in 1825 in the midst of the first Anglo-Burmese war, the British public could consume Krao as a prize, a souvenir of imperial conquest, for with her hairy naked body and monkeylike nature, Krao was emblematic of all that was wild, lawless, and savage in the lands at the edge of empire.[54] To emphasize her savagery, Farini circulated portraits of Krao that underscored not only her simian characteristics but also her essential primitiveness. Even when clothed in the trappings of middle-class respectability, Krao was placed in a natural and explicitly savage environment, either leaning against rocks or perched on the stump of a tree. The most explicitly "wild child" image of her was made around 1884. This souvenir carte de visite produced in Liverpool depicted Krao in a jungle setting. Here she is completely naked, which accentuates her hairy body. Her hair surrounds her face like a lion's mane (a trope of other hirsute freak performers), and her right leg is raised to rest upon a rock in order to better expose her flat, hairy, and thus primitive feet. This image was reproduced in Britain as a woodcut and was used as part of the promotional material for her 1887 reappearance at the Aquarium. But here, significantly, the artist introduced a small beaded loincloth for the sake of modesty (figure 6.1).

However, just as Krao epitomized the primitive nature of colonial subjects, so too was she quickly domesticated by the media, who underscored how easily she had been civilized since her arrival in Britain. Her pamphlet and the press reports of her exhibition return repeatedly to the success of the civilizing process, for this wild monkey-child was regularly held up as a well-behaved, charming little girl. If Krao's pamphlet figured the Indochinese as wild and savage—the tribe of hairy people to which Krao supposedly belonged lived in a state "as low and as bestial as the beasts of the field"[55]—her capture was construed as a rescue, for she was saved from this savage life and civilized. When Bock declared to Prince Kromolat of Burma that Krao would be "far better cared for in Europe [by Farini] than she possibly could [be] in the wild country" that was her home, the prince replied that he had indeed heard of "the Great Showman" and at once acquiesced to her removal "on condition that she should be formally adopted by Mr. Bock, on behalf of Mr. Farini, as his adopted daughter."[56] While the fictitious prince's admiration for Farini was inserted into the story to aggrandize the showman,

Figure 6.1

Krao, the Missing Link. Photo courtesy of Bodleian Library, University of Oxford, John Johnson Collection, Human Freaks Box 4, Handbill for "Krao" 1887.

it also served to underscore the dominant imperial ideology that figured colonial peoples as grateful recipients of Western culture.

The final phrase of Krao's pamphlet asserted that this "daughter of a tribe of hairy men and women, Now makes her appearance before the civilised world."[57] But much of the media coverage of her exhibition also focused on the success of Krao's own process of civilization. Her ability to speak English was often noted, as were her good manners. Like an appropriately grateful immigrant, Krao was apparently so taken with her new home that she announced her "intention of residing in England."[58] Argued the anthropologist A. H. Keane, Krao recognized her own good fortune and had "so far adapted herself to civilised ways, that the mere threat to be sent back to her own people is always sufficient to suppress any symptoms of unruly conduct."[59] Similarly, her parents had, according to her souvenir pamphlet, been equally "anxious" to leave their native land and accompany Bock back to England.[60] Ironically, the freak show, seen by many to be voyeuristic, prurient, and immoral, was in this context cast as a civilizing force. As Rosemarie Garland-Thomson has similarly argued in relationship to the "nondescript" hirsute attraction Julia Pastrana, her "exploitation becomes a salvation; her colonization becomes a conversion; and her display becomes a testimony."[61]

Krao's formal adoption by Farini confirmed that she could not only be successfully transplanted but also transformed into a little English girl. Krao's adoption officially anglicized and domesticated her, and her adaptability to her new father was often noted. She appears "to be happy enough in her new position," remarked the *Daily News*, "and to regard her papa, as she calls Mr. Farini, with feelings of affection."[62] Other journalists maintained that she appeared "much attached" to Farini, "her kind foster parent,"[63] and indeed she bore the surname Farini throughout her life. Not only did her adoption normalize and Westernize Krao by locating her within a Victorian family unit (making her, as one newspaper noted, not only "hair apparent, but heir apparent"[64]) but also several newspaper reports highlighted the fact that she had been vaccinated.[65] If by the 1880s all British children were compelled to be vaccinated, they were also required to be educated. The *London Figaro* noted that before long the "Board School officers will be looking up Miss Krao" and will likely "insist [on] her passing her standard like any other young lady of colour located in this country."[66] By advertising her vaccination, and the possibility of her education, Farini accentuated Krao's admittance into British society through the rites and rituals of Western childhood.

As part of this discourse of successful civilization, Farini often clothed Krao in the dress and elegant black boots of a middle-class girl, although her costume always left her hairy arms and legs exposed. In one souvenir photograph she is garbed in an elaborate hat and ruffled dress, resembling the clothes of a Victorian fashion doll.[67] These "civilized" images of Krao served as the basis of an illustration that appeared in American papers when she first crossed the Atlantic. In the Peru

(Indiana) *Republican* in 1885, a well-groomed and neatly dressed Krao was depicted sitting beside a younger and decidedly more simian version of herself, adapted from the image that first appeared on her promotional pamphlet.[68] The illustration suggests the distance she has traveled from savage to civilized in the space of a mere two years. If Krao was a trophy of empire, she was therefore also an object lesson in imperial relations. Her representation as a charming child, happily adapting to English life, underscored Britain's role as a civilizing force and its ability to turn even the most primitive peoples into good British subjects.

The Darwinian and Social Darwinian messages of Krao's exhibition are clear; indeed, her success stemmed in large part from Farini's ability to cast Krao as an educational act rather than as a freak. However, it is hard to ignore that at least part of Krao's appeal, particularly in the decades around the turn of the century, derived from the implicit sexuality of her partially exposed hirsute body. While she was not primarily an erotic performer, Krao's body could be, and clearly was, read as sexually available. The very act of displaying one's body publicly rendered the female performer, regardless of the content and nature of the performance, a sexual object. Thus many female freaks, particularly bearded women, who were also transgressing gender boundaries, attempted to underscore their femininity, and thus to contain their sexuality, by promoting themselves as wives and mothers—models of heterosexual, procreative, middle-class domesticity. However, Krao's act required her to exhibit more of her body than bearded ladies, whose difference was manifest only above the neck. Indeed, by the end of the nineteenth century Krao was regularly depicted reclining in a jungle setting, like other hirsute acts, in the highly eroticized pose of an odalisque.[69] Her costume, a version of which she wore throughout her career, was similar to those preferred by female acrobats (like the scandalous Zaeo) whose performances were structured to allow male viewers to see as much of the female body as possible, and whose aerial feats permitted the audience to look up at their spread legs from a strategic vantage point. By evoking both the female acrobat and the odalisque in her promotional materials, Krao's promoters used sex to sell her act.

However, it was not merely the erotic poses and skimpy costumes but in fact the hairiness of her body itself that suggested Krao's sexual availability. Since at least the Renaissance, the hairy female body had been associated with animalistic lust.[70] By the nineteenth century hirsuteness had become a marker of the primitive or savage body, which was in turn bound up in notions of unbridled, perverse, and pathological sexuality.[71] That Krao grew hair where "normal" women did not titillated audiences in ways similar to the half-woman/half-man whose gender bending also suggested a polyvalent and thus excessive sexuality. In her early twenties Krao had not only cultivated a great mane of hair but was also sporting a full beard and mustache. By exposing female body and facial hair for all to see, Krao made visible that which generally went unseen: her body hair and her beard evoked pubic hair, a preoccupation of Victorian pornography, and thus she permitted male audience members access to an erotic, if not necessarily feminine, aspect of the sexualized female body.

The eroticization of Krao found its fullest expression in France in 1886. The French media transformed the previously innocuous carte de visite of a nine-year-old Krao in her jungle setting into an image of a considerably older, sexually aggressive, and sexually available young woman. This illustration, which appeared on a poster advertising her exhibition in a private room at the café-concert the Alcazar d'Eté (a competitor of the Folies-Bergère, where King Theebaw's "sacred hairy family" was exhibited in 1887), had clearly been adapted from the British woodcut seen in figure 6.1, but its tone and meaning had changed. Instead of confronting the viewer with a direct and passive stare, more animal than human, Krao looks over her left shoulder and grins suggestively at her viewers in a coquettish come-on. Her legs and thighs are considerably more curvaceous, and she rises up on her toes to exaggerate the curved arches of her feet. Similarly, a picture of a nude Krao seated on the lap of a scientist was significantly altered in a French cartoon to emphasize the lasciviousness of the scientist and the sexual availability of what was now clearly a young woman.[72]

The French overtly sexualized Krao, even at this very early stage of her career, revealing heightened anxieties, as Diana Snigurowicz has argued, over the sexual connotations of female hirsuteness, which suggested bestiality, zoophilia, and interspecies breeding.[73] For the British, the erotic nature of Krao's act seems to have been more implicit. The media coverage of Krao's exhibition in Britain, in contrast to her publicity materials, emphasized not her bestial qualities but her humanity and, indeed, her femininity. There was little question that Krao was in fact a young girl with more human than simian characteristics. Most newspapers reported that she had "lovely" or "lustrous" eyes. Even her own pamphlet drew attention to what was obviously seen as her best feature: "How many a fair lady will envy Krao those full and sparkling eyes! How their dark luster would be set off on a fair skin!"[74] This remark implied that despite the existence of "several British subjects who are uglier than Krao,"[75] she could never be truly beautiful as her dark skin (hairy or not), the clearest marker of her racial difference, precluded this. Nonetheless, as the newspapers all indicated, she showed "truly feminine delight" in the clothes and jewelry and satin slippers she was provided with.[76] This feminization of Krao suggested that she was not only flirtatious but possibly available. Maintained one reporter, this "pretty little girl" exhibited "the elementary coquettishness of her sex," asserting her "fair sex through and through her hirsute appearance."[77] Indeed, *Punch* suggested knowingly that she was ready to receive company: "Entrance without knocking, ask for the Hairy Belle," a sentiment that Farini clearly endorsed, for he placed this quote on the promotional pamphlet itself.[78]

Krao's evening appearances at the Star of Erin music hall in Dublin in 1883, even more than her daytime exhibition to learned professionals in her underclothes, underscored the erotic readings of her body. According to Shane Peacock, Farini's biographer, "Each night the lights were dimmed, primitive music played and she slowly emerged onto the stage . . . in a short blue dress with red stockings and shoes, her side turned to the crowd and her face partially covered. . . . When she came fully into the footlights and dramatically lifted her head to the audience there was always an audible gasp. . . . But once again her most striking characteristic was her personality—she was a charming, charismatic performer who enjoyed being on stage.[79] The music hall, as opposed to the pseudoscientific setting of the Aquarium, encouraged Krao to perform her freakish bodily difference in dramatic and sexually provocative ways that explicitly located her as "primitive" Other. Her performance, complete with music, lighting, and costume, prefigured that of Josephine Baker, who self-consciously manipulated the discourses of primitive sexuality to market herself as an exotic, and therefore erotic, act.

When Krao returned to Britain in 1887 the Aquarium program maintained that "Old friends will be astonished at her development,"[80] hinting at her body's maturity. Seven years later the *English Mechanic* reported that while on exhibit in Germany, Krao had received a marriage proposal, a not uncommon phenomenon for sideshow freaks, which she had refused because "she had learned too much independence during her wild life in the woods."[81] However, it was not until the turn of the century that Krao's sexuality generated concern in Britain. In 1899, when Krao reappeared at the Aquarium, an irate member of the public wrote to the London County Council to complain about her exhibition. The shocked correspondent maintained that in the "interest of decency" the act should be withdrawn. "The revolting inference in the attraction" is that the public should "behold the result of copulation between a woman and one of the most filthy beasts." Such an exhibition, it continued, might lead to the logical next step: an exhibition of the woman and the monkey, the "authors of the horror exhibited."[82] While the LCC investigated and found "nothing whatever in the exhibition or the costume of the woman that could call for any remark whatever,"[83] Krao clearly elicited anxieties over bestiality. This letter writer misunderstood Krao's claim to be half-woman, half-monkey, as she continued throughout her adult career to advertise and promote herself as "the missing link," not as a product of interbreeding. This misreading nonetheless reveals the sexual fantasies and anxieties suggested by both Darwinism and imperialism, for sexual unions between man and monkey, it has been argued, were both implicit in Darwin's theory and part of "pornotropic" fantasies dating back to the early modern period.[84]

Krao's sexuality, while not the primary focus of the act, thus served to enhance the dominant imperial and sociobiological message of her exhibition. For in the late nineteenth century the discourses of evolution, imperialism, and primitive sexuality were deeply imbricated as Britain justified colonialism by promoting it as a civilizing mission. Her long-term success, evidenced by the fact that she was one of the highest paid freaks in the Ringling Brothers lineup,[85] was thus due to her ability literally to embody the relationship between primitive sexuality, imperial ideology, and Darwinian theory. For by displaying her hairy body, Krao reinforced the profound difference between evolved British bodies and "primitive" Others. Her hirsuteness, and thus essential savagery, reassured the British public, across the class spectrum, of its racial, national, and imperial superiority. At the same time she continued to serve as proof of the success of the civilizing process. As "the best-liked of freaks," who "never complained," Krao was, according to "the fat lady," her longtime friend, destined straight for the ultimate rewards of Christian civilization: "If any one has gone to heaven," she proclaimed, "that woman has."[86] Audiences across the United Kingdom thus swarmed to see "Krao, the Missing Link" because she provided the British public with perfect proof of their supreme status on what her pamphlet called "the Darwinian chain of evolution" that joined "molecule to man."[87]

Notes

1. *Krao, The Missing Link. A Living Proof of Darwin's Theory of the Descent of Man,* c. 1883. British Library, Evanion Collection, item 2474.

2. Throughout this essay I will be employing the nineteenth-century terms for the countries that make up the region we know today as Southeast Asia. I am using Victorian terminology because I am interested in British fantasies about the countries known today as Laos, Thailand, and Myanmar.

3. Shane Peacock, "Africa Meets the Great Farini," in *Africans on Stage: Studies in Ethnological Show Business,* ed. Bernth Lindfors (Bloomington: Indiana University Press, 1999), 84.

4. Erroll Sherson, *London's Lost Theatres of the Nineteenth Century* (London: John Lane, 1925), 296.

5. Ibid., 297.

6. Administrative County of London, Sessions of the Licensing Committee, October 9, 1889. London Metropolitan Archives LCC/MIN/10, 891.

7. Tracy C. Davis, "Sex in Public Places: The Zaeo Aquarium Scandal and the Victorian Moral Majority," *Theatre History Studies* 10 (1990): 1–13.

8. *Krao,* 1.

9. Michael Mitchell, *Monsters: Human Freaks in America's Gilded Age* (Toronto: ECW Press, 2002), 46.

10. Nigel Rothfels, "Aztecs, Aborigines, and Ape-People: Science and Freaks in Germany, 1850–1900," in *Freakery,* ed. Rosemarie Garland-Thomson (New York: New York University Press, 1996), 162.

11. For the conventions of ethnological display see Lindfors.

12. *Morning Post,* January 1, 1883, 2.

13. *Krao,* 13.

14. Ibid., 12.

15. Ibid., 14.

16. Qtd. in Shane Peacock, *The Great Farini: The High-Wire Life of William Hunt* (Toronto: Viking, 1995), 290.

17. *Sporting and Dramatic News,* January 6, 1883, 425.

18. Many thanks to Shane Peacock for sharing this image with me.

19. Edward Caudill, "Victorian Satire of Evolution," *Journalism History* 20, nos. 3/4 (1994): 107–15.

20. Leo Henkin, *Darwinism in the English Novel, 1860–1910* (New York: Corporate Press, 1940).

21. James W. Cook, Jr., "Of Men, Missing Links, and Nondescripts: The Strange Career of P. T. Barnum's 'What-is-It?' Exhibition," in Garland-Thomson, *Freakery.*

22. Diana Snigurowicz, "Sex, Simians, and Spectacle in Nineteenth-Century France; or, How to Tell a 'Man' from a Monkey," *Canadian Journal of History* 34, no. 1 (1999): 60.

23. *Billboard,* February 21, 1914, 32.

24. *Krao,* 1.

25. Ibid., ii.

26. Ibid., ii–iii.

27. *Morning Post*, January 1, 1883, 2.

28. *Sporting and Dramatic News*, January 6, 1883, 425.

29. Z. S. Strother, "Display of the Body Hottentot," in Lindfors, 31.

30. Francis T. Buckland, *Curiosities of Natural History* (London: Macmillan, 1900).

31. Peacock, *Great Farini*, 298.

32. *Krao*, ii.

33. *Bell's Life in London*, January 6, 1883, 7.

34. *Krao*, 11.

35. *Nature*, January 11, 1883, 245.

36. *Nature*, April 19, 1883, 579.

37. *Scientific American*, April 21, 1883, 247.

38. *British Medical Journal*, January 6, 1883, 28–29.

39. *Daily News*, January 1, 1883, 2.

40. *London Figaro*, January 6, 1883, 4; *Morning Advertiser*, January 2, 1883, 2.

41. *Land and Water*, January 6, 1883, 14.

42. Fred Bradna, *The Big Top: My Forty Years with the Greatest Show on Earth* (London: Hamish Hamilton, 1953), 197.

43. James McKenzie, *Strange Truth. The Autobiography of a Circus Showman, Stage and Exhibition Man*. Unpublished manuscript, Brunel University Library, 218.

44. Anne McClintock, *Imperial Leather* (New York: Routledge, 1995), 30.

45. Patrick Brantlinger, *Rule of Darkness: British Literature and Imperialism, 1830–1914* (Ithaca, NY: Cornell University Press, 1988).

46. In 1883 the *British Medical Journal* suggested that Laos was part of Burma; in 1894, once Laos had been absorbed into French Indochina, the *English Mechanic* nonetheless maintained that it was part of Siam.

47. Deborah Deacon Boyer, "Picturing the Other: Images of Burmans in Imperial Britain," *Victorian Periodicals Review* 35, no. 3 (2002): 216.

48. *Krao*, 5–6.

49. *Strand*, March 1897, 408–9.

50. *What we know of Waino and Plutaino, Wild Men of Borneo. And some of the latest Popular Songs*, c. 1878, National Fairgrounds Archive, University of Sheffield. See also Robert Bogdan, *Freak Show: Presenting Human Oddities for Amusement and Profit* (Chicago: University of Chicago Press, 1988), 121–27.

51. *Krao*, 6.

52. Ibid., 7.

53. Ibid., 9, 11.

54. John Johnson Collection, Bodleian Library, Oxford University, London Play Places Box 10. For a similar argument about the Kohinoor diamond at the Crystal Palace, see Lara Kriegel, "Narrating the Subcontinent: India at the Crystal Palace in 1851," in *The Great Exhibition of 1851*, ed. Louise Purbrick (Manchester, UK: Manchester University Press, 2001).

55. *Krao*, 7.

56. Ibid., 12.

57. Ibid., 14.

58. *The Broad Arrow*, January 6, 1883, 22.

59. *Nature*, January 11, 1883, 245.

60. *Krao*, 11.

61. Rosemarie Garland-Thomson, "Narratives of Deviance and Delight: Staring at Julia Pastrana, the 'Extraordinary Lady,'" in *Beyond the Binary: Reconstructing Cultural Identity in a Multicultural Context*, ed. Timothy B. Powell (New Brunswick, NJ: Rutgers University Press, 1999), 94.

62. *Daily News*, January 1, 1883, 2.

63. *Bell's Life in London*, January 6, 1883, 7; *Land and Water*, January 6, 1883, 14.

64. *Land and Water*, January 6, 1883, 14.

65. *Daily News*, January 1, 1883, 2; *The London Figaro*, January 6, 1883, 4.

66. *The London Figaro*, January 6, 1883, 4.

67. Peacock, *Great Farini*, 289.

68. *The Peru Republican*, April 24, 1885.

69. Snigurowicz, "Sex, Simians, and Spectacle," 76–77.

70. Mary E. Fissell, "Hairy Women and Naked Truths: Gender and the Politics of Knowledge in *Aristotle's Masterpiece*," *William and Mary Quarterly* 60, no. 1 (2003): 43–74.

71. Sander Gilman, "Black Bodies, White Bodies: Toward an Iconography of Female Sexuality in Late Nineteenth-Century Art, Medicine and Literature," in *"Race," Writing and Difference*, ed. Henry Louis Gates, Jr. (Chicago: University of Chicago Press, 1986); George W. Stocking, Jr., *Victorian Anthropology* (New York: Free Press, 1987).

72. These images are reproduced in Sabine Lenk, ed., *Grüße aus Viktoria: Film-Ansichten aus der Ferne* (Basel: Stroemfeld, 2002), 48, and Diana Snigurowicz, "Spectacles of Monstrosity and the Embodiment of Identity in France, 1829–1914" (Ph.D. diss., University of Chicago), 455–56.

73. Snigurowicz, "Sex, Simians, and Spectacle," 78.

74. *Krao*, 12.

75. *News of the World*, December 31, 1882, 5.

76. *The Times*, January 2, 1883, 9; *Daily News*, January 1, 1883, 2.

77. *Land and Water*, January 6, 1883, 14.

78. *Krao*, ii.

79. Peacock, *The Great Farini*, 297–98.

80. Royal Aquarium Programme, April 30, 1887.

81. *English Mechanic and World of Science*, December 28, 1894, 429.

82. Unsigned letter to Clerk of London County Council, December 22, 1899. London Metropolitan Archives, LCC/MIN/10, 891.

83. Inspection of Places of Public Entertainment Report, Royal Aquarium, January 2, 1900. London Metropolitan Archives, LCC/MIN/10, 891.

84. Snigurowicz, "Sex, Simians, and Spectacle," 67; McClintock, 22; Londa Schiebinger, *Nature's Body* (Boston: Beacon Press, 1993), 95.

85. According to contract documents Krao was paid $50 for the 1916 season, as much as Frank Lentini, the spectacular three-legged boy. Many thanks to Fred D. Pfening for sharing his collection of contracts with me.

86. *New York Times*, April 19, 1926.

87. *The Broad Arrow*, January 6, 1883, 22.

PART III

Empire, Race, and Commodity

THIS SECTION takes up a triad of related concerns: empire, race, and economics. While the essays in this section also speak to the "marketing" strategies of part I and the scientific discourses of part II, they are brought together here around the theme of empire making. Marlene Tromp's essay looks at the place of the Indian freak exhibits in England, proposing that we must read Indian performers in the social context of empire and English-Indian relations. Kelly Hurley's essay on the Victorian mummy obsession points to the ways that the anxieties over great ancient nonwhite civilizations were managed through the uncanny double of the white mummy—a figure revealing a commodity and sexual fetish that, like the cultural management of the freak, balms fears of racial degeneration or disappearance provoked by imperial activity. Rebecca Stern's discussion of Julia Pastrana, the hair-covered "Bear Woman," suggests that anxieties about empire were addressed in negative prescriptions for womanhood embodied in this famous masculinized/feminized performer. In all of these essays, the political and social implications of empire are laid against the freak show performer or the metaphor of the freak to enrich our understanding of both in their British context.

7

EMPIRE AND THE INDIAN FREAK

The "Miniature Man" from Cawnpore and the "Marvellous Indian Boy" on Tour in England

MARLENE TROMP

Performers in the Cultural Context

The published scholarship on freaks and freak shows in the nineteenth century has been dominated by studies of the American context, and for this reason, there has been little written on the question of freakery with regard to the colonial relationship between England and India. Gayatri Chakravorty Spivak has argued that we must read every Victorian text as a commentary on imperial relations since those tensions were so fundamental to the nineteenth century.[1] Tales and texts about Indian freak performers in England would certainly demand such an analysis. This essay explores one manifestation of the colonial relationship by looking at two freak performers who exhibited themselves from the mid-century to its end: Mohammed Baux, the thirty-seven-inch-tall "Miniature Man of India," and Laloo, the "Marvellous Indian Boy," who had a parasitic twin embedded in and emerging from his torso. What the promotional materials of these two performers suggest is that, during a significant period in English-Indian relations, freakery was one of the many discourses that helped construct—as well as destabilize—the rhetoric of empire and, further, that the discourse of freakery was as profoundly marked by those of race and power relations as the rest of the culture.

Both Mohammed Baux and Laloo were billed as and marketed by more than the most overt aspect of their physical freakishness— although, of course, those bodily differences featured prominently in their advertisements. Their race and ethnicity were profound markers of their perceived dissimilarity from the English viewing audience, in spite of the fact that—if normalcy is determined by predominance—those who were ethnically Indian would then, and now, be far more "norma- tive" than their Anglo counterparts in terms of sheer numbers. How- ever, power relations are also a part of how we understand and define normalcy and freakishness, and the Indianness of these two performers underscored their difference and inevitably the thematics of British- Indian relations as well as its attendant power structures. Sara Suleri has noted the ways in which British narratives of India often displaced images of Indian beauty or personhood with a "horrified reading of the Indian body as out of control, swelling with an internal evil or wearing evil on its skin in a hideous reminder of the grotesquery encoded within the colonial will to aestheticize." In this way, she argues that such nar- ratives attempt "to read bodily mutation as a purely Indian property, in order that the infection of India can be confined to the Indian race."[2] Indeed, much of the energy of the narratives surrounding these perform- ers reifies imperial sensibilities and marks Indians as the inferior object of observation. I explore these themes—as well as the failure of such gestures of containment—as they are manifested in both an explicit and a more subtle understanding of social, political, and economic aspects of the narratives surrounding Baux and Laloo.

The potential value in such a course of inquiry is evidenced by the scholarship on former slaves and Asians who were exhibited in the United States simply because of this aspect of their identity. Afri- can Americans and East Asians were staples of American freak shows. P. T. Barnum's first great success, Joice Heth, was a former slave who was billed as the 161-year-old one-time nurse of the infant George Wash- ington. Heth had no "disability" or disfigurement. She was simply an elderly black woman—and that was enough to make her marketable to a white, middle-class American audience. Her presence in Barnum's traveling show both spoke to and exploited the ongoing anxieties about the history of slavery and race relations.[3] Critics such as Benjamin Reiss and James W. Cook have identified the Heth exhibit as an index of contemporary American social issues.[4] Other scholars have recognized the role of what Edward Said has called "Orientalism" in the American freak show as well. John Kuo Wei Tchen has examined "classical freaks" like Chang and Eng, the "Siamese Twins," but he has also highlighted performers who took to the stage *simply because* of their Asian identity or dress, as in the case of "Afong Moy."[5] Tchen argues that the characterization of these performers, as well as responses to their exhibits, was based on American ideologies of race and difference. Certainly, race and power relations with regard to former slaves and the influx of Chinese laborers into the United States created a social landscape in which being black or Chinese enfreaked an individual enough to justify his or her exhibition on stage.

Similarly, the Indian Colonial Exhibition and the "India in London" exhibition made India a sideshow for British public consumption. In Britain, inhabitants of the colonies had a relationship to their white colonizers that echoed the race relations between powerful white Americans and both former slaves and Asian immigrants. Thus, like these racialized "others" in America, Indian performers in Britain were particularly marketed with regard to racial and social relations in their advertisements. These facts make the case of a performer such as Mohammed Baux, the thirty-seven-inch-tall "Miniature Man of India," an intriguing study. One of the things that set Baux and other Indian performers apart from other traveling show people was their race and political identity. In Baux's case, the exhibition of his colonized and racially other body gave him a potential advertising edge over the dozens of other performing little people. Of the thirty-one different handbills and pitch cards for "dwarves" in the John Johnson Collection of Printed Emphemera at the Bodleian—the largest single category of freak performers in the collection—only a small percentage is for nonwhite performers, and all of these highlight their "foreignness" as a key feature in their pitch and often in their names. For example, Lucia Zarate, a small Mexican woman, is introduced with the explanation that she comes from a "swarthy people of Spanish or mixed Spanish and Indian race. . . . Lucia is rather like a monkey: she is dark of complexion, and her features are of the Aztec type."[6] Her darkness, perceived animality, and racial otherness—here, tamed for presentation to a polite audience—mark her more dramatically in the advertisement than her size. Similarly, another handbill begins: "Just Arrived! The 8th Wonder of the World!! Don Santiago de los Santos, From Philipina Island, near

China, Being the Smallest Man in Existence is King of All Dwarfs." His geographical origins are an identifying feature (though they appear in a smaller typeface than his name, which also provides an indicator of his ethnic difference). Other freak performers, too, bore these national/ethnic markers, such as "The African Lion-Faced Lady, Madame Howard," and "The Spotted Indian from Kingston, Jamaica." In all of these cases, the color of the performers' skin and its relationship to their identity was key in the narratives offered about them. A newspaper advertisement of Baux, for example, highlighted his Indian origins and offered a woodcut image of him with dark skin, accentuated by a white high-collared shirt. It was, in part, his darkness and Indianness that made him an object of interest to his English audience, and—as I will explain below—the very fact that he was a dwarf underscored these thrilling aspects of his identity.

Race and the Dwarf

Baux's size likely amplified his Indianness for both the scientific and popular audience. Dwarves were often perceived to be a particularly *racialized* group, in spite of the fact that "dwarf" was an umbrella term that encompassed three categories of small people: homologous communities later known as "pigmies"; apparently small individuals within "normal" racial groups; and people whose growth was stunted as a result of disease. While individuals whose bodily difference was the result of rickets were less frequently identified along racial lines (though class played a key role in understanding this phenomenon), the boundaries were blurred between the other two groups—"pigmies" and genetically small individuals in a larger community of those who were not dwarves. This confusion of boundaries is evident in journals such as *Chamber's, Nature, Science,* and *Popular Science,* which were filled with speculation on the possibility of "dwarf races," who were typically believed to be particularly fierce, "extremely courageous and wonderfully active,"[7] or—at the worst—no better than "murderous savages."[8] This blurring often marked the individual dwarf as "racialized" and potentially threatening, a fact that marked Baux's identity as both a dwarf and an Indian.

Dwarves were often identified as a potentially "prehistoric race,"[9] and physically small nonwhite individuals who lived in a homologous community were considered genetic throwbacks to this race. They were imagined to have either "Mongolian eyes, yellow, broad square faces . . . and red hair" or "broad faces and mahogany-colored woolly hair"—features that were characteristic "of dwarf races everywhere."[10] Another writer described the "reddish complexion which [was] characteristic of almost all dwarf races, and which one of [his] informants describe[d] as 'like that of the Red Indians of America.'"[11] While some writers acknowledged that there could be no dwarf race "in purely scientific terms" because dwarves were "anomalies,"[12] racial dwarves were still believed to exist in areas such as southern Africa, North Africa (particularly Morocco), and India, or simply, the "East,"[13] and inquiries regarding searches for them pepper the popular scientific journals.

The perceived, and largely uncritically accepted, relationship between race and dwarfism ramped up the social valence of Baux's perceived racial identity and made his enfreakment particularly raced. When we understand that Africans and Asians were enfreaked simply by virtue of their ethnic background, we can see the ways in which nonwhite dwarves were doubly enfreaked. The apparent race and ethnicity of a performer could add another layer to his or her freakishness. So entrenched was this racialized way of thinking about dwarves that white European little people were considered by many to be explicitly "non-racial" dwarves who could not transmit their condition to their offspring[14]—in spite of the fact that European dwarves often evidenced the hereditary quality of their condition through the close relatives with whom they shared their condition. Particularly well known to Europeans were the eighteenth century's famous Count Joseph Boruwlaski and his sister Anastasia.

When Anglo dwarves toured, their whiteness became a "normalizing" characteristic, emphasizing their relationship to the audience and providing the thrill of proximity. Stereotypes of dwarfish savagery were muted, unless the individual's class visibly marked him or her. Whereas the handbills and accounts of nonwhite dwarves were often characterized by a kind of grotesque wonderment, General Tom Thumb—whose wealth was popularly noted—and Londoner Princess Lottie were praised for their physical attractiveness, genteel attainments, and the "simple" miniaturization of a beautiful Anglo norm that they seemed to offer. Anglo dwarves were depicted as living dolls, formed to enchant the public but evoking the human nonetheless. Edwin Calvert, a well-known little person, was described as "sharp and intelligent . . . a clever performer on the violin; a great mimic of birds and animals [who] could dance some of the most fashionable ancient and modern dances."[15] Princess Lottie was admired for her "blonde, blue eye[d, and] delicate" beauty.[16] These individuals, like Count Boruwlaski before them, catered to the court's and the middle-class public's "penchant" for "men in miniature,"[17] even donning "court dress" to charm their audience. White dwarves were often feminized or infantilized, and the focus of the gaze drawn away from any element of strength or power and turned to the "perfect [miniaturized] models of symmetry and beauty"[18] that they were believed to represent. Marriages were often celebrated with great fanfare between Anglo dwarves, "normalizing" their lives even further—and turning a pretty profit. The "American Midgets," General Mite and Millie Edwards, were married in Manchester and garnered a full-page spread in the *London Illustrated News* in June of 1884, and the marriage of Tom Thumb (Charles Stratton) and Lavinia Warren, who was described as a "perfect beauty" with "faultless form,"[19] had a similarly impressive presence in the society pages.

In contrast, nonwhite dwarves, while they were sometimes feminized by virtue of their size, were frequently marked as savage, even subhuman. While white dwarves clearly experienced social oppression—particularly evident in the cruelly dismissive representations of unrequited love with "normal" folk—they suffered a different kind of dehumanization than most nonwhite dwarves did. Like Lucia Zarate, who was described as a "monkey," the Chinese dwarf Chung or Chang-Mow, who toured England from mid-century through 1865 with a Chinese giant, was described as in stark contrast to the most famous Anglo dwarves, his failure to achieve the same beauty as the white dwarves particularly emphasized. Chung was "not so well-proportioned a figure as Tom Thumb";[20] he was instead a "wretched little dwarf" and an "unfortunate little mannikan."[21] The perceived racial inferiority transformed them from attractive human miniatures into potentially dangerous and unquestionably inferior figures of only marginal humanity.[22]

Managing Indian Danger: Mohammed Baux

Mohammed Baux's advertisement evoked the thrill and novelty of difference through his Indianness and his racialized enfreakment. This alone, given the cultural context into which he entered, would have situated him as a potentially threatening or anxiety-producing figure. This anxiety would have certainly been enhanced by the fact that Baux made his tour of England just three years after the "Indian Mutiny" or First Indian War of Independence, and English anxieties about the impossibility of containing and controlling the colony and its subjects reverberated through the announcement of Baux's arrival and his exhibition in the country—alongside attempts to manage those anxieties. Baux's advertisement remembers Cawnpore, the site of the infamous Indian Mutiny. In the wake of decades of abuses and outrages, a group of Sepoys held more than a hundred English women and children in close quarters in an empty house for two weeks, ran them through with swords, then dragged the few survivors and dead out of the house, stripped them, and threw them down a well. This event, which shocked and horrified the English public, became a "public symbol of . . . Indian atrocity,"[23] an indicator of the culture's barbarity, lack of civilization, and antagonism (characteristics that had also been particularly associated with dwarves). In the framework of Cawnpore, Indianness itself *was* atrocity. These perceptions justified to many English the extension and increased force of imperial control and brutal retaliation against the Indian people, just as the September 11 attacks on the World Trade Center and the Pentagon justified, for many, a retaliatory invasion of Iraq.

Baux's pitch narrative exploits his size, his Indianness, and the events in India to make him a saleable show. His body provided a material and visually charged link to the events at Cawnpore. Indeed, "curiosities" such as Baux may have been the only living representation of Indianness that many nonmilitary English at mid-century would have encountered. Moreover, Baux was, himself, the "son of a Sepoy"[24]—a description bound to trigger some consternation. The racialized notions of nonwhite dwarves as savage and of dwarves in general as "irascible"[25] may have increased these anxieties. Popular belief in moral depravity as an inherent characteristic of nonwhite or working-class dwarves was often underscored in the scientific discourse, which suggested that "personal deformity [could be in] singular unison with . . . moral depravity."[26] As the flesh and bones, so went the soul. These beliefs paired neatly with the many of the social values that buttressed imperialism, like the conviction that the English were the necessary civilizers of the Indians. Assessments about the social significance of Baux's physical stature and his attendant moral, emotional, and intellectual capacity could only have underscored sensibilities about people already perceived as morally incomplete or dwarfed.

More than simply "justifying" imperialism, however, Baux's advertisements also offer qualifiers that attempt to mitigate the tensions produced by such intense cultural anxieties and memories. Baux's notice indicates that his father was "discharged as being unfit for duty," a description that suggests that he was not fit for service and distances him from the Indians' violent and ultimately effective resistance to English rule. In addition, while it is uncertain what Baux wore during his performances, he appears in the woodcut advertisement in a *British* military officer's mess dress: with a cutaway-style frock coat with vest, ribboned epaulettes, gold lace, gold-trimmed cuff flaps, white shirt, and black bow tie; an officer's forage cap (and perhaps also gloves) sit on the chair beside him—not the turban worn by the Sepoys (figure 7.1). His apparent abandonment of Indian dress for English military attire suggests an effective martial management of Baux, as well as his fealty to the British. While his appearance in an English uniform could have also evoked anxieties about an Indian usurpation of English power, mitigating gestures can be read as attempts to "[reify] colonial terror into the safety of the collectible thing," as Sara Suleri describes it.[27] To alleviate some of the anxiety inevitably produced by the evocation of Cawnpore, the smallest Indian, neatly contained in English military dress, appears at the pleasure of his betters.

Baux's small size, one of his most "saleable" features in terms of its materiality and the metaphor it offered, may have also been read as comfortingly manageable. Baux's size, of course, features prominently in the handbills because it is one of the central points of difference that drew paying audiences—but the language with which this feature is described did more. In contrast to the savagery imputed to nonwhite dwarves, his size may also have worked to defuse the threat implied in his Indianness, marking him as emotionally and socially submissive. Indeed, these very characteristics are underscored in his description. He was often, we are told, "invited by the most distinguished native and British residents [in India] to their houses, where he was always a welcome visitor from his amiable conduct and pleasing manners." His passivity and politeness are highlighted in the wake of the advertisement's discussion of the events at Cawnpore. Baux explains, "in his own words," that he was only saved from destruction during the massacre "because he was a dwarf, and never did any harm, and could fight nobody." Remarkably, unless we read Baux himself (or his Indian brother, with whom he was traveling at the time) as *English,* there is no reason why he should have been targeted during the initial rebellion at Cawnpore where the colonizers were the victims of the violence. Were he a British loyalist, mentioning this fact would seem the most direct means of refuting his involvement in the violence, though it still would mark him as a figure with the potential for such savagery. However, the strange claim that

MOHAMMED BAUX, THE MINIATURE MAN OF INDIA.
FROM A PHOTOGRAPH BY JOHN WATKINS.

Figure 7.1
Mohammed Baux, the Miniature Man of India. Photo courtesy of
Bodleian Library, University of Oxford, John Johnson Collection,
Human Freaks, Box 1, clipping of Mohammed Baux.

Baux's stature, passivity, and unwillingness to fight saved him—strange
because children, who were no less small or defenseless, were, in fact,
slaughtered at Cawnpore—shifts his identity from dangerous rebel to
"English subject" and subject *to* the English, moves that would certainly
have made him more attractive to an English audience. If we imagine
his comments to refer to the British retaliation at Cawnpore, then we

are called upon to read him as so extraordinarily passive and power-less as to be beneath notice in the military response—a significant and politically comforting characterization of Baux (and Indians in general) given the sweeping, brutal repression that followed.

Such narratives would have certainly participated in the sociopolitical reclamation of the event, just on the heels of its occurrence, emphasizing Baux's identity as the "good Indian"—mastered by and humbled before his "betters," even while his presence evoked the anxieties embedded in his Indianness. Indeed, he becomes the kind of Indian described in Macaulay's "Minute on Indian Education": English speaking and genteel by English standards, in spite of his Indianness. The group Macaulay imagined would be a "class [of] interpreters between us [the English] and the millions whom we govern; a class of persons, Indian in blood and colour, but English in taste, in opinions, in morals, and in intellect."[28] Baux's advertisement describes his "unembarrassed manners," his ability "to converse in English," his "remarkable . . . gentlemanly deportment," and his "mental qualities[, which are] rather above than below the ordinary standard."

A general perception of Indian passivity and weakness stood along-side the narratives of Indian barbarity and savagery and served to temper English anxieties about the colony and its people as well as to provide justification for empire. These tales were embodied in representations of Indian dwarves in general. One scientific journal identifies a group of racial "Hindoo dwarfs" as wholly passive and emasculated. These men were "in speech and intelligence . . . indistinguishable from ordinary natives of India. . . . They marry ordinary native girls, and the female children grow up like those of other people. The males, however, though they develop at the normal rate until they reach the age of six, then cease to grow, and become dwarfs. These stunted specimens of humanity are almost helpless, and are quite unable to walk more than a few yards."[29] This narrative suggests that this group of Indian males, "indistinguishable from ordinary natives of India," is incapable of achieving masculine maturity, evoking a common British metaphor for the colonized nation as "helpless" and stunted. In spite of the physical and sexual maturity indicated in their ability to produce offspring, they are depicted as lacking the virility or power to live in the world as adult males; they are feminized and reduced.

Suleri explains that "the feminization of the colonized subcontinent remains the most sustained metaphor shared by imperialist narratives from ethnographic, historical, and literary fields. . . . The 'strength' of the colonizer is always delineated against the *curious attractions* of the colonized race's 'weakness.' . . . While colonized effeminacy ostensibly indicates whatever is rotten in the state of the colony, the hysterical attention that it elicits provides an index for the dynamic of complicity that renders the colonizer a secret sharer of the imputed cultural characteristics of the other race."[30] The enfreaked Indian becomes a metonymy of English-Indian relations, an embodiment of the simultaneously threatening, enthralling, and starkly feminized characterization of the nation and its people.[31] As Edward Said argues, narratives of India were dominated by "on the one hand, surveillance and control over India; on the other, love for and fascinated attention to its every detail."[32] The spectacle of the freak allowed for a surveillance of the Indian that offered a pleasing fantasy of control; it also permitted a fascinated and often eroticized attention to the Indian body and culture. The impossibility of the nation's management and control evidenced in Baux's case is underscored in Laloo, another performer who made his mark in the last decades of the century. The abundance of materials surrounding Laloo also demonstrates the failure of narrative containment, as well as the increasing discomfort with imperialism as the century progressed.

Social Parasites and the Empire: Laloo

Laloo, the "Marvellous Indian Boy,"[33] was highly popular both on the public exhibition circuit and in the scientific community in the 1880s and beyond. On the landscape of Laloo's overdetermined and "doubled" body, we find both justifications of and anxieties about empire. Laloo had a parasitic twin embedded in and protruding from his chest (figure 7.2). The twin's arms, torso, and legs extended out of the autosite's body just above his waistline. His highly medicalized "pitch" offers a detailed discussion of the "half body" (the "parasite") in relation to "the Boy" (the "autosite").[34] Described as a "double monstrosity" in many of the medical discussions of his case, Laloo evokes the multiplicative layering of deformity and race seen in Baux's case. Like Baux, Laloo's ethnicity and national origin, highlighted by his "very dark complexion" and regular references to his Indianness,[35] feature prominently in descriptions. Laloo was dehumanized like other nonwhite performers, being unreflectively compared to both a spider monkey and a "cocoanut" in one report on his case in the *British Medical Journal* (*BMJ*) and to a sideshow "foetal pig" in another.[36] These starkly Orientalist

Figure 7.2

Laloo. Photo courtesy of Bodleian Library, University of Oxford, John Johnson Collection, Human Freaks, Box 2, pitch book for Laloo.

characterizations render him even more enfreaked, more animalized, more distant from both his viewing audience and the scientific community. Further, the *BMJ*, while overtly rejecting the cause in his particular case, acknowledged the belief that Indianness often served as the very source of deformity when it explained that "early Oriental marriages" were often regarded "as the cause of monstrosity" such as Laloo's.[37]

As with other nonwhite performers, Laloo is alternately feminized and marked as threatening. His effeminization, studied at length by Nadja Durbach, echoes the feminization of other freak performers, a move that certainly evokes the "Orientalist paradigm in which the colonizing presence is as irredeemably male as the colonized territory is female."[38] Durbach has located a discussion in the *Indian Medical Gazette* regarding an unnamed figure that is almost certainly Laloo, which clearly elucidates the sexual and gender blurring that fed into social and political rhetoric regarding India. The buttocks of the parasite are described as bearing a "[striking] resemblance . . . to those of a female."[39] In spite of the evident, though "stunted," penis on the parasite, the *smell* of the parasite's genital area is described as being "similar to that of female organs," and elevations on the area are described as resembling the labia majora.[40] Even the integument between the parasite and autosite is described as having "mammae."[41] In the last decades of the century, during which there was a keen cultural awareness of India's resistance to empire and an increasingly explicit cultural articulation of the social tensions regarding imperialism, this rhetoric clearly works to feminize Indianness, offering metaphors that mitigate imperial anxieties about the potential masculine power of their "inferiors."[42]

In Laloo's case, the depiction of physical differences features more subtle markers of this process than those in Baux's. Here, we can read Laloo's "autosite" and "parasite" as metaphors for England and India, respectively. Political and social commentary depicted England as the supplying host and India as the vampiric parasite—a diversion of valuable resources in terms of both money and manpower, particularly in the wake of the Sepoy Rebellion in the 1850s.[43] Parliamentary and public debates were rife with the argument about the costs of "maintaining" the colony. Patrick Brantlinger's *Fictions of State* points to the ways in which empire grew with and was read against English national debt and economic need. The "uncontrolled micturation"[44] of the parasite can be read as a sign of the autosite's inability to control itself, an index of the finances being "pissed away" on the colony. This interpretation of India persisted in spite of the fact that England was drawing enormous natural and human resources from the nation.[45] As Emily Haddad has argued, economic questions served as a justification for empire and "a necessary point of contact between capitalist desire and the civilizing mission."[46] Moreover, medical reports suggestively described the parasite as "accessory parts,"[47] as an unnecessary appendage (though the physicians acknowledged that to remove the parasite would likely end the life of the autosite). Similarly, the English government often regarded India as an excess appendage in spite of its economic interrelationship with the nation. So apt is this comparison that one article on Laloo refers to the relationship between the autosite and the parasite as a "commonwealth," language that quite explicitly evokes the national relationship between England and her colonies.[48]

These relations were often figured through parallel metaphors of maternity and economic expense, both of which resonate in the discussion of the relationship between autosite and parasite. Frequently, England was read as maternal, nurturant, of its colonies,[49] and India was described as parasitic on the crown. Bill Ashcroft has noted that the "trope of the child . . . absorbed and suppressed the contradictions of imperial discourse itself."[50] Colonized people were often read as childlike—in need of the nurturing, civilizing force of the colonizing nation. Sudipta Sen fleshes out this familial metaphor, citing one used by Reverend William Tennant. "Providence," he indicated, "had cast 'many millions into [Britain's] arms, for their protection and welfare.'"[51] Underscoring the Kantian roots of this sentiment, Sen notes that "everyone regard[ed] the Commonwealth as the maternal womb."[52] It is significant then that Laloo, around whose neck the arms of the twin are frequently wrapped, is described as having the appearance of a "mother holding her babe for the purpose of suckling."[53] Laloo becomes the mother country, and his twin, the breastfeeding colony. In this one complex Indian body, English notions of "care" and feeding for the parasitic colony, as well as the colony's supposed leeching of British resources, emerge.

Moreover, the favorable rhetoric used to describe the autosite highlights the imagined cultural and intellectual dominance that undergirded much of the ideology of empire. Just as the maternal metaphor suggested superior strength, maturity, and power of the mother figure as compared to the child, the autosite's ascendancy over the parasite generates a figure of imperial power. The autosite's "body [is] properly developed, and [his] head remarkably well formed. He is very intelligent, and good-looking, and his health is excellent." The parasite, on the other hand, is referred to either in medical terms, or in language that points to its passivity and impotence: the upper extremities "[lie] flabbily over the left half of the abdomen of the boy" and the lower limbs, and the lower limbs are described as a "mass hang[ing] slantingly downwards." The hands of the parasite lack the "humanizing" opposable thumb on the right hand and the joints are small and ankylosed, mobile only at the behest of the autosite. Again, like the mother managing her burdensome and demanding child and the nation its demanding colony, the stronger autosite still "complains of feeling the weight [of] the Half Body."[54] Moreover, in the discussion of the gestation of Laloo, mention of Laloo's biological mother is largely absent—her presence is treated as irrelevant, as if Laloo was self-generated. Even in a discussion of his "monstrosity," scientific researchers described the production of Laloo as beyond the power of his parents, collectively, and his mother, independently.[55] We might read the erasure of Laloo's mother—except as an origin of his Indianness—as an emblematic dismissal of the relevance of Indian history or cultural context, except for the ways in which it figured into Britain's contemporary relationship to the colony. It appears, in fact, that Laloo himself is the progenitor for both the autosite and parasite—as Britain was seen as responsible for the civilized rebirth of the Indian nation. Indeed, Laloo's "whole" body (the autosite) is described as more favored and "normal," the very source of life for the partial—headless, mindless—parasitic body attached to the whole. The parasite is essentially without head and heart, mind and morality, and these functions are supplied by the superior body of the autosite, as they were imagined to be provided by the colonizing nation.[56]

What is, of course, most striking about this delineation of the "two" bodies is that treating them as entirely separate entities makes little sense, something the pitch narrative highlights when it notes that "on pricking the skin over any part of the Half Body it is sensitive, as the pain is complained of by the Boy." Further, these are twins—not just of similar but identical genetic material—and are "developed from the same ovum."[57] The biological correspondence and connection implied in these remarks underscores the intimate relation that interrupts the rhetoric of difference. Indeed, it is the fact that the two embryos were inadequately separated that creates the double-bodied structure of Laloo in the first place. Inevitably embedded, then, in this narrative of difference is one of sameness and kinship, a theme that interferes with and undermines the rhetoric of superiority. Homi Bhabha has argued that imperial narrative always bears the marks of such undermining tensions and that "disclosing the ambivalence of colonial discourse also disrupts its authority."[58] A closer study of the body of text surrounding Laloo demonstrates that although many of these elements I have described seem a simple recapitulation of imperial rhetoric—equating the "whole," life-giving, and intellectual portion with the imperial state and the "attached" and parasitic portion to the colony—equally present is a critique of colonial power, which marks the power as a (potentially unethical) seizure of resources by the "stronger" of the two bodies. The pitch book describes at length the biological formation of the bodies and in this way demonstrates these disruptions: "One placenta pushes back the weaker one, and thus interferes with, or impedes, the circulation of the less favored foetus. . . . Notwithstanding this change, the circulation in the less favored foetus . . . still goes on. It is insufficient to nourish or develop the upper parts of the body, as the head and trunk, but the lower extremities fully, and the upper limbs partially share the supply, and go through imperfect development and growth. Thus the less favored foetus receives its nutritive supplies from the normal foetus."[59]

The "interference" of the stronger fetus seems selfish, almost barbaric; it "pushes back the weaker one"—language that implies bullying mistreatment, not a generous, maternal care. Indeed, in this account, the elimination of all intelligence and rationality and the focus on the body of the "less favored" fetus is caused by the seizure of resources and uneven distribution of those resources by the stronger fetus. The "imperfect" development of the twin is an outcome of the excessive consumption of supplies by the larger placenta. This language was also present in the socially circulating tensions about British rule, evident in parliamentary debates about the politics of imperial engagement and appearing alongside the rhetoric that seems to praise colonial power. Reading the "head" as underdeveloped and the body as "imperfect" as a result of the intervention of the stronger fetus speaks to the ways in which the colonies might have been dwarfed and damaged by the intervention of the imperial state.[60] Moreover, the autosite, while legible as a metaphor for imperial power, was, of course, himself Indian, a fact that also destabilizes the binary of superiority.

A tension thoroughly imbricated in imperialism, as Laloo's pitch book suggests, is the role of economics and class in relation to the abased other. Whereas American culture (and freak show sensibility) were founded upon a "faith in individualism[,] progress," and upward mobility,[61] the British had a different consciousness of the class system. The "self-made man" was an American construct that shaped much of the social construction of the working freak and of the managers and exhibitors of freaks.[62] Tchen suggests that American culture and the performances such as those he discusses were shaped by a cultural belief structure "infused with . . . faith in individualism and progress [in which] the ethic for individual self-improvement unleashed the pursuit of individual desires and the cultivation of one's own abilities." Indeed, this was dependent, in part, upon articulating "the nation's contradictory mix of not being like Europe: individual egalitarianism, pluralist consumerism, white supremacy, and cultural admixture."[63]

While differences (and similarities) in the conceptions of class between the United States and Britain are manifold and complex, the American celebration of consumer capitalism was more muted in Britain. Indeed, if a novelist such as Anthony Trollope could have his popularity undermined by explaining in his autobiography that economic need drove much of his writing, and if Spiritualist mediums were derided as frauds unless they were unpaid or could achieve distance from the production of income, we can perhaps understand the ways in which it was vital for anyone with pretensions to class mobility to do the same and why it would be distasteful to the public to see performers evidence the economic drive that undergirded their exhibition, even if this need was evident. For example, it was after Joseph Merrick, the Elephant Man, was removed from the public circuit by Frederick Treves (literally from a "shop") and transplanted to a hospital that he could begin a round of visits with the privileged.

In Laloo's case, as in that of many other Indian performers, the economic exigencies of his self-exhibition served to debase him further, a tension underscored by the economic relations between England and India that I have already described. The BMJ demonstrates this in one short piece that, while not referring to Laloo by name, has been identified by Durbach as discussing his case. This piece, though explicitly about the "posterior dichotomy" in Laloo's body, almost exclusively discusses the finances of Laloo as an "extraordinary spectacle." It announces that "several thousand rupees were collected" when Laloo was exhibited in Bombay and that "an enterprising Parsee gentleman has advanced the lad's father a thousand rupees in expectation of the success" of his exhibition.[64] Indeed, Laloo is ultimately conflated with both the economics of display and the marketplace in which he appears when the author indicates that a "report of the Sudder Bazaar case, drawn up by a competent anatomist, would be of great interest."[65] To refer to Laloo himself by the name of the bazaar in which he exhibited and to describe the Bazaar case as the body that requires examination renders Laloo almost entirely as a financial interest rather than a human being. Similarly, relations with Indians were often treated and debated as questions of economic interest rather than as those of a nation of human beings. One of the concerns associated with Laloo's appearance in England was the claim that he was prohibited from appearing in the Indian Exhibition "owing to some question of the right of his guardians to make a show of him."[66] This commodification of the heavily raced Laloo happens much more unabashedly than that of most other freak show performers and degrades him further.

Ultimately, meditations on the colonial relationship, including these economic aspects, are depicted as vexing and vexed. The most damning discussion of the economic relations appears in the work of Bland Sutton, a teratological expert and an expert on Laloo himself. In his report, Bland Sutton fleshes out the economic exploitation of a body such as Laloo's, along with the implications of such a relationship. "Parasitic [twins] are almost in all cases so extremely valuable as sources of gain in fairs, shows, and large cities that the parents, or the unscrupulous individuals who get possession of these children, will not permit operative interference" or surgical "normalizing" of the body. Moreover, "the children rarely survive the interference."[67] The overt recognition that union between the parasite and autosite produces great wealth is paired with the notion that it would be a form of unwelcome "interference" to disrupt the relationship between the two and that it could potentially cause the death of the autosite, as well. This illustration of the biological and economic interdependence implicates England in the financial exploitation of Laloo. Ultimately, the language of "double monstrosity" that permeates discussions of Laloo suggests that both Britain and her colony become monstrous—though profitably so—when connected. It implies that the autosite (Britain, in my argument about this metaphor) would not be whole without the parasite, and, without the interference of the autosite, the parasite (India, in this discussion) might have formed into a whole and healthy individual on its own.

This is not the only representation of the potentially poisonous aspects of the imperial relation for the mother country that we may read as a metaphor offered in discussions of Laloo. Another is embodied in the discussion of Laloo's intestines. This revealing metaphor expresses worries about the potential dangers that lie in the exchanges between the autosite and parasite, particularly in terms of their effect on the autosite. These concerns suggest the perceived hazards—economic and social—of imperial relations. The scientist-author laments that the parasite, for which he indicates there is "distinct evidence [of] an intestine, . . . would be a source of danger to an autosite, especially should the parasitic diverticulum be to the least degree pervious where it joins the autosite's intestines."[68] Since the parasite in Laloo's case had no anus but only a "dimple," this meant that it could not pass excrement as it did urine. The concern was that the parasite utilized food energy and that with no place for passage of feces, this structure would require the movement of the excrement back to the autosite. This would be most threatening in the case that there existed some perforation or permeability in the connection between the autosite's and parasite's intestines and thus would cause the internalization of the parasite's feces in the body of the autosite. As a metaphor for imperial relations, this language seems to suggest that damage done or "waste" created in the relationship between Britain and her colonies from the British expenditure of resources would rebound on the British themselves, circulating in the interconnected exchange of material and social structures.

Empire and the Freak

I have suggested, in the case of both Mohammed Baux and Laloo, that we must follow Spivak's admonition to understand the way in which narratives of the period comment on imperial relations. Here I have argued that dwarves, like Baux, entered into a social fabric that already had a particular understanding of dwarfishness and that this understanding was complicated by cultural perceptions of Indianness and of the imperial relationship. Baux's materials express both a desire to contain the colonial other and anxieties about the inability to do so. These contradictory impulses were apparent in many kinds of narratives that spoke to England's empire. The tensions in this narrative point to the way in which there was, increasingly, discomfort with the work of empire in the world. Decades later, we see this discomfort amplified in the uniquely positioned body of Laloo. Unlike Baux, who had a relatively common and well-known bodily difference, Laloo's singular body was of exceptional scientific and social interest. In Laloo, the metaphoric parallels to the imperial relationship are more complexly embodied, but they reveal what might be described as a more profound degree of general dis-ease with the engagement between Britain and the Indian colony, especially as it regards the use and distribution of economic and other material resources. In this way, both Baux and Laloo demonstrate how freakery emerged as one of the discourses that spoke to imperial relations. It also demonstrates the way in which freakery must not be perceived as marginal to Victorian culture or irrelevant to mainstream social issues. The rhetoric of freakery expresses tensions that were integral to the culture and was certainly a part of the way in which the culture worked through them. More thorough investigation and explication of freakery on tour in England will help us flesh out international relations and understand the rhetorics of difference and disability that helped make them possible.

Notes

1. Gayatri Chakravorty Spivak, "Three Women's Texts and a Critique of Imperialism," in *Feminisms,* ed. Robyn R. Warhol and Diane Price Herndl (New Brunswick, NJ: Rutgers University Press, 1991), 798–814.

2. Sara Suleri, *The Rhetoric of English India* (Chicago: University of Chicago Press, 1992), 89.

3. Her exhibition spoke in complicated ways to American racial politics. While it was her body (her race and age) that were figured as the center of her draw, the thematics of her appearances on stage were also significant. Her exhibition yoked slavery and American patriotism, rather than tragedy, through her fond remembrances of the first president in her performances. Her remarkably "long" life, her animated engagement with the audience, and her public success seemed to suggest that her life—and by extension, perhaps those of others—had not been hindered by her enslavement. Still, her very identity as a sideshow freak undermined the rosier picture painted on the surface.

4. James W. Cook, *The Arts of Deception: Playing with Fraud in the Age of Barnum* (Boston: Harvard University Press, 2001), 3; and Benjamin Reiss, *The Showman and the Slave: Race, Death, and Memory in Barnum's America* (Boston: Harvard University Press, 2001).

5. John Kuo Wei Tchen, *New York Before Chinatown: Orientalism and the Shaping of American Culture, 1776–1882* (Baltimore, MD: Johns Hopkins University Press, 2001), 114.

6. "The Pigmies in Piccadilly," *Illustrated London News* (November 27, 1860): 517.

7. R. G. Haliburton, "Some Further Notes on the Existence of Dwarf Tribes South of Mount Atlas," *Asiatic Quarterly* 4 (1892): 80.

8. W. C. Preston, "Dwarf Negroes of Andaman Islands," *Littell's Living Age* 203 (1894): 307.

9. William McPherson, "Racial Dwarfs in the Pyrenees," *Nature* 47 (1892–93): 295.

10. Ibid.

11. Haliburton, 80.

12. G. H. L., "Dwarfs and Giants," *Fraser's Magazine for Town and Country* 54 (1856): 140. For contrary opinions, see "Extremes of Humanity: Dwarfs and Giants," *Chamber's* (1889): 378–80.

13. W. A. Seaver, "Giants and Dwarfs," *Harper's* 37 (1869): 208.

14. Haliburton, 79.

15. "Dwarfs and Giants," *Leisure Hour* 9 (1860): 109.

16. John Johnson Collection, Bodleian Library, Oxford University. "Human Freaks," Box 1. "Dwarfs Named."

17. "Dwarfs and Giants," *Leisure Hour,* 110.

18. Seaver, 209.

19. "Little People," *Harper's Weekly* (January 31, 1863): 66–67.

20. "The Chinese Giant," *Illustrated London News* (30 September 1855): 200.

21. Ibid.

22. This characterization was carried over in cases in which the dwarf was perceived as working class. For example, an 1889 pathological study of a man executed for the attempted murder of his wife and child in 1819 (Jonathan Hutchinson, "An Account of the Skeleton of the Norwich Dwarf," *Transactions of the Pathological Society of London* 40 [1889]: 229–35) suggested that the dwarf's "personal deformity was in singular unison with his moral depravity." The dwarfish body was perceived as an index of moral development, which was linked intimately to class or race. As the pathologist remarked of the Norwich dwarf, "a general impression is formed that he was a man of very inhuman character. This fact becomes of great interest in connection with the singularly brute-like formation of the bones of his extremities" (230).

23. Lillian Nayder, "Rebellious Sepoys and Bigamous Wives," in *Beyond Sensation: Mary Elizabeth Braddon in Context,* ed. Marlene Tromp, Pamela Gilbert, and Aeron Haynie (Albany: SUNY Press, 2000), 38.

24. "Mohammed Baux, the Miniature Man of India" advertisement, Bodleian Library, University of Oxford, John Johnson Collection, Human Freaks, Box 1. All quotations are from this advertisement.

25. G. H. L, 150.

26. Hutchinson, 20.

27. Suleri, 95.

28. Thomas Babington Macaulay, "Minute on Indian Education," 2 February 1835. *Bureau of Education Selections from Educational Records, Part I (1781–1839),* ed. H. Sharp (Calcutta: Superintendent, Government Printing). Cited on http://www.mssu.edu/projectsouthasia/history/primarydocs/education/Macaulay001.htm.

29. A. T. Fraser, "Hindoo Dwarfs," *Nature* 49 (1893–94): 35.

30. Suleri, 16, emphasis added.

31. In another twist in this tautological construction of identity, the vexed quality of the dwarfishness becomes a metaphor for Anglo-Indian relations in another narrative of the Indian Mutiny. Though the British engaged in a brutal military retaliation, there were Indian survivors, many of whom were sent to an island penal colony. This island was inhabited by a reportedly savage, cannibalistic "dwarf" race. As Preston indicates, "When the Indian Mutiny of 1857 had been suppressed and

justice overtook some of its principal instigators . . . the mutinous Sepoy regiment was condemned to be transported to the Adaman Islands, in the Bay of Bengal. The men were horror-stricken. They would much rather have been shot. And no wonder. It seemed, indeed, that their fate would be terrible. The islands were not far away; barely six hundred miles from the Gufli mouth of the Ganges, but little was known of them except that they were inhabited by a race of murderous savages, and that the malarious climate made health impossible and speedy death certain" (307). The violence of the "dwarf race" becomes one way to manage the dangers of the mutinous Indian subjects. Baux, like Macaulay's ideal Indian, becomes a representative from the savage place to embody the subdued savage.

32. Edward Said, *Culture and Imperialism* (New York: Vintage, 1994), 161.

33. I am deeply indebted to Nadja Durbach, whose essay on Krao appears in this collection, for sharing with me her insights on Laloo from her as-yet-unpublished essay, "Two Bodies, Two Selves, Two Sexes: Siamese Twins and the Double-Bodied Hindoo Boy," which offers a fine discussion on sexuality, identity, and freakery.

34. *An Interesting Treatise on the Marvellous Indian Boy Laloo: Brought to this Country by M. D. Fracis* (New Walk, Leicester: W. Willson Printer, n.d.), Bodleian Library, University of Oxford, John Johnson Collection, Human Freaks, Box 2.

35. "Parasitic Foetus," *British Medical Journal* (February 11, 1888): 312.

36. Ibid.; "The Case of Parasitic Foetus," *British Medical Journal* (February 28, 1888): 437.

37. "Parasitic Foetus," 436.

38. Durbach, "Two Bodies."

39. "Monstrosity," *Indian Medical Gazette* (July 1886): 220.

40. Ibid.

41. "Parasitic Foetus," 436.

42. As Suleri has argued, "the Indian subcontinent is not merely a geographic space upon which colonial rapacities have been enacted, but is furthermore that imaginative construction . . . from which colonial and postcolonial imaginations have drawn . . . their most basic figures for the anxiety of empire" (5).

43. See especially debates such as those over military expenditure that appear in the London *Times* (e.g., H. W. Norman, "Military Expenditure in India," *Times* [October 31, 1871]: 4, col. E).

44. "Parasitic Foetus," 437.

45. One particularly disturbing Rudyard Kipling short story, "At the End of the Passage," offers a capsule of the debates that were carried on in Parliament regarding the cost of the colony. A group of officers in India discuss a newspaper clipping about these parliamentary debates. The article in the clipping complains that "the masses . . . get [nothing] from [India], which [England has] step by step fraudulently annexed. . . . [The aristocracy] take good care to maintain their lavish scales of income . . . while they themselves force the unhappy peasant to pay with the sweat of his brow for all the luxuries in which they are lapped" (in *Victorian Ghost Stories*, ed. Michael Cox and R. A. Gilbert [New York: Oxford University Press, 1993], 330). The men complain that they have no luxuries and get very little.

46. Emily A. Haddad, "Tennyson, Arnold, and the Wealth of the East," *Victorian Literature and Culture* 32, no. 2 (2004): 373–91.

47. "Monstrosity," 219.

48. "Parasitic Foetus," 436.

49. See Kalpana Ram's "Maternity and the Story of Enlightenment in the Colonies: Tamil Coastal Women, South India," in *Maternities and Modernities,* ed. Kalpana Ram and Margaret Jolly (New York: Cambridge University Press, 1998).

50. Bill Ashcroft, "Primitive and Wingless: The Colonial Subject as Child," in *Dickens and the Children of Empire,* ed. Wendy S. Jacobson (New York: Palgrave, 2000), 184.

51. Sudipta Sen, *Distant Sovereignty: National Imperialism and the Origins of British India* (New York: Routledge, 2002), 86. While noting the domestic dynamic and paternalistic rhetoric implied here, Sen does not speak to the *maternal* quality of this passage, which is certainly suggested by its gendering.

52. Ibid., 88.

53. *Interesting Treatise,* 6.

54. Ibid., 4, 5, 8.

55. "One can entirely understand deformities being transmitted from the parents—indeed the subject is beyond question; but although nearly everyone, I think, will acknowledge that maternal impressions produce birth marks and other deformities, still it is hard to believe that such impressions would cause *excess of paris*" ("Monstrosity," 221, emphasis in original).

56. While the *Treatise* describes the biological necessity for the fact that the twins' bodies are the same sex (6), Laloo's handbills describe the twin as a *girl:* "BOY and GIRL Joined Together" (Bodleian Library, University of Oxford, John Johnson Collection, Human Freaks, Box 2). This phenomenon evokes Sara Suleri's fascinating thesis in *The Rhetoric of English India.* It also echoes the sexualization of the Indian body and the relationship between the social work of imperialism and the social work of gender as described in Anne McClintock's *Imperial Leather: Race, Gender, and Sexuality in the Colonial Contest* (New York: Routledge, 1995).

57. *Interesting Treatise,* 5, 6.

58. Homi K. Bhabha, "Of Mimicry and Man: The Ambivalence of Colonial Discourse," in *Modern Literary Theory: A Reader,* ed. Philip Rice and Patricia Waugh (London: Edward Arnold, 1996), 234.

59. *Interesting Treatise,* 7.

60. Even narratives (such as Rudyard Kipling's *Gunga Din* and *Kim*) that discussed wholly "normal" Indians betrayed what Mathew Chacko calls an "imperial ethnographic impulse, like an effort to categorize an alien species" (personal communication, August 4, 2005), a feature that laid the groundwork for the exhibition of Indian bodies (in the way that Tchen describes of Chinese in America).

61. Tchen, xvi.

62. Cook, 26.

63. Tchen, xvii, xix.

64. "Case of Posterior Dichotomy," *British Medical Journal* (August 29, 1885): 404.

65. Ibid., 405, emphasis added.

66. "Parasitic Foetus," 437.

67. J. Bland Sutton, *Tumors: Innocent and Malignant* (London: Cassell & Company, Ltd., 1894), 375.

68. "Parasitic Foetus," 437.

8

THE VICTORIAN
MUMMY-FETISH

H. Rider Haggard, Frank Aubrey,
and the White Mummy

KELLY HURLEY

She was so beautiful that I was wont to creep in hither with a lamp and gaze at her. . . . I learned to love that dead form, that shell which once had held a life that no more is. I would creep up to her and kiss her cold face.

—H. Rider Haggard, *She*

They were both very, very fair to look upon—he handsome as a god, she as beautiful as a goddess; but their faces were not flushed with the warm blood of youth or health, or even of life at all. They . . . were but dead automatons made to move and act by some occult power, as might persons walking in their sleep.

—Frank Aubrey, *King of the Dead*

FRANK AUBREY'S *King of the Dead* (1903) describes a lost white race hidden away in the wilds of the Brazilian rainforest. The novel's "Myrvonians," encountered by a small band of English men and women, are the heirs of a civilization older and more advanced than that of ancient Egypt, and their mighty empire once stretched all across the Americas, from "what is now Alaska to Cape Horn." The present-day Myrvonians are merely the pitiful "remnant of a once proud, dominant, conquering race,"[1] though their leader, Lyostrah, a powerful scientist-magician, hints darkly that his people will once again issue forth from their jungle stronghold to conquer the countries of the world, England

among them. Subtitled "A Weird Romance" to underscore its indifference to realist narrative conventions, *King of the Dead* deploys many of
the "weird" plot elements common to imperial Gothic fiction at the
fin de siècle,[2] including the discovery of a lost white civilization, the
threatened invasion of England, occult science, cannibalism, and men-
acing indigenous flora and fauna.[3] Most notably, *King of the Dead* features mummies. Millions of mummies lie preserved in the labyrinthine
catacombs of the city's necropolis, awaiting resurrection. These millions,
the reader gradually learns, will make up Lyostrah's conquering army
once they have been revived by a combination of advanced electricity,
"Will-force," and dark magic, wielded by Lyostrah and his companion
priestess, Alloyah. Even now dozens of resuscitated mummies roam the
city by night, attacking unsuspecting citizens and cannibalizing their
corpses.

As is the case in H. Rider Haggard's *She* (1887), a clear influence for
King of the Dead, Aubrey's mummies have been immaculately preserved
by a process of embalming that is now a lost art. "What impresses you
most," says a character who has visited the catacombs, "is the wonderfully life-like appearance of these mummies. They are not dried up, as
are the mummies of Egypt. . . . The dead appear as though actually
alive; they seem to be sleeping, or . . . temporarily stupefied."[4] Haggard's
novel also features a necropolis, a hollowed-out mountain within whose
hundreds of caves are laid out the mummies of the long-extinct people
of Kôr, a forgotten white race whose empire spread across Africa more
than six thousand years ago. Their science of embalming was also far
superior to that of the Egyptians, their probable descendants: "the flesh
to all appearance was still flesh. . . . It was not shrunk or shrivelled, or
even black and unsightly, like the flesh of Egyptian mummies, but plump
and fair, and . . . perfect as on the day of death."[5]

The mummy is a recurring figure in British imperial Gothic fiction at
the fin de siècle, when interest in Egyptian and other ancient cultures
was being fueled by museum exhibits, popular lectures on art, archeology, and history, and the increasing availability of "exotic" artifacts for
private collection. Fictional mummies may be hideous and fearsome,
like the "horrid, black, withered thing" brought back to life in Arthur
Conan Doyle's "Lot No. 249" (1892),[6] or surpassingly beautiful, like
Queen Tera in Bram Stoker's *The Jewel of Seven Stars* (1903). They may
serve as objects of necrophiliac sexual desire, as we see in the quote from
She that began this essay, or they may arouse the acquisitive desire of a
scholar-collector such as Professor Braddock in Fergus Hume's *The Green*

Mummy (1908). When fictional mummies are resuscitated, they may be fallen in love with and even married, as happens at the conclusion of George Griffith's *The Romance of Golden Star* (1897). Or the reanimated mummy may turn murderer and thus take its vengeance against British imperialist rapacity, like the eponymous mummy in Guy Boothby's *Pharos the Egyptian* (1899).

The overdetermined figure of the mummy serves any number of symbolic functions in late-Victorian imperial Gothic fiction, but the mummy always recurs as an object disproportionately and irrationally infused with affect, desirability, portent—as a fetish-object, in other words. Both commodity fetish and sexual fetish,[7] mummies are also fetishized as magical objects that are simultaneously embodied and disembodied, corporeal and transcendental. While this essay will be concerned with fin-de-siècle mummy fiction in general, I am particularly interested in the figure of the *white* mummy developed in *She* and *King of the Dead*, a figure that serves as an uncanny double for the late-Victorian subject in a process both fearsome and pleasurable. By entertaining the fantasy of the perfectly preserved mummy, both novels fetishize the beautiful white body, but not the body in all its materiality—rather a fantasy body that will never decay and thus is not truly corporeal in an important sense. Moreover, given the thousands upon thousands of flawless white corpses that rest in seeming suspended animation in the catacombs of their forgotten cities, the mummy can be said to symbolize not just the potential immortality of the (white) subject but also the potential immortality of the (white) empire. The mummy thus functions as a prophylactic against the possibility of racial extinction, an ongoing anxiety in "lost white civilization" novels such as Haggard's and Aubrey's, wherein dead or dying degenerate white empires serve as potential monitory doubles for the British empire.

The Mummy as Freak

Gothic monsters like the resuscitated mummy exist neither fully within nor entirely without the parameters of "the human," and they violate other boundaries crucial within human culture, such as the boundary between life and death, or between natural and occult phenomena.[8] Compare Rosemarie Garland-Thomson's discussion of nineteenth-century freak show exhibitions of anomalous humans such as "conjoined twins, the spectacularly deformed, the hirsute, the horned, the gigantic, and the scaled."[9] Freaks were thought to exist at the very limits of human identity and thereby to call into question what it meant to be a human subject in a human body. Of particular interest are the liminals: the indeterminately sexed; the "living skeletons"; the wild men, "missing links," dog- and lion-faced boys, and others of ambiguous species identity. As Elizabeth Grosz argues, such freaks are seen as "intolerable" anomalies "whose existence imperils categories and oppositions dominant in social life" and who "exist outside and in defiance of the structure of binary oppositions that govern our basic concepts and modes of self-definition."[10]

Elsewhere Garland-Thomson connects the "extraordinary" and admixed body of the freak to the strange monsters of mythology: "centaurs, griffins, satyrs, minotaurs, sphinxes, mermaids, and cyclopses," whose composite forms "gesture towards other modes of being and confuse comforting distinctions between what is human and what is not."[11] The late-Victorian Gothic, too, is populated by phantasmatic liminals: "undead" figures such as the mummy and the vampire, shape- and sex-shifting entities, post-Darwinian species hybrids, devolutionary or otherwise transformative bodies that cannot hold their human shape.[12] One can imagine a freak show front man hawking the fin-de-siècle Gothic: come read about the vampire-mummy, the beast-people, the beetle-woman, the fungus-man, the tentacled boy, the prehistoric survivals, the ape-man.[13]

For the Victorians, mummies were also freakish by virtue of their exotic foreignness. On the one hand, "enfreakment" is the hypostasis of physical disability or difference into freakishness. The person who is legless, unusually hirsute, hermaphroditic, and so on, is subsumed within the totalizing identity of "freak."[14] But in the nineteenth century, enfreakment was also the hypostasis of racial and cultural difference into freakishness. Non-Europeans were exhibited side by side with, or at the same venues as, people who were physically anomalous, with both groups identified as freaks. Zulus, Central and North American Indians, Khoikhoi, and Bosjesmans might be dressed up and presented as wild men, missing links, species nondescripts, and survivors of lost races—or simply displayed to Londoners as weird ethnographic specimens. Ethnographic freak shows sought both to thrill their Victorian audiences and to educate them (nominally at least) about the customs and habits of the strange peoples at the far edges of the empire.[15]

The Victorians tended to regard present-day non-Europeans contemptuously or condescendingly, as uncivilized barbarians, whereas the ancient Egyptians were respected as a scientifically and culturally advanced people. Nonetheless, as imperial spectacle, ethnographic freak shows provide a useful context for the sensational Egyptian exhibits and events that were fashionable in England throughout the nineteenth century: the extravagant Valley of the Kings show in 1820; public unwrappings of mummies in the 1830s and 1840s; the Nile panorama at Egyptian Hall; popular lectures on ancient Egyptian culture and history; and museum displays of Egyptian mummies and other artifacts.[16] Moreover, as the other essays in this section argue, the ethnographic freak show helped articulate Victorian racial and national identity in complex and sometimes contradictory ways, and this was no less true of the Egyptologist's "freak show." In the one case, Victorian audience members felt both complacent superiority to the "primitives" exhibited at the ethnographic freak show and discomfort at the thought of their evolutionary kinship, and thus likeness, and the "indistinct, elusive line that separates civilization from barbarism."[17] Similarly, while exhibits on ancient Egypt, with their bizarre animal-headed deities, scarabs, hieroglyphs, and mummies, seemed exotically strange to Londoners, they also served to remind the Victorians of the ephemerality of great imperial powers like their own.

The mummy in particular worked to mediate the British empire's concern about its own mortality, as I will argue below. Already a freakishly "undead" figure—a corpse awaiting the resurrection promised by a half-comprehended, long-extinct religion—the mummy becomes further "enfreaked" when reanimated by Gothic fiction. To enfreak is to infuse an anomalous subject or phenomenon with affective *frisson*, just as the Gothic does by marking the anomaly as uncanny. Phenomena take on nonspecifiable, intense meaningfulness in excess of their own reality. This is also the strategy of fetishism.

Fetishism

The word *fetish* signifies an object, or parts or attributes of objects, which by virtue of association to sentiment, personality, or absorbing ideas, exert a charm . . . or at least produce a peculiar impression which is in no wise connected with the external appearance of the sign, symbol or fetish.

—Richard von Krafft-Ebing, *Psychopathia Sexualis*

In his important article series on fetishism, William Pietz discusses the historical origins of this concept that would be developed in the nine-teenth century by anthropology, economic theory, sexology, and psy-choanalysis. The pidgin word *fetisso* derived from the Portuguese *feitiço*, alluding to the magical practices of the peasant classes in the late Middle Ages. The *feitiço*, as opposed to the *idolo* (a "freestanding statue repre-senting a spiritual entity"), was an object worn close to the body, such as a charm or amulet, "which itself embodied an actual power resulting from the correct ritual combination of materials." Unlike the idol, an object of worship, the *feitiço* had a more limited and specific instru-mentality, being employed "to achieve a concrete, material effect."[18] Thus *feitiço* alludes to an idiosyncratic and contingent practice of magic suited to the occasion (albeit subject to traditional ritual): to a religious practice that is flexible rather than idolatrous, and oriented toward the material rather than the transcendent.

Mary Pratt uses the phrase "contact zone" to describe the "space of colonial encounters" wherein geographically and culturally disparate peoples meet and "establish ongoing relations," relations usually char-acterized by conflict and inequality.[19] The concept of *fetisso* emerged in just such a contact zone in the sixteenth and seventeenth centuries: the West African coast, where first Portuguese then Dutch traders initi-ated commercial relations with various black African societies. Fetish discourse attempted to negotiate "the problematic of the social value of material objects as revealed in situations formed by the encounter of radically heterogeneous social systems."[20] That is, European merchants engaged in the exchange of commodities found themselves baffled by the markedly different economic, social, and religious values their new trade partners assigned to material objects. Black Africans were derided for their willingness to exchange gold for inexpensive "trifles" such as colored cloth and shells and for their general overvaluation of suppos-edly worthless items, for "just as blacks seemed to overestimate the economic value of trifles, so they were perceived to attribute religious value to trifling objects," *fetissos* that often appeared to be chosen at random.[21] During this early modern European encounter with extreme cultural difference, then, a period of crisis that revealed the "nonuni-versality and constructedness of [European] social value,"[22] the idea of the *fetisso* allowed Europeans to try to comprehend and engage with, as well as derogate and contain, an alien value system.

They themselves being subject to a protocapitalist overestimation and mystification of commodities, sixteenth- and seventeenth-century Europeans traders struggled to comprehend the mysteries of the *thing*, whose value to one person or culture might seem incommensurate with its innate qualities. Pietz argues that "the discourse on fetishism represents the emerging articulation of a theoretical materialism" particular to modernity and at odds with existing philosophical systems.[23] Within this nascent secular and antiplatonic tradition, objects appear in all their suchness, referring to nothing but themselves. But fetish discourse shows how the material object, however meaningless because of its intractable materiality, can nonetheless be infused with meaningfulness. The significance attributed to the object might be arbitrary and irrational, and human overinvestment in a *mere thing* might signal primitivism to the ethnologist, false consciousness to Karl Marx, perversion to the sexologist, neurosis to Sigmund Freud. But when they become fetishes, even mere things have a "shine" about them, to use Freud's word from his 1927 essay on fetishism.[24] Objects come to life when singled out by human need or desire.

For Marx, the unexpected liveliness of inert objects is yet another symptom of human beings' estrangement from the products of their own labor and from one another under capitalism. In *Capital* (1867) he argues that straightforward "articles of utility" become fetishized commodities, taking on a "mystical" quality incommensurate with their use-value, when humans interact only through the exchange of products, not the sharing of labor. The "definite social relation between men" is displaced by "the fantastic form of a relation between things,"[25] and things become more substantial, more evocative, than their human owners. Attending to the Gothic undertones in Marx, Nicholas Daly shows how the Victorian narrative of the reanimated mummy demonstrates the commodity's uncanny ability to take on a life of its own, particularly in the consumer-driven economy of the later nineteenth century when commodities might be desired not because of their usefulness but because other consumers had marked them as desirable. In mummy love stories, Daly argues, "the relations of subjects and objects are problematized so that objects become subjects, and subjects come under the spell of objects."[26]

Within mid- and late-Victorian anthropology, fetishism alluded to the religious practices of non-European "primitive" peoples who worshiped and made use of inanimate objects, plants, and animals thought to be invested with magical powers or properties. Fetishists were scorned for their naïve and superstitious relation to the natural world, their irrationality, and the arbitrary, unsystematic nature of their religious practices.[27] The Amahagger in *She* (a hybrid, degenerate, cannibalistic race descended from the people of Kôr) set fire to the mummy-corpses and use them as torches "to light up a savage *fetish* dance" where they dress up as and imitate animals, a ritual Holly describes as "fiendish," "hideous," and "grotesque."[28] In *The Jewel of Seven Stars*, when van Huyn opens Queen Tera's tomb, one of the Bedouins who accompanies him proves himself a fetishist by breaking off the mummy's seven-fingered right hand "to use . . . as an Amulet, or charm," which his fellows "regard with special awe and reverence." Van Huyn disapproves of these Bedouins as a "callous," greedy, and superstitious lot. However, *Jewel* makes clear that Europeans are no less fetishistic than the "primitive" Arabs they deride. Trelawny displays the freakish mummy hand as the ultimate fetish object, assigning it pride of place within his magnificent collection: the hand rests upon a "cushion of cloth of gold as fine as silk," which is nested within an intricately engraved case of crystal and gold, which in turn rests upon an "exquisite" alabaster table.[29]

The European's liability to fetishism was amply documented by nineteenth-century sexologists such as Richard von Krafft-Ebing, who understood fetishism as a form of obsessive sexual behavior. The libido becomes fixated on an object associated with a person (or with masculinity or femininity in general), which object then, inappropriately, itself becomes the focus of desire, "produc[ing] feelings of delight and even ecstasy."[30] Like all sexual deviancies, fetishism was considered a degenerate practice, thus linking the European to the "primitive" subject as Marx's model of commodity fetishism had done.[31]

Freud's subsequent work produced a much more singular definition of the fetish: "the fetish is a substitute for the woman's (mother's) phallus which the little boy once believed in and does not wish to forego." In Freud fetishism represents an extreme and aberrant response to the always traumatic perception of sexual difference, when the little boy first catches sight of his mother's genitals and discovers that she has been "castrated."[32] The discovery serves as a blow to his narcissism: both the narcissistic belief that he is the sole point of reference and everyone else is just like him, and the "narcissism which Nature has providentially attached to this particular organ," since the boy fears that the father who castrated the mother might castrate him as well. If the trauma of the realization of difference is too great, the boy denies the mother's castration and designates an object to serve as the nonexistent maternal phallus, investing it with libidinal affect. Often this object is determined by a "last impression received before the uncanny traumatic one": underclothes, the foot or the shoe or the stocking glimpsed as the boy peered up his mother's dress, or velvet and fur, which "reproduce . . . the sight of the pubic hair which ought to have revealed the longed-for penis."[33]

Jacques Lacan has shown how "imagoes of the fragmented body" that recur in dreams—scenarios of the mutilation, dismemberment, and the dehiscence of the body—are terrifying because they disrupt the subject's fantasy of itself as a coherency or *gestalt*.[34] But for the (male) fetishist, the dismembered body part, rather than serving as a nightmarish reminder of the inchoate nature of the subject, signifies a more or less successful consolidation of the subject through containment of the difference of the Other. The fetish "remains as a token of triumph over the threat of castration and a safeguard against it." But it is only partially successful, as Holly's experiences with part-objects will demonstrate, because the fetish also hypostatizes the moment of trauma: "the horror of castration sets up a sort of permanent memorial to itself by creating this substitute."[35] When Holly picks up a perfectly preserved mummy foot in his sleeping chamber, he launches into a sentimental paean to femininity, imagining the foot's owner as a harmless "blushing maid" and "perfect woman." "Shapely little foot! Well might . . . the lips of nobles and of kings have been pressed upon its jewelled whiteness." But when Holly's first glimpse of the dread Ayesha is a disembodied "beautiful white hand" appearing through the curtains, he is "fill[ed] . . . with a nameless terror."[36]

As Garland-Thomson points out, in Freudian discourse women are *naturally* freakish (mutilated, castrated) because of their departure from a male norm.[37] The putatively castrated woman becomes even more freakish when she is phantasmatically reinvested with the phallus, as is the case with Ayesha and still more clearly with Tera. Tera's physical anomaly—the extra fingers on her right hand, which is the locus of her extraordinary powers—marks her as a "phallic woman," one whose bodily excess both symbolizes and helps her to consolidate her inappropriately masculine potency. The snakes growing out of Medusa's head, the sixth and seventh fingers on Tera's hand:[38] these phallic symbols out of place, these grotesque extrusions on the female body, hypostatize the fearsome possibilities of sexual liminality and sexual dissonance and render them monstrous, just as the enfreakment of the hermaphrodite renders them monstrous.

It is a "technical rule," Freud reminds us in "Medusa's Head," that "a multiplication of penis symbols signifies castration."[39] The phallic woman signifies castration simply because she is a woman, and already castrated, but also because she is herself a castrator, and thus a figure of terror to men. Ayesha murders Kallikrates with her supernatural powers and threatens similarly to "blast" Holly and Leo when they anger her; Tera places Trelawny in a coma and attempts to rip off his hand at the wrist as her own was ripped off.[40] Within Freud's formulation, nonetheless, the phallic woman is an oddly reassuring figure. The snakes on Medusa's head "serve actually as a mitigation of the horror [of castration], for they replace the penis, the absence of which is the cause of the horror."[41] And indeed, when Perseus brandishes it as a weapon—as a fetish—Medusa's decapitated head greatly augments his masculine puissance. Tera's disembodied hand with its extra fingers is both a disquieting symbol of castration and a fetish-object which confers power and thus comfortingly belies the possibility of castration. Fetishism substitutes a phantasmatic but potent object for a lost one, or one whose loss is threatened. Working from Freud, we can consider the ways in which the fetish serves as a *compensatory mechanism* at the cultural as well as psychosexual level. It compensates for a perceived lack, as I will discuss below.

The (Im)Material Body

Trelawny is a fanatical collector: as his assistant, Corbeck, says, when Trelawny "makes up his mind that he wants to find a particular thing, . . . he will follow it all over the world till he gets it." *Jewel* displays, if not outright disapproval, at least a certain uneasiness with European tomb robbing and the systematic confiscation of artifacts. And yet that uneasiness may stem from the overwhelming British fascination with Egyptian culture no less than British exploitation of it. Corbeck describes Egyptology as a madness, an addiction, and an obsession that has absorbed his entire life and Trelawny's as well.[42] When Ross sits among Trelawny's Egyptian artifacts he seems to lose himself, becoming overpowered by the mysterious atmosphere seemingly generated by the collection itself. "There were so many ancient relics that unconsciously one was taken back to strange lands and strange times. There were so many mummies, or mummy objects . . . that one was unable to forget the past. . . . More than once as I thought, the multitudinous presence of the dead and the past took such hold on me that I caught myself looking round fearfully, as though some strange personality or influence was present. . . . All at once I sat up. I had become lost in an absorbing reverie. The Egyptian smell had seemed to get on my nerves—on my memory—on my very will."[43]

As Pratt points out, "transculturation" works in both directions, unequal power dynamic notwithstanding. Both colonizer and colonized are transformed within the "contact zone" of imperial encounter, even more so when the contact zone begins to extend back "from the colonies to the metropolis."[44] The fruits of imperial conquest—knowledge about and artifacts from alien cultures—are returned to England itself, so that domestic subjects, too, might experience the shock of encounter with extreme cultural difference. In mummy fictions such as *Jewel*, "Lot No. 249," and *The Green Mummy*, where English bedrooms and sitting rooms are crowded with "sepulchral ornaments," scarabs, "brilliantly tinted mummy cases" full of their "embalmed dead," and statues of animal-headed deities,[45] "domestic space . . . is increasingly experienced as foreign; the present is increasingly infiltrated by what it has designated as archaic."[46]

Pietz argues that the fetish "not only originated from, *but also remains specific to*," cross-cultural exchanges and negotiations.[47] In general, we may see the Victorian mummy-fetish as symptomatic of dissonances within the British empire at home and abroad, including anxieties about the health of the empire, concerns about the legitimacy of its mission, and the narcissistic shock of the repeated encounter with radical cultural difference. (I will have more to say about this in the final section.) Pietz argues further that the various fetish discourses attribute to the fetish an ability to "create the illusion of a natural unity among heterogeneous things"[48] and to seem to reconcile conflict or contradiction. For instance, in Freud the fetish compensates for the loss of a bodily organ, the mother's phallus, that never existed in the first place. A tangible object is substituted for a phantasmic one, and the child simultaneously "retains th[e] belief" in the woman's phallus and "gives it up."[49] Working from Pietz, Anne McClintock suggests that the fetish "marks a crisis in social meaning as the embodiment of an impossible irresolution. The contradiction is displaced onto and embodied in the fetish object, which is thus destined to recur with compulsive repetitiveness," for fetishes "do not resolve conflicts in value but rather embody in one object the failure of resolution."[50]

What are the contradictions and crises that the late-Victorian mummy-fetish embodies and vainly attempts to resolve? First, like the commodities exchanged between the sixteenth-century Dutch and West Africans, the mummy illustrates the stubborn problem of translating value across the gulf of cultural difference. Professor Braddock acquires the green mummy in order to unwrap it and "examine into the difference between the Egyptians and the Peruvians, with regard to the embalming of the dead," and because the emeralds hidden in its casket will finance his life's passion, Egyptological research. Don Pedro demands the mummy's return because the Inca Caxas was his ancestor, "my own flesh and blood." For him Braddock is engaged in the "desecrat[ion]" of a rich and deeply personal cultural heritage, while the scientist-scholar dismisses Don Pedro as irrational and "uncivilized."[51] Just as the reanimated mummy represents the commodity that holds its would-be possessor in thrall, as Daly argues, it is also an object of scholarship that comes to haunt its would-be investigator. Since Great Britain enjoyed the power to enforce its own system of valuation as the "correct" one, a vengeful mummy such as Boothby's Pharos the Egyptian may be said to incarnate the bad conscience of empire, as well as enacting a kind of return of the oppressed. "Ah, my nineteenth-century friend, your father stole me from the land of my birth, . . . but beware, for retribution is pursuing you, and is even now close upon your heels."[52]

The mummy-fetish represents an attempt to come to terms with not only the new global culture but also a modern secular, scientific culture and its discontents. Rapid and continuous technological change had led to alienation and anomie, as Max Nordau argued in his famously cranky polemic *Degeneration* (1892), and Victorian science was maligned for having stripped away all mystery from "this prosaic age."[53] Evolution theory, geology, and paleontology in particular proved incompatible with traditional religious belief and offered no spiritual alternative in its stead. In *The Place of Enchantment*, Alex Owen describes late-Victorian occultism as a secular movement that nonetheless pursued "metaphysical quests, heterodox spiritual encounters, and occult experimentation, each of which seems to signal the desire for unorthodox numinous experience in a post-Darwinian age." Rejecting the anthropological orthodoxy that science necessarily superseded religion in the evolution of cultures, late-Victorian occultists brought scientific methods to bear on their topic and argued that magical phenomena could be rationally demonstrated and validated.[54] Mummy fiction also seeks "to mobilize a reworked notion of science in the name of the religion of the ancients,"[55] imagining cultures in which science and thrilling magic are so seamlessly blended that they are indistinguishable from one another.

Ayesha appears both omniscient and immortal, can read minds and "blast" her enemies with her bare hands, yet she insists that "there is no such thing as magic," only "a knowledge of the secrets of Nature."[56] Lyostrah shows his English friends "marvellous" devices that he admits might seem like "downright black magic," and "yet they are merely developments of other lesser inventions and discoveries that are perfectly familiar to you," like electricity and wireless telegraphy.[57] *The Jewel of Seven Stars*, David Glover argues, "is striking in its use of scientific discovery as a springboard for metaphysical conjecture, bringing questions of immortality or reincarnation into the world of radium and X-rays" and the most up-to-date Victorian sciences of mind.[58] *Jewel* explores both the magical nature of such phenomena as the human unconscious and the exciting possibility that ancient magic might be susceptible to factual explanation.

Most of all, science and magic are reconciled across the body of the mummy. The scientist-sorceress Ayesha, enswathed in her white wrappings, is like a beautiful living mummy. In *She* the myth of reincarnation is proven as sober fact when Leo meets his perfect double, his mummified ancestor Kallikrates. Lyostrah resuscitates the mummies from the necropolis using rays from a rare indigenous "lightning plant"[59] and controls them through hypnosis. The mummy hand is "a central point or rallying place for the items or particles of [Tera's] astral body. That hand . . . could ensure her instantaneous presence in the flesh, and its equally rapid dissolution." Trelawny, in fact, hopes that when Tera's mummy is resuscitated and her ancient wisdom brought to life in the modern West, she will reconcile *all* oppositions: she "can link together the Old and the New, Earth and Heaven, and yield to the known worlds of thought and physical existence the mystery of the Unknown."[60]

The mummy is an incarnate oxymoron: a decaying body preserved from decay. It speaks to the afterlife, to the prospect of immortality and the transcendence of the body. But the mummy is also a *corpse*— "the utmost of abjection," as Julia Kristeva says.[61] Pietz emphasizes the "untranscended" physicality of the fetish,[62] relating this to a theoretical materialism characteristic of modernity. As I have argued elsewhere, late-Victorian materialist sciences, particularly the evolutionary sciences, described an "untranscended" human subject bound to the earth by the contingencies of natural selection, instinct, and the instability of the flesh.[63] Thus the most difficult cultural work the mummy-fetish is asked to perform is to conjoin the human body, in all its ineluctable materiality, with the immaterial world of the spirit. Like the Freudian fetish, the mummy-fetish serves a compensatory function: in a secular and post-Darwinian age it reinvests the human body, a body that has become a mere thing, with numinousness. Again like the Freudian fetish, which simultaneously acknowledges and denies the unwelcome "truth" of the mother's castration, the mummy-fetish simultaneously acknowledges and denies the untranscended materiality of the human subject.

Decline and Fall

> Kôr is fallen! No more shall the mighty feast in her halls, no more shall she rule the world, and her navies go out to commerce with the world. Kôr is fallen! and her mighty works and all the cities of Kôr, and all the harbours that she built and the canals that she made, are for the wolf and the owl and the wild swan, and the barbarian who comes after.
>
> —H. Rider Haggard, *She*

Late-Victorian popular fiction charts a paradoxical anxiety about Great Britain's imminent and inevitable decline during the decades when the empire was in fact at its height, solidifying its worldwide dominance. Such literature responded to and perhaps aggravated widespread concerns about late nineteenth-century British deficiencies, real and perceived: Britain's loss of global economic ascendancy, its often fraught relationships with its colonies, its internal weakness due to social and cultural degeneration and decadence. In 1871 England was invaded and ignominiously defeated by the Prussians in Sir George Tomkyns Chesney's best-selling *The Battle of Dorking,* and dozens more stories of England besieged by European powers were published in the wake of *Dorking*'s success.[64] Stephen Arata has described the late-Victorian novel of "reverse colonization," such as Stoker's *Dracula* (1897) or Richard Marsh's *The Beetle* (1897), which depicts Britain as the target rather than the instigator of imperial aggression, in danger of "being overrun by 'primitive' forces" from "outside the civilized world."[65] Dystopian novels such as Richard Jefferies's *After London* (1885) represent a future England that has imploded and relapsed into feudal barbarism. In Jefferies the capital city itself has become an abject necropolis, a vast, toxic swamp filled with chemical pollutants, sewage, and the decomposed remains of London's unburied millions.

A corollary to these late-Victorian narratives of moribund England was an often morbid fascination with actual dead civilizations, especially

ancient Egypt.[66] Amelia B. Edwards, famous for her public lectures and
popular writings on archeology and Egyptian culture, describes Egypt
as a city of the dead rather than a living nation in *Pharaohs, Fellahs
and Explorers* (1891). "It has been aptly said that all Egypt is but the
façade of an immense sepulchre." Estimating that at least 731 million
mummies were interred in the days of the Pharaohs, Edwards notes
that "there are probably at this moment more ancient Egyptians under
the soil of Egypt than there are living men and women above it." The
thousands of as-yet-unexcavated tombs and tumuli might make Egypt
seem something like a "great museum" awaiting its British curators,[67]
but they also served as a melancholy reminder of the inevitable decline
and fall of even the greatest civilization.

Novels such as *She* and *King of the Dead* also provide a somber medi-
tation on the ephemerality of empires. "Time after time have nations,
ay, and rich and strong nations, learned in the arts, been and passed
away and been forgotten, so that no memory of them remains," Ayesha tells Holly. The long-ago people of Kôr "conquered till none were
left to conquer,"[68] but they fell suddenly, to a catastrophic plague, and
their massive state works have lain in silent ruins for six thousand
years. Myrvonia was once a mighty empire, but it came to know "evil
times. . . . Little by little they lost a province here, a territory there,
until even their original country became overrun by invaders, and little
was left to them save the memory of their former glory."[69] More pointedly, both of these white empires serve as potential monitory doubles
for Great Britain. The citizens of Kôr were once a high-living, luxurious
people, but the plague swept across their decadent empire and laid them
low. The Myrvonians once boasted of their technological superiority
and military dominance, but there came a shameful time when they
could not retain their colonies or even safeguard their own borders.

In these two novels, however, the white mummy serves as a fetish
object that compensates, or attempts to compensate, for the prospective
decline and fall of the white empire. While both necropolises showcase
the spectacle of mortality, they simultaneously deny mortality's power.
The thousands upon thousands of white mummies in Myrvonia and Kôr
have defied death and decay. "Nearly all the bodies, so masterly was the
art with which they had been treated, were as perfect as on the day of
death thousands of years before."[70] This fantasy of a white body that is
flawless and unchanging has its corollary in the fantasy of immortality,
or near immortality: both Ayesha and Lyostrah have plumbed the secrets
of nature and enjoy long life in undiminished youth and beauty.

In the catacombs of Myrvonia it is the city-state itself, the body of the empire, that seems to have been suspended in time. *King of the Dead*'s mummies are grouped together in "natural" arrangements—scenes of kings holding court, citizens at work, and so forth—and sealed behind glass as if in a museum. Moreover, Myrvonia's catacombs conceal a mighty living-dead army poised to conquer and rule, with its "soldiers, fully dressed, and equipped with complete arms and armour, standing in long rows, their officers beside them, as though on parade." Lyostrah looks forward to a "Second Empire": when he has succeeded in resuscitating the eight million dead of Myrvonia, "the ancient glories of this people shall be revived, [and] they will issue forth once more as a conquering nation, subduing everything and everybody that may stand in their way."[71]

But if the mummy-fetish represents an attempt to deny the corruption of the body and the fragility of empire, the repressed returns in both novels, in scenes of overwhelming body horror—iconic scenes of white enfreakment. Located beneath the catacombs of Kôr is an "enormous pit" full of heaped-up plague-corpses, imperfectly mummified by heat and time rather than human arts. "It was nothing but one vast charnel-house, being literally full of thousands of human skeletons, which lay piled up in an enormous gleaming pyramid, formed by the slipping down of the bodies at the apex as fresh ones were dropped in from above. Anything more appalling than this jumbled mass of the remains of a departed race I cannot imagine, and what made it even more dreadful was that in this dry air a considerable number of the bodies had simply become desiccated with the skin still on them, and now, fixed in every conceivable position, stared at us out of the mountain of bones, grotesquely horrible caricatures of humanity."[72] These mummies even get resuscitated in a way, for Holly disturbs a skull that "bring[s] an avalanche of other bones after it, till at last the whole pit rattled with their movement, even as though the skeletons were getting up to greet us." In Holly's dreams these corpses march across their "imperial home" in battle formation: "thousands and tens of thousands—in squadrons, companies, and armies—with the sunlight shining through their hollow ribs."[73] Meanwhile, *King of the Dead*'s reanimated mummies do not remain Lyostrah's obedient subjects but begin to engage in "ghastly, hellish revelries" and sexual "debaucheries," and to hunt the living citizens of Myrvonia, ripping their throats out and devouring them. "Every face was that of a corpse, save as to the eyes, which blazed with a ferocity more like that of a beast of prey than of a human being.

... Blood ... still dribbled from their chins on to their clothes."[74] At this particular freak show, the white spectator comes face-to-face with *itself*, in uncanny semblance.

In Holly's dream the multiplication of white mummy-corpses symbolizes not the potential immortality of the white empire but the nightmare of imperial decline. A "bodiless voice" accompanies the dead army's progress across a deserted city, lamenting ceaselessly: *"Fallen is Imperial Kôr!—fallen!—fallen!—fallen!"*[75] In *King of the Dead* the white mummy, far from succeeding in spiritualizing the material body, serves to collapse the figure of the European degenerate and the cannibal savage into one most grossly corporeal body, and to point toward the white subject's liability to degeneration and even devolution. The interrelated fantasies of reanimation and reincarnation, of the immortality of the flesh and the undying glory of empire, cannot be sustained: they crumple under the weight of the body itself, in all its untranscended materiality.

Notes

1. Frank Aubrey, *King of the Dead: A Weird Romance* (New York: Arno Press, 1978), 50–51.

2. Patrick Brantlinger coins the phrase "imperial Gothic" to describe a characteristic late-Victorian "blend of adventure story with Gothic elements," that is, supernaturalist or uncanny incidents and themes. See *Rule of Darkness: British Literature and Imperialism, 1830–1914* (Ithaca, NY: Cornell University Press, 1988), 227.

3. Aubrey had already perfected this formula in *The Devil-Tree of El Dorado: A Romance of British Guiana* (1896) and *A Queen of Atlantis: A Romance of the Caribbean Sea* (1899).

4. Aubrey, *King of the Dead*, 185.

5. H. Rider Haggard, *She* (New York: Penguin, 2001), 116.

6. Arthur Conan Doyle, *The Best Supernatural Tales of Arthur Conan Doyle* (New York: Dover Publications, 1979), 81.

7. In his excellent chapter on nineteenth-century mummy narratives, Nicholas Daly shows how the mummy comes to serve simultaneously as commodity fetish and sexual fetish within a late-Victorian economy increasingly fueled by consumption rather than production. See *Modernism, Romance and the* Fin de Siècle: *Popular Fiction and British Culture, 1880–1914* (Cambridge: Cambridge University Press, 1999), 84–116.

8. On the liminal status of the mummy, see David Seed, "Eruptions of the Primitive into the Present: *The Jewel of Seven Stars* and *The Lair of the White Worm*," in *Bram Stoker: History, Psychoanalysis and the Gothic*, ed. William Hughes and Andrew Smith (New York: St. Martin's Press, 1998).

9. Rosemarie Garland-Thomson, *Extraordinary Bodies: Figuring Physical Disability in American Culture and Literature* (New York: Columbia University Press, 1997), 57.

10. Elizabeth Grosz, "Intolerable Ambiguity: Freaks as/at the Limit," in *Freakery: Cultural Spectacles of the Extraordinary Body*, ed. Rosemarie Garland-Thomson (New York: New York University Press, 1996), 57. See also Garland-Thomson, *Extraordinary Bodies*, 69–70.

11. Garland-Thomson, "From Wonder to Error—A Genealogy of Freak Discourse in Modernity," in Garland-Thomson, *Freakery*, 1.

12. The prevalence of such literary representations can be related to the rise of biological and sociomedical discourses such as evolutionism, degeneration theory, and sexology, which served to dismantle traditional notions of "the human" during the late nineteenth century. See Kelly Hurley, *The Gothic Body: Sexuality, Materialism, and Degeneration at the* Fin de Siècle (Cambridge: Cambridge University Press, 1996).

13. See E. Heron and H. Heron, "The Story of Baelbrow" (1898); H. G. Wells, *The Island of Dr. Moreau* (1896); Richard Marsh, *The Beetle* (1897); William Hope Hodgson, "The Voice in the Night" (1907); Arthur Machen, *The Three Imposters* (1895); John Buchan, "No-Man's-Land" (1898); and Phil Robinson, "The Hunting of the 'Soko'" (1881).

14. Garland-Thomson, "From Wonder to Error," 10.

15. See Robert D. Altick, *The Shows of London* (Cambridge, MA: The Belknap Press, 1978), 268–87; Bernth Lindfors, "Ethnological Show Business: Footlighting the Dark Continent," in Garland-Thomson, *Freakery*; and Z. S. Strother, "Display of the Body Hottentot," in Bernth Lindfors, ed., *Africans on Stage: Studies in Ethnological Show Business* (Bloomington: Indiana University Press, 1999). In this collection, see Nadja Durbach, "The Missing Link and the Hairy Belle: Krao and the Victorian Discourses of Evolution, Imperialism, and Primitive Sexuality." For a discussion of ethnographic freak shows in Germany and the United States, see Nigel Rothfels, "Aztecs, Aborigines, and Ape-People: Science and Freaks in Germany, 1850–1900," in Garland-Thomson, *Freakery*; and Rachel Adams, *Sideshow U.S.A.: Freaks and the American Cultural Imagination* (Chicago: University of Chicago Press, 2001), 25–59.

16. See Daly, 95–102; Altick, 206, 244–46.

17. Altick, 287.

18. William Pietz, "The Problem of the Fetish, I," *Res* 9 (1985): 5; "The Problem of the Fetish, II," *Res* 13 (1987): 36–37. The final article in the series is "The Problem of the Fetish, IIIa," *Res* 16 (1988): 105–23.

19. Mary Louise Pratt, *Imperial Eyes: Travel Writing and Transculturation* (London: Routledge, 1992), 6.

20. Pietz, "Fetish I," 7.

21. Pietz, "Fetish II," 41.

22. Pietz, "Fetish I," 9.

23. Ibid., 6.

24. Sigmund Freud, "Fetishism," in *Sexuality and the Psychology of Love*, ed. Philip Rieff (New York: Collier Books, 1993), 204.

25. Karl Marx, *Capital: A Critique of Political Economy*, vol. 1, trans. Samuel Moore and Edward Aveling (New York: International Publishers, 1967), 71–72.

26. Daly, 111.

27. See Pietz, "Fetish II," 41–43; Anne McClintock, *Imperial Leather: Race, Gender and Sexuality in the Colonial Contest* (New York: Routledge, 1995), 185–89.

28. Haggard, 219–22, emphasis added.

29. Bram Stoker, *The Jewel of Seven Stars* (Oxford: Oxford University Press, 1996), 101, 100, 81.

30. Richard von Krafft-Ebing, *Psychopathia Sexualis: A Medico-Forensic Study*, trans. Harry E. Wedeck (New York: G. P. Putnam's Sons, 1965), 46.

31. See Robert A. Nye, "The Medical Origins of Sexual Fetishism," in *Fetishism as Cultural Discourse*, ed. Emily Apter and William Pietz (Ithaca, NY: Cornell University Press, 1993).

32. Freud, 205.

33. Freud, 205, 207. However, Freud also acknowledges that it is "not . . . possible to ascertain the determination of every fetish." The "selection of individual fetishes is in part conditioned by accidental circumstances" (207, 204), and, moreover, the libido is capable of cathecting *any* object.

34. Jacques Lacan, "Aggressivity in Psychoanalysis," in *Écrits: A Selection*, trans. Alan Sheridan (New York: W. W. Norton & Company, 1977), 11.

35. Freud, 206.

36. Haggard, 116, 145.

37. Garland-Thomson, *Extraordinary Bodies*, 19.

38. Conveniently enough, *The Jewel of Seven Stars* associates the two things. Trelawny says that the first glimpse of the ruby cradled in Tera's hand "struck me with a shock almost to momentary paralysis. I stood gazing on it . . . as though it were that fabled head of the Gorgon Medusa with the snakes in her hair, whose sight struck into stone those who beheld" (99).

39. Freud, "Medusa's Head," in *Sexuality and the Psychology of Love*, 202.

40. Charles Bernheimer argues that Freud's model of fetishism is particularly useful for discussing fin-de-siècle culture, not because of Freudian theory's "claim to universality" and transhistorical relevance, but because castration was "the seminal fantasy of the decadent imagination," arising from fin-de-siècle misogyny and sexual hysteria. See Bernheimer, "Fetishism and Decadence: Salome's Severed Heads," in *Fetishism as Cultural Discourse*, ed. Apter and Pietz, 62.

41. Freud, "Medusa's Head," 202.

42. Stoker, 69. As David Glover writes in his introduction to *Jewel*, "Egypt is treated as if it were some ominous state of mind, irresistibly taking hold of the lives of all who come into contact with it" (xiii).

43. Stoker, 29–30.

44. Pratt, *Imperial Eyes*, 6. In the imperial Gothic, colonizers may experience transculturation as regression to a more primitive state, or "going native," like Fleete in Rudyard Kipling's "The Mark of the Beast" (1890). See Brantlinger, 229–30.

45. Fergus Hume, *The Green Mummy* (New York: G. W. Dillingham Company, 1908), 20, 22.

46. Daly, 100.

47. Pietz, "Fetish I," 7, emphasis added.

48. Ibid., 9. Pietz explains further that for Marx, "the term was useful as a name for the power of a singular historical institution to fix personal consciousness in an objective illusion." For sexologists such as Alfred Binet, "the origin of the fetishistic fixation was in the power of a singular personal event to structure desire" (9).

49. Freud, 206. Freud notes that a fetish "constructed out of two opposing ideas is capable of great tenacity" (209).

50. McClintock, 184.

51. Hume, 11, 167, 178, 166.

52. Guy Boothby, *Pharos the Egyptian* (London: Ward, Lock, & Co., 1899), 49.

53. Stoker, 140.

54. Alex Owen, *The Place of Enchantment: British Occultism and the Culture of the Modern* (Chicago: University of Chicago Press, 2004), 7–8.

55. Ibid., 8.

56. Haggard, 155.

57. Aubrey, *King of the Dead*, 41.

58. David Glover, *Vampires, Mummies, and Liberals: Bram Stoker and the Politics of Popular Fiction* (Durham, NC: Duke University Press, 1996), 81–82.

59. Aubrey, *King of the Dead*, 119.

60. Stoker, 151–52, 184.

61. Julia Kristeva, *Powers of Horror: An Essay on Abjection*, trans. Leon S. Roudiez (New York: Columbia University Press, 1982), 4.

62. Pietz, "Fetish I," 7.

63. See Hurley, *Gothic Body*, especially 23–38.

64. See I. F. Clarke, *Voices Prophesying War: Future Wars, 1763–3749*, 2nd ed. (Oxford: Oxford University Press, 1992), especially 27–56.

65. Stephen Arata, *Fictions of Loss in the Victorian* Fin de Siècle (Cambridge: Cambridge University Press, 1996), 108.

66. See Richard Pearson, "Archaeology and Gothic Desire: Vitality Beyond the Grave in H. Rider Haggard's Ancient Egypt," in *Victorian Gothic: Literary and Cultural Manifestations in the Nineteenth Century*, ed. Ruth Robbins and Julian Wolfreys (Houndmills, UK: Palgrave, 2000), 219–24.

67. Amelia B. Edwards, *Pharaohs, Fellahs and Explorers* (New York: Harper & Brothers, 1891), 4–5, 11–12.

68. Haggard, 83–84.

69. Aubrey, *King of the Dead*, 131.

70. Haggard, 187.

71. Aubrey, *King of the Dead*, 185, 135, 132.

72. Haggard, 184–85.

73. Ibid., 185, 210.

74. Aubrey, *King of the Dead*, 211, 220.

75. Haggard, 210, emphasis in original.

OUR BEAR WOMEN, OURSELVES

Affiliating with Julia Pastrana

REBECCA STERN

GIVEN THE taxonomical purposes to which her unusual body was deployed in Victorian culture, it is appropriate that I first "met" Julia Pastrana in a box. In the summer of 1996, I was in Oxford doing research at the John Johnson Collection of Printed Ephemera, a glorious resource for research on British popular culture, which holds the disposable artifacts of everyday life. Street ballads, broadsides, playbills, valentines, beauty books, illustrations, and newspaper clippings are all carefully indexed in boxes that open like giant storybooks. Pastrana's story—or at least the version of it I first encountered—resides in a box labeled "Human Freaks 2." Powerful, compelling, and disturbing, both the woman's image and the stories that accompany it are startling, even within the lexicon of "Human Freaks."

In "Human Freaks 2," among handbills promoting mermaids and mermen, the Aztec Lilliputians (actually mentally retarded microencephalic children) and the small-footed Chinese lady, are the two clippings that generated this essay.[1] The first is a handbill trumpeting the London appearance of Julia Pastrana, the Nondescript, otherwise known as the Bear Woman, appearing at the Regent Gallery in 1857. The second is an etching from an 1862 issue of the *Penny Illustrated Journal*, promoting with equal vivacity a "New and Unparalleled Discovery in the Art of Embalming . . . As Exemplified in the Appearance of Julia Pastrana," available for viewing later at the Burlington Gallery, 191 Piccadilly. When I first came upon these bits of paper, I was intrigued by the illustration of a dark, bearded woman holding a flower in the first advertisement, and then horrified but fascinated by the second depiction of the same woman, dead, embalmed, and propped upright *sans* flower in a glass cage.

Not surprisingly, the range of sources about Pastrana deliver variously credible accounts of the story behind these documents, yet most all agree that Pastrana was born to an indigenous tribe in Mexico during Victoria's early years on the throne. She suffered from two rare congenital disorders, due to which her face and body were covered in long dark hair and her gums were so overgrown as to appear to be a second set of teeth.[2] Abandoned as a child, she was taken in by the governor of Sinaloa, in whose house she was working as a serving girl when an American promoter discovered her in the 1850s and convinced her to join the ranks of physical "freaks" who were increasingly being exhibited for money in the United States. Pastrana was a very good performer—so good, in fact, as to attract both large audiences and considerable competition for her commerce. Her second manager, Theodore Lent, persuaded her to marry him in 1858 as a means, according to various sources, of ensuring that her profits would continue to come to him. After extended international touring, Pastrana became pregnant by Lent and, in 1860, was delivered of a son who shared her congenital traits. The boy lived only hours, Pastrana herself only a few days after him. According to the sparse primary information left by her few acquaintances, she spoke three languages, sang beautifully, and was an intelligent, kindly woman, normal in all aspects but that of appearance.[3]

Until her death, Pastrana maintained an active career as the Bear Woman, the Baboon Lady, and the Ugliest Woman in the World, among other monikers. However, in one of those plot twists that prove truth stranger than fiction, her career continued, and *continues* beyond her death. Lent, her clever capitalist husband, sold the corpses of his wife and child to a pioneer in the science of embalming, one Professor Sokolov, who treated the bodies and placed them in Moscow Imperial University's anatomical museum. When Lent realized that he might still exhibit his wife—and profitably add his child to the mix—he fought to buy back their bodies. His success opened the second phase of Pastrana's career, during which she and her son were exhibited as embalmed corpses. This career continued into the 1970s when she toured in the United States with the traveling Million Dollar Midways. Her body now resides in the basement of the Institute of Forensic Medicine in Oslo and is ostensibly available only for medical research.[4] As a coda to the story, Theodore Lent married a second bearded woman, Marie Bartels, whom he persuaded to be exhibited as Julia's sister, "Zenora Pastrana," initially alongside the corpse of his former wife.[5] He lived and worked with her for more than a decade. His death followed a mental collapse, during which he reportedly ran naked through the streets of St. Petersburg, tearing up banknotes and throwing them into the Neva River. Not surprisingly, current renderings of Pastrana find decided satisfaction in her husband's melodramatic end.

In nineteenth-century England, alongside Darwinian discourse, early anthropology, "civilizing" missions, and efforts to create more equitable forms of citizenship for both women and nonwhites, Pastrana's spectacular body was generally deployed to pose decidedly Victorian questions of classification.[6] More recently, various artists have taken Pastrana out of her original context and repackaged her surprising image for modern audiences with modern concerns. The disturbing story of an intelligent woman in a disruptive body—married, sold, stuffed, and circulated—and the image of that body have together attracted the attention of scholars so diverse as Richard Altick, Coco Fusco, Rosemarie Garland-Thomson, and Matthew Sweet, as well as that of various poets, musicians, dramatists, and screenwriters. Beyond her remarkable success as a live performer in her own era, and as a lifeless exhibit for more than a century following her death, her appeal has proved enduring for current audiences: just in the past decade, representations of Pastrana have multiplied in both number and complexity. Her body signified powerfully for the Victorian audiences that viewed her initially, and it continues to signify powerfully now.

In this essay I want to emphasize the mobile effects of spectacle, the ways in which socially discordant bodies resonate with cultural meanings, and how the same body may mean quite different things even at the same cultural moment. I will focus primarily on Pastrana's significance with regard to the Victorian culture in which she lived and died, but I also want to stress the boundaries of that reading and question whether current theoretical perspectives adequately describe the mechanics of freakery. In so doing, I will be utilizing various of the most common strategies for analyzing "freak" culture, which by and large deploy discourses of Othering, by now a familiar critical dynamic wherein exhibited bodies become legible only through a rhetoric of negation that articulates the subject's differences from the body on display. "Normalcy" thus emerges through a series of "nots," the most famous of which is the viewing subject's "not me."[7] This implicit rejection of "abnormal" bodies is roughly accurate in discussing the general attitude in Victorian culture wherein exhibitions emerged as a form of entertainment alongside a fascination with compartmentalizing the world into infinitely smaller boxes.

I find it rather problematic, however, that beyond the paradigm of Othering, the most benign options that modern theory has to offer spectators both modern and historical are pity and misguided worship. Pity emerges as a positive variation on Othering that elevates the viewing subject through a rhetoric of sentimentality. According to Garland-Thomson, empathy for the body on display "posit[s] an exchange of feeling so that the other inspires elevating and humanizing sensibilities in the self which then projects those sentiments back onto the other. This sentimental economy merges *identification through pity* with *differentiation through otherness* to produce Pastrana as the hybrid construct of the sensitive monster, whose role it is to instruct, edify, and thus construct the middle-class canonical self. Her viewers become better people, citizens higher on the ladder of bourgeois respectability, through looking at Pastrana."[8] Pity, in other words, is inevitably a form of superiority. Despite its gestures of identification, it bestows grace from above, thus maintaining the distance of radical difference. And pity does accurately describe some Victorian responses to Pastrana: many records report the exclamation, "Poor woman!" while one of Lent's promotional catalogs suggests that the viewer who attends "with the expectations of seeing some frightful monster . . . will be puzzled amazingly to account for his share of the milk of human kindness, and the abundant juiciness of his own heart."[9] Similarly, various scholars have argued that the reverence of both audiences and critics maintains the freak's Otherness, simply inverting the position of the spectator (looking up to versus looking down upon). Mary Russo, for example, criticizes the movement that emerged in the 1960s to identify with the freak (to "freak out") as a means of expressing "the secret self." Russo's objection—that such impulses are "nostalgic and idealizing"—is well taken, as is her point that "real freak" communities often overtly reject "regular bodied" members.[10] Denigration, pity, and reverence, that is, all *use* the body of the Other as an occasion to construct some element of the self, and do so without recognizing the desire, will, or subjectivity of that Other.

However apt this limited range of perspectives may seem for describing exhibition culture, neither renunciation, nor idealization, nor pity adequately describes the tenor of many deployments of Pastrana's image, which bespeak what I will be terming affiliation. Affiliation is an effort toward alliance, collaboration, and understanding; it recognizes difference but neither fetishizes nor seeks to erase it. It does not escape the problems of projection: especially when one engages with a figure long deceased, a truly reciprocal relationship is impossible. Therefore, affiliation maintains the troublesome risk of co-optation, but it also recognizes its desires and its stakes. It is, that is to say, a form of engagement that attends to and is consciously answerable for its own inevitable liabilities.[11]

The efforts toward affiliation in many current representations of Pastrana have forced me to return to and reconsider my readings of various Victorian engagements with her. Lent's remarks above, for example, seem clearly to promote Pastrana as a vehicle of "instruct[ing], edify[ing], and thus construct[ing] the middle-class canonical self."[12] However, his metaphors ("the milk of human kindness," the juicy heart) also suggest the potential for less predictable forms of engagement that have boundaries more permeable than awe, pity, or dismissal allow. In addition, then, to analyzing representations of Pastrana over the years, I will be working through those analyses to both illustrate and augment the scholarly lexicon that describes the relationship between ordinary and extraordinary bodies.[13]

Exhibition Perspectives: Spectacle and Dirt

Two theoretical approaches predominate in modern readings of exceptional bodies; both underscore the exclusionary—or disciplinary—aspects of display. First, Mary Russo's comments on the relationship between spectacle and gender in *The Female Grotesque* emphasize the cultural processes activated by the female body out of bounds:

> There is a phrase that still resonates from childhood. . . . It is a harsh, matronizing phrase, and it is directed toward the behavior of other women: "She [the other woman] is making a spectacle out of herself."
>
> Making a spectacle out of oneself seemed a specifically feminine danger. The danger was of an exposure. . . . For a woman, making a spectacle out of herself had . . . to do with a kind of inadvertency and loss of

boundaries: the possessors of large, aging, and dimpled thighs displayed at the public beach, of overly rouged cheeks, of a voice shrill in laughter, or of a sliding bra strap—a loose, dingy bra strap especially—were at once caught out by fate and blameworthy.[14]

In this passage, Russo concentrates on the relationship between the production of proper gender identity and the disciplinary function of classifying disorderly women as spectacles through "a kind of inadvertency and loss of boundaries." The act of identifying, or taxonomizing, women explicitly *constructs* boundaries where they are most needed, where the potential for likeness overshadows the clarity of difference. The spectacular body thus exposes the appearances and behaviors that bound normalcy, the *cordon sanitaire* beyond which propriety must not pass; the spectacle offers an inverse example of the "normal." Such bounding seems accurate for a nineteenth-century culture in which merely to court the gaze, even within the private space of the home, was to play at the margins of feminine grace. The excessive visibility a woman hazarded in acting up or out provided substantial fodder for contemporary authors—think of Austen's Maria Bertram, Brontë's Blanche Ingram, Eliot's Gwendolen Harleth—and, subsequently, has fueled a profusion of feminist and cultural studies scholarship.

A woman who put herself on display *beyond* the private space of the home was even more troublesome: until late in the century, professional acting was commonly denigrated.[15] As the Victorian moralist Dinah Mulock Craik argued, the actress was perilously close to the prostitute: "the general eye becomes familiar, not merely with her genius, but her corporeality."[16] Elsewhere, Craik observes that a woman who seeks the spotlight "is a creature so anomalous that she cannot fail to do enormous harm, both to her own sex and to the other. She ceases to be the guardian angel she was meant to be, and becomes an angel-faced devil, working woe wherever she appears."[17] Craik's alarm may be amusing, but her strategy of species segregation is part of a larger dynamic that models the Victorian subject's proper relationship to bodies on display. When Craik divides women into two classes, angels and devils, she expects her readers to understand which one is in the house and which is categorically excluded. The angel-faced devil defines by negation the very *species* of proper womanhood. Deploring the woman who seeks the spotlight, Craik relies upon a Victorian lexicon that condemns social behavior through racialization, so that the "angel-faced devil" becomes a dangerous hybrid.

As a form of boundary blurring, hybridity was of widespread interest in an era obsessed with taxonomy. Pastrana offered a walking metaphor for disorder: standing at the crossroads of male and female, animal and human, savage and civilized, Pastrana's body refused to keep *this* separate from *that*. As Garland-Thomson has argued, "Her body was explicated as a boundary violation, a confusion of categories, a puzzlement."[18] Pastrana epitomized the hybrid's potential to muddy the waters of classification.

In analyzing such border cases, many scholars have turned to Mary Douglas's notion of dirt as "matter out of place" to explain Victorian formulations of racial, national, and class difference, categories that exhibition culture both complicated and clarified. According to Douglas, "Dirt . . . is never a unique, isolated event. Where there is dirt there is system. Dirt is the by-product of a systematic ordering and classification of matter, in so far as ordering involves rejecting inappropriate elements."[19] In regarding Victorian exhibitions, dirt provides a remarkably useful metaphor for understanding the tenuous line between savagery and civilization, and for contextualizing the implications of *social* dirt for these categories of identity. In Pastrana's case, her social transgressions as the female body on display were mapped onto her body in what seemed to be a form of species deviance.

In general, the Victorians linked concepts of difference with ideologies of race and empire, many of which were deployed in the interest of keeping individual bodies in line. The vast number of late-Victorian soap advertisements that promoted the idea that racial color *is* dirt worked both to shore up the sanctity of white British identity and to inculcate the various forms of supervision inherent in it. The ads thus drew upon notions of dirt, species, and nation to suggest that racial color exceeds the specificity of raced bodies. For example, in one increasingly infamous Pears' advertisement, a black boy peers almost fearfully into a tub of seemingly opaque water as a white boy, sporting a crisp white apron, hands him a bar of Pears' soap (figure 9.1). In the diptych's second plate, the bather reappears, washed white from his neck down, peeking at his reflection in a mirror held by his aproned attendant. No longer suspicious but wide-eyed with wonder, the black boy regards his transformed body, his leg displacing the tub's slogan now that his body stands as testimony to it: Pears' soap, matchless for the complexion, has expanded the parameters of possibility, turning on its ear that old fabular maxim about the impossibility of washing an Ethiop white.[20]

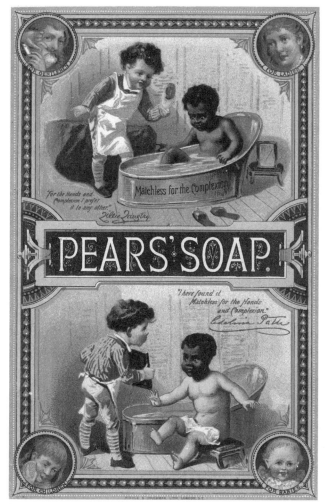

Figure 9.1
Pears' Soap advertisement. Courtesy of the Bodleian Library, University of Oxford, John Johnson Collection, Diptych of Black Boy and White Boy, Pears' Soap, Box 5.

The ad's ideology seems fairly straightforward, as it suggests in none too subtle terms not only that Pears' is fabulous soap but also that racial color is equivalent to dirt and that blacks, if only they would "clean themselves up," might be as white as the next Briton.[21] However, just as Pastrana's image offers various interpretive possibilities, the ad as it was printed in the 1890s is irreducible to a simplified racial spectrum of black and white. In the strikingly vivid original, both the soap and the "black" boy are brown, and the cheeks of the white boy's face, as well as of those that peer in, out, and down from the corners of the ad, are a rosy pink. Just as it is important that the Crayola crayon with which I used to color white faces was once called "flesh" but is now more correctly labeled not "white" but "peach," the pink cheeks of the "white" faces in this ad only approximate the whiteness Victorian culture held in such high regard. Color proves to be a cultural condition that can, perhaps, be washed off but also, conversely, can "soil" racially white bodies, thereby bringing them into the realm of cultural visibility and censorship. Even in racist soap ads, that is, dirt is less the stuff of bodily content than of proper bodily management.

Another ad, in which a bar of Pears' soap crests an exotic horizon as "The Dawn of Civilization," more clearly articulates the link between behavior, racial color, and social purity (figure 9.2). Printed in the 1890s, this ad explicitly refers back to the mid-century practice of exhibiting foreign peoples. These exhibitions aligned racial color with social dirt through the rhetoric of spectacle, catching out foreign or deviant ("uncivilized") bodies and behaviors and making them "blameworthy." Echoing the works of Edwin Chadwick and other sanitary reformers who clearly linked "civilization" with "clean" living, the exhibition effectively excluded behavioral others from the civilized world. Few middle- and upper-class visitors attended the free display of "savage" life that Chadwick, Henry Mayhew, and others had discovered at home in the slums of England, but the middle-class public was fascinated with and regularly visited the displays of "real" savages at Vauxhall Gardens, Leicester Square, the Egyptian Room, and other such venues.[22]

Exhibitions in which peoples of foreign lands were put on display for "Civilized White People," as one handbill calls them, gained popularity in England throughout the Victorian period.[23] Crowds flocked to see the Aztec Children, the Algerine Family, the Small-footed Chinese Lady and Family, the Zulu Kafirs, the Ojibbeway Indians, the Pigmy Earthmen, and Julia Pastrana, the Bear Woman, among others. These exhibitions brought the literally exotic into safe spaces where, for between 1s and 5s, visitors learned not only about the habits of "savages" abroad but also that civilized whiteness required more than having pale skin. By aligning display (the principal of exhibition) with racial color and cultural barbarism, these exhibitions tacitly erected the guidelines that regulated civilization and, hence, inclusion within the category of "white."[24] The exhibition, then, exceeded its function of teaching its audience how wonderful it was to be a British citizen; it also, as Charles Dickens demonstrates in his essay "The Noble

Figure 9.2
Pears' Soap "The Dawn of Civilization." Courtesy of the
Bodleian Library, University of Oxford, Dawn of Civiliza-
tion, John Johnson Collection, Pears' Soap, Box 4.

Savage," effectively employed the threat of racializing the insurgent
white body. Underlining the ways in which exhibitions were lessons in
proper British behavior, the author writes, "if we have anything to learn
from the Noble Savage, it is what to avoid."[25] Dickens's "what to avoid"
had nothing whatever to do with the color or decoration of one's body.
It entailed characterological traits that antonymically summed up British civilization. A good Briton is not "cruel, false, thievish, murderous,"
nor "conceited, tiresome, bloodthirsty, [or] monotonous."[26] Proving that
his concept of savagery has no relation to skin color, Dickens compares
the Zulu Kafirs to the Irish:

The chief makes a speech to his brothers and friends, arranged in single file. No particular order is observed during the delivery of this address, but every gentleman who finds himself excited by the subject, instead of crying "Hear, hear!" as is the custom with us, darts from the rank and tramples out the life, or crushes the skull, or mashes the face, or scoops out the eyes, or breaks the limbs, or performs a whirlwind of atrocities on the body, of an imaginary enemy. Several gentlemen becoming thus excited at once, and pounding away without the least regard to the orator, that illustrious person is rather in the position of an orator in an Irish House of Commons. But, several of these scenes of savage life bear a strong generic resemblance to an Irish election, and I think would be extremely well received and understood at Cork.[27]

Dickens is only one of a plethora of Victorian thinkers who illustrate how the exhibition could be mobilized as a disciplinary medium that taught its audience to Other the bodies on display. Condemning the white Irish alongside the black Zulus for their collective lack of civilization, Dickens illustrates the ease with which the white body might take on the attributes of the savage. If one exceeded the parameters of civilized British behavioral codes, if one acted like a "savage," these exhibits implicitly suggested, one might well become one. The exhibition, therefore, was a form of public entertainment with the potential to be a powerful ideological tool.

Pastrana in England

I want to offer multiple readings of Pastrana's body as it appeared in Victorian culture. I begin here with the standard disciplinary reading that I have been developing thus far and that, until recently, had been my *only* reading of her significance for Victorian viewers.

Within Victorian rhetorics of dirt and spectacle, exhibitions of Pastrana's dark-complexioned, hair-covered body crystallized in reverse a prescription for Victorian white womanhood, materializing literally the fabular consequences—ostracism, racial or species segregation, and an unappealing masculinity—with which Victorian culture threatened ostentatious women. Her appearances were part of a much larger operation that, in effect, inculcated the mechanics of social discipline.[28]

The handbill advertising Julia Pastrana's 1857 appearance in London's Regent Gallery, for example, elucidates how Pastrana's paradoxical body worked to articulate and to police the borders of femininity (figure 9.3). It describes Pastrana as both animal and young lady, both masculine and feminine, both foreign and utterly domestic. The description of *"Miss Julia Pastrana, the NONDESCRIPT"* remarks:

> This curious and very interesting little lady . . . has thick black hair upon the nose, forehead, and every part of her face and person, excepting the front of the neck, hands, and feet; . . . she has very pretty whiskers, beard, and moustache; her eyes are large and fine . . . ; her form and limbs are quite perfect, with wonderfully small hands and feet. Altogether Miss Julia is the most singular, curious, and pleasing specimen of humanity in the world, and will entertain her audiences by dancing
> THE HIGHLAND FLING,
> AND SINGING
> ENGLISH AND SPANISH ROMANCES.[29]

The handbill clearly articulates Pastrana's exhibitions within the discourses of dirt and spectacle, using her body and its display to promote female docility, reticence, and modesty within the field of vision. Encouraging audiences to disregard the more "normal" aspects of Pastrana's identity, it presents Pastrana as an odd disjunction of feminine ability and hirsute excess, not merely a "human curiosity" but also a parable about the consequences of female display. Through functional solicitation rather than evasion of the gaze, this rendition of Pastrana's exhibitions suggests, first, Pastrana's audacity in putting herself on stage, and that departing from social constraint had literal somatic consequences: the "very interesting little lady" who made a spectacle of herself would be rewarded for her troubles with a fall into color and a preponderance of body hair. Advertisements such as this one note that, although she can "Cook, Wash, Iron, [and] Sew," at her exhibitions Pastrana leaves off domestic employment to dance and sing. The "thick black hair upon the nose, forehead, and every part of her face and person, excepting the front of the neck, hands, and feet" thus seems to narrate her truancy from kitchen and hearth—one handbill even remarks explicitly, "In 1854, Julia getting tired of housework [in Mexico], left for the United States to be exhibited."[30]

Furthermore, various printed materials promoting the 1857 show at the Regent describe Pastrana as a "Digger Indian." According to one London pamphlet, "Travellers say that of all the Aborigines known within limits of the Western Continent, the Digger Indians are certainly

REGENT GALLERY,
69, & 71, QUADRANT, REGENT STREET.

GRAND & NOVEL ATTRACTION.

Miss JULIA PASTRANA,
THE NONDESCRIPT
Known throughout the United States and Canada, as the
BEAR WOMAN.
Where she has held her Levees in all the *Principal Cities*, and created the greatest possible excitement, being pronounced by most eminent *Naturalists and Physicians* the WONDER OF THE WORLD.

WILL HOLD HER LEVEES
At the Regent Gallery, Every Day,
COMMENCING ON MONDAY, JULY 6th, 1857,
Morning 11 to 1, and 3 to 5, Evening 8 to 10. No Evening Entertainment on Saturday.

STALLS, 3s.   AREA, 2s.   GALLERY, 1s.
Stalls can be procured at the Box Office, Regent Gallery, every day between 10 & 5, without extra charge

Miss JULIA PASTRANA'S Pedigree,
In 1830, several Root Digger Indian women went some distance from their homes to bathe; on returning, Julia's mother got lost, and lived in the mountains six years, some hundreds of miles from any human beings. She was then discovered by a Mexican with this child, but two years of age, who was then receiving its support from nature's fount. This woman loved the child dearly, though not willing to own it as hers. The mother died soon after, and the child went to Pedro Sanchez, Governor of the State of Sinaloa, where she learned to Cook, Wash, Iron, Sew, and speak the Spanish language. In 1854, Julia getting tired of housework, left for the United States to be exhibited.

A description of Julia Pastrana, the NONDESCRIPT.

This curious and very interesting little lady is 23 years of age, 4 ft. 6 in. in height, and weighs 112 lbs.; she has thick black hair upon the nose, forehead, and every part of her face and person, excepting the front of the neck, hands, and feet: the flesh upon the forehead is from one-half to three quarters of an inch in thickness; the ears are longer than usual, and covered with hair; she has very pretty whiskers, beard, and moustache; her eyes are large and fine, the centre being so jet black that the pupil is scarcely perceptible; her nose is without cartilage from the bridge downwards, and very pliable; her mouth is elongated, lips thick, back teeth perfect and very fine, with double gums in the upper and lower jaws in the front part of the mouth, but only one row of front teeth, which are covered when the gums are closed, they being in the back gum of the lower jaw, which extends much more than ordinary, and the angle of the face is very different; her hair is black, straight and abundant; her form and limbs are quite perfect, with wonderfully small hands and feet. Altogether Miss Julia is the most singular, curious, and pleasing specimen of humanity in the world, and will entertain her audiences by dancing

THE HIGHLAND FLING,
AND SINGING
ENGLISH AND SPANISH ROMANCES.
She dresses with great taste, in rich Spanish and other costumes, and after each performance, comes among the audience to converse and answer questions. JULIA PASTRANA is sociable and polite, and besides being undoubtedly

The Greatest Living Natural Curiosity,
She is a Lady in every respect, and not only Scientific Men take great interest in her but also Ladies & Children are highly amused at her strange appearance, her Dancing & Singing

Description of the Root-Digger Indians to which Tribe Julia's Mother belonged

These remarkable beings inhabit the Mountains, in Mexico, and live in caves with animals of different description, such as Bears, Monkeys, Squirrels, &c., between which and themselves they know no difference; their food consists of grass, roots, insects, barks of trees, &c.

They have no hair on any part of them except their heads, their stature is from three to four feet; and they weigh from eighty to ninety pounds, they have intellect, their dispositions are very much of the monkey order, very spiteful and hard to govern.

No description of this wonderful creature, and greatest of all living curiosities, can be given so minutely as to be at all satisfactory, the public are therefore respectfully invited to call and see her and judge for themselves.

W. BRICKHILL, Steam Machine Printer, Kennington and Walworth Roads.

Figure 9.3
Handbill for Julia Pastrana's 1857 appearance in London's Regent Gallery. Courtesy of the Bodleian Library, University of Oxford, Julia Pastrana, Regent Gallery Handbill, Human Freaks, Box 2.

the most filthy and abominable. They come into the world and go from it with as little purpose as other Carnivorous animals."[31] Although the same pamphlet marks her difference from her tribe—"the case is quite the reverse with Julia Pastrana"—its rhetoric of civilization and filth ally both her body and her performance with animalistic, uncivilized behavior. The fact that the category of "Digger Indian" is an invention of nineteenth-century writers lays bare the desire to classify the performing, masculine, nondocile female body as barbaric and animalistic.[32]

Arthur Munby's long poem "Pastrana" takes a similar tack, going so far as to disallow the term "woman" to describe not only Pastrana but also women who offer themselves up for visual consumption in general. The poem begins with Munby's speaker at the zoo, regarding "a big black ape from over the sea," who "sputter'd and grinn'd in a fearsome way."[33] Fascinated and disgusted by the grinning female baboon, the speaker returns to his inn, only to be terrified when he recognizes the "baboon lady" amongst a large dinner party of "gentles and simples, ladies fair, / And some not fair though fine" (9). Of one of the gowned, bejeweled women amongst the party of fifty at his inn, the speaker muses:

> Sure, I remember those bright brown eyes?
> And the self-same look that in them lies
> I have seen already, with strange surprise,
>   This very afternoon;
> Not in the face of a woman like this,
> Who has human features, and lips to kiss.
> But in one who can only splutter and hiss—
>   In the eyes of a grim baboon! (10)

Munby's fantastical tale articulates the symbolic propensity for women to slide into barbarity, as the ape on display at the zoo materializes in the "fine" woman at the "sumptuous inn." Much of the poem's panic derives from the speaker's fear that first the baboon and then the woman will break free of her restraints (a literal chain in the case of the former, a symbolic collar in the latter) and "get at" him (6, 8). And yet, in an oddly sensitive symmetry, he realizes that he has "gotten to" the baboon, provoking her ire by staring. "Why do you stare at me so?" he imagines her asking (5), and concludes that

> She did not like my scrutiny;
> And she meant to know the reason why

A human mortal such as I
        Should trouble her state at all. (8)

In one of the poem's more telling moments, the speaker articulates explicit anxiety about women who look back. His discomfort emerges from her returned stare, from the "singular look in her bright brown eye . . . [which] meant too much and it reach'd too high / For one of an apelike kind" (6). When he finds this "singular look" repeated in "the self-same look" of his dinner companion, he immediately begins to suspect her qualification to socialize with polite company. Both the baboon and the gazing woman disturb the speaker's confident viewing position and hence unsettle his comfortable manhood.

The polemic of the returned gaze that Munby presents may explain, at least in part, the appeal of Pastrana's postmortem performance as "The Embalmed Nondescript, Exhibiting at 191 Piccadilly." Her capacity for response suspended, her body rendered passive, mute, and visually inert, Pastrana's embalmed corpse has had a long and illustrious career that, as I note above, continues to this day. As Janet Browne and Sharon Messenger observe, "Her literal transformation into a pickled object made it easier for curious spectators to gaze without embarrassment."[34] The 1862 exhibition carried forward the mid-Victorian discourses of race and gender that implicated white women through the bodies of women of color, but it neutralized Pastrana's capacity to look or talk back.

In her Burlington Gallery exhibitions, Pastrana's tightly corseted, short-petticoated corpse stood upright in a glass cage, her brown body explicitly cast as a performer. While the head that topped that body maintained her radical difference from the English showgirl, it also revealed an usually unseen "truth" about the showgirl's body: Pastrana was unbonneted, her hair in disarray, her features set in an angry, rebellious stare, and her beard and moustache prominent. The sensationalized display of Pastrana's embalmed corpse exposed the showgirl as a deformed creature who brought her body into the public sphere for money, who all too self-consciously performed the attributes of femininity.

In an etching from the *Penny Illustrated Journal* (figure 9.4), Pastrana appears as the shade within Victorian white womanhood in general. Behind the glass case in which Pastrana stands is a white couple, a top-hatted man and a bonneted woman. While the man stands three-quarters to the outside of the case so that most of his body and nearly

Figure 9.4
Julia Pastrana, etching from the *Penny Illustrated Journal*. Courtesy of the
Bodleian Library, University of Oxford, Julia Pastrana, Embalmed Nonde-
script, Human Freaks, Box 2.

all of his head are clearly visible, the woman stands fully behind the
double layer of glass that encloses the outlandishly outfitted, bearded
corpse. The glass is a complexly fluid barrier that not only obscures
the white woman's face and body but also, because she stands behind
and only slightly off-center to Pastrana, casts her as Pastrana's shadow.

This strange inversion—white middle-class lady as shadow of brown hermaphroditic showgirl—maintains and complicates the relationship between the two women: here are not simply a viewing subject and a viewed object, for the shadow-woman is not clearly white, although her dress and white husband imply that she is so. Behind the protective glass that boxes Pastrana, the woman appears a dusky gray. Shadowing Pastrana's brown skin, beside a man who is clearly white, the bonneted woman exhibits the "savage" potential that lies behind and within the whiteness of the Victorian middle-class white woman—much as Munby's speaker feared. The exhibition of "the embalmed nondescript" reduces Pastrana's humanity to an ugly lesson about the "truth" of corrupted female nature—the showgirl becomes an unsexed, nonwhite creature, a woman whose masculinity has pushed through her skin in the shape of "very pretty whiskers, moustache, and beard," a woman who exceeds the boundaries of "nature," whose dead/undead body stands upright as a lesson to the visiting public about the monstrous spectacle all women have the potential to become.

Pastrana Resurrected

Here I want to change gears, to formulate a rather different reading of Pastrana's dynamic image, for despite these clearly punitive components, there were other factors at play in Pastrana's exhibitions that demand consideration. In raising this alternate set of interpretive possibilities, I will be turning to recent interest in Pastrana's story and image, before circling back to the Victorian context I have read thus far.

In the years since we first "met," Pastrana has been resurrected with a vengeance, reemerging as a powerful symbol, adorning the covers of magazines, books, and playbills. It is not terribly surprising (if nonetheless disappointing) that some of these current representations replicate the dynamics of the freak show, trafficking in sensationalized speculation and hyperbolic phrasing with little regard for truth. For example, Christopher Hals Gylseth and Lars O. Toverud's book-length biography of Pastrana, just printed in English in 2003, is more melodrama than scholarship; it includes gruesome photos and vast stores of material the authors could neither know nor research. (For example, Gylseth and Toverud write knowingly that Pastrana "no doubt believed that she was the only one in the world to be doomed to a life of such loneliness. Could any man ever love a bearded woman? And would she ever find such a man? . . . And if it occurred, would he love her for her own sake? Only time would tell; and she had other things to think about.")[35] Despite their avowed desire to produce a sympathetic rendering of her life and experiences, these authors continue the trajectory of what might be best described as sideshow representation, portraying Pastrana's strange body so as to produce shock, horror, fascination, and monetary gain.

There are, however, a growing number of exceptions to the grotesque mode of depiction. As opposed to the Othering so commonly associated with the "normal" subject's relationship to the "freakish" body, many of these more recent representations articulate a defiant association—an affiliation—with Pastrana. It seems little coincidence that this happens as our culture increasingly assimilates tattooed, pierced, and even scarified bodies, but the current turn to Pastrana often has less to do with her physical differences than with a range of human emotions: suffering, longing, triumph, defiance.

A great many current interpreters have fastened upon Otto Hermann's remarks about Pastrana in his book *Fahrend Volk,* in which he notes her kindness and records her (perhaps apocryphal) final words, spoken in reference to her husband: "He loves me for my own sake."[36] While I have found no other record, nor any Victorian interpretations, of these words, they seem central to many modern renditions of her. For example, in Hollywood, the home of plastic surgery, a cinematic Pastrana is in the works and has been under way for some years now. Claire Noto's original script cast Lent and Pastrana as beauty and the beast (Lent being the beauty—originally to be played by Richard Gere). Noto's version appealed to American culture's fascination with remaking fairy tales, and gave the bear woman a happy ending. When I spoke with Steve Longey at the film's original home, Permut Presentations, back in 2000, he described it as a story with a universal theme, a "classic love story."[37] Meg Richman, who revised Noto's script, and the new production company, Sobini Films, has changed the spin somewhat, retaining the love story but making it more tragic than classic. As it stands now, *Fortune of Love,* the movie, is "the beautiful and unusual true story of a dashing showman of freaks, who pursues a woman, rumored to have the face of a beast, in the hopes of displaying her on stage. Driven by his hunger for success, riches and power, he seduces Julia Pastrana into joining his troupe but . . . against all of his initial instincts, he begins to fall in love with her."[38] This filmic version of Pastrana's life inverts the animalistic significance of her body in Victorian culture: here, savagery resides in Lent's "instincts" against loving "the ugliest woman in the world." In the twenty-first-century rendition, Pastrana's body becomes an occasion for educating the "dashing" man into a proper appraisal of *inner* beauty, so that the film might more accurately merit the title "Civilizing Theodore Lent."

In that the story remains a tragic love story in which, according to Robin Schorr, president of production at Sobini, Lent "loves her but can't quite admit it to himself," the Hollywood Pastrana is clearly reminiscent of Garland-Thomson's "sensitive monster, whose role it is to instruct, edify, and thus construct the middle-class canonical self." Working to complicate current definitions of beauty, the film draws upon Pastrana's body to shake up not only how an audience measures attractiveness but also how they envision the possible shapes of love. However, the "sensitive monster" in this script also reframes the definition of disability. Schorr says that she was drawn to the project because she sees Pastrana as a woman born with an enormous strike against her who refused to see herself as unlucky. The film finds Pastrana complicated and inspirational, a woman who, Schorr says, "has a life spirit that's weirdly contagious" to both her audiences and those in her life.[39] This rendition of Pastrana has the potential to communicate to her viewers a sense not only of their own "normalcy" but also that cowardice is a less visible form of disability. Within the film's own lexicon, therefore, the "bear woman" appears distinctly abled.

A 1993 song by the Ass Ponys also turns to Hermann's records to treat the romantic theme: "she said he loves me for my own sake," the chorus of "Julia Pastrana" repeats. While the song's minor chords and sing-along rhythm may invoke the distancing pulse of pity, they also invite commiseration with the emotional poignancy of longing, across a gulf of bodily difference.[40] Pastrana is no edifying lesson here; rather, the Ass Ponys render her story familiar and readily inhabitable; she is a woman deluded by desire, but no more so than many of us have been. Similarly, poet Wendy Rose also writes alliance. In her 1985 poem "Julia," Rose speaks from the embalmed Pastrana's perspective: "Oh my husband / tell me again / this is only a dream / I wake from warm," she pleads, finding in her Pastrana the embodiment of marital betrayal and of the death in (and of) marriage during an era of rampant divorce. In another poem, "Sideshow," Rose returns to Pastrana to interrogate her label as "The Ugliest Woman in the World": the poem is direct address, rather than a dramatic monologue, and the speaker honors Pastrana's subversion of feminine beauty, and claims relationship to her:

I call you
the most beautiful she-wolf,
the highest-flying canary,
the most ancient song,
the most faithful magic.
I call you
my mother and my sister
and my daughter and me.[41]

Alongside the reverent, transcendent imagery of flight and melody, Rose's familial lexicon seems an insistent departure from spectatorship. Instead, Rose dispenses with methodologies of looking and thinking that rely upon rigid definitions of human and animal, let alone self and other.

Visual artists have more of a challenge in representing Pastrana without replicating the exploitative dynamics of making a person into an object. A case in point is Holley Bakich, who has produced a series of sculptures depicting sideshow "freaks." Bakich has little interest in teaching her audience to assume proper middle-class sympathy. Rather, she writes, "'Freaks' have, for the most part, an extraordinary acceptance of themselves often lacking in so-called 'normal' people."[42] Her Pastrana is positively joyous: a smiling figure in a cheerful, brightly colored dress, perched on a bright pink stage festooned with ribbons and cloudlike flowers (figure 9.5). Bakich embroidered the dance costume by hand and "painstakingly sewed all the little hairs onto her leather body for a more realistically hairy effect."[43] Unlike the majority of promotional materials that presented Pastrana in profile, this rendition gives her back the potential to look: Bakich's Julia faces her audience straight on. Beautiful, vivid, and almost buoyant, this Pastrana is decidedly designed to project self-possession. Kathleen Anderson Culebro's painting for the New York production of *The True History of the Tragic Life and Triumphant Death of Julia Pastrana, the Ugliest Woman in the World* similarly challenges audience expectation by obscuring Pastrana's head behind a swath of fabric that (nonetheless) names her and her function in Victorian culture (figure 9.6). The body gracefully balanced on one toe, as was Pastrana in many of her promotional posters, is oddly hairless, an artistic choice that recuperates the possible options for the draped head. The headless woman in advertising—such as beer and automobile commercials—would generally imply that a woman's head does not really matter. Culebro's painting, however, emphasizes the ways in which Pastrana's title ("the Ugliest") was more a function of narrative

Figure 9.5
Julia Pastrana sculpture by Holley Bakich. Reproduced with kind permission of the artist.

than fact. The sprightly pose of the veiled woman becomes playful, engaged, and ludic, suggesting that this woman has a sufficiently settled head on her shoulders to allow her to dance through the words that cover her over.

The play itself, for which Culebro produced the painting, is by British playwright Shaun Prendergast. It premiered in London in 2000 and

Figure 9.6
Kathleen Anderson Culebro's painting for the New York production of *The True History of the Tragic Life and Triumphant Death of Julia Pastrana, the Ugliest Woman in the World*. Reproduced with kind permission of the artist, Kathleen Anderson Culebro, Artistic Director of Amphibian Stage Productions.

made its New York debut in November 2003 (Culebro was the artistic director of the New York production). Like Culebro's painting, the play repeatedly emphasizes the importance of language to our experiences of the people and situations we encounter. In Prendergast's script, Lent explicitly proposes,

> Hell, words'll hit you like spitballs
> Right in the kisser, nose to nose
> Upfront and personal . . .
> For the price of a ticket,
> You can get every superlative known to Mr Webster.[44]

And the audience will need a whole dictionary of words to process what Prendergast gives them. The play is meant to be staged in pitch darkness, forcing the audience to rely upon sound and smell to piece together the story.[45] Although Pastrana is the only member of the cast to be embellished by physical description, she nonetheless remains unseen, so that one never "knows" what one sees.[46] Disrupting the visual dynamics of the freak show, Prendergast's play is explicitly confrontational, "displaying" an exceptional woman whose physical exceptionality he renders invisible.

The play opens with traditional sideshow barkers hawking admission:

> We got Siamese twins and sheep with two heads
> And a boy with the face of a fish.
> And ghost trains and geeks
> And the wild child of Borneo.
>
> And armless wonders and legless wonders and limbless wonders
> And parasitic twins. Will wonders never cease?[47]

These opening lines catalog the distinctions of Victorian freak culture—disability, nationality, hybridity, exceptionality—but offer no visual clue to Pastrana for the first four pages. And then, as Prendergast puts it, "her sweet voice gives the first bodily descriptions in the play." The audience's apprehension of Pastrana's appearance is therefore inescapably enmeshed with the sound of her own voice, made all the more "sweet" for the barkers' harsh cries at the threshold. In the contrast lies an implicit critique of sideshow culture but also a reminder that, to the best of our knowledge, Pastrana was integrally involved in her own representation.[48]

Like Suzan-Lori Parks's *Venus*, Prendergast's Julia is hardly a simple story of exploitation.[49] Both plays emphasize "scientific" and popular exhibitions as spaces of exchange in which spectators depart with their various forms of data, but the exhibited woman is also a subject who takes home something she considers valuable. Prendergast's Pastrana reminds us that the original was a very successful and strategic performer of ugliness—and she was *not* the ugliest woman in the world (he offers Grace McDaniels, "the Mule-Woman," to illustrate). Pastrana made a career of *performing* ugliness and, despite her severely limited options for a "normal" life, she made a successful and relatively comfortable existence for herself.

In his effort to intervene in established narratives about exhibitions and audiences' responses to them, Prendergast took great pains not to put words into Pastrana's mouth, and he refused to dictate how the audience should feel (he terms didactic theater "disastrous"). Instead, the playwright aimed "to constantly ask the audience what they thought," offering them options of response and granting them "permission to be curious." Real curiosity entails asking questions without foregone conclusions, which allows for interactions that move beyond, or beside, appropriation and negation. And, Prendergast says, the politically correct climate of recent years has all but closed down such possibilities. When the play was staged in New York, the cast and crew handed out promotional cards in Washington Square Park. "Come see *The Ugliest Woman in the World*," they said brightly to passersby, offering cards printed with Culebro's painting. According to Culebro, various people chided the performers: "We think all women are beautiful," one couple responded, while others shook their heads in disgust. (For the record, plenty of theatergoers responded positively: the New York production was so successful as to extend its run.)[50] These dismissive responses may initially seem compassionate, but they also smack of the same social training that insists one not "make a spectacle of oneself": it's not polite to stare. However, in refusing to let its audience actually *see* (or stare at) "the ugliest woman in the world," and yet offering them a vision of her life though language, sound, and smell, the play makes visible other components of identity, producing not only more complicated characters but also a "viewing" experience that confronts the complexity of how the experience of viewing works.

These representations of the "bear woman" depart radically from those generally discussed in "Pastrana studies," or with regard to Victorian freakery in general. What disciplinary messages they offer have little to do with proper behavior, ostentation, or domestic duty. In addition, with the exception of Culebro, who respectfully insists upon giving Julia her proper Spanish pronunciation, they elide the dynamics of racial, national, and species difference that so powerfully informed

Victorian exhibition culture. Gylseth and Toverud's lurid biography and Matthew Sweet's desire to spend "one night with the delectably furry Julia" offer salient reminders that these forms of Othering live on, and that various current readers and viewers encounter even the most empowering of these modern Pastranas only to validate Lennard Davis's assertion that "most Americans react to the idea of disability with good wishes and a silent prayer to the effect that 'there but for the grace of God go I.'"[51] Culebro agrees, stating that "we're not all that much more evolved" than Victorian audiences. Yet I think both would concur that there exist other potential relationships to the anomalous body that are reducible neither to estrangement, nor to reverence, nor to custodial relations of pity.[52]

Reading Affiliation

To be quite personal about it, none of these terms adequately sum up my own experience. As a woman who has struggled all of her life alternately to approximate or to dismiss unattainable standards of beauty, my attraction to Pastrana derives from her embodiment of the persistent failure of female bodies to meet the mark, and of an existential longing for acceptance in a social world where such acceptance is rare. In an age when women in Western culture routinely undergo freakish rituals (Brazilian waxing, fad dieting, Botox injections, liposuction) in order to conform to "normal" standards of attractiveness, I find it no coincidence that Pastrana has reemerged as a figure of resistance and empowerment.[53]

To be sure, in part my response initiates me into the "position of stewardship over the other" that Rosemarie Garland-Thomson criticizes, yet I want to argue that it does so in a manner better described as affiliation than any other term modern theory offers. To the best of my understanding, too, affiliation more accurately designates the various investments of other scholars and interpreters of unusual bodies. Many of us have very personal stakes in resurrecting these figures, in telling these stories. Many of us embrace spectacular bodies not only to mark our differences from them, and not simply to mediate our own differences from the conventions of normalcy, to articulate our own inabilities to fit neatly into a box, but also to work toward some form of social intervention. Alongside viewers' capacities to feel horror, superiority, or pity, that is, there is the potential for them also to experience feelings of association or alliance that are engaged and ethically conscious. At the New York performances of Prendergast's play, Culebro circulated a petition to have Pastrana's remains returned to Mexico for a proper burial. Bakich writes that she intends her sculptures as "homage." Schorr remarks that she finds Pastrana "inspirational," a woman who urges us "to think of what we might all do with ourselves if we had such a will." And, without naming names, I can identify a great many academics whose bodies or personal histories resonate with the individuals on whom they work.

Current deployments of Victorian freaks offer models that might— and ought—to expand the parameters of how we read not only our own encounters with "the Other" but historical encounters as well. In that interest, therefore, I want to return to some of the Victorian materials I have already read to suggest how the complexity of these representations makes clear that Pastrana's significance, even in Victorian culture, was emphatically plural. In closing, I would like to consider some of those options both for Victorian culture and for cultural criticism in general.

While it may be easy to disqualify the authenticity of alliance in those Victorian accounts that deem Pastrana a "perfect woman" or remark upon her inherent ability to waltz, other accounts significantly complicate dominant theoretical paradigms for describing relations to the extraordinary body. In the etching of "the embalmed nondescript," for example, while the echoing position of the bonneted woman may articulate the disciplinary cautions I explore above, one may also read in it a quiet sign of empathy with the disruptive body in the case. One might wonder about the meaning of that glass cage, and in particular about the woman's right hand, imprisoned under her husband's arm. Neither woman, that is, appears to have many options for mobility. Similarly, for all of its hyperbolic misogyny, Munby's poem also articulates a surprising recognition of women's lack of sovereignty within Victorian culture. The speaker initially remarks of the baboon,

> I must confess I was glad to see
> That her chain was made fast to the walnut tree;
> So she could not manage to get at me,
>   Were she ever so much inclined; (6)

But he also notes that, as she "gazed at herself, and fondly eyed / Her steel-bright collar and chain: / She seem'd as blithe as a bride full-drest"

(6). The analogy with the imprisonment of marriage becomes even more complex as the baboon, enraged by the speaker's superior stare, ceases to be so pleased with her accoutrements and begins to mangle and gnaw at the "massive chain," until she has flattened some of its links into strips (7). Later, when the speaker notes that the woman at his inn also wears a "white metallic thing / That shines on her throat, like the gleam of a ring" (10), the comparison is complete: the collar appears an enlarged version of the nuptial band. The speaker secures our sympathies to the collared woman when the innkeeper throws a gray shroud over her head, pinions her arms to her chair, and carries her off, fighting and screaming. Flummoxed by this complex and disturbing series of events, the speaker asks no questions

> For in fact I dreaded to hear her tale;
> That very word made me turn quite pale,
> When I call'd to mind her long wild wail
>   Of anger and despair . . . (12)

Does the thought of her tale make him blanch because of the homonym with the tails of animals at the zoo, suggesting that the woman ought to be locked up? Or is it that the audible wail proves narrative enough, articulating the "anger and despair" of the marital condition? Even as Munby's speaker states his "dread" of either of the imprisoned female creatures' "getting to" him, his narrative expresses sympathy with, albeit mixed with fear of, imprisoned female figures. The "long wild wail" he records exceeds barbarity, registering "despair" as well. It is clear that Pastrana did "get to" Munby, and that she did so complexly—not enough, perhaps, to revise his expectations of femininity and civilization, but sufficiently to prompt contemplation, curiosity, and exploration.

Elsewhere, Wilkie Collins's depiction of the troublingly hirsute but explicitly engaging Marian Halcombe in *The Woman in White* emerges shortly after Pastrana's first London appearance. Walter Hartright's first response to Marian repeats almost verbatim the rhetoric that various handbills used to promote Pastrana. Consider, for example, his admiration of "the rare beauty of her form" and "the unaffected grace of her attitude" when Marian's back is turned toward him. His admiration turns to shock when he first sees her face:

> Never was the old conventional maxim, that Nature cannot err, more
> flatly contradicted—never was the fair promise of a lovely figure more

strangely and startlingly belied by the face and head that crowned it. The lady's complexion was almost swarthy, and the dark down on her upper lip was almost a moustache. She had a large, firm, masculine mouth and jaw; prominent, piercing, resolute brown eyes; and thick, coal-black hair, growing unusually low down on her forehead. . . . To see such a face as this set on shoulders that a sculptor would have longed to model—to be charmed by the modest graces of action through which the symmetrical limbs betrayed their beauty when they moved, and then to be almost repelled by the masculine form and masculine look of the features in which the perfectly shaped figure ended—was to feel a sensation oddly akin to the helpless discomfort familiar to us all in sleep, when we recognise yet cannot reconcile the anomalies and contradictions of a dream.[54]

The "anomalies and contradictions" that Marian Halcombe provokes for Walter Hartright seem explicitly indebted to the literature that promoted and responded to Julia Pastrana. Consider, for example, the Regent Gallery handbill, which remarks, "her eyes are large and fine, the centre being so jet black that the pupil is scarcely perceptible," "her mouth is elongated," "the lower jaw . . . extends much more than ordinary," "her hair is black, straight, and abundant; her form and limbs are quite perfect," and of course, "she has thick black hair on the nose, forehead, and every part of her face and person."[55] As Richard Collins observes, "Marian's 'modest graces of action' are reflected in the dancer Pastrana's 'good and graceful figure'; Marian's 'clear, ringing, pleasant voice' is echoed in the singer Pastrana's 'sweet voice.' Indeed, Collins's description of the 'highly-bred' Marian could almost stand in for that of Julia Pastrana with her 'great taste' in the arts and her linguistic skills."[56] Wilkie Collins's depiction of his hero, "charmed by the modest graces of action through which the symmetrical limbs betrayed their beauty when they moved, and then . . . almost repelled by the masculine form and masculine look of the features in which the perfectly shaped figure ended," describes thoroughly many a Victorian man's response to Julia Pastrana. And yet, Marian Halcombe emerges as one of Collins's most intelligent and admired heroines. While Hartright initially finds her an "error" of nature, and his initial reaction to his contradictory responses is decidedly feeble—he is "charmed" yet "repulsed" by Marian—he ultimately comes to rely on Laura Fairlie's savvy, engaging half-sister. To be sure, she is not a serious romantic figure in the novel; Count Fosco's admiration for her notwithstanding, Marian never marries. Nonetheless, through her, Collins offers a representation of the hirsute woman that expands, rather than reifies, the parameters of acceptability.[57]

Pastrana's Victorian exhibitions thus seem to have elicited a range of responses that included not only discrimination, not only pity, but recognition and affiliation as well. That is not to say that these responses evade the dynamics of proprietorship, exploitation, or distortion.[58] Indeed, the problem of replicating sideshow dynamics is familiar to academics who work on freakery: we reproduce images, we cite handbills, we resurrect the call to "look at this!"—just as I have asked you throughout this essay to look at "the ugliest woman in the world." Generally, scholarship of freaks is politically inflected, meant to reappraise the original dynamics of representation.[59] Often, such reappraisals offer the opportunity to condemn sideshow culture as exploitative and cruel, or to educate modern readers into a more humane perspective on what we now term the dis- or differently abled body.

Alternatively, my aim in this essay has been to reappraise the exploitations of freakery, not as a means to "correct" those "bad" Victorians who went to see Pastrana, but rather to add to our resources for reading her and other extraordinary bodies. Modern renditions of Julia Pastrana have augmented the potential meanings I now find in the Victorian texts I have known for many years, and have expanded a theoretical vocabulary the "abilities" of which had come to feel limited. The dynamics of affiliation do not escape the problems of exploitation, nor do they avoid the intense problematics involved in "speaking for" another person. However, they can significantly complicate both how we envision the work we do and how we understand the cultures and bodies we explore.

Notes

1. These are reproduced later in this essay as figures 9.3 and 9.4.

2. Pastrana's "bearlike" appearance was due to gingival hyperplasia and congenital hypertrichosis terminalis. See Jan Bondeson, *A Cabinet of Medical Curiosities* (Ithaca, NY: Cornell University Press, 1999), 241–42.

3. The source most frequently cited with regard to Pastrana's life is Otto Hermann, *Fahrend Volk* (Leipzig: Weber, 1895).

4. The grossly Gothic introduction to Christopher Hals Gylseth and Lars O. Toverud's 2003 biography suggests that less "serious" researchers also have access to her body. The following, in any case, is not standard medical discourse: "In the vaults in Oslo, the flickering light reveals the contents of the hospital's basement room. . . . All at once, you are inside medicine's innermost chamber of horrors. Twisted shadows are cast upon the walls. . . . Light filters through turbid liquids of varying colour and uncertain composition to reveal a macabre collection of body

parts. An amputated foot, a pale hand the colour of wax, a human embryo, a gray-ish brain, something of knotty, indefinable form (a tumour?), a detached, deformed elbow . . . In one far corner, there is an indeterminate apparition . . . it has vaguely human contours. What is it? A stuffed ape?" (ix–x). Christopher Hals Gylseth and Lars O. Toverud, *Julia Pastrana: The Tragic Story of the Victorian Ape Woman*, trans. Donald Tumasonis (Phoenix Mill, UK: Sutton Publishing, 2001, 2003).

5. For more on Bartels, see Frederick Drimmer, *Very Special People: The Struggles, Loves, and Triumphs of Human Oddities* (New York: Amjon Publishers, 1973), 374–76. Bondeson notes that her disorder was radically different from Pastrana's; Bartels's was secondary hypertrichosis.

6. Rosemarie Garland-Thomson argues convincingly that Pastrana is best understood in her status as hybrid. She writes, "Pastrana's body confused in several ways a number of the orthodox categories of being upon which the social structure was hung." She cites "five foundational oppositions that structured the nineteenth-century social order[:] . . . human/animal, civilized/primitive, normal/pathological, male/female, and self/other." See "Narratives of Deviance and Delight Staring at Julia Pastrana, the 'Extraordinary Lady,'" in *Beyond the Binary: Reconstructing Cultural Identity in a Multicultural Context*, ed. Tim Powell (New Brunswick, NJ: Rutgers University Press, 1999), 90.

7. Lennard J. Davis neatly sums up the historical background to this approach, noting that the term "normal" emerges in English in the late eighteenth and early nineteenth centuries, alongside the new science of statistics. Prior to that period, bodies had been understood within the discourse of the "ideal," whereby no actual body measured up. However, Davis argues, "the new ideal of ranked order is powered by the imperative of the norm and then is supplemented by the notion of progress, human perfectibility, and the elimination of deviance, to create a dominating, hegemonic vision of what the human body should be." See "Constructing Normalcy: The Bell Curve, the Novel, and the Invention of the Disabled Body in the Nineteenth Century," in *The Disability Studies Reader*, ed. Lennard J. Davis (New York: Routledge, 1997), 17. See also Davis's *Enforcing Normalcy: Disability, Deafness, and the Body* (London: Verso, 1995).

8. Rosemarie Garland-Thomson, "Making Freaks: Visual Rhetorics and the Spectacle of Julia Pastrana," in *Thinking the Limits of the Body*, ed. Jeffrey Jerome Cohen and Gail Weiss (Albany: SUNY Press, 2003), 142, emphasis added.

9. Qtd. in *Account of Miss Pastrana, the Nondescript; and the Double-Bodied Boy* (London: E. Hancock, J. W. Burrows, Printer, [1857]), 12.

10. Mary Russo, *The Female Grotesque: Risk, Excess, and Modernity* (New York: Routledge, 1995), 76, 84. "The secret self" derives from Leslie Fiedler's influential study of freakery, published in 1978. Fiedler's study has come under considerable fire for its overly reverent perspective: as Brian Rosenberg notes, Fiedler renders the freak an "art-object, described in terms usually reserved for painting and poems" (302). Robert Bogdan writes that although Fiedler sets out to critique the dynamic of the freak show, he nonetheless replicates it by making the freaks themselves, rather than their audiences, the subjects of his study. See Leslie Fiedler, *Freaks: Myths and Human Images of the Secret Self* (New York: Simon and Schuster, 1978); Brian Rosenberg, "Teaching Freaks," in *Freakery: Cultural Spectacles of the*

Extraordinary Body, ed. Rosemarie Garland-Thomson (New York: New York University Press, 1996); and Robert Bogdan, *Freak Show: Presenting Human Oddities for Amusement and Profit* (Chicago: University of Chicago Press, 1988).

11. My colleague Mindy Fenske has been instrumental in helping me consolidate my intuitions about affiliation. Fenske's essay "The Aesthetic of the Unfinished: Ethics and Performance" (*Text and Performance Quarterly* 24 (2004): 1–19) argues for an interpretive practice that refuses both closure and the illusion of conciliation, and offers a model of ethical engagement that foregrounds the problems of reciprocity.

12. See Garland-Thomson, "Narratives."

13. See, for example, Guy Debord's 1992 introduction to *The Society of the Spectacle,* originally published in 1967, in which he justifies his assertion that he is "not someone who revises his work": "A critical theory of the kind presented here needed no changing—not as long, at any rate, as the general conditions of the long historical period that it was the first to describe accurately were still intact." I am suggesting, contra Debord, that such revision is decidedly necessary. Guy Debord, *The Society of the Spectacle,* trans. Donald Nicholson-Smith (New York: Zone Books, 1995), 7.

14. Russo, 213.

15. I draw upon this perspective as stereotype but acknowledge its lack of historical complication. In actuality, the stage provided possibilities of income and class transcendence for women of various classes, and many actresses did manage to secure an opinion of respectability from all but the most excruciatingly religious judges. Nonetheless, the majority of popular print materials roundly denounce women's participating in the profession of acting and the principles of female display in general. See Tracy Davis, *Actresses as Working Women: Their Social Identity in Victorian England* (New York: Routledge, 1991).

16. Dinah Mulock Craik, *A Woman's Thoughts About Women* (London: Hurst and Blackett, 1858), 58.

17. Dinah Maria Mulock Craik, "Concerning Men. By a Woman," in *Concerning Men and Other Papers* (London: Macmillan, 1888), 7–8.

18. Garland-Thomson, "Making Freaks," 131.

19. Mary Douglas, *Purity and Danger: An Analysis of Concepts of Pollution and Taboo* (London: Routledge and Kegan Paul, 1966), 35.

20. Karen Newman discusses this trope within and beyond its role in Renaissance literary representation. See "'And wash the Ethiop white': Femininity and the Monstrous in *Othello,*" in Newman, *Fashioning Femininity and English Renaissance Drama* (Chicago: University of Chicago Press, 1991).

21. See chapter 5 of Anne McClintock, *Imperial Leather: Race, Gender and Sexuality in the Colonial Contest* (New York: Routledge, 1995), and chapter 3 of Carol Mavor's *Pleasures Taken: Performances of Sexuality and Loss in Victorian Photographs* (Durham, NC: Duke University Press, 1995) for other extended discussions of the role of soap in constructing whiteness. Incidentally, soap ads are the stuff of late-Victorian England, a point that Mavor and McClintock rather problematically elide. Exhibitions relied upon a similar logic as soap advertisements, but as I discuss below, exhibition dynamics and implications are not simply interchangeable with

those of Pears'. The Unilever Corporation, which now owns Pears', in no way endorses or supports the rhetoric of these historical advertisements.

22. Cf. Edwin Chadwick, *Report on the Sanitary Conditions of the Labouring Population of Great Britain,* and Henry Mayhew, *London Labour and the London Poor* (Edinburgh University Press, 1842; 1965).

23. Handbill promoting the Aztec Children, 1853. Bodleian Library, John Johnson Collection, Exhibition Catalogues 34.

24. Beyond the groups of people in foreign attire, these exhibitions also displayed the biases by which those who failed to conform to British standards of civilization were deprived of cultural, international, and racial power.

25. Charles Dickens, "The Noble Savage," in *The Works of Charles Dickens,* Vol. 13 (Boston and New York: The Jefferson Press, n.d.), 231. Originally printed in *Household Words* (June 11, 1853).

26. Ibid., 226.

27. Ibid., 230–31.

28. The messages of these exhibitions were, not surprisingly, explicitly gendered. Saartjie Baartman, otherwise known as "the Hottentot Venus," both ushered the practice of exhibition into the nineteenth century and established a corporeal stereotype for primitive sexuality. Medical men, authors, and a wide variety of spectators learned through Baartman's steatopygia that there was a link between distended physiology and an eroticism that was neither English nor white. Popular discourse surrounding Baartman established a precedent that compounded display, corrupt femininity, racial color, eroticism, and dirt, a conglomeration that was transferred to Victorian prostitutes and to other white women who too bawdily entered the field of vision. For more on Baartman, see Richard Altick, *The Shows of London* (Cambridge, MA: Belknap Press, 1978).

29. "Grand and Novel Attraction. Miss Julia Pastrana, The Nondescript." Regent Gallery handbill, 1857. Bodleian Library, John Johnson Collection, Human Freaks 2.

30. Ibid.

31. *Account of Miss Pastrana,* 6.

32. "Digger Indian" is an invented category, ostensibly including the Shoshonees or Snakes, and the Utahs. According to the *Account of Miss Pastrana,* "The term 'Digger' is applied to all of these Indians, wherever located, in consequence of the method of procuring their food, which consists principally of grass-hoppers, anils and wasps. They are very fond of a certain little animal which the Bible tells us greatly afflicted the Egyptians in the days of Pharaoh. The California grass-hoppers, however, mainly compose their mess" (6). According to Garland-Thomson and Bondeson, the term is entirely apocryphal.

33. Arthur Munby, "Pastrana," in *Relicta: Verses* (London: Bertram Dobell, 1909), 5. Future citations are parenthetical and refer to page numbers.

34. Janet Browne and Sharon Messenger, "Victorian Spectacle: Julia Pastrana, the Bearded and Hairy Female," *Endeavour* 27, no. 4 (2003): 159. See also Garland-Thomson, "Narratives." The *Era* remarked that her body "*might, but for the silence of the tongue, be regarded as still living*" (March 16, 1862, quoted in Burlington Gallery handbill, John Johnson Collection, Human Freaks 2; original emphasis).

35. Gylseth and Toverud, 6. See also note 4, above, and their account of her birth, marked by "a horrified shriek [that] echoes through the forest" (1). The book is so terribly bad that even the sensational Matthew Sweet condemns it as so much "fanciful detail and hindsighted moralizing." But Sweet's review of the book in the *London Independent* is little better in approach. Despite his critique, he takes the occasion to indulge in his own fetishized objectification: "Of all the eminent Victorians I'd like to have round for dinner," he writes, "Julia Pastrana the Baboon Lady tops the list. . . . She'd stroke her luxuriant beard, and reveal whether her marriage to her manager, Theodore Lent, was a love-match. . . . Oh for one night with the delectably furry Julia!" *London Independent* (21 December 2003): 13.

36. Hermann, 125. See, for example, Garland-Thomson, "Narratives," 100.

37. Interview by phone (December 18, 2000).

38. Sobini Films, *Fortune of Love* (formerly *Julia Pastrana*). Available at http://www.sobini.com, under "Packaging." Accessed October 3, 2007.

39. Interview by phone with Robyn Schorr (May 26, 2004).

40. The song's final stanza is also memorable: "poor julia was injured inside / and soon followed her son to the grave / her husband had them mummified / and toured until he went insane."

41. Wendy Rose, "Julia" and "Sideshow," in *A Gathering of Spirit: A Collection by North American Indian Women*, ed. Beth Brant (Ithaca, NY: Firebrand Books, 1984, 1988).

42. Holley Bakich, "The Bakich Sideshow," available at http://www.geocities.com/holleybak/julia.html. Other representatives in her collection include the three-legged man, Francesco Lentini; Robert Wadlow, the world's tallest man; Baby Thelma, a "fat lady"; Prince Randion, the "caterpillar man"; Johnny Eckhardt, "the half boy"; William Henry Johnson, otherwise known as "Zip"; and Horace Ridler, the "zebra man."

43. Ibid.

44. Shaun Prendergast, "Julia Pastrana: The Ugliest Woman in the World," 1–2. Unpublished script, received through the author's kind consideration.

45. Amphibian Productions, which put on the play in New York, revised the staging to include roughly three minutes of light at the outset to help establish ambiance. Prendergast fought stridently against this choice, feeling that it removed the audience's visual curiosity about the other characters, which was integral to the play's democratic ethic.

46. Prendergast notes that he was striving to make Julia Pastrana a real person, one who "went home at the end of a day, who had a cup of tea, who had a nice house." Interviews with Shaun Prendergast, by phone April 22, 2004, and in London, May 13, 2004. All subsequent quotations derive from these conversations.

47. Prendergast, "Julia Pastrana," 2–3.

48. For a critique of exhibited people's consent, see David A. Gerber, "The 'Careers' of People Exhibited in Freak Shows: The Problem of Volition and Valorization," in Garland-Thomson, *Freakery*, 38–56. Gerber rightly points out that few "freaks" had many options for "normal" employment. I find problematic, however, his refusal to allow their careers *as* careers, especially when the performers conceived of them as such.

49. Much of the disturbing power of Parks's play derives from its complicated arguments about the Hottentot Venus's "exploitation." While the doctors, showmen, and audiences that come to see the Venus are clearly exploitive, her Venus is an explicitly willing participant. Suzan-Lori Parks, *Venus: A Play* (New York: Theatre Communications Group, 1997).

50. Kathleen Anderson Culebro, interview by phone (March 4, 2004). All subsequent quotations derive from this conversation.

51. Lennard J. Davis, *Bending Over Backwards: Essays on Disability and the Body*, ed. Lennard Davis and Michael Berube (New York: NYU Press, 2002), 1–2. One might locate the following response to Prendergast's play within a similar context: "we're left to question our own lives through the harrowing, soul-wrenching story of Julia. A woman who simply yearned to fall in love, have a child, own a house and live life. . . . Now when's my next waxing appointment?" Available at http://www.beautynewsnyc.com/newsletteroctober2003/play.html. Accessed April 17, 2004.

52. "The sentimental relationship is nonreciprocal as it elevates the self into a position of stewardship over the other." Garland-Thomson, "Making Freaks," 141.

53. There is room for further scholarship in the "freak show" of *The Swan*, a Fox network reality TV show, in which perfectly acceptable, if ordinary, women submitted themselves to a "Dream Team of experts" including cosmetic surgeons, a cosmetic dentist, a personal trainer, a "life coach," and a therapist, so that they could become beautiful. For more on *The Swan*, see the cover story of *People* from June 7, 2004.

54. Wilkie Collins, *The Woman in White*, ed. John Sutherland (New York: Oxford University Press, 1998).

55. "Grand and Novel Attraction." See also the record of Victorian naturalist Francis T. Buckland, who spoke with Pastrana during her 1857 London levees: "Her eyes were deep black, and somewhat prominent, and their lids had long, thick eyelashes; her features were simply hideous on account of the profusion of hair growing on her forehead, and her black beard; but her figure was exceedingly good and graceful." *Curiosities of Natural History*, vol. 4 (London: Bentley, 1903), 41. Richard Collins also notes this concordance in his essay "Marian's Moustache: Bearded Ladies, Hermaphrodites, and Intersexual Collage in *The Woman in White*," in *Reality's Dark Light: The Sensational Wilkie Collins*, ed. Maria K. Bachman and Don Richard Cox (Knoxville: University of Tennessee Press, 2003).

56. Richard Collins, 41.

57. Richard Collins argues that Marian's "defect . . . made her all the more appealing" to readers, noting that various "men responded [to her] by proposing marriage" (132).

58. Shaun Prendergast has said overtly, "I exploit Julia just as much as Lent did." Perhaps in degree, but not in kind: it is clear to me that Prendergast's exploitation is not "the same as" Lent's.

59. Garland-Thomson writes that it "excavates the meanings of embodied differences and explores how the body has been understood over time." See "The Beauty and the Freak," *Michigan Quarterly Review* 37 (1998): 459.

PART IV

Reading and Spectating
the Freak

THIS LAST SECTION asks questions about the literary and photographic—and thus, *cultural*—production of freaks, of their embodiment in various kinds of "text." Through English fiction and through images, we can plumb the politics of material representation of freakery in nineteenth-century England. Martha Stoddard Holmes's essay takes up Victorian novelist Wilkie Collins's depictions of both marriage and the disabled body to ask questions about how the "irregular" and freakish were not simply sites of charity but also of eroticism. Melissa Free looks at both Collins and Charles Dickens to ask how the enfreaked characters demonstrate anxieties that underscore notions of freakishness when they suggestively represent alternative sexualities. Both of these essays build upon the broader social notions of English identity and freakery offered in previous sections. Finally, Christopher Smit closes the collection with a provocative theoretical discussion that challenges notions of freak representation and volition in the foundational work of Rosemarie Garland-Thomson and others, reading the freaks as active and enabled participants in their own production.

10

QUEERING THE MARRIAGE PLOT

Wilkie Collins's The Law and the Lady

MARTHA STODDARD HOLMES

IRREGULARITY MARKS the marriage plot that is the core of Wilkie Collins's *The Law and the Lady*. If domestic novels often seal their happy endings with marriage, this one uses the conjugal rite to set its problems in motion. The first chapter, inauspiciously titled "The Bride's Mistake," introduces Valeria Brinton, one of Collins's heroines of "irregular features," whose excesses ("too pale" of complexion, "too dark" of hair and brows) generate the use of "too" nine times in five sentences of description.[1] The groom, Eustace Woodville, is also presented as distinctive in demeanor and body; he is melancholy and prematurely bald, and he walks with a limp. The newlyweds' emotional dynamic and the early days of their marriage are also atypical, even in the context of Victorian culture. Both are "bewildered" after the ceremony, and the groom is tearful in the honeymoon carriage.[2] Valeria's mistake—signing the marriage register with her married, not maiden, name—foreshadows a much more serious irregularity in this marriage. On the honeymoon, a meeting with a stranger who turns out to be Valeria's mother-in-law leads to the discovery that her husband has married her under a false name; he is really Eustace Macallan. When Eustace refuses to tell Valeria his reasons for the deception, she discovers through some very creative private detective work that he has been tried for the murder of his first wife, Sara, and still bears the stigma of a Scottish "not proven" verdict. Finally, after Valeria confronts him with what she has learned of his troubles and reaffirms her love for him, Eustace disappears, leaving behind an apologetic letter advising his wife to seek an annulment. The opening narrative of newlywed happiness is thus truncated, leaving room for a much different story to enter and inhabit the novel. Instead of being about love and marriage, most of *The Law and the Lady* is about Valeria Macallan's search outside of marriage for the evidence that will allow her to normalize her husband's irregular public identity and thus begin her domestic life.

The search leads her to one of the most interesting characters Wilkie Collins ever created. Miserrimus Dexter's first appearance in the novel, in the pages of the report Valeria reads of Eustace's trial, returns a *frisson* of actual sensation to the sensation novel: "Gliding, self-propelled in his chair on wheels, through the opening made for him among the crowd, a strange and startling creature—literally the half of a man—revealed himself to the general view. A coverlid, which had been thrown over his chair, had fallen off during his progress through the throng. The loss of it exposed to the public curiosity the head, the arms, and the trunk of a living human being: absolutely deprived of the lower limbs."[3] If by 1875 a murder trial in a sensation novel is for readers a pleasurably familiar encounter with a genre convention, Dexter's extraordinary body offers a disruptive new kind of reading pleasure. Bilaterally limb-deficient from birth, he is also a gender puzzle:

> To make this deformity all the more striking and all the more terrible, the victim of it was—as to his face and his body—an unusually handsome and an unusually well-made man. His long silky hair, of a bright and beautiful chestnut color, fell over shoulders that were the perfection of strength and grace. His face was bright with vivacity and intelligence. His large clear blue eyes and his long delicate white hands were like the eyes and hands of a beautiful woman. He would have looked effeminate but for the manly proportions of his throat and chest, aided in their effect by his flowing beard and long mustache, of a lighter chestnut shade than the color of his hair. Never had a magnificent head and body been more hopelessly ill-bestowed than in this instance! Never had Nature committed a more careless or a more cruel mistake than in the making of this man! (173)

Appearance is only the first layer in Dexter's many fascinations, but my purpose is to explore only one of them: his complex relationship to

Valeria's disrupted marriage plot. I will argue for Dexter's centrality not simply to the puzzle of who killed Sara Macallan but more crucially to the novel's endorsement of irregular bodies, relationships, and situations as the powerful and pleasurable foundations of Victorian social life. As the limit case in a continuum of social and sexual behaviors explored, indulged, and finally repudiated by the plot, Miserrimus Dexter functions as a queer sort of marital aid. The desires associated with his extraordinary body and unconventional behavior are essential to the success of Valeria's middle-class marriage, even if she must relinquish these desires, and Dexter himself, by the novel's end.

In making this argument, I diverge from recent critics' emphasis on Dexter as a character whose meaning derives from the history of "monsters" and "freaks," as well as from my usual critical practice of reading atypically embodied Victorian characters as "disabled," with meanings to be elaborated by looking at the historical record of disability's formation as a socioeconomic category and a social identity.[4] Rather than either domesticated freak or disabled person, I choose to read Dexter as a queer and "critically" disabled character. Through his atypical body's work as desire's instrument, conduit, and register, Dexter generates important messages about the failures of heteronormativity and able-bodiedness as social systems.

Accordingly, while my analysis shares most scholars' focus on the long period in which Valeria is separated from her husband, my concerns are different from theirs. The core of the novel is usually regarded as the "detective" narrative in which Valeria's adventures allow her to accumulate the evidence that ultimately clears her husband's name of any suspicion of having murdered his wife. In contrast, I am more interested in the contexts in which Valeria gathers these clues and the other knowledge she accumulates in the process. While *The Law and the Lady* is indeed a detective story, propelled by the suspense of the genre, it is also an excursion into a world of nonnormative, nonmarital pleasures and miseries. The curiosity and desire of detection set the novel and Valeria in motion, but these energies soon diverge from the limited object of clearing Eustace's name and spill out toward far more enticing objects. While Eustace is away, the novel luxuriates in Valeria's separate but not solitary growth as a woman who is neither married nor single, with a group of "odd" and—I will argue—"queer" men, of whom Dexter forms the core; he is only the most visible thread in a fabric of queerness that organizes and gives substance to this marriage plot.

Through Dexter, Collins affirms the literal and figurative reliance of marriage on practices and characters marked as marginal or even antithetical to the system of compulsory heterosexuality. Hetero-able normativity, as Collins posits it, clearly relies on the queer, disabled energy Dexter generates: not just to point out its limits but actually to keep it—and its institutions—running. If detection clears Eustace's name, queerness revives the marriage, even while unveiling its flaws. Valeria's development in relation to these men reinstates her marriage, while suffusing that reinstatement with a sense of loss.

My exploration of the particular gender/sexuality/ability trouble that Dexter generates is guided by Robert McRuer's concept of "queer theory and critical disability."[5] McRuer posits compulsory able-bodied-ness as a correlate to Adrienne Rich's compulsory heterosexuality: No one achieves either impossible state of "full" heterosexuality or able-bodiedness, but these dominant identities are nonetheless naturalized as essential and normal states that produce the alternatives (or "aberrances") of queerness and disability. Working with the ideas of Judith Butler, McRuer further argues for the social compulsion to continue the practices that constitute the two "impossible" identities of heterosexuality and able-bodiedness, so that noticeable gaps occur when someone fails to perform them. Queerness and disability are not simply parallel identities but by-products of mutually dependent systems: "the system of compulsory able-bodiedness that produces disability is thoroughly interwoven with the system of compulsory heterosexuality that produces queerness."[6]

McRuer draws both on Butler and on Michael Warner's critique of heteronormalcy to posit a key distinction between "virtual" and "critical" disability perspectives: "In contrast to a virtually queer identity, which would be experienced by anyone who failed to perform hetero-sexuality without contradiction and incoherence (i.e. everyone), a critically queer perspective could presumably mobilize the inevitable failure to approximate the norm." Similarly, "everyone is virtually disabled, both in the sense that able-bodied norms are impossible to achieve fully and because we will all experience disability if we live long enough," but critical or "severe" disability would mobilize the gaps between the normative and disabled body to generate "ability trouble" that might move us to "[reimagine and reshape] the limited forms of embodiment and desire proffered by the systems that would contain us all."[7]

As I will illustrate, Collins's work is full of such gaps, playfully and painfully wedged open by the performative presence of Miserrimus Dexter. We can view Dexter's refusals and failures to participate fully in heterosexuality or able-bodiedness as a critique of these systems and their cruel compulsions. As Collins develops Dexter as an integral and significant character, not simply a "material metaphor" who generates a story on others' behalf, Miserrimus's performances affirm his membership in the human community whose institutions he illuminates.[8]

In calling Dexter "queer," or "critically disabled," and later using the terms "camp" and "crip," I consciously deploy usages and words that were absent in 1875.[9] I will close by arguing, however, that a socially responsible reading of Dexter dictates the anachronism. While a key tenet of disability studies has been to recover disabled people's history and the historical dynamism of disability as a social category, historicist (rather than metaphoric or essentialist) readings of literary representations of human variation can be necessary but not sufficient as a means to more ethical scholarship.

Analyses that work analogically, by finding (for example) a historical figure "like" Dexter to use as a key to his meaning, can be particularly problematic. If there is a noticeable disjunction between the character and his or her historical analogue, this interpretive method can actually counteract the goal of reinstating disabled people into history. The analogue can be a Procrustean analytical bed whose effect is to reinscribe disability as an essential difference in persons rather than as a representational mode, minority group identity, or civil rights issue. History that does not fit can appear to humanize, while firmly redrawing the able/disabled binary and boundary. This has been the case with Miserrimus Dexter. Only a reading that makes use of our present theoretical moment can unpack the character, much less the novel's usefulness as a tool for social justice.

Valeria first encounters Dexter in a book in the library of a Major Fitz-David who forms the primary connection between her family and Eustace's. An old friend of Valeria's uncle whose evasive response to inquiries about Eustace before the wedding caused the uncle to advise against the marriage, Fitz-David is Valeria's first good lead in her quest for the truth about why Eustace has married her under a false name. Taken with her person (Valeria has for the first time in her life applied makeup, intuiting that it will help her appeal to the aging roué), Fitz-David leaves her alone in the library to make her own search, secretly watching her through a partly closed door.

Dexter's vehement defense of Eustace in the trial report inspires Valeria to find and speak to him. She visits with Dexter four times, in the course of which he cooks for her; composes and performs a song in her honor; misleads her regarding the truth about Sara Macallan's death; makes sexual advances toward her; and inspires her interest, disgust, pity, fear, anger, compassion, and forgiveness, before giving her, against his will and in the context of his mental dissolution, the key to the buried evidence of the truth that will restore Eustace's good name. In the process, Dexter also gives Valeria training in the range of practices, pleasures, and sorrows that can characterize adult relationships.

"The Hero of My Dreams"

Valeria first visits Dexter in the company of her mother-in-law, who offers a modicum of support for her husband's deserted wife. The chapters aptly titled "Miserrimus Dexter: First View" and "Miserrimus Dexter: Second View" continue the court report's pattern of tracing the visual details of Dexter's body in appraisal and erotic appreciation:[10]

> I saw plainly now the bright intelligent face and the large clear blue eyes, the lustrous waving hair of a light chestnut color, the long delicate white hands, and the magnificent throat and chest. . . . The deformity which degraded and destroyed the manly beauty of his head and breast was hidden from view by an Oriental robe of many colors, thrown over the chair like a coverlid. He was clothed in a jacket of black velvet, fastened loosely across his chest with large malachite buttons; and he wore lace ruffles at the ends of his sleeves, in the fashion of the last century. . . . The one defect that I could discover in his face was at the outer corners of his eyes, just under the temple. Here when he laughed, and in a lesser degree when he smiled, the skin contracted into quaint little wrinkles and folds, which looked strangely out of harmony with the almost youthful appearance of the rest of his face. . . . Speaking of him . . . from a woman's point of view I can only describe him as being an unusually handsome man. . . . A young girl, ignorant of what the Oriental robe hid from view, would have said to herself, the instant she looked at him, "Here is the hero of my dreams!" (213–14)

A few of the layers of Valeria's appreciation bear comment. First, the pleasure encompassing comments about "deformity" and "defect" is based on attributes that, like the earlier passage, describe a beauty not dependent upon Dexter's overtly manly parts, and the manly parts themselves are the site of wonderful ambiguity. Some critics interpret the last passage to mean that the Oriental robe hides a nothing, the absence of a penis.[11] As he is described as born "legless," however, I would suggest that the passage is equally legible as saying that the robe hides the end of Dexter's torso and the sockets of his hips—or even, that "what the Oriental robe hid" is what it would hide in any adult male: Valeria here articulates "a young girl's" premarital ignorance of what male genitals look like—an ignorance she presumably can no longer claim.

If the first inference is correct, however, how much queerer a situation emerges, one in which the links between biological sex, cultural gender, sexual practices, and the larger realm of desire are inescapably broken. Regardless of how we read the scene, it affirms McRuer's assertion of the mutual imbrication of sexual orientation and disability, both of which it troubles along with gender norms. As Teresa Mangum asserts, "His unclear sexual status and complex gendering are presented as his greatest deformities, motivating the spectator's guilty gaze."[12] This is a scene whose queerness is generated by Dexter's hybrid appearance, which inconsistently traverses the registers of disability, gender, and age; it is fully mobilized, however, by relational looking. It cannot be located solely in Miserrimus as an object, but it has to be equally anchored in Valeria (and the readers) who objectify him in curious and desiring ways.[13]

"What are those things, Mr. Dexter? and are we really going to eat them?"

On the next visit, following Valeria's similar appraisal of him, Miserrimus elaborates the queerness of his social body:

I have dressed, expressly to receive you, in the prettiest clothes I have. Don't be surprised. Except in this ignoble and material nineteenth century, men have always worn precious stuffs and beautiful colors as well as women. A hundred years ago a gentleman in pink silk was a gentleman properly dressed. Fifteen hundred years ago the patricians of the classic times wore bracelets exactly like mine. I despise the brutish contempt for beauty and the mean dread of expense which degrade a gentleman's costume to black cloth, and limit a gentleman's ornaments to a finger-ring, in the age I live in. I like to be bright and beautiful, especially when brightness and beauty come to see me. (232)

As Dennis Denisoff has noted, Dexter here is doing what we would now term "camping it up," consciously troubling the gender conventions of his time, not simply through dress but also through practices such as embroidery, which he does to compose himself when the conversation agitates him.[14] In Butler's terms, he has moved from "virtually" to "critically" queer. Later, Dexter dons a white cap and apron, pours Valeria a goblet of Clos Vougeot, "the king of burgundies," and cooks her the first truffles Valeria has ever eaten:

> He pierced and produced to view some little irregularly formed black objects, which might have been familiar enough to a woman accustomed to the luxurious tables of the rich; but which were a new revelation to a person like myself. . . . When I saw my host carefully lay out these occult substances of uninviting appearance on a clean napkin, and then plunge once more into profound reflection at the sight of them, my curiosity could be no longer restrained. I ventured to say, "What are those things, Mr. Dexter? and are we really going to eat them?"
>
> He started at the rash question, and looked at me, with hands outspread in irrepressible astonishment.
>
> "Where is our boasted progress?" he cried. "What is education but a name? Here is a cultivated person who doesn't know Truffles when she sees them!"
>
> "I have heard of truffles," I answered, humbly, "but I never saw them before. We had no such foreign luxuries as those, Mr. Dexter, at home in the North."
>
> Miserrimus Dexter lifted one of the truffles tenderly on his spike, and held it up to me in a favorable light. "Make the most of one of the few first sensations in this life which has no ingredient of disappointment lurking under the surface," he said. (245–46)

While he cooks, Valeria explores the macabre curiosities that decorate his room, including plaster casts of murderers, "a frightful little skeleton of a woman," and the skin of a Marquis. Not surprisingly, she finds the truffles less than savory after this appetizer: "On the marble slab were two plates, two napkins, two rolls of bread—and a dish, with another napkin on it, on which reposed two quaint little black balls. Miserrimus Dexter, regarding me with a smile of benevolent interest, put one of the balls on my plate, and took the other himself. 'Compose yourself, Mrs. Valeria,' he said. 'This is an epoch in your life. Your first Truffle! Don't touch it with the knife. Use the fork alone. And—pardon me;

this is most important—eat slowly.' I followed my instructions, and assumed an enthusiasm which I honestly confess I did not feel." (248) The luxuriant scene develops both Collins's hobbyhorse of the superiority of French to British culture and, more significantly, the growing relationship between a confidently queer man and a resilient young woman whose marital traumas have not dulled her readiness to explore life. It is exactly the kind of scene that might have developed Valeria and Eustace's marriage. The relationship between Dexter and Valeria is not unlike Carolyn Dever's description of the "affirmative, loving, nonmarital bonds" between same-sex couples that are a regular feature of Collins's marriage plots.[15]

Cripping It Up

Dexter's camping it up is interwoven with wonderful scenes in which Dexter uses his social body and the gazes that constitute it in a conscious, critical way that returns power to him—"cripping it up," as it were. Aware of Valeria's transfixed gaze, he decides that rather than explode in his pink coat, he will exercise:

> In an instant he was down on the floor, poised on his hands, and looking in the distance like a monstrous frog. Hopping down the room, he overthrew, one after another, all the smaller and lighter chairs as he passed them; arrived at the end, he turned, surveyed the prostrate chairs, encouraged himself with a scream of triumph, and leaped rapidly over chair after chair on his hands—his limbless body now thrown back from the shoulders, and now thrown forward to keep the balance—in a manner at once wonderful and horrible to behold. "Dexter's Leap-frog!" he cried, cheerfully, perching himself with his birdlike lightness on the last of the prostrate chairs when he had reached the further end of the room. "I'm pretty active, Mrs. Valeria, considering I'm a cripple." (259)

Later, he courts and counters the stares of the household of Benjamin, the aged bachelor and family friend in whose house Valeria resides after her husband leaves her. Valeria and Benjamin return home to find a distraught and offended housemaid complaining of a "Thing" having been carried into the library that "curdled my blood." Valeria finds Dexter "arrayed in his pink jacket, fast asleep in Benjamin's favourite armchair! No coverlid hid his horrible deformity. Nothing was sacrificed to conventional ideas of propriety, in his extraordinary dress. I could hardly wonder that the poor old housekeeper trembled from head to foot when she spoke of him" (292). Upon being disturbed, Dexter smiles "as innocently as a waking child" and greets Valeria sweetly, then disarms and discomposes Benjamin before the other gentleman can say a word: "'Excuse my getting up, sir. . . . I can't get up—I have no legs. You look as if you thought I was occupying your chair? If I am committing an intrusion, be so good as to put your umbrella under me, and give me a jerk. I shall fall on my hands, and I shan't be offended with you. I will submit to a tumble and a scolding—but please don't break my heart by sending me away'" (293). Directing his comments both at Benjamin and at the reader, Dexter both embodies the disabled body's failure to conform to expectations and calls our attention to the gaps. This might be what moving from "virtual" to "critical" disability might look like.

Fab Four:
Queer Eye for the New Wife of an Accused Murderer

The surprise with which other characters greet Dexter can distract us from noticing his multiple affinities with the other men in the plot, many of whom are simply closer to normative on the normative-queer continuum they share with the novel's most extreme character. Dexter seems extraordinary with his beautiful garments and bracelets, his "Black Museum" of Sadean objects and his paintings of cruelty. The aging roué Fitz-David, however, is queer by degrees, with his moustache and eyebrows dyed to match his brown wig, his meticulous and beautiful dress, and the album Valeria finds on her search for the court report. Fitz-David's album, in which he commemorates his past dalliances with locks of hair and the dates on which he broke things off with the women in question, is no less a fetish collection than Dexter's skins, only less extreme. Further, Fitz-David is a friend of Valeria's clergyman uncle, and both Fitz-David and Dexter are Eustace's friends, thus connecting not only Fitz-David but also Dexter with the novel's larger male community.

Dexter, with his pink jacket, perverse wit, and unabashed elitism about beauty and cuisine, combines with Fitz-David, Benjamin, and the lawyer Playfair to form a sort of Victorian *Queer Eye for the Straight Guy* crew.[16] They give Valeria the secret to her husband's innocence, but they also provide her another possible secret to marriage: its need for an excursion into that which is not marriage, the ebullient and eroti-cally charged life they inhabit. These men—or Fab Four—initiate and transform Valeria in ways not dissimilar to how *Queer Eye*'s Fab Five initiated and transformed various unhygienic, hair-troubled men with underdeveloped social and sartorial skills. If the Fab Five molded these fellows into men who could propose to their girlfriends, stop embarrass-ing their teenage daughters, or catch up with their hip wives, Dexter et al. introduce Valeria to the pleasures of the adult world, including makeup, grooming, cuisine, and couture.

Collins's queer world does not exclude women or married people. Valeria evolves a substantial interest in and attraction for Mrs. Hel-ena Beauly, whom Eustace desired and would have married (had he not married his first wife Sara to save Sara's reputation after she had behaved immodestly out of passion for him). Helena is desirable not only because she is the woman Eustace desired before her, nor because she may hold a clue to Sara's death, but also because she is a woman who has adventures, such as disguising herself as her maid in order to visit a masked ball—"not at all a reputable affair" including "all sorts of amusing people . . . ladies of doubtful virtue . . . and gentlemen on the outlying limits of society" (267). Another representative of this social circle is Lady Clarinda, who recounts Helena's adventure and dismisses as "What stuff!" Eustace's disapproval of the masked ball. Only briefly in the plot, Lady Clarinda is nonetheless a character Valeria takes the time to describe physically in great detail. The younger woman notes that Clarinda wears her hair exactly like Valeria's, and she speculates on Clarinda's mix of elite breeding and simplicity: "If you had accepted her for what she was, on the surface, you would have said, Here is the model of a noble woman who is perfectly free from pride. And if you had taken a liberty with her, on the strength of that conviction, she would have made you remember it to the end of her your life" (264–65). The passage itself enacts Valeria's imaginative taking of such a liberty, her interest in the woman and fear of being rebuffed.

Other women, including Eustace's dead wife, draw Valeria's atten-tion as models of adult women's passionate feelings. Karin Jacobson observes that Valeria's knowledge of Sara's unseen (because she is physi-cally plain) desire "creates a space for the representation of a sexually desiring woman and . . . sanctions the representation of herself as sexu-ally passionate for Eustace."[17] In fact, Sara is one of a series of displaced versions of herself Valeria sees, including Sara, Beauly, Dexter, Clarinda, Mrs. Macallan, and even Dexter's intellectually disabled cousin Ariel and Fitz-David's paramour Miss Hoighty. Her mimetic attraction to the women in Eustace's former social circle is yet another version of the queer desires the novel circulates.

Rejection: *The Queer Scandal of Disabled Sexuality*

In meeting these characters, Valeria acclimates herself to her husband's own social history. The goal of this education cannot be deferred forever, though many readers wish that it could. While the middle of the novel richly illustrates the idea of a continuum of fluid gendered and sexual identities, Collins does not leave us in a utopian realm of imagining that any place on the continuum is as acceptable as any other. I want to close with a passage that illustrates best of all how heterosexuality and able-bodiedness are, as McRuer argues, imbricated systems, and how these compulsions work in the context of *The Law and the Lady*.

When Dexter arrives uninvited in Benjamin's house, Valeria meets with him alone. He has by this time introduced Valeria to his own sexuality, but she has not narrated it as such, possibly to cover her own knowledge of what lies beneath the Oriental robe, or because of her inability or refusal to connect sexual desire with a disabled man. Dexter has queried her on the terms of the separation with her husband, contrived to have her move around the room so he can watch her walk, and noted her resemblance to Sara, the dead woman he loved; he has even grabbed her hand in agitation while discussing the trial. For her part, Valeria has noted his exceptional beauty; feared his mood changes; experienced his wild, bardic harp music; eaten his truffles and drunk his wine; and decided that he is not, despite others' assessment, mad. She has responded to his touch with chills and a rebuke. At the start of their conversation at Benjamin's house, then, Valeria's feelings for Dexter are clearly not limited to the compassion of an able-bodied woman for a disabled man.

In this scene, Dexter affirms his love for the dead Sara and his sorrow that anyone might suspect him of bringing about her death. When Valeria moves close to him, avowing she feels no such suspicion, he holds her hand and "devour[s] it with kisses" (299). Valeria's first-person account makes the scene immediate and sensory: "His lips burned me like fire. He twisted himself suddenly in the chair, and wound his arm around my waist" (299). For the *Graphic*, the illustrated "family" periodical in which the novel was first serialized, this was "an attempted violation" of a heroine we soon find out is not just married but preg-nant.[18] I would suggest that the scandal is more complicated. The scene dramatizes the breaking of a particularly Victorian (and later) compact in which disabled people can be objects of sympathy and financial sup-port as long as they refrain from disrupting a cultural frame that denies them agency and sexuality. Dexter's advance, especially occurring in response to sympathy, is a direct violation of this social compact. In another layer, for this act to be truly "scandalous" it has to be a "styl-ized repetition" of a heteronormative and able-bodied act—"attempting to kiss the heroine." This, of course, it is, as is Valeria's initial rebuff. For the advance to be forgivable, however—and on the terms it is for-given—is an indication of its ultimate failure. Dexter's disability makes this a queer kind of scandal, as the close of the scene articulates.

When Benjamin arrives in response to her cry for help, Valeria says, "You can't lay your hand on a cripple" (299), and watches from in hid-ing as Dexter's servant takes him away: "The rough man lifted his master with a gentleness that surprised me. 'Hide my face,' I heard Dexter say to him, in broken tones. He opened his coarse pilot-jacket, and hid his master's head under it, and so went silently out—with the deformed creature held to his bosom, like a woman sheltering her child" (300). While it domesticates and infantilizes Dexter, this last view also alerts us to the sadness and shame that are significant constituent factors in both queer and disabled identities within most cultural frameworks.[19]

Here I want to touch again on the notion of compulsion rather than volition that Annamarie Jagose reminds us is central to Butler's theories of the performance of gender.[20] It is possible for much of the novel to simply delight in Dexter's moments of camping and cripping it up as voluntary practices in which he pleases himself, partly through his control of social situations. Significantly, Collins continues to the point of the burning kisses that mark the limits of Dexter's volition, and on to the image of him cradled in the arms of the servant. The novel thus reminds us that the dictates of "normal" sexualized behavior, especially in conjunction with atypical embodiment or any other socially stigma-tized attribute, are only flexible up to a point. Beyond that point lies the shame of failure, itself as ritualized and compulsory as the successful kiss that Valeria and Eustace share early in the novel.

Valeria's excursion into queer life, similarly, is not a playful or vol-untary departure of marriage but one catalyzed by marital trauma and Eustace's rejection. The biggest secret of the book overall, and the one Dexter imparts to this wife-in-training, may be not only the variety of practices and pleasures that underpin human relationships but also the shame and sadness that pervade them, especially in the context of a regime of normalcy. Valeria's rejection of Dexter's queer, crippled body mirrors, as Jacobson points out, Sara's rejection of Dexter and also Eustace's rejection of Sara; it further suggests the fear Valeria has of Eustace's rejection. The impossible ideal of a mutually desiring heterosexual union, then, exists nowhere in the rich fabric of mismatched desires, misunderstandings, depression, and failure that Collins charts so fully in this novel. No one achieves it: it is merely Dexter and Sara who are the unhappiest victims of the system of compulsory heterosexuality and bodily normalcy.

Despite her identification with Dexter's experience, however, Valeria's rejection of his queer, crippled body is necessary to shore up this impossible ideal. If Dexter invokes both a celebratory rejection of conventions and an abject failure to meet them, both subversion and failure are finally contained by convention. My reference to *Queer Eye for the Straight Guy* is purposefully connected to this dynamic. Nominally a celebration of queerness (and a fairly assimilationist version of it at that), the object of the show was to produce or reinforce heterosexual marriages; the use of queer handmaidens to produce straight marriages, however, is one of the things the show naturalized and trained us not to query. The middle of the novel is a time of generic jouissance (the pleasure of suspense and detection) as well as the pleasure of sex/gender/ability disorder, with Dexter at the heart of both threads. These narrative threads, however, are dynamic and purposeful no less than the degenerative disease, or disease of degeneration, that gradually burns out his volatile presence; all three move toward closure, unknotting at once. Dexter gives up his secrets; Eustace, who has had a serious illness, returns home with his wife; and the lawyer Playfair solves the mystery.[21]

The passion that Dexter articulates for Valeria, however, is the last trace of sexual energy in the book. In their final meeting, he involuntarily gives up, in a deranged speech, the piece that completes the puzzle of Sara Macallan's death: Sara poisoned herself after Dexter gave her the diary in which Eustace wrote of his distaste for her. Valeria returns to a subdued marriage, changed not only by Eustace's illness and the birth of a son but also by what she has learned in Dexter's company of the dimensions of human pleasure and pain. Soon after, she learns that Dexter's mental and physical dissolution have ended in his death. It is in this subdued and mournful mood that Collins leaves us, connected through Valeria to Dexter as a fully evolved character whose failures to meet the impossible identities of able-heteronormalcy are never completely domesticated and smoothed over. Dexter's irregularity persists as that which exposes the fissures and failures of the marriage plot, marking above all how much it depends on the very energy it needs to repudiate in the form of characters like him.

Butler's *Bodies That Matter* offers a useful model of how to read this ending. Rather than the abject body that "fails to materialize" within the discourse of "sex," forming the "necessary 'outside' . . . for the bodies which, in materializing the norm, qualify as bodies that matter," Dexter intermittently and partially materializes that norm to the extent that we see both the limits of its constructedness and the losses it produces. And instead of simply producing "a field of deformation, which, in failing to qualify as the fully human, fortifies those regulatory norms," Dexter argues for "a radical rearticulation of what qualifies as bodies that matter, ways of living that count as 'life,' lives worth protecting, lives worth saving, lives worth grieving."[22] It is tempting to end a reading of *The Law and the Lady* there, with grief. There is no resolution—inside or outside the novel—to the sense of loss Dexter's death produces. Perhaps this is the point: his death, the marriage of Fitz-David, and the birth of Valeria's son combine to produce the troubled affect and affective meaning that shape the novel's end.

McRuer discusses films such as *As Good as It Gets* as examples of invoking "the crisis of authority that currently besets heterosexual and able-bodied norms" only in order to resolve it.[23] This is always a charge that critics have leveled at the Victorian novel, and more particularly the sensation novel: its ultimate goal is to conserve and reiterate the status quo. In *The Law and the Lady*, it is true that order of a sort is restored with Valeria and her husband's reunion and the birth of their son. That this resolution follows on the heels of the deaths of Miserrimus and Ariel and the marriage (and instant aging) of Major Fitz-David suggests that the excision of nonnormative bodies, practices, and pleasures from the plot is a precondition of its resolution. The elegiac affect hanging over this happy ending, however, tells us otherwise. Dever memorably characterizes Victorian "legal" marriage as "a sinkhole of deception, hostility, abuse and grubby materialism at worst, and at best a site of placid, jog-trot boredom." As we close *The Law and the Lady*, the Macallan marriage is not either of these, but the base from which it moves forward is a refusal of awareness: the letter revealing how Eustace's rejection of his first wife led to her suicide remains sealed, so that only Valeria and the reader have access to the shame and pain or rejection experienced by Sara Macallan—and Miserrimus Dexter. At the same time, we remember the novel's middle and its affirmation of *The Law and the Lady* as a key example of Collins's "erotically pluralist novels."[24]

So while the ending repudiates queerness and disability, it does so in a way that shows both the compulsoriness of the rejection and the loss it entails. What enables both the loss and its meaning is Dexter's imbrication within the web of human relationships, as part of that human circle rather than its "outside." The novel itself demands that we make sense of Dexter on these terms.

Critical Cul-de-Sacs

While there are relatively few essays devoted to *The Law and the Lady*, Dexter figures prominently in most of them. He is also noted in most book-length studies of Collins. Called an "effeminate dwarf" and "half-human monster," he has often been read biographically, as a figure for the author; metaphorically, as a figure for the plain Victorian woman, or the female detective; or historically, as a referent for the Victorian popular and/or medical "curiosity" or for nineteenth-century theories of psychology, physiology, and hereditary degeneration.[25] Despite their differences, most critics from 1951 to the present have made sense of Dexter in ways that reiterate his separation from the world.

Any reading of Dexter as metaphor is problematic from the start, given how thoroughly developed he is as a *character*, as opposed to a *figure*, especially in comparison to Eustace. More to the point, Dexter as a metaphor must be distanced from the human circle in order to shed light on characters like Valeria, who are only temporarily displaced from a normative community role and long to return to it (and whose longing to return is partly what makes them "normal"). His gender-scrambling appearance and behavior, for example, are for Mangum "simultaneously a reminder of and distraction from the failure of those crucial boundaries between male and female, masculine and feminine" that Valeria's detective work enacts, a useful elucidation of Valeria's situation but not of Dexter's own engagement in the world of gendered energies.[26]

The historicist readings that inform the work of Mangum, Taylor, Rosner, Denisoff, and others are provocative and important, but still troubling in their effects. Mangum's thoughtful study of the novel's interweaving of cultural constructions of gender and disability features an important section on the ways in which the novel anatomizes the visual dynamics between the atypically embodied and "norms," positioning *The Law and the Lady* as part of a larger history of medical, popular, and literary displays of anomalous bodies, including the work of Geoffroy-St. Hilaire and Gould and Pyle; Bartholomew Fair; Tod Browning's film *Freaks*; and Katherine Dunn's novel *Geek Love*. When her essay moves from the novel's recurrent emphasis on curiosity to a reading of Dexter through the analogues of Victorian "curiosities" or working-class "freaks" such as Joseph Merrick or the American Hervey Leech, however, it limits itself in important ways. While Leech, like Dexter, was characterized by "perfect symmetry, strength, and beauty" above the waist and the capacity for "feats of leaping," as Mangum herself notes, theatrical display is not Dexter's context.[27] If Collins did use Leech for a template, retaining aspects of Leech's bodily configuration and exaggerating others (removing the limbs entirely), he also specifically moved Dexter away from these public arenas of singularity and into a domestic space—however queer that space might be—and a circle of human relations that includes, at least for a time, both "freaks" and "norms." Dexter's privacy and the class status associated with it are in fact marked by the text; his estate is a crumbling holdout against the Victorian suburbs Collins so detested; his habits of couture and cuisine are funded by (crumbling) hereditary privilege. While the coded visual distance—scopophilia, even—between the curious reader and Dexter is compelling to consider, the fact that the novel critiques this visual dynamic between disabled and nondisabled people makes it a vexed key to the historical meaning of Dexter.

Further, this visual dynamic, and the economic relations historically affiliated with it, do not hold up in the novel. Many of Dexter's displays, like the courtroom entrance, are self-choreographed performances in which it is abundantly clear who decides when the coverlid will fall off. Rather than supplicate able-bodied characters' pleasure and money, Dexter's bodily shows produce discomfort in everyone but himself. Even if Collins's own display of Dexter as curiosity—and of curiosity about Dexter—is behind the character's self-exposures, these are significant gaps in socioeconomic context, public affect, and narrative power between the character and his proposed analogues.

A more precise way of discussing Dexter and his relationship to the web of human relationships is through the discourse of degeneration in which he and his developmentally disabled cousin "Ariel" are variant expressions of the same hereditary taint. This is one of the points Jenny Bourne Taylor makes in her analysis of Dexter's links to Victorian theories of consciousness and psychology, which were often closely connected to hereditarian thought. Within that discourse, Dexter's advances toward Valeria are scandalous not just because she is married (and, we later learn, pregnant), but because the pre-eugenic discourse of degeneration argues that no one should have procreative sex with Dexter. Scientific interest, however, is not the primary energy the narrative invests in him. Mary Rosner's reading of Dexter variously as a "monster" or mutant, a man with an unhealthy body and mind, and a sideshow freak does not resolve the problem. Dennis Denisoff is more persuasive in his focused connection of Dexter with Max Nordau's theories of the degenerate artist.

Yet another historicist tack that no scholar has explored might be to read Dexter as a representation of the double amputees that were not that unusual either in industrialized and post–Crimean War Britain or in our own age of war veterans.[28] This "normalizing" reading, however, would require us to elide all the extravagance Collins insists on investing in Dexter, just as the other historicist readings require us to see him as detached from social life and domesticity.

None of these historical analogues is a very good fit with Dexter, and this is actually part of the novel's point. Locating Dexter within late-Victorian culture, Collins pointedly delineates the confusion and ambivalence in other characters' responses to Dexter in a way that richly suggests his cultural constructedness. Is he a "crippled gentleman," a "wretched crippled creature," a "Thing" that curdles the looker's blood, a "deformed creature," "a Portent," "an Indian idol"? There is no clear consensus of how to talk about a man with Dexter's body, much less about the feelings he evokes.[29] And, despite a series of rich and interesting analyses, critics have been similarly frustrated. We have not yet found a way to consider either Dexter's failures or subversions of convention in full context of the human community without in some way retooling the character to fit our critical purposes.

And yet, I would argue, this is exactly the work we still need to pursue, both as scholars and as citizens. If we have attached Dexter to particular cultural gaps, we have not considered those gaps as filled with energy that might be mobilized against the oppression of particular kinds of bodies and practices within Victorian culture or our own. Further, if as Mangum argues, "encounters with Victorian sensation writers' obsessive attention to physical deformities embarrass, even shame twentieth-century readers," we have not done much in the way of exploring the dynamics by which that shame is written on the bodies of characters such as Dexter or transferred to our own readerly bodies. The critical frameworks we have used to discuss Dexter have thus diminished the power of Dexter's critique of normative bodies and practices, useful both in Collins's time and in our own era of social inequities.

A substantial part of the pleasure of reading *The Law and the Lady* originates in the dramatic, curious presence of Dexter, who catalyzes the novel's most memorably playful and bleak moments, but a productive critical analysis must avoid using the alterity of the past as a *cordon sanitaire* for that pleasure. Critics have become more suspicious of metaphoric, unhistoricized readings of literary representations of human difference; but historicist readings have their own pleasures and dangers. Locating Dexter in the Victorian freak show, for example, not only tinkers with the plot of Collins's novel but also preserves our enjoyment of this character in an imagined Victorian tableau in which our readerly spectatorship has no relationship to our extrafictional practices of living and looking. This approach may subtly reinforce disabled *figures'* separation from actual human *communities*, keeping alive the concept of "The Disabled" as an undifferentiated group of people distinguished by their essential difference from nondisabled people. Alternately, historicist readings that invoke an equality discourse (Dexter as normal disabled person) run the risk of removing the pointed commentary on social relationships that figures such as Dexter enact. There are no easy formulas, then, for ethical readings of representations of human variation. As scholars of literature and culture, we need both to historicize carefully and to ask what our work and its use of history make possible. As the analysis of characters such as Dexter inevitably suggests the place of disabled people in contemporary social relations, we need to consider which historicist readings actually help return disabled figures to the human community, and which ones reinscribe disability as radical difference under the cover of history and its legitimating power.

Conclusion

We may have only recently found the critical tools—a combination of queer theory and critical disability studies—that will let us make full meaning of Miserrimus Dexter, reclaiming him as part of the human circle. We can make more nuanced sense of that circle by including

Dexter in it. We may also be able to move, through Dexter, beyond the critical approach of identifying stereotypical ways of representing the sexuality of disabled people. If a critical commonplace has been that disabled men, for example, are culturally constructed as castrated, meaning either feminization or asexualization, queer theory allows us to consider the many representations that exceed that phallocentric framework—those in which disabled male characters are in fact highly sexualized, but in whom "sex" is complexly nuanced, not unitary or anchored to biological givens.[30]

A critical disability and queer reading allows us to consider Dexter beyond the terms of metaphor or figuration and more in terms of a material representation of the relationships that exist and might exist among a range of embodiments and sexualities. To put it very simply, disability-centered and queer readings might open up the novel's messages in wider ways and to a wider group of readers, including those for whom bodies and desires like Dexter's are viable subject positions rather than curiosities. Such an opening of the text might also invite new ways to position the character and the novel in their Victorian cultural web, in which the conventions Collins flouted throughout his life may have been less consistently rigid than we have imagined.

Notes

1. Jeanne Fahnestock, "The Heroine of Irregular Features: Physiognomy and Conventions of Heroine Description," *Victorian Studies* 24, no. 3 (Spring 1981): 325–50.

2. Helena Michie points out that in nineteenth-century literature and life alike, "the most famous honeymoon stories are stories about failure," from Frankenstein and Tess of the D'Urbervilles to John and Effie Ruskin. See *Victorian Honeymoons: Journeys to the Conjugal* (Cambridge: Cambridge University Press, 2006), 1.

3. Wilkie Collins, *The Law and the Lady* (1875; Oxford: Oxford University Press, 1992), 173. Subsequent references are cited parenthetically in the text.

4. See, for example, Martha Stoddard Holmes, *Fictions of Affliction: Physical Disability in Victorian Culture* (Ann Arbor: University of Michigan Press, 2004).

5. See Robert McRuer, "As Good as It Gets: Queer Theory and Critical Disability," *GLQ* 9, nos. 1–2 (2003): 79–105; and "Compulsory Able-Bodiedness and Queer/Disabled Existence," in *Disability Studies: Enabling the Humanities*, ed. Sharon L. Snyder, Brenda Jo Brueggemann, and Rosemarie Garland-Thomson (New York: MLA, 2002), 88–99.

6. McRuer, "Compulsory," 89.

7. Ibid., 95, 96.

8. See David Mitchell and Sharon Snyder, *Narrative Prosthesis: Disability and the Dependencies of Discourse* (Ann Arbor: University of Michigan Press, 2000).

9. My reading of Dexter as "queer" should not be read as positioning him in a homo/heterosexual binary, but rather noting his power to confuse that binary. His object choices, which are consistently feminine, mark him as heterosexual; his performances of gender explicitly disrespect the binary; and the desires he articulates and mobilizes in others are disruptively unconventional. Here my exploration might be productively considered in conversation with Melissa Free's essay in this volume. Free explores queerness as homosexuality and distinguishes it from the quality of "freakishness" that is valued in the novels she discusses. Regardless of Collins's novel predating the use of the term "homosexual," I argue that Dexter's queerness cannot be accommodated by this term.

10. We learn later in the novel that the account we read of Dexter's courtroom entrance is not an extract from the report but Valeria's paraphrase, a fascinating narrative device.

11. See, for example, Teresa Mangum, "Wilkie Collins, Detection, and Deformity," *Dickens Studies Annual* 26 (1998): 296.

12. Ibid., 294.

13. The portrait of Dexter combines a number of the visual rhetorics of disability that Rosemarie Garland-Thomson identifies in her important essay "The Politics of Staring: Visual Rhetorics of Disability in Popular Photography," in Snyder et al., 56–75. The novel's illustrations, as Mangum observes, provide a strange countereffect: instead of rendering Dexter's manly and womanly appeal, they portray him as a "round-shouldered, sad-faced elderly gentleman in a wheelchair" (287–88).

14. See Dennis Denisoff, "Framed and Hung: Collins and the Economic Beauty of the Manly Artist," in *Reality's Dark Light: The Sensational Wilkie Collins*, ed. Maria K. Bachman and Don Richard Cox (Knoxville: University of Tennessee Press, 2003), 34–58.

15. See Carolyn Dever, "The Marriage Plot and Its Alternatives," in *The Cambridge Companion to Wilkie Collins*, ed. Jenny Bourne Taylor (Cambridge: Cambridge University Press, 2006), 112.

16. The show aired on the Bravo television network from 2003 to 2006 and again beginning in October 2007.

17. Karin Jacobson, "Plain Faces, Weird Cases: Domesticating the Law in Collins's *The Law and the Lady* and the Trial of Madeleine Smith," in Bachman and Cox, 305.

18. Collins was privately and publicly infuriated by the editors' censorship of this section of the novel. See Jenny Bourne Taylor, "Appendix" to *The Law and the Lady*, 415–18.

19. See Michael Warner, *The Trouble with Normal: Sex, Politics, and the Ethics of Queer Life* (New York: The Free Press, 1999). Much of his book explores shame as a constitutive factor in the construction of queer identities and the public politics of AIDS.

20. Annamarie Jagose, *Queer Theory: An Introduction* (New York: New York University Press, 1996), 86–87.

21. Eustace's return is catalyzed only by his illness; Valeria continues her detective work in secret, against his wishes, through Playfair, until she can finally give her husband the means to declare his innocence. The ending leaves unopened the letter from Sara Macallan that tells of her suicide in response to Eustace's unspoken rejection, thus clearing him legally while indicting him in other ways. This plot element echoes *The Moonstone*'s similar one of rejection and a hidden/buried letter that publicizes it.

22. Judith Butler, "Introduction," *Bodies That Matter* (New York: Routledge, 1993), 16.

23. McRuer, "Compulsory," 97.

24. Dever, "Marriage Plot," 114, 112.

25. See Kenneth Robinson, *Wilkie Collins: A Biography* (London: Bodley Head, 1951); Catherine Peters, *The King of Inventors: A Life of Wilkie Collins* (Princeton, NJ: Princeton University Press, 1991); Mary Rosner, "Deviance in *The Law and the Lady*: The Uneasy Positionings of Mr. Dexter," *Victorian Newsletter* 106 (Fall 2004): 9–14; Jenny Bourne Taylor, *In the Secret Theatre of Home: Wilkie Collins, Sensation Narrative, and Nineteenth-Century Psychology* (London: Routledge, 1988); and Denisoff. For a useful summary of twentieth-century readings (to the 1980s) of Dexter, along with her own intelligent reading of him, see Sue Lonoff, *Wilkie Collins and His Victorian Readers: A Study in the Rhetoric of Authorship* (New York: AMS, 1982), 163–67, 259n49.

26. Mangum, 295.

27. Unlike Dexter, as Mangum notes, Leech did have legs, albeit exceptionally small ones. See *London Times*, April 27, 1847. For more on Leech, see James W. Cook, Jr., "Of Men, Missing Links, and Nondescripts," in *Freakery: Cultural Spectacles of the Extraordinary Body*, ed. Rosemarie Garland-Thomson (New York: New York University Press, 1996), 139–57. Garland-Thomson's collection makes significant contributions to the cultural history of "freaks."

28. For recent work on the history of amputees and prosthetics, see David Gerber, *Disabled Veterans in History* (Ann Arbor: University of Michigan Press, 2000), and *Artificial Parts, Practical Lives: Modern Histories of Prosthetics*, ed. Katherine Ott, David Serlin, and Stephen Mihm (New York: New York University Press, 2002).

29. In this, Dexter is a precursor of the "nameless deformity" of Edward Hyde in Robert Louis Stevenson's "The Strange Case of Dr. Jekyll and Mr. Hyde," published in 1896.

30. Part of this complexity is historical; some theorists argue for an un-self-conscious sexualization of disability before the Victorian era, followed by the rise of charity and the instantiation of a disabled master identity of charitable object that was, at least officially, incompatible with that of sexual object or sexual being (despite or because of the ease with which the two identities may be collapsed). Thanks to Leila Granahan for raising the question of disabled representations that do not fit critical commonplaces any more than they do popular-culture stereotypes.

11

FREAKS THAT MATTER

The Dolls' Dressmaker,
the Doctor's Assistant,
and the Limits of Difference

MELISSA FREE

———•———

THE POWER to transform belongs to freaks in Charles Dickens's *Our Mutual Friend* (1865) and Wilkie Collins's *The Moonstone* (1868). Physically challenged, visibly disfigured, emotionally isolated, and sexually deviant (in truth or innuendo), *Our Mutual Friend*'s Jenny Wren and *The Moonstone*'s Ezra Jennings are viewed as freaks by other characters in their respective novels. In a world in which impairment, deformity, slander, and queerness are grounds for abjection, Jenny and Jennings navigate unfriendly borders by sharpening their insight, honing their sensitivity, and developing their imaginations. Thus empowered, they manage to not only survive but also make themselves useful, reading and communicating unarticulated desires that others find incomprehensible. In their service as interpreters—of the lovelorn and the dying—these outcast figures, sacrificing their own queer attachments, become critical aids to the traditional heroes and heroines whose lives they transform and save. In the limited but representative contexts of these two Victorian novels, marriage (the crux of Victorian society) is the product of epiphany facilitated by—even *contingent* on—freakery, the powers of a sacrificial body serving as a nexus of difference. A textual receptacle for nonnormative desire, race, and physicality, the freakish body matters because of rather than in spite of that which makes it different, though its ostensible value resides in its ability to bolster the normative. Useful in establishing order but necessarily disposable once that order is restored, queer freakishness is the conduit transformed—or destroyed—in the process of generating heterosexual union.

Charles Dickens introduces the character of Jenny Wren as a freak who is yet far more than a "queer little comicality."[1] "A child—a dwarf—a girl—a something," she calls out to the visitors on her doorstep to come in: "I can't get up . . . because my back's bad, and my legs are queer. But I'm the person of the house" (271). "[A] child in years" but a "woman in self-reliance and trial" (498), Jenny is a "Doll's Dressmaker"[2] who supports both herself and her alcoholic father. Rejected and taunted by other children and plagued by pain and loneliness, Jenny uses her imagination to endure a brutal childhood, one in which she is "surrounded by drunken people" (277). Her intense familiarity with physical and emotional suffering and her heightened imaginative faculty, which help her survive difference, further mark her as different. "Far from blurring the contradictions of Jenny's make-up, Dickens heightens the inconsistencies. She is compounded of opposites."[3] She is at once silly and serious, creative and practical, abrasive and tender, young and old, deformed yet angelic. Jenny's duality exists both beneath and on the surface; it is noticeable—visible—much like that of Ezra Jennings, whose "doubleness is inscribed on his body, making him a walking set of contrasts."[4]

An "explicitly cross-category figure,"[5] Jennings is visually and hermeneutically striking. A doctor's assistant, he has become an opium addict in his attempt to manage the pain of his own mysterious, debilitating, and agonizing ailment. He suffers equally, however, from his status as an outcast, the result of others' discomfort with "his appearance [and] mixed race, and the stigma of some 'horrible accusation'" that hangs over him.[6] Unattractive, striking, and of indeterminate age, his "remarkable" body "produce[s] an unfavorable impression"—disgust, distrust, "downright terror," and, at best, pity—in others: "Judging him by his figure and his movement, he was still young. Judging him by his face, . . . he looked [old]. . . . [H]is fleshless cheeks had fallen into deep hollows, over which the bone projected like a pent-house. . . . His marks and wrinkles were innumerable. From this strange face, eyes, deeply sunk in their orbits—looked out at you. . . ."[7] Observing that his "complexion [is] of a gipsy darkness," his nose is the nose of "the ancient people of the East," and his hair is starkly black and white, divided arbitrarily, as by a "freak of Nature," "without the slightest gradation of grey to break the force of the extraordinary contrast" (321), Blake guesses that "there was the mixture of some foreign race in his English blood" (367). For Jaya Mehta, "Jennings's appearance—his gypsy complexion, his asiatic nose, his parti-colored hair"—signals and "affronts" "the code of racial segregation. . . . His very body figures the mingling of East and West."[8] "The bastard child of the British Empire," "imperialism's shameful secret,"[9] Jennings was "born, and partly brought up, in one of our colonies. My father was an Englishman; but my mother - - We are straying away from our subject . . .'" (366). Collins suggests but does not explicate Jennings's colonial heritage,[10] an allusion enhanced by Jennings's placement of Henry Mackenzie's *The Man of Feeling* (1771), which includes an anti-imperialist diatribe, in Blake's bedroom on the night of the reconstruction of the theft.[11] On the skin and in the blood, Jennings is tainted—marked as different.

Treated poorly by his family for reasons not specified and hounded by "slander that was death to [his] character" (374)—by rumor and innuendo—Jennings's malady is an English malady. Perceived as a contaminative subject, he is actually the victim of colonial subjugation, "the violence and cruelty of British imperialism which obscures its motives and accuses its victims."[12] Despite Jennings's ill-founded reputation, Blake *needs* the help of the gypsy-skinned stranger, whose liminal status makes him an able translator. In order to secure it, however, he must confess his own suspected criminality, for only then does Jennings become willing to assist. Born to a colonial subject on colonial soil, Ezra is not only permitted but requested to enter the inviolate English family circle, and thus he becomes "simultaneously the outcast [and] the . . . detective" who "interpret[s] and explain[s]" the insensible mumblings (of Dr. Candy) that no one can else understand.[13] Like his counterpart in *Our Mutual Friend*, Jennings's importance—to others in the novel and to the novel itself—hinges on his status as an outsider, precisely because his familiarity with the unusual makes him an able translator of words spoken at the edge of death.

Jenny and Jennings are meant to be recognizably freakish, but their roles are more complex than those generally attributed to Victorian freaks and monsters—that is, as conduits for sympathy, horror, or discipline. Henry James, simplistically—dismissively, even—described Jenny as a "pathetic character, . . . a little monster [who] belongs to the troop of hunchbacks, imbeciles, and precocious children who have carried on the sentimental business in all Mr. Dickens's novels."[14] More recently and more searchingly, Judith Halberstam has interpreted the Gothic monster as "the place of corruption," noting that its Victorian manifestations represent "a symptomatic moment in which boundaries between good and evil, health and perversity, crime and punishment, truth and deception, inside and outside dissolve. . . . Gothic fiction . . . produces the deviant . . . opposite which the normal . . . can be known."[15] In her Foucauldian reading of the Gothic's "significant role in the history of discipline and punishment," she adduces that "the Gothic monster is precisely a disciplinary sign, a warning of what may happen if the body is imprisoned by its desires or if the subject is unable to discipline him- or herself fully and successfully."[16] Though the freakish characters of Victorian fiction, two of whom I examine here, should indeed be read in light of their relationships with more traditional characters, they do far more than stabilize notions of the normative. Indeed, the gallery of freaks who populate the fiction of the nineteenth century should also be read for their capacity to construct themselves. Rejected by society, they become more than self-reliant; they become useful. "[I]ndustrious [and] virtuous," and possessing "a secret sympathy or power" (OMF 332, 809), Jenny and Jennings "give . . . new life" (MS 410) to others, demonstrating that difference can be (re)generative. Without these freaks, the next generation—"little Miss Harmon[. . .]" in *Our Mutual Friend* (883) and the child Rachel is carrying in *The Moonstone*—would not exist. In their own way, Jenny and Jennings are an intrinsic part of (pro)creation.

Freaks That Desire

Our Mutual Friend corroborates Janet Todd's contention that "although the action in the [Victorian] novel usually takes place in the heterosexual plot, its sentiment may be centered in female friendship."[17] Jenny's love for Lizzie, the virtuous heroine who nominates Jenny as her closest ally despite familial objections, is laden with romantic nuances. At every opportunity, Jenny's hand "cre[eps]" (283) or "st[eals] up to her friend's" (333), her arm slips "round her friend's waist," or she "manage[s] a . . . touch or two of her nimble hands" (403). On one occasion, Jenny "rock[s] herself on Lizzie's breast" (405). Sitting before the fire, brushing out her own and Lizzie's hair, Jenny "lay[s] a cheek on one of [Lizzie's] dark folds, seem[ingly] blinded by her own clustering curls to all but the fire, while the fine handsome face and brow of Lizzie [are] revealed without obstruction in the somber light" (403). "Lizzie-Mizzie-Wizzie," Jenny affectionately calls out to her friend at sunset on this "sultry night," the first time that we see the pair alone together, "'This is what your loving Jenny Wren calls the best time in the day and night'. . . . Her real name was Fanny Cleaver; but she had long ago chosen to bestow upon herself the appellation of Miss Jenny Wren" (283).

Here, in what Helena Michie describes as a "confession scene, an oddly erotic centerpiece to the novel,"[18] we are told of the one change that Jenny effects upon not another but herself. Though far from nominal, the change she makes is her name itself. Unlike Jennings, who, despite the protection it would afford him, "scorn[s] the guilty evasion of living under an assumed name" and keeps his own "ugly" name (375, 322), Jenny Wren discards her given name, Fanny Cleaver, and creates the name by which she is known. Her new appellation fits her, as the narrator points out, because Jenny, like the "bird whose name she ha[s] taken" (403), is uncommonly bright-eyed and watchful, qualities that serve her in interpretation—reading and reading *for* other people. Jenny's original name was not wholly unsuitable if one considers the contradictory double meaning of "cleave" (from which Cleaver is derived): to bring together and to tear apart. Jenny herself acts as a cleaver, simultaneously bringing together (Lizzie and Eugene) and splitting apart (Lizzie and herself) in a single action: discovering a word. Also, like the word "cleave"—and like Ezra Jennings—Jenny is inherently contradictory.

Perhaps Jenny rejects the name of Fanny Cleaver because of its sexual—and homosexual—suggestiveness. The name "Fanny" would have been considered rather crude in nineteenth-century Britain given that, then as now, fanny "referred to female genitals."[19] "Cleave," a name that Daniel Defoe's Moll Flanders takes for herself during her most promiscuous period, is also a word that has historically connoted the sexual. Writes David Blewett, "In the slang of [Defoe's] time an immoral woman was said to be one who would cleave."[20] Less than a century and a half later, Victorian readers would also have been familiar with this association. Sedgwick writes that "Fanny Cleaver is a name that hints at aggression—specifically, at rape, and perhaps at homosexual rape," and contends that the name signals "two scenes in *Our Mutual Friend* whose language . . . strongly suggest[s] male rape."[21] I would argue for a reading of Fanny Cleaver that is closer to the source: Jenny's real name, mentioned only once—in the intimate fireside scene referred to above—connotes her own homosexual, wholly unaggressive desire for Lizzie, a one-sided (homo)sexual attraction that is never consummated, a cleaving that never occurs.[22]

Having disclosed the fact but not the history of Jenny's name change, the narrator cedes to Jenny: "I have been thinking . . . as I sat at work to-day, what a thing it would be, if I should be able to have your company till I am married, or at least courted. Because when I am courted, I shall make Him do some of the things that you do for me. He couldn't brush my hair like you do, or help me up and down stairs like you do, and he couldn't do anything like you do; but he could take my work home, and he could call for orders in his clumsy way. And he shall too. *I'll* trot him about, I can tell him!" (284). "Jenny, of course, has . . . sexual desire," writes Michie, who points to such "fantasies of an erotic future" as evidence;[23] but the erotic, contrary to Michie's opinion, cannot be found in Jenny's description of her imaginary husband, someone more servant than lover, more nuisance than pleasure. The erotic, rather, is evident in the intimacy between the "loving Jenny Wren" and her "Lizzie-Mizzie-Wizzie," whose gentle touch Jenny welcomes and who can do for her what, Jenny tells Lizzie, a husband cannot. Since Victorian portrayals of children are often "coded ways of thinking and writing about the erotic," writes Michie, Dickens, "by making Jenny a child and a cripple[,] outlines a safe space for the articulation of female sexuality"—queer (Jenny) and otherwise (Lizzie).[24] Charley's language regarding his sister and the "'extraordinary companion'" to whom she has "giv[en] herself up" (449) underscores the domestic, one-sidedly romantic nature of the relationship. Charley deems it "one of [Lizzie's] romantic ideas" (450) and, afraid the liaison will hamper her chances of marriage, warns Lizzie that Jenny's "way is not your way as Mr Headstone's wife" (460)—or, implicitly, as *a wife*. When Lizzie is in hiding, Jenny, with "tears . . . in her eyes," confides in Riah: "I feel so much more solitary and helpless without Lizzie now, than I used to feel before I knew her" (494). Riah commiserates, mentioning the loss of his own romantic partner, his wife.

As Jenny focuses much of her attention on Lizzie, so is Ezra Jennings preoccupied with assisting Franklin Blake. "What is the secret of the attraction that there is for me in this man?" Jennings wonders, in regard to Blake, in a journal entry in *The Moonstone*. "How useless to ask these questions!" he concludes, "Mr Blake has given me a new interest in life. Let that be enough, without seeking to know what the new interest is" (393). The reader, however, *is* interested in the nature of Jennings's attraction. The content of the unspecified accusations against Jennings, the "Evil report" that follows him, further invites speculation (374). "'Unspeakable,'" according to Sedgwick, "is a favorite Gothic word,"[25] and "homosexuality, still according to Sedgwick, becomes equivalent to the unspeakable in Gothic romance"[26]—as well as, I would argue, in Gothic-inspired texts such as *The Moonstone*. The "unspeakable" accusations that plague Jennings function like the elusive, unnamable specters that haunt the protagonists of the Gothic, "the first novelistic form in England to have close, relatively visible links to male homosexuality."[27] While there is every reason to believe that the accusations against Jennings are false, the *possibility* of their homosexual content evokes queerness and is supported by Jennings's cohabitation with Candy, in whose arms he dies, exclaiming "Kiss me!" (456); his excitable references to Blake, whom he watches during the opium experiment with a throbbing heart and beating temples until at last, "I was obliged to look away from him—or I should have lost my self-control" (419); and the innuendo-laden scene between Jennings and Rachel at the experiment's conclusion, in which Jennings finds Rachel kissing Blake. "'You would have done it,' she whispered, 'in my place'" (425). It is, in fact, Jennings's experiment that allows Rachel to take her place, by taking *his* place as Blake's closest ally and dearest companion. The happy couple gone to London, Jennings confesses that his "brief dream of happiness is over" (425). Just as Jenny without Lizzie feels "solitary and helpless" (494), so Jennings without Blake feels "friendless and lonely" (425). Of course, neither character is actually unloved or alone—Jenny has Riah, just as Blake has Candy. Though unable to articulate it with precision, what they both are is lovelorn.

Freaks That Attract

While the majority of characters in *Our Mutual Friend* and *The Moonstone* are put off by the visible peculiarities of, respectively, Jenny and Jennings, Lizzie and Blake are drawn to these characters against the will of others. "You talk as if you were drawn or driven [to that] little crooked antic of a child, or old person, or whatever it is" (OMF 278), Charley Hexam reprimands his sister in an unsuccessful effort to undermine the relationship with Jenny that he thinks will make it difficult for Lizzie to "rise" in the world. Refusing to adhere to her brother's wishes, Lizzie independently elects to continue lodging with Jenny. Consider Lizzie's choice in light of Todd's contention that, in the Victorian novel generally, "[f]emale friendship is the only social relationship [that] the heroine actively constructs. The family commonly selects the lover (or the man nominates himself), where the woman chooses the friend."[28] In the virtuous heroine's nomination of Jenny as her closest ally—and domestic partner—we see her independence asserted through her approval of and affection for the unconventional Jenny, who, contrary to Charley's predictions, facilitates rather than deters Lizzie's social transformation. Though an affair of the heart, so to speak, rather than of social ambition, Lizzie's unconventional alliance with Jenny enables Lizzie to become both lady and wife.

A similar attraction exists between Jennings and Blake. Knocking on the door as Blake speaks the words, "I don't know of a living person who can be of the slightest use to me," Jennings enters Blake's life, immediately taking his "attention captive" (321). Shortly thereafter, at a crowded railway station, the two men's "eyes me[e]t at the same moment" (321). "[T]he irrepressible Ezra Jennings"—Blake's description—next appears in image, as Blake finds himself "idly drawing likenesses from memory"—"a dozen portraits at least"—of the man who, like a lover, he cannot get out of his mind (356). Though both his "appearance" and his reputation, "speaking from the popular point of view, w[ere] against him[,] it is not to be denied," writes Blake, "that Ezra Jennings made some inscrutable appeal to my sympathies, which I found it impossible to resist" (364). Flouting public opinion and the judgment of the faithful steward Betteredge, Blake allies himself with the bizarre-looking stranger, exhibiting a trust that is by no means misplaced. Standing at "a place where the highway . . . branched off into two roads . . . watch[ing Jennings] walking farther and farther away from me; carrying farther and farther away with him what I now firmly believed to be the clue of which I was in search," Blake "rash[ly]" decides to call Jennings back, a decision that Blake knows "might be the turning point of [his] life" (372). As Peter Thoms points out: "The importance of Blake's eventual decision to confide in Jennings is emphasized by the way Collins suspensefully plays out the choosing with Blake finally halted in doubt at the figurative fork in the road. . . . It can be argued, then, that the most significant moment in Blake's quest is not his reunion with Rachel but his union with Jennings, a decisive act of communion from which all the rest proceeds. Reunion with Rachel is the motivation for his quest and its symbolic fulfillment, but understanding Jennings more satisfactorily represents Blake's personal development."[29] Blake not only understands but also *approves* of Jennings, though his endorsement alone is inadequate to remove the stigma of difference from the outcast doctor. In choosing him as a companion and ally, however, Blake inadvertently gives Jennings the chance to demonstrate his worth to others. Employing his differences, his interpretive and imaginative skills, on the hero's behalf, Jennings makes the most of the opportunity and displays abilities that no one else possesses in an unselfish act that proves Blake's innocence and secures him the hand of his beloved. This relationship between central and marginalized character, in which the latter demonstrates his value by assisting the former, directly parallels the dynamic between Lizzie and Jenny; as in Dickens's novel, a powerful emotional same-sex attachment is at the heart of freakish sacrifice.

Freaks That Dream

If sacrifice is compelled by emotional attachment, it is enabled by the imagination. For Jenny and Jennings, fantasy, "a condition made necessary by pain"—both physical and emotional—"is also enabling"—an asset.[30] For these suffering characters, fantasy, the realm of the imagination, is not only a shelter from the intolerable; it is also a means of sating unquenchable desires, queer or otherwise, and a practical resource that makes them of use. Deprived of grandparents, a mother, and a sober father, Jenny is further isolated by her small stature, bad back, and queer legs, which prevent her from playing with other children and fuel their cruelty toward her. To withstand their taunting, Jenny makes do with imaginary playmates, "long bright slanting rows" of children who swoop down and make her "light," giving her "delicious ease and rest" (298). Though Jenny's children leave her as she grows older and her physical pain diminishes, she continues to smell flowers that are not really there and to hear birds that "sing better than other birds" (290). As for her home life and the challenges of social interaction, Jenny bears her father's alcoholism by envisioning herself as the parent of a troublesome child, whom she threatens, scolds, and disciplines. In uncomfortable situations with adults who intimidate her, she tells riddles, peers through imaginary glasses, and brings dolls to life as moral arbiters—as we see with "Mrs Truth. The Honourable" (397), who sits in judgment of Bradley Headstone. An imaginary "Him" (284) who will one day come to court and marry her serves to keep worries about her future at bay. Unable to extend her vision to preclude her future husband's drunkenness, Jenny imagines "boiling liquid bubbling" down his throat in place of alcohol (294). Her world—even the world of her imagination—may be darkened by alcohol, but Jenny will deal with it—with "Him," as with her father—creatively.

Until she meets Lizzie, Jenny's interaction with women is limited to the imagination. Just as, while a young child, Jenny watched children only from a distance, generating playmates from the realm of make-believe, so as an adolescent she creates doll-companions, turning live women into the dolls she earns her living clothing. "Making . . . perfect slave[s]" of the women she admires, Jenny "make[s] great ladies try [her] dresses on" (496, 495). Catching sight of someone who strikes her fancy, she "take[s] particular notice of her, and run[s] home and cut[s] her out and baste[s] her," then comes back to examine her again, imagining her adorned in her dolls' clothing, as she has imagined her dolls clothed in theirs. "When they go bobbing into the hall from the carriage, and catch a glimpse of my little physiognomy poked out from behind a policeman's cape"—gazing, thus, illicitly—"I dare say they think I am wondering and admiring with all my eyes and heart, but they little think they're only working for my dolls!" (496). Michie describes Jenny's sewing as "a metaphor for the possibility of . . . female transformation and transfiguration,"[31] but it is also a metonym for her queer desire. Her scissors, thread, and needles give form to her longing: shaping with her eyes, caressing with her hands, Jenny makes virtual contact with women otherwise beyond her reach.

As Jenny makes use of fantasy for income, so she employs it in changing her name. Shedding the name that identifies her queer desire, the former Fanny Cleaver elects to call herself Jenny Wren, the name of the bird-heroine in various "Cock Robin" stories that proliferated in the nineteenth century. A plain dresser who refuses to array herself in wedding finery, she is widowed on her wedding day. Though the dolls' dressmaker has a happier ending than that of her nursery-rhyme counterpart, she is similarly disinterested in her own transformation into the traditional image of femininity. *Our Mutual Friend*'s queer Jenny Wren transforms not herself but others, turning ladies into dolls, her best friend into a lady, and the real-life clergyman who presides over her father's funeral into a "doll clergyman [capable of] uniting two of my young friends in matrimony" (804). In a reversal of the Cock Robin story, in which the wren participates in a marriage ceremony that devolves into a ritual of death, Dickens's young Wren defeats death by means of marriage, using her imagination as a means of communicating with Eugene and uncovering the word that, in securing Eugene's marriage, saves his life.

Other fairy tales that Jenny invokes include Jack and the Beanstalk, Little Red Riding Hood, and, most frequently, Cinderella. Michie claims that Jenny "names herself 'Cinderella,'" and in so doing "sets in motion the multiple ironies of the fairytale subtext."[32] Jenny, however, does not explicitly name—or ever call—herself Cinderella; rather, she invites the name by calling Riah "godmother" (492) and actuates the fantasy by pretending that Riah possesses the capacity to grant her wishes—sobriety for her father, freedom from her physical problems, and the return of days gone by when she and Lizzie shared a home. Jenny's play-acting as Cinderella is indeed ironic, a temporary indulgence while Lizzie, the novel's true Cinderella, is in hiding. Sitting at the fireside, telling fortunes, Lizzie cannot imagine herself into the role of Cinderella, cannot envision herself as the lady that flickers before her in the "hollow down by the flare" (404). Jenny does this for her, reading her veiled fantasies of love for Eugene as imaginative texts of unarticulated desire, just as she later reads Eugene's fevered wish to make Lizzie his wife. Interpreting and articulating other people's desire, Jenny herself acts the part of fairy godmother, transforming the working girl into a lady and wife—and in so doing sacrificing her beloved Lizzie to Eugene. These fairy-tale allusions made by the girl with the Rapunzelesque hair underscore Jenny's linguistic, emotional, and practical capabilities: living in the real world but utilizing fancy to do so, she speaks two languages, ultimately serving as a translator not only between the realms of fantasy and reality but also between those of health and illness, childhood and adulthood, queerness and conventionality, margin and center.

Like Jenny, Jennings is, of necessity, resourceful, creative, and capable. When "the one man who had befriended" him lies dying before his eyes (368)—Mr. Candy having fallen ill after secretly dosing Blake with opium—the doctor's assistant defies the advice of "two physicians of established local repute" (367), whose treatment views differ from his own. Detecting a "feebleness" in Candy that the others are unable to sense (367), Jennings administers stimulants, though he knows that in doing so he drives his colleagues from his—and his patient's—bedside: "If I had been a happy man, if I had led a prosperous life, I believe I should have sunk under the task I had imposed on myself. But *I* had no happy time to look back at, no past peace of mind to force itself into contrast with my present anxiety and suspense—and I held firm to my resolution through it all" (368). "Death and I fought over the bed" (368), and Jennings's stimulants prove life-saving. Distinct by admission, though not, he tells us, unnatural, Jennings explains to Blake the burst of tears that follows: "Physiology says, and says truly, that some men are born with female constitutions—and I was one of them!" (369). Thus, Collins suggests, genetically coded intuition (a "feminine" trait) as well as circumstantial wretchedness enables Jennings's service to others. Daring (limit pushing, in essence), perseverance (easily applied, suggests Jennings, when one's life is a misery), and diagnostic (interpretive) and creative capabilities are the instruments at the freakish Jennings's disposal in his facilitation of Candy's physical recovery and, as we will see shortly, of Blake's salvation. What the other physicians—like the novel's other detectives—lack, Jennings possesses and freely gives.

The last exertions of Jennings's life are spent on behalf of Blake, the former suffering the extremes of opium use to withstand the pain of his illness. "The progress of [his] disease has gradually forced [him] from the use of opium to the abuse of it" (375), and Jennings considers giving it up, since the "frightful dreams" that plague him while he is under its influence are worse than "the physical suffering" he must withstand without it (396). "A slight return of the old pain" is even "welcome" for its ability to "dispel the visions" of the past that opium inevitably brings on. Phantoms of the dead, "empty space," "hideous . . . phosphorescen[ce]," and a grotesque image of "the one beloved face which I shall never seen again" are the substance of his nightmares (392). Perhaps generously, perhaps addictively, perhaps both, Jennings persists in his use of the drug because, he claims, the pain he would endure without it would slow his progress toward vindicating Blake. His nervous system "shattered," his nights a "horror" (375), Jennings is nonetheless aided by opium in his investigation. Not only does it sustain—even as it tortures—Jennings, opium proves to be the key to the riddle of Blake's unconscious theft—the key only the doctor's assistant can determine, because of his firsthand experience with the effects of the drug. Functioning as a sort of imaginative potion for unlocking the truth, opium determines Blake's innocence by demonstrating his guilt—his narcotic, unconscious, well-meaning abduction of the diamond—in an experiment conducted by Jennings. Free from calumny, Blake begins a new life, while Jennings, spent, finishes his own. Opium in *The Moonstone* is double-edged: a coping mechanism for Jennings and the means by which he clears Blake's name, it is also the precipitous factor in his own demise. In Jennings's narcotic nightmares, we see fantasy in excess. In his intuition-inspired assistance to Candy and Blake, we see imagination that proves useful. Where even the imagination turns on the much maligned outcast, it benefits those whom he serves.

Freaks That Translate

The help of these characters, though freely given, is actively solicited, in *The Moonstone* by a man who finds himself unexpectedly a criminal suspect and in *Our Mutual Friend* by a man pummeled into a state of incomprehensibility—to all but Jenny Wren. Mangled and immobilized by a savage beating and near drowning, Eugene Wrayburn asks that Jenny be sent to his sickbed. His summons is unexpected given that previously these characters have appeared together in only two scenes, in which, enduring Jenny for the sake of Lizzie, Eugene quickly grows "weary of the person of the house" (289). Though their mutual love for Lizzie may motivate Jenny's readiness to go to him, Eugene beckons her not for any comfort she can offer Lizzie but for the help she can offer him. Referring to Jenny's imaginary children, Eugene simultaneously acknowledges and requests the assistance of her powerful interpretive skills. Little more than a child herself, Jenny does for Eugene what her children did for her: read and ease pain as no one else can. Jenny's familiarity with pain, her heightened imagination, and her sensitivity to unmet, often unexpressed, desires, some of those very aspects that make her different, make her valuable to the wounded Eugene on his "death bed." Able to do more than merely sympathize, Jenny listens to, observes, and assists Eugene with the patience that pain has taught her, easing, turning, altering, adjusting, recognizing, and soothing Eugene's pain with a "delicacy of touch" and a "fine . . . perception" learned through suffering and possessed by her alone (809). Although Eugene is unable to move so much as a hand, Jenny, "through this close watch-ing . . . attain[s] an understanding of him that" is incomprehensible to even his best friend, who sees "the little creature" as "an interpreter between this sentient world and the insensible man" (809). Nursemaid *and* matchmaker, Jenny interprets and articulates Eugene's desire to make Lizzie his "Wife" (811), as she earlier interpreted Lizzie's unde-clared love for Eugene, thus enabling the marriage that allows Eugene to flourish, physically and otherwise. Wrayburn enters the novel as a mere reflection in the Veneerings' mirror, "buried alive at the back of his chair" (53). As Albert Hutter writes, "long before his near drowning and rescue by Lizzie, he is badly in need of resuscitation, if not resur-rection."[33] But Hutter, like the fictional Mortimer, fails to note that Jenny also plays a role in Eugene's resuscitation. The medium through which love is conducted, Jenny literally translates desire, in an act that ultimately saves Eugene's life. Mortimer predicts that Eugene's "noble wife" turns out to be the "preserver of [his] life" (812), but this occurs only through Jenny's mediation. In the novel's final pages, the gentleman Twemlow publicly argues that Lizzie is a lady because her marriage to Eugene makes her so; readers, however, know that Jenny, with her discovery of the "Word" ("Wife") and its communication to Mortimer, is the person truly responsible for Lizzie's accession to the status of lady (811). It is a gift—and a sacrifice. Hiding within her "golden bower," weeping at the wedding of Eugene and Lizzie as she weeps at the bedside parting of Eugene and Mortimer, Jenny is really weeping for herself and for the loss of her "particular friend."[34]

As Jenny translates Eugene's wishes for Mortimer, so does Ezra Jennings, in *The Moonstone*, interpret the ailing Candy's words for Franklin Blake. In so doing, he, too, facilitates a marriage for his favored companion, rendering himself, at least partially, redundant. Admittedly having "attempted to make [his] poor friend's loss of memory the means of bettering his acquaintance with" Blake (376), Jennings's ultimate goal—for which he makes the ultimate sacrifice—is Blake's happiness. Unwilling to dismiss Candy's words as nonsense, Jennings decodes and relays their meaning. Familiar with intense pain, colorful dreams, and the power of imagination, Jennings uses the same "principle which one adopts in putting together a child's 'puzzle,'" gives "order and shape" (370) to "the patient's 'wanderings'" (369), and "penetrate[s] through the obstacle of disconnected expression to the thought that was underlying it connectedly all the time" (382).

His translation of Mr. Candy's discursive exertions, insensible to all but himself, is insufficient on its own to prove Blake's innocence. Jennings's notes, which "produce . . . the [words] which Mr Candy himself would have used if he had been capable of speaking connectedly" (382), serve only as a guide to his "bold experiment" (384). No mere *scientific* experiment, Jennings's experiment is an *imaginative* one that hinges on the same "element of intuition" that he employed in saving Candy's life.[35] Just as on that earlier occasion, Jennings's colleagues looked down on what seemed to them "like unreasonableness" (663), so, too, on the night of the experiment do Betteredge and Blake demonstrate doubts about Jennings's instincts. Chiding Bruff for having "no more imagination than a cow!" (415), Jennings proceeds with his attempted recreation of the past, which, like Jenny's enactment of the Cinderella fantasy, is compounded of "multiple ironies."[36] A man who admittedly believes that "we should all be happier . . . if we could but completely forget!" (365), Jennings is also "a man with no future [who] help[s] a friend recover his past,"[37] "renew[ing]" a love "which is of [his] bringing back" (394).[38]

The Limits of Difference

In facilitating the marriage of the same-sex companion to whom each is affectionately devoted, Jenny and Jennings use skills that only they possess, thereby demonstrating the functionality of difference. The negative connotations of freakishness, these novels seem to tell us, are matters of faulty perception; while inflexible and morally questionable characters mock and fear freaks, open-minded and redeemed characters support them. Eugene's request that Jenny come to his sickbed is a sign of his moral rehabilitation: now that he is morally fit, he comprehends Jenny's value, just as now he recognizes Lizzie's true worth—her fitness to be his wife. And just as Lizzie, privileged because of her marriage to Wrayburn, is recognized by Twemlow as a lady, Jenny, privileged "because of her association with Mrs Eugene Wrayburn," is recognized by the Harmons "as having a claim on their protection" (875). In *The Moonstone*'s conclusion, Bruff and Betteredge, who had doubted Jennings, acknowledge their wrong, ask his pardon, and sign a written statement in support of him as "atonement" (423). Regeneration—spiritual and moral reformation—prevails.

Unlike freakishness, same-sex bonding is not a matter of perception but of extent, so while freakishness has its merits, *queerness*, manifestly, does not. The taint of homosexual attachment carries with it the penalty of marginality to the degree that that taint persists. Having served her purpose at Eugene's bedside, Jenny takes up a "new and removed position" from which she is no longer able to "see the sufferer's face," enabling Lizzie to take her rightful—soon to be legally sanctioned—"station by [his] pillow" (812). Having overseen Eugene's transformation, Jenny relinquishes her central location, retreating to the corner of the room, the edge of the text. In her final scene—an interlude within a chapter titled "Persons and Things in General" (4.16)—Jenny, less proud than we have seen her previously, meets Sloppy, the "cabinet-mak[er]," for the first time. "And what do you think of Me?" she asks. "'Out with it!' said Miss Wren, with an arch look. 'Don't you think me a queer little comicality? . . . I am lame.'" Freed from the euphemisms of a "bad back" and "queer legs," Jenny takes her crutch in hand, demonstrating—and narrating—her walk for Sloppy. "Hoppetty, Kicketty, Pep-peg-peg. Not pretty; is it?" (881, 882). In the moment in which she enters the world of heteronormativity, meeting and accepting "Him," Jenny asserts her lameness. Spoken, the lameness emerges, as, unspoken, the queer disappears. The nubile Jenny is left with only one sign of difference—which must be named so that the unnamed can be extinguished. As a final act, Jenny hands Sloppy the doll she has made for Lizzie's daughter: "'Take care of her, and there's my hand, and thank you again.' 'I'll take more care of her than if she was a gold image,' said Sloppy, 'and there's both *my* hands, Miss, and I'll soon come back again'" (883). The "her" with which Sloppy is entrusted is not just the doll. It is also Jenny herself, the "Her" for whose hand, we are to presume, he will shortly return. Further, and more critically, it is Jenny's (queer) desire that, transferred to him—not necessarily as object but surely as *bearer*—becomes heteronormative.

Ezra Jennings, unlike Jenny Wren, remains not only associated with the possibility of homosexuality but also, inescapably, infused with colonial blood. Whereas Jenny can grow up and out of deviant desire, Jennings can outgrow neither the queerness of his "female constitution [. . .]" (369) nor the darkness of his skin, both of which mark him from birth.[39] Although, like the dolls' dressmaker, Jennings removes himself from the bedside of the man (whose character) he resurrected, allowing the novel's heroine to take his place, unlike Jenny he remains other as a result of queer domesticity (continued cohabitation with Candy), inherent gender deviance, and race. The taint, then, that remains with Jennings is both literal and elusive: dark skin that he cannot shed and dark rumors that he cannot outrun. Franklin's absolution and reunion with Rachel, both facilitated by Jennings, are in many ways the equivalent of a rise to manhood across his back, the back of a queer, colonial body that deteriorates in its final efforts to assist the heterosexual Englishman.[40] Though Blake and Jennings once coexisted in a "fraternity of guilt,"[41] Blake's guilt, while real, was only temporary. Absolved of wrongful intent, Blake is wholly redeemed. Jennings's "guilt," on the other hand, though unjustified, is never disproved. "His story is"—and remains—"a blank" (455) and death his only haven from unnamed "disgrace" (374). His request that his story die with him, that he be buried with his letters, notes, journal entries, and manuscripts in an unmarked grave, underscores the tragedy of queer erasure and colonial exploitation. Homosexual desire, though *transmutable* (as with Jenny), is inassimilable when racially other. Freakishness may have its merits, but, finally, queerness and "darkness" do not (321). The lame can use crutches, the queer body can pass, but the colonial body, the racial hybrid, like the queer character who persists in his associations, must be made to disappear.

Aggregates That Threaten

"Queer theorists," writes Robert McRuer, "are now used to unpacking how performances of heterosexuality depend on gay bodies and their repudiation," but they do not address how these performances are "relat[ed] to ability and disability."[42] McRuer has called for "an alliance between queer theory and critical disability" in order "to affirm, strategically, that the two activities are in many ways of a piece."[43] Similarly, Judith Butler has argued that "collective disidentifications"—the feminist and the queer are her examples—"can facilitate a reconceptualization of which bodies matter and which bodies are yet to emerge as critical matters of concern."[44] The challenge is to bolster power through strategic alliance without inadvertently supporting the rhetoric of sameness that, in collapsing difference, obscures it. How do we value the queer, the disabled, the politically, socially, even geographically marginalized without, as McRuer wisely warns we should not, "serv[ing] as metaphors for each other"?[45] In other words, how do we work "collective disidentification[. . .]" to political advantage without sacrificing the very differences that we have worked so hard to disentangle from the dust mounds of history, literary and otherwise?

Furthermore, how flexible is the queer? And how flexible do we want it to be? Providing background for his analysis of the 1997 film *As Good as It Gets*, McRuer describes how twentieth-century bodies "placed in an inevitable heterosexual relationship and visually represented as able" are reliant on "other bodies"—"invariably queer and disabled"—that "must function flexibly and *objectively* as sites on which the epiphanic moment"—a moment of "clarity that . . . allows the protagonist to carry, to the close of the narrative, a sense of subjective wholeness that he or she lacked previously"—"can be staged."[46] The "heteronormative epiphany" translates into an "expansion" of identity[47] and is coupled with a retraction of the other. In examining two of Victorian fiction's most memorable freaks, I have tried to show the ways in which, because of their queer coding, they elucidate the uses of queer bodies and abilities. Further, I have demonstrated that in the limited contexts of *Our Mutual Friend* and *The Moonstone*, the freakish body matters *because of its flexibility.* Well before there was a big screen, difference was, in its own way, shown to be procreative. At the same time, however, it was quite specifically not self-generating: in producing heteronormativity, it was itself consumed. Flexibility leaks (difference) even as it yields (the norm). Another's gain, you might say, is the other's loss. This loss might, as in the case of Jenny, be one of (queer) otherness itself; it also might, as in the case of Jennings, in whom the taint of sexual and racial difference remains, mean the loss of life; and it might simply mean, as in *As Good as It Gets,* that "disability, . . . queerness," and the character who embodies them, "having served their purpose, . . . are then hustled offstage together."[48]

McRuer argues that "the homophobia and ableism represented" by this film enact a "new, improved, and flexible homophobia and able-ism," one that is *"unique to the past few decades."*[49] While I certainly do not agree with the novelty of flexible bigotry, I am otherwise in accord with McRuer's assessment. Merely modernized versions of flexible freak-fetishism, the self-congratulatory impulses of flexible homophobia and ableism are also self-deceiving, masking an imperative to deny behind a willingness to tolerate. How do we counter this more subtle form of violence?[50] By yet more flexibility? How can we, scholars of the queer, the disabled, and the colonial, intent on recovery and reinscription, use flexibility to our advantage without falling into the traps it so often sets—traps, such as those of sacrifice, elision, and disappearance? Is it really possible to form the kind of alliances, the collective disidenti-fications suggested by McRuer and Butler, without glossing over the multiple differences of the abjected body, those multiple differences so dangerously "compelled to pass under the sign of the same"?[51] Which differences will we find ourselves hustling offstage?

These are important questions, as evinced by the fact that two of us in this collection (Martha Stoddard Holmes and I) have grappled with them—and both, interestingly, via Collins's work. Stoddard Holmes makes broad use of the term "queer," reading Dexter, a leg-less, wheelchair-bound character in *The Law and the Lady* (1875), "as a queer . . . character" based on "his atypical body's work as desire's instrument, conduit, and register."[52] He is one of several "'queer' men" whose association with Valeria, the novel's heroine, helps "revive[. . .] [her] marriage."[53] Dexter, "half man, half chair,"[54] is "only the most vis-ible thread in a fabric of queerness that organizes and gives substance to [the] marriage plot. . . . Hetero-able normativity, as Collins pos-its it, clearly relies on the queer, disabled energy Dexter generates."[55] In Stoddard Holmes's interpretation, the queer includes "[t]he desires associated with [Dexter's] extraordinary body and unconventional behavior"; Valeria's "mimetic attraction to the women in Eustace's former social circle"; the desires and behaviors of the other "'odd'" men she terms, à la *Queer Eye*, the "Fab Four"; and, more broadly still, "the variety of practices and pleasures that underpin human relationships."[56] In this theoretical amalgamation, nuance itself become coextensive with the queer. In valuing difference by queering difference, Stoddard Holmes inadvertently devalues—by co-opting—the queer.

Frequently convergent though rarely if ever equivalent, differences—the queer and the postcolonial, for example, as in my reading of the doctor's assistant—should be textually distinguished, regardless of which theoretical approaches to difference are applied. If we fail to do so, we risk replicating some of the problems we are attempting to confront, problems such as the disregard of historically contingent hierarchies of differences, the elision of differences, the naturalization of associations between the abject, and the correlative reinforcement of the normative as a realm apart. Think, for example, of the conglomeration of obsessive-compulsive disorder and bigotry in the character of Melvin in *As Good as It Gets:* the two "are repeatedly linked, narratively and visually, and the link is naturalized, [though] there is nothing natural about this link."[57] When Melvin medicates his illness, his bigotry diminishes, suggesting "that there is no material separation between disability and serious flaws in character."[58] Similarly, physical and mental disability are collapsed in the aforementioned Dexter of *The Law and the Lady,* who deteriorates mentally as he deteriorates physically.[59]

A 2005 call for papers for a panel titled "The Queer Space of the Postcolonial" sought papers that read postcolonial space as queer space.[60] Instead of the intersection that I had anticipated, I found an appropriation.

> This panel proposes to explore the ways in which the postcolonial nation and subject are seen through literature to inhabit what Judith Halberstam, in *In a Queer Time and Place: Transgender Bodies, Subcultural Lives,* terms "queer space." If we do, indeed, "detach queerness from sexual identity," we can begin to imagine those spaces which function in non-normative time patterns and across spaces which escape conventional definition. . . . [T]he rendering of the "postcolonial" as queer allows for ways in which literatures can be seen to be revealing narratives which must necessarily work against the concepts of space and time which have been defined by the normative values of the West.[61]

The proposed panel stretches what Halberstam herself, on the first page of *In a Queer Time and Place*, admits is "perhaps [the] overly ambitious claim that there is such a thing as 'queer time' and 'queer space.'"[62] "Queer time" is, for Halberstam, a post-AIDS phenomenon;[63] it is an "adjustment in the way in which we think about time," which allows for "new ways of understanding the nonnormative behaviors that have clear but not essential relations to gay and lesbian subjects. . . . 'Queer space' refers to place-making practices within postmodernism in which queer people engage . . . ."[64] Queer, in other words, is not merely synonymous with the nonnormative; it is not, simply, other. Though Halberstam is willing to "detach queerness from sexual identity," she asserts, again on page 1, that "queer uses of time and space develop, at least in part, in opposition to the institutions of family, heterosexuality, and reproduction."[65] A misappropriation of Halberstam, the call for papers nonetheless—perhaps, all the more—illustrates my concerns about not only "collective disidentifications" but also the increasingly inattentive use of "the queer." Having concluded my reading of the call for papers, I was left wondering: What place is there for the queer *within* the postcolonial, when the postcolonial *is* the queer? Imagine, for a moment, reading the queer as postcolonial. Who would dare? Is the former proposition any less problematic, even if well intended? What would be gained by such an endeavor? What would be lost? Queer difference is real difference—even as it is sameness (like and unlike that against which it is defined, but by no means equivalent to other forms of "difference")—and to appropriate it at the expense of its historical—though admittedly continually emergent—meanings, to move not through but utterly beyond its association with socially deviant desires, identities, affinities, tendencies, behaviors, and bodies—is to reinter the queer body in the anonymity of mass abjection. A young scholar, I hesitate to entrench myself in this position, but it is, now, where I stand. I do not object to theoretical alliances, but I suggest we form them with caution, treating our subjects with distinction.

Specificity, fortunately, assists us by struggling to assert itself. The fictions that I have examined demonstrate how even when they are, finally, swallowed whole by the text, queer, disabled, dark bodies force us to consider the ways in which they are "fully human,"[66] fully unique. The poietic power that Jenny and Jennings, *because* "freaks," possess, their ability to "draw[. . .] people together and reconstruct[. . .] community,"[67] distinguishes them. The representational connections between freakishness, queer desire, racial hybridity, and disability examined here in the context of the nineteenth-century novel, but also, clearly, evident elsewhere, illustrate the ways in which such categories—and the people who manifest them—have been, and continue to be, both valued and devalued. Perhaps these associations, conflations, and sometime elisions have something to teach the politically motivated theorist who wishes to form practical and theoretical alliances without merely reordering hierarchies of difference, without incurring further loss.

Notes

Thanks to Leila May for calling Professor Tromp's emerging *Freaks* collection to my attention; to Marlene Tromp for her many helpful suggestions, both precise and general; as well as to Cannon Schmitt, Pat Kennedy, Siobhan Somerville, and the anonymous reviewers at The Ohio State University Press for comments on various drafts.

1. Charles Dickens, *Our Mutual Friend* (London: Penguin, 1985), 881 (hereafter cited parenthetically with the abbreviation *OMF* where needed).

2. "I'm a Doll's Dressmaker," says Jenny (273). Although when Jenny speaks of her occupation she uses the singular form of "doll," all other such references, including the two chapter headings in which she figures (4.10 and 4.11), use the plural: "dolls' dressmaker" (880). One wonders what Dickens had in mind in creating this consistent discrepancy—what he had in Jenny's mind, that is. Did Jenny envision always the one doll as she worked? And was Lizzie this muse? Except above, where I quote Jenny, I will also use the more accurate plural form of the word.

3. Malcolm Andrews, *Dickens and the Grown-up Child* (Iowa City: University of Iowa Press, 1994), 86.

4. Tamar Heller, "Blank Spaces: Ideological Tensions and the Detective Work of *The Moonstone*," in Heller, *Dead Secrets: Wilkie Collins and the Female Gothic* (New Haven, CT: Yale University Press, 1992), 156.

5. Jenny Bourne Taylor, "Lost Parcel or Hidden Soul: Detecting the Unconscious in *The Moonstone*," in Taylor, *The Secret Theatre of the Home: Wilkie Collins, Sensation Narrative, and Nineteenth-Century Psychology* (London: Routledge, 1988), 189.

6. Alexander Welsh, *Strong Representations: Narrative and Circumstantial Evidence in England* (Baltimore, MD: Johns Hopkins University Press, 1992), 234.

7. Wilkie Collins, *The Moonstone* (London: Penguin, 1994), 364, 409, 321 (hereafter cited parenthetically with the abbreviation *MS* where needed).

8. Jaya Mehta, "English Romance: Indian Violence," *Centennial Review* 39, no. 3 (Fall 1995): 628, 631.

9. Ronald R. Thomas, "Minding the Body Politic: The Romance of Science and the Revision of History in Victorian Detective Fiction," *Victorian Literature and Culture* 19 (1991): 242; Mehta, 628.

10. Collins quite pointedly constructs Jennings as a multiracial character. His

model for him, a doctor's assistant whom he met while on a walking tour with Dickens, was a strikingly *pale* man: "What was startling in him was his remarkable paleness, [his] extraordinary pallor. There was no vestige of colour in the man" (qtd. in Nuel Pharr Davis, *The Life of Wilkie Collins* [Urbana: University of Illinois Press, 1956], 250, citing Charles Dickens and Wilkie Collins, *The Lazy Tour of Two Idle Apprentices and Other Stories* [London: Chapman, 1890], 26).

11. Heller drew my attention to the significance of Mackenzie's novel in *The Moonstone* (190n8). In it, Mr. Harley condemns the "conquests in India" as exploitative and lawless (Henry Mackenzie, *The Man of Feeling* [London, Paris, and Melbourne: Cassell, 1893], 150). The British, he notes, "drained the treasuries," "oppress[. . .] the industry of their subjects," and rule by a militia "covered with the blood of the vanquished" (151).

12. Thomas, 242. See also Melissa Free, "'Dirty Linen': Legacies of Empire in Wilkie Collins's *The Moonstone*," *Texas Studies in Literature and Language* 48, no. 4 (2006): 359–61.

13. Heller, 156; Taylor, 189.

14. Henry James, quoted in Leslie Fiedler, *Freaks: Myths and Images of the Secret Self* (New York: Simon & Schuster, 1978), 269.

15. Judith Halberstam, *Skin Shows: Gothic Horror and the Technology of Monsters* (Durham, NC: Duke University Press, 1995), 2.

16. Ibid., 72.

17. Janet Todd, *Women's Friendship in Literature* (New York: Columbia University Press, 1980), 2.

18. Helena Michie, "'Who Is This in Pain?': Scarring, Disfigurement, and Female Identity in *Bleak House* and *Our Mutual Friend*," *Novel: A Forum on Fiction* 22, no. 2 (1989): 211.

19. Eve Kosofsky Sedgwick, *Between Men: English Literature and Male Homosocial Desire* (New York: Columbia University Press, 1985), 225n5.

20. David Blewett, Introduction to Daniel Defoe, *Moll Flanders* (London: Penguin, 1989), 7.

21. Sedgwick, *Between*, 164.

22. No other critic of whom I am aware has identified Jenny as queer, while only one critic whom I encountered, Alexander Welsh, notes the "homoeroticism" of the Jennings plot (234).

23. Michie, 212.

24. Ibid.

25. Eve Kosofsky Sedgwick, *The Coherence of Gothic Conventions* (New York: Methuen, 1986), 4.

26. Halberstam, *Skin Shows*, 65, paraphrasing Sedgwick.

27. Sedgwick, *Between*, 91; emphasis added. Recall that Jenny and Jennings are both physically—*visibly*—marked as different.

28. Todd, 2.

29. Peter Thoms, "'Detective-Fever': The Quest for Understanding in *The Moonstone*," in Thoms, *The Windings of the Labyrinth: Quest and Structure in the Major Novels of Wilkie Collins* (Athens: Ohio University Press, 1992), 151–52, 153.

30. Here, Helena Michie writes specifically of Jenny, although her assessment is applicable to Jennings as well (211).

31. Ibid., 210.

32. Ibid., 211.

33. Albert Hutter, "Dismemberment and Articulation in *Our Mutual Friend*," *Dickens Studies Annual* 11 (1983): 153.

34. Dickens, 823, 272. See also Michie, 210.

35. Ross C. Murfin, "The Art of Representation: Collins's *The Moonstone* and Dickens's Example," *ELH* 49 (1982): 663.

36. Michie, 211.

37. John R. Reed, "The Stories of *The Moonstone*," in *Wilkie Collins to the Forefront: Some Reassessments*, ed. Nelson Smith and R. C. Terry (New York: AMS, 1995), 97.

38. "Both [Rachel and Blake] first express their love for each other to Jennings" (Timothy L. Carens, "Outlandish English Subjects in *The Moonstone*," in *Reality's Dark Light: The Sensational Wilkie Collins*, ed. Maria K. Bachman and Don Richard Cox [Knoxville: University of Tennessee Press, 2003], 257). We have already seen how Jenny performs a similar function for Lizzie and Eugene.

39. Sedgwick cites Jean Baker Miller (*Toward a New Psychology of Women* [Boston: Beacon, 1976], chapter 1), who distinguishes between "temporary" and "permanent" inequality. Miller's logic—"gender difference marks a structure of *permanent* inequality, while the relation between adult and child is the prototype of the *temporary* inequality that in principle—or in ideology—exists only in order to be overcome" (qtd. in Sedgwick, *Between*, 194)—supports my contention that Jenny's youthful freakishness is potentially temporary—or at least assimilable—whereas Jennings's gender "deviance" and racial "difference" preclude his incorporation into the normative.

40. This analysis was suggested to me by Lillian Nayder's "Agents of Empire in *The Woman in White*" (in *Victorian Newsletter* 83 [Spring 1993]): "The growth of the imperial hero, in Collins's novel [*The Woman in White*] and in Victorian literature generally, is only made possible by the primitive conditions of the 'savages,' since it is measured by the ability to withstand or resist them" (5).

41. Welsh, 224.

42. Robert McRuer, "As Good as It Gets: Queer Theory and Critical Disability," *GLQ: A Journal of Lesbian and Gay Studies* 9, nos. 1–2 (2003): 85.

43. Ibid., 97.

44. Judith Butler, *Bodies That Matter: On the Discursive Limits of Sex* (New York: Routledge, 1993), 4.

45. McRuer, 99.

46. Ibid., 84. In his discussion of "flexible bodies," McRuer cites Emily Martin, *Flexible Bodies: Tracking Immunity in American Culture from the Days of Polio to the Age of AIDS* (Boston: Beacon, 1994).

47. McRuer, 92, 96.

48. Ibid., 95.

49. Ibid., emphasis added.

50. "Queers and people with disabilities should insist, inflexibly, that we will not serve as metaphors for each other and will not simply be tolerated, especially when that tolerance is used, paradoxically, to shore up heterosexual, able-bodied perspectives that continue to subordinate queerness and disability" (ibid., 99).

51. Ibid., 96, quoting himself from *The Queer Renaissance: Contemporary American Literature and the Reinvention of Lesbian and Gay Identities* (New York: New York University Press, 1997), 22.

52. Martha Stoddard Holmes, "Queering the Marriage Plot: Wilkie Collins's *The Law* and *the Lady*," in this volume, 239.

53. Ibid., 240.

54. Wilkie Collins, *The Law and the Lady* (London: Penguin, 1998), 193.

55. Stoddard Holmes, 240.

56. Ibid., 239, 248, 240, 246, 250.

57. McRuer, 91.

58. Ibid.

59. This problematic overlap goes uninterpreted by Stoddard Holmes.

60. Rebecca F. Romanow, "CFP: The Queer Space of the Postcolonial (9/15/05; NEMLA, 3/2/06–3/5/06)," online posting, June 15, 2005, Literary Calls for Papers Mailing List, http://cfp.english.upenn.edu/archive/Gender-Studies/0134.html.

61. Ibid.

62. Judith Halberstam, *In a Queer Time and Place: Transgender Bodies, Subcultural Lives* (New York: New York University Press, 2005), 1.

63. Ibid., 2–6.

64. Ibid., 6.

65. Ibid., 1.

66. Butler, 540.

67. Thoms, 154.

12

A COLLABORATIVE AESTHETIC

Levinas's Idea of Responsibility and the Photographs of Charles Eisenmann and the Late Nineteenth-Century Freak-Performer

CHRISTOPHER R. SMIT

L **OOKING AT** original prints of the photographs taken by Charles Eisenmann and the freak-performers he worked with in the late nineteenth century is an amazingly surreal event. The pictures are quite small, only three inches by four inches, and are delicate to the point of fragile. They are, as will be described below, cartes de visite, an early form of popular photography that emerged in the 1850s. Each carte is now housed in its own plastic sheath, alerting the contemporary viewer that fingerprints are not welcome and that any handling of the photographs is meant to be brief, temporary, a moment to be cherished. Yet the moment is not entirely pleasant. Rather, my session of viewing Eisenmann's photographs of freaks was as bizarre as it was beautiful, as strange as it was sublime, and as privately powerful as it was publicly perverse.

My session with Eisenmann and the freaks took place in the Syracuse University Library, in their special collections office. The pictures in front of me seemed false; years of movies and television tricked my mind into believing that what I was seeing were produced images, tailored fakes of monstrous bodies. But they were not fake. Though posed and staged with precision, the bodies, faces, and eyes I was studying were real. They were the freaks of the Victorian age, and they were forcing me, calling me, to look at them. My gaze was grasped by JoJo, the dog-faced boy; Moses Jerome, the elephant boy (see figure 12.1); Charles Tripp, the armless wonder; Harvey Wilson, the human skeleton; Anne Jones, the bearded lady; and hundreds more freak-performers who sat with Eisenmann in his studio between the years 1879 and 1890. My session with the photographs was brief, but their images remain etched in my memory. I was not repulsed, nor was I morally offended, by these photographs. Rather, I was, and continue to be, deeply moved by pictures I had studied for so long yet never had the opportunity to feel, touch, or see in that way.

My viewing of the Eisenmann photographs is contextualized by a scholarly project of the last fifteen years to interpret and readdress what most critics see to be a horrific portion of disability history, roughly shelved between 1840 and 1940. Within these years, in both Britain and the United States, there is evident a rise in the production, distribution, exhibition, and consumption of the different, or *freakish*, body, most clearly seen in sideshows, novelty museums, and, of course, the sale of photographs. Consequently, those photographs produced by Eisenmann and the Bowery freaks are interwoven within a practice of exhibition of the disabled body that prospered during these one hundred years. They were vital parts of a growing economy of amusements and spectacle that would eventually come to represent an era in which people with disabilities could cast their bodies as commodity, selling their likenesses to any interested audience. The issue of whether or not these freak-performers freely chose this practice, or if they were forced in front of the camera, has been the axis on which some of the current analytical pursuits of freakery have spun. Several scholars have theorized the self-awareness of the freak, criticized the apparent oppressive structures of the freak show formula, and articulated the social construction of the freak-performer, all in the name of claiming some authoritative description of the nineteenth-century thirst for the display of physical and mental difference.[1]

The tenor of this work, while varying in competence and eloquence, is attached to one central question: who was the freak, and how was his or her life lived? Different answers arise from each study, yet surprisingly, each uses a similar methodology. The dominant approach to the exhibition of people with disabilities during the time period from ca.

Figure 12.1
Unknown photographer, ca. 1859. Moses Jerome (ele-
phant boy) carte de visite. Ronald G. Becker Collection,
Special Collections Research Center, Syracuse University
Library.

1840 to 1940 has been cultural and political. While such an approach
has established a freak discourse within the humanities more generally, it has also forced our current understanding of the freak to remain
centered on issues of power. Besides a few rogue studies that attempt to
reread the freak-performer as an economic and artistic hero, the majority of the work being written on freaks figures the freak, or the person
with physical, mental, or behavioral difference being exhibited, as a

powerless victim of a cultural and economic system of objectification.[2] The freak described in this body of work is not a "freak-performer." Indeed, performance implies volition. Rather, the freak in these texts became an emblem of social discrimination, drawn heavily from a backdrop of twentieth-century disability political activism, in which freakery, objectification, and spectacle are read as misrepresentations of disability by an able-bodied society.

I am not discrediting the gains made by such a reading of freakery, but I do wish to question its methodology as well as its assumptions about the experience of disability. On a methodological level, contemporary freakology establishes a linear cause-and-effect narrative that posits that freak exhibition, in all its forms, was mainly a practice initiated by able-bodied entrepreneurs and audiences. The consequences of this spectacle lust was mainly felt by those individuals exhibited, namely, people with mental and physical deformities. Historical research, cultural analysis, and political theory are employed to draw this conclusion. Due to this methodology, a distinct, disempowered disabled subject emerges from the pages of these studies; expressed as inevitable bearers of bad luck, Victorian freaks are read as disabled protagonists trapped in an era wherein their bodies were simply viewed as consumable. They are, seen through the eyes of the field of disability studies, "the creatures that time forgot."[3]

I feel that it is imperative for current studies of disability, freakery, and the spectacular body to reconsider the assumption of powerlessness of people with disabilities from the Victorian period.[4] It is the aim of this essay to reread the exhibition of freaks and offer an alternative persona for the freak-performer, via an aesthetic and philosophical methodology of dialogicism. Surprisingly, only a small number of articles and books have been written about the freak show, and these concern themselves with photography of freaks in particular. Furthermore, it is clear that aesthetics has played little or no part in the pursuit of understanding the formation and maintenance of the freak identity during the Victorian period. Working off of a dialogical methodology garnered from the writings of Emanuel Levinas, the comments that follow attempt to shed new light on the importance of image construction on the part of the freak, a process that places the freak-performer directly in the action of promotion, self-representation, and exhibition. Rather than assume an able-bodied catalyst in the showing and viewing of freaks, I examine a dialogical relationship between the photographer, specifically Charles Eisenmann, and the freak subjects who worked *with* him, not for him.

Levinas and Responsibility: A Philosophy of Reciprocity

In his essay "Ethics as First Philosophy," Emanuel Levinas posits that the relationship between the I and the Other is not only reciprocal but also something for which individuals feel responsible. Explaining that responsibility for the Other preexists self-consciousness, Levinas offers a model of interaction between the I and the Other that, when applied to the current understanding of freak exhibition, could dramatically alter the ways in which we conceptualize the relationship between disabled bodies and photography. He writes, "The summons to responsibility destroys the formulas of generality by which any knowledge or acquaintance of the other man re-presents him to me as my fellow man."[5] Levinas's conceptualization of responsibility challenges scholars to reconsider a reading of objectification and to explore a given text as an interaction between disability and nondisability based on responsibility. Most important in his descriptions of responsibility is a call to accept the conditions of misunderstanding and imperfection that taint all interactions with, and representations of, otherness.

Using Levinas as the inspiration for a dialogical analysis of freak photography will allow a theoretical space for the shortcomings present in the relationships and artistic expressions negotiated between the disabled and able-bodied. Whereas many contemporary freakologists see the historical exhibition of disability as primarily an able-bodied action, which segregates the disabled and nondisabled experience being addressed, Levinas urges us to reexamine these issues and texts. It is through this action that mediated forms of disability can become more usefully interrogated by the media and disability critic. Because there remains no useful justification for a split between disability and nondisability in this model, more can be learned about the ways the two might potentially find cohesion. Cultural union, which Levinas calls *verbundenheit*, can be achieved only through commitment, dialogue, and responsibility, all of which, I argue, can be seen in the photographs taken from Eisenmann's studio in the Bowery at the close of the nineteenth century.

In *Existence and Existents*, Levinas pondered the nature of experience, particularly of the self. In this discussion, he posits the following about the condition of time and subjectivity: "If time is not the illusion of movement, pawing the ground, then the absolute alterity of another instant cannot be found in the subject, who is definitely *himself*. This alterity only comes to me from the Other. . . . The dialectic of time is the very dialectic of the relationship with the Other, that is, a dialogue which in turn has to be studied in terms other than those of the dialectic of the solitary subject."[6] The self, written here as the accumulation of the instant, is never in isolation, nor is it ever fully rid of relational qualities. Such a definition of the "instant," it should be noted, goes against the classical ideas of the self, which Levinas limited experience to the subjectivity of the individual.

This line of argument, this move away from solitary existence toward an almost reciprocal mode of being, is what characterizes the Levinasian philosophical system as dialogical. Like Martin Buber had done fifty years earlier in *I and Thou*, Levinas, through a variety of texts, searches for an understanding of self, and subjectivity, that encompasses the reality of coexistence.[7] Contemporary critics understand the exhibition of freaks and freak photography through an isolated self, whether it be the self of the freak or the powerful, nondisabled audience member or photographer. And to be fair, it must be acknowledged that when a twenty-first-century eye peers at the pictorial evidence of the freak, community, reciprocity, and even love are the last things that one might claim to see there. Yet by using a different approach to these images, one garnered from dialogical philosophy, much more can be seen; changing the lens changes the photograph.

In short, Levinas works to articulate a manner of living, one deeply involved with ethical action. He argues that wisdom, and the very creation of knowledge itself, can never occur without an awareness of the Other. Through the writings of Husserl and Heidegger, he posits that there is further reason to believe that there is a strong correlation between knowledge and being.[8] Thus, "knowing" is marked as a sort of *mastery* over truth—being, or existence, becomes the object or property of knowledge—which is anchored in the present but still connected, through representation, to the past and the future.[9] And still, Levinas is insistent on the fact that all of this mastery, knowledge building, and being must not occur, as it has always been assumed to by classical philosophers, in isolation. "Thought is an activity, where something is appropriated by a knowledge that is independent, of course, of any finality exterior to it, an activity which is disinterested and self-sufficient and whose self-sufficiency, sovereignty, *bonne conscience* and happy solitude are asserted by Aristotle. 'The wise man can practice contemplation by himself,' says Book Ten of the *Nicomachean Ethics*."[10] Levinas rejects this classical view by asserting that the Other is forgotten when one figures knowledge this way.[11] Knowledge, as he places it, occurs only in the maturation of responsibility toward the Other, a process that is solidified by a selfless love of the Other, comparable only to a devotion for God.[12]

When these ideas are applied to freak photography, Levinas allows an alternative understanding of the nineteenth-century exhibition of the different body due mainly to his belief that action and knowledge are never done in isolation. In other words, dialogical philosophy works as a way of denying power to only one self or individual. What we see emerging, then, is an ethical and pictorial moment based on the reciprocal actions of empowered freak-performers and photographers. I do not offer this argument as a conclusion with any finality but rather as an alternative understanding of Victorian-era representation of freak-performers. Even in this volume, some essays show us that for some freak-performers, empowerment and dialogue were never an option. Furthermore, it should be noted that the financial success of any given freak carte de visite was strictly regulated by a market with its own specificities of form and content. Such stringent requirements, all of which were fueled aesthetically, should certainly be seen as a breakdown, or at least a restriction, in the mutuality and reciprocity idealized by Levinas.

Even with these and other regulations and realities in mind, it is still vital to reimagine political and aesthetic relationships. Without risking such interpretations, disabled historical players remain static in roles and remain as powerless as their interpreters fear they have always been. My reading of Levinas, and subsequent research of Eisenmann and the Bowery freak-performers, have led me to the following conclusion: while some photographs of freak-performers are no doubt evidence of a systematic oppression and objectification of physical and mental difference, there is aesthetic and philosophical reason to see something quite different when we view Eisenmann's photographs. Indeed, there can be seen a new aesthetic, one based on a dialogical, and thus equal, inventive, and mutual action between the nondisabled photographer and the disabled subject. And no pictures illustrate this new aesthetic better than those created by Eisenmann and his freak-performer subjects.

The Eisenmann Studio: Cartomania and the Bowery

In 1854 scientist and inventor André Disdéri patented a multilensed camera that would come not only to revolutionize the mass production of photographs in the public market but also to initiate a new mode of looking at and collecting pictures of the different body.[13] Convinced that photography could, and should, be in the hands of the masses, Disdéri worked hard to take the technological and chemical processes made popular by Daguerre and Fox Talbot, both instrumental in the early stages of photographic development, out of its upper-class environment and make them more widely accessible. His camera, fitted with eight lenses, would consequently produce eight small images on one sheet. These miniature portraits, or cartes de visite as they were called, were then cut into individual photo cards by the patron and handed out at parties, social engagements, and the like (see figures 12.3, 12.4, and 12.5, for example). The years between 1860 and 1900, labeled by some photo historians as a period of cartomania, saw a rapid rise and decline of cartes. At the height of its popularity, the carte business proved to be a lucrative endeavor for professional photographers. In 1850, when the trade was first beginning, there were 938 registered professional photographers in the entire United States. When Charles Eisenmann opened his studio in the Bowery in 1879, he was one photographer among ten thousand working to find the most abundant source of sitters and subjects.[14]

Attempting to understand the wide appeal of the carte craze at the end of the nineteenth century is a task that requires both cultural and technological evidence. As Peter Hamilton and Roger Hargreaves suggest, "The evident appeal of the *carte* lay in its uniformly small size and its relatively low price. . . . [They] could be bought individually from a wide range of outlets including stationers, booksellers, print sellers, and luxury good emporia. To be depicted on a *carte* was not the preserve of the rich, powerful and famous but a pleasure open to ever-widening strata of society. By the early 1860s it was possible to visit a studio and have your image reduced, formatted, and packaged in exactly the same way as that of an emperor or a queen."[15] The carte de visite market was the most significant shift of who owned, and thus defined, photography of the nineteenth century. Prior to this point in the history of the medium, portraits, the most popular (and available) mode of photography, were the luxury of primarily the upper class. The carte changed this by lowering the cost of sitting for a picture, but it also added a sense of collection fever that fit into a growing middle-class sensibility in the United States and Britain.

Alongside the actual production of cartes came a new form of self-identification for the middle classes of Europe and the United States—the family and individual portrait. Most sitting rooms during this time had an elaborately decorated photo album that visitors were encouraged to look through and admire.[16] Serving the purpose of status and identity, the photographs included in these albums worked not only as pictorial entertainment but also as markers of class, prestige, and often idiosyncratic style. Among the photographs of family members were often portraits of vaudeville entertainers, dignitaries, and other celebrities that the owners of the albums had purchased from studios; the most popular cartes in the early years of the process were of Napoleon III and Abraham Lincoln.[17] Owning these cartes indicated the purchaser's social significance and wealth, but the process became increasingly financially accessible as the century progressed.

As early as 1840, the exhibition of the different body via photography had already been initiated by the freak show entrepreneur. In 1842 P. T. Barnum, perhaps the most notorious exhibitor of extravagant bodies and fascinating creatures, opened the American Museum on lower Broadway in New York. It is Barnum's work with circuses, freak shows, exotic exhibits, and other amusements that truly marks the second half of the nineteenth century as being an unprecedented time of disability-based entertainment. Furthermore, it is, in part, thanks to Barnum that the photographed image of the freak-performer took hold like it did, pictures being Barnum's media of choice in both advertisements and souvenirs.[18] Carte collectors, then, by the early 1850s, could include in their photo albums of family and friends pictures of General Tom Thumb, the famous midget, or Charles Tripp, the armless wonder.

While the carte craze can, and should, be seen through the eyes of the historical collector, the middle-class patron, and the professional photographer, it is most important for the present discussion to consider the effect it had on the subjects of the photographs themselves—the freak-performers. It is crucial to understand that cartes allowed the freak-performer a virtually unending source of capital in the latter half of the nineteenth century. Although most of the freak-performers whose photographs are discussed below also worked with Barnum and other exhibitors on a contract of performance, their primary source of income seems to have been from personal sales of their own likenesses. This fact alone should begin to help formulate a new identity for the historical freak: rather than simply belonging to a class of mistreated entertainers as many freakologists have argued, the freak-performer was actually an entrepreneurial figure, a savvy businessman or woman, and a decisive creator of image and product. However, I do not see these individuals as independent, and thus all-powerful, players in the philosophical or economic sense. Their employment of their own bodies, as objects, was made a lucrative process by a cultural and economic milieu of spectacle and fascination. The dark reality is that in order to capitalize on their own freak identity, these performers had to concede, and buy into, a market that no doubt caused a great deal of harm to people with mental and physical disabilities.

Yet it would be a mistake to end our analysis here. When we have the courage to look deeper into the lives of these freak-performers and speculate, based on material research, about the philosophical underpinnings of the freak phenomenon, much more can be said. In my pursuits of Charles Eisenmann, and the freak-performers with whom he worked, I have seen much more than isolation, objectification, and horror. Freak-performers, as I see it, needed to work with a professional photographer. And it is this idea of "working with" that should be of the utmost importance to us. Rather than remain powerless in what we, with twenty-first-century eyes, see as a state of inactivity as a result of dreadful oppression, it is possible to rewrite a portion of the freak experience as being proactive. Some freak-performers knew what they were doing, knew why they were doing it, and knew that they needed to foster and sustain relationships with able-bodied folks to keep doing it. In short, the process of taking, organizing, and distributing the freak-performer carte needed to be a dialogical process. And such a process found its impetus in the thriving communities in the Bowery of New York City.

The Bowery, which extended for roughly three city blocks, was filled with shops that ranged from ethnic specialty food markets, small taverns, and pool halls to newsstands and, of course, photography studios. Among the more popular establishments in the neighborhood, especially after 1860, were the dime museums. By 1880, in fact, the Bowery held more dime museums than any other area in the United States.[19] The dime museum was essentially a localized, which is to say nontouring, version of the historical freak show; any eager patron could pay the entrance fee (obviously a dime) and be entertained by both live performances or immortalized exhibits of freaks. It should be noted that as well as freaks, other amusements were housed in the dime museum, including replicas of the guns used by Jesse James and the blood of a "real life African warrior"—in short, any spectacle that would attract an audience. The freak-performer, however, stole most of the shows being produced. It was within this context that Charles Eisenmann, an immigrant from Germany in 1868, set up his studio and beckoned the would-be patron with the following advertisement: "If you want photographs to sell of yourself this is the place where you can get them CHEAP QUICK AND GOOD. When in New York call and sit for negatives; if not convenient to sit write for instructions how to send negatives, send for latest price list. The Eisenmann Studio, 229 Bowery, NY."[20] Pitching himself as both a photographer and a printer, Eisenmann quickly established himself as one of the Bowery's most successful studio photographers. While some of this success was surely the result of self-promotion, his work does immediately strike the viewer as being inspired and original. Although he would take photographs of anyone willing to pay the one guinea for a sheet of eight photographs, his talents seemed to lead him toward a career of working with freaks.

According to Eisenmann's biographer Michael Mitchell, the photographer worked with hundreds of freaks, among them some of the most famous freak-performers of the day, including Myrtle Corbin, the Texas Giant Brothers, bearded Jane Dearer, Maximo and Bartola, Millie Chistine, Admiral Dot, and Charles Tripp.[21] His popularity with the freak-performers can perhaps be explained by the stellar quality of the photographs, or even by the competitive prices he seems to have charged. The argument forwarded by the following analysis, however, wishes to demonstrate that it is also possible to posit that Eisenmann found favor with the Bowery freak-performer because of the photographer/subject relationship he was able to foster in his approach to freak cartes. As alluded to above, there were several photography studios in New York to which the freak-performer could go. None of these competitors did nearly as well as Eisenmann did, especially with regard to the pictures being discussed here. I am convinced that Eisenmann's photographs of freak-performers were so abundant, and thus so successful, because he approached the process, as did the subjects he worked with, in an entirely new aesthetic—what we now, following our discussion of Levinas, might label here the collaborative aesthetic.

The typical carte de visite was constructed intentionally to communicate, almost instantly, a sense of grandeur and dignity. Props, elaborate backdrops, and elegant costuming were employed to raise the cultural capital of the photograph as well as the subject therein. As Mitchell suggests: "This theatrical aggrandizement of the sitter was a photographic commonplace of the day. In Eisenmann's studio . . . it was a collaborative taste. Both the client and the photographer made the choices that shaped the end result. In making these sets available to his clients Eisenmann had, of course, considerable influence on the final result. But there is a consistency in setting with those clients who returned regularly over the years which demonstrates that they made the fundamental decision as to how they wished to appear. The details and execution were left to the photographer."[22] Here, then, is a rare situation in which the disabled body is on an even playing field with the person taking the photograph. Here, as Levinas might suggest, is a dialogical scenario in which the self and the Other, the disabled and nondisabled, are working together under conditions of responsibility.

It would be difficult to offer material proof of such collaboration. Instead, what I am suggesting here is actually a new way of looking. This manner of looking, guided by dialogical philosophy, urges the viewer (and reader of this essay) to spot the emergence of a new pictorial presentation of the different body in the photographs of Eisenmann. This collaborative aesthetic challenges us, as Levinas would phrase it, not to obliterate the other through representation but rather to empower them in our looking—to take note of their action in a scene where they are normally denied it. Levinas encourages the individual to rethink the way in which he or she reads the very presence of the Other. Concerned with the self's interpretation of "presence," in both proximity and theory, Levinas challenges his readers to contemplate how they meet the Other. His understanding is that the Other, or the other person in front of the self, is wrongly perceived as a mere representation—an image without consequence.[23] Claiming the Other in this fashion marks the death of the Other: "The alterity of the Other is the extreme point of 'thou shall not kill' and, in me, the fear of all the violence and usurpation that my existing, despite the innocence of its intentions, risks committing. Here is the risk of occupying . . . the place of the Other and, thus, in the concrete, of exiling him, dooming him to a miserable condition in some 'third' or 'fourth' world, bringing him death."[24] In hopes of clarifying this sentiment and aligning it with our current discussion, it may be useful to associate what Levinas here calls the "third or fourth world" with a photograph, specifically a photograph of a disabled body. Exiled as it were to a place of pure representation, the disabled subject of a picture is in no way *real* to the observer. Rather, he or she becomes, as Levinas would phrase it, a victim of unconscious usurpation. The world of the picture, then, resembles the world alluded to above and essentially destroys the Other, which in this example would be the person with a disability. Being just an image without engagement removes the essence of the subject's individuality.

The discussion below emerges from a purely philosophical and aesthetic interpretation. I want to acknowledge that what follows is not a declaration of historical proof, but a theoretical analysis. The Levinasian methodology that follows sets out in its task with some core assumptions that differentiate it from current writing on the subject: first, through an understanding of pure representation as being the eventual death of the Other, the subjects discussed below are seen as being active agents who are deeply involved with their own representation. Second, existence is never isolated—we are, unknowingly at times, connected to the Other through the very notion of history. This being the case, pictorial representation becomes an emblem of interaction, a citation of human connectedness, which serves to illustrate the fact that we are bound to (wo)mankind through even our own existence—the relationship between the photographer and the subject is made concrete through the picture they create together. Third, and finally, the methodology below is bound to Levinas's claim of ethics as first philosophy. Here, the idea that knowledge, whether historical, cultural, or aesthetic, can never be made by the self alone helps us contemplate the fact that a photograph is never singular in nature. Photographs are never, as some have suggested, the dream and execution of just the person behind the camera. Nor can they be the work of just the subject. They are, because of the inevitable force of ethics and responsibility, the documents of collaborative, interactive action.

Identifying the Collaborative Aesthetic: Eye Contact, Return Visits, and Intention

The presence of any subject of a photograph is fairly reliant on their eyes; conveying emotion, carrying nonverbal messages, and illuminating personality, the eyes of the subject are perhaps the most vivid indicators of that subject's essence. Certainly, in both the United States and Britain, this has been the case for portraiture photography since its inception in the 1840s. In addition, photographs of the disabled body have also shown the importance of eye contact, clearly illustrated in photographs taken by the physician Hugh W. Diamond in 1848 of asylum inmates. In most of Diamond's pictures the subject rarely looks directly into the camera, leaving him or her a passive object to be viewed without engagement.

The most striking examples of this enforced passivity can be seen in what could be called the body-centric motif of medical photography described in Meegan Kennedy's essay on "Poor Hoo Loo" in this volume (see also figure 12.2). In these types of photographs the potential for eye contact is simply erased by the choice to hide or avert the face of the subject. What is left is simply the extraordinary body, the spectacle of flesh and disfigurement. In some ways, though to a lesser extent, Diamond's photographs initiate the body-centric motif as well. The subjects of his photographs are not "present" by means of identity but rather by their medical condition. They remain disempowered, a condition marked here by a lack of direct eye contact and a forced perspective employed by the camera. The collaborative aesthetic rarely allows this type of perspective. Eisenmann and the Bowery freak-performers were initiating a new mode of disabled presence, one clearly seen in the use of direct eye contact.

A clear example of this can be seen in Eisenmann's photograph of an unidentified bearded lady, a subject identified in the archives by her age, twenty-three (figure 12.3). Dressed in what appears to be a wedding dress and holding a memento from the marriage ceremony, the subject here is in perfect accord with traditional carte scenes. The appearance of her formal attire, the stature of the dress, are contrasted and intensified by the presence of her fully grown beard. Because this woman's eyes face the camera (and viewer) directly, I would argue that there is no aesthetic space for uncertainty. This subject positions her gaze with confidence.

An even more convincing example of this confidence can be seen in a portrait taken by Eisenmann of Rosie Lesslie (figure 12.4). The archive of Eisenmann's work shows that a large number of the photographer's subjects were what were known as fat ladies or fat men. Although not as immediately recognizable as disabled or disfigured, the fat lady/fat man appears to have been a lucrative freak identity in the nineteenth-century amusement market. Lesslie is included in this section, however, primarily for the eye contact that this picture, as well as others not included, displays. Again, as with the previously discussed photo, the freak-performer takes no shame in visually addressing the camera. Furthermore, as with many of the Eisenmann photographs, Lesslie is a confrontational subject—her gaze here taunts the viewer as if to say, "Go ahead, take a good look."

This is a drastically different subject than we would typically see of people with disabilities from this era. Lesslie, as an empowered figure, knows that her likeness will be more profitable if it is unabashed in its presentation. Robert Bogdan helps contextualize Lesslie's empowered positioning by pointing to the fact that most freak-performers employed a rather pompous response to their audiences. Convinced by his research

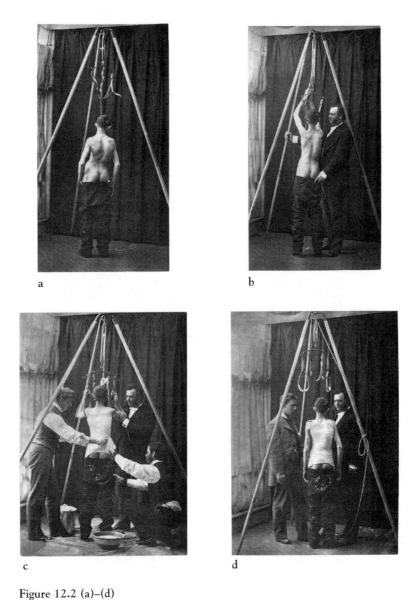

a   b

c   d

Figure 12.2 (a)–(d)
J. E. Mayall (attributed), English (b. U.S., 1810–1901). Doctor and suspended
patient. Lewis A. Sayre, *Spinal Disease and Spinal Curvature* . . . , 1877, woodbury
type, Museum Collection. Courtesy of George Eastman House.

Figure 12.3
Charles Eisenmann, ca. 1879–90. *Unidentified Bearded Lady, Age 23*/Ronald G. Becker Collection, Special Collections Research Center, Syracuse University Library.

that the label of "freak" was not an identity but rather a social construction, Bogdan posits that freak-performers were empowered, career-minded individuals. He argues, "During its prime the freak show was a place where human deviance was valuable, and in that sense valued. Modern social scientists advocate a view of people with physical, mental, and behavioral anomalies as stigmatized, rejected and devalued. While this viewpoint may reveal part of the story of people who were exhibited [freaks], it leaves out a great deal. Some were exploited, it is

Figure 12.4
Charles Eisenmann, ca. 1879–90. *Rosie Lesslie—fat lady/*
Ronald G. Becker Collection, Special Collections
Research Center, Syracuse University Library.

true, but in the culture of the amusement world most human oddities were accepted as showmen. They were congratulated for parlaying into an occupation what, in another context, might have been a burden."[25] What makes Bogdan's model of the freak-performer, and freak exhibition more generally, unique is that it no longer casts freaks as historical victims, and hence freaks have at least a theoretical opportunity here to play a role in their own lives.

Bogdan, consequently, posits that freak-performers, under their own doing, took happily the title "freak," for with such a label there came immense popularity, national fame, and a great deal of money.[26] The major goal of the freak-performer, as for any performer working in the independent amusement world at the end of the nineteenth century, was to "dupe" the unsuspecting audience. And their duping was the best one of them all: able to charge a decent fee for stage shows as well as photographs of themselves, the freak-performer conjured a living from simply being. Rather than seeing this as something for which to be ashamed or by which to be isolated, Bogdan claims it offered these people with disabilities power in a culture and era that otherwise kept them on the fringes of society: "As freaks sat on the platform, most looked down on the audience with contempt—not because they felt angry at being gawked at or at being called freaks, but simply because the amusement world looked down on 'rubes' in general. Their contempt was that of insiders toward the uninitiated. For those in the amusement world it was the sucker who was on the outside, not the exhibit."[27] Here the freak-performer is a valued member of a culture of amusement; an economically astute individual, deeply involved with his or her own well-being; an artist; and an active agent, overpowering his or her nondisabled audience.

The pictures taken in Eisenmann's studio make even more clear the fact that these individuals knew what they wanted to portray and would search however long they needed to in order to find the right photographer for the job. Again, here is evidence for a dialogical reading of the freak carte de visite. Lesslie and other freak-performers were reliant on a good photographer just as much as said photographer was on good subjects, especially those that made return visits. And so, the responsibility and reciprocity outlined by Levinas above also carried with it an economic component in the collaborative aesthetic. Lesslie understood that in order to sell a good number of cartes she would need a quality product: this type of product was most likely judged by the photographer's prices, the location of the studio, and, most importantly, how well the person behind the camera could create the desired effect. Eisenmann, as is being proven here, fulfilled all of these criteria for the freak-performer, and thus he conducted much of his business with different bodies.

And he did have many return visits with freak-performers, the fact of which is a second characteristic of the collaborative aesthetic being outlined here. The return visit, characterized by at least three or more sittings over time, is indicative of the collaborative aesthetic and its dialogical element, due to the presence of choice and selection on the part of the freak-performer. Pointing again to an empowered disabled subject, a return visit indicates a discerning eye on the part of the freak-performer, as well as an awareness that it was only with Eisenmann that such photographs could be taken. Consider, for example, the many cartes taken by Eisenmann of Rosie Wolf, a midget-performer of the day (figure 12.5[a]–[f]). In these six photographs, four of which seem to be from different visits, we see Wolf in different outfits, with various backdrops (nature, inner hall, stairway). In several of the pictures she poses alone, while she is pictured with a violin in another. The significance of these six separate photographs is twofold. First, the perspective Eisenmann uses in all the cartes of Wolf is the same—she is pictured in such a way as to accentuate her minuteness. Notice that the camera is placed at a considerable distance from the subject, a method commonly used to enhance the size of a smaller sitter. The fact that all six poses, while positionally different, are shot from the same distance suggests that Wolf returned to Eisenmann in order to reproduce the desired effect. She had found a camera operator whose perspective had met her requirements, and consequently she wanted to continue working with him.

Second, and as a consequence of this first conclusion, the six pictures included here work to suggest that there was in fact a relationship being fostered between Wolf and Eisenmann. I am not attempting to posit here that Eisenmann and the freak-performers who sat for him were close friends. While this may have been the case, I am only willing to argue here that at the very least a professional relationship seems to have been clearly established between the two. Again, this is evidence of a dialogical interaction. For further evidence of this it is useful to look at a notorious collection of photographs taken of Chauncy Morlan.

Based on the many pictures of Morlan included in the Becker Collection of Eisenmann photographs, it seems that he was one of the photographer's most faithful collaborators. In his first sitting with Eisenmann (figure 12.6) we see a young man dressed in an elaborate suit coat. In this picture, Morlan appears to be tentative, apparently uneasy about the process of being photographed. However, as the progression of his visits continues there is a distinct change in not only his demeanor but also his courage to be photographed (figures 12.7, 12.8, and 12.9). Morlan's decision to sit nude for Eisenmann shows a willingness to be vulnerable beyond the intimacy already being enforced by the sessions in which he was clothed. The man pictured nude in these three pictures,

Queen-Midget, ⚜ The German Rose.
Age 16 years.   Height 33 Inch.   Weight 38 pounds.

a

Eisenmann, Photo-   229 Bowery, N.Y.

b

Eisenmann, Photo-   229,Bowery, N.Y.

c

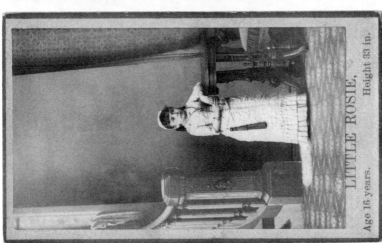

Figure 12.5 (a)–(f)

Charles Eisenmann, ca. 1879–90. *Rosie Wolf—midget*, 1–6/Ronald G. Becker Collection, Special Collections Research Center, Syracuse University Library.

Figure 12.6
Chauncy Morlan (young with coat)

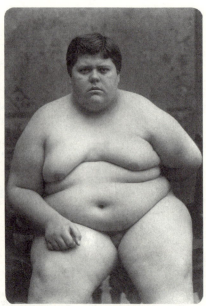

Figure 12.7
Chauncy Morlan (nude, direct stare)

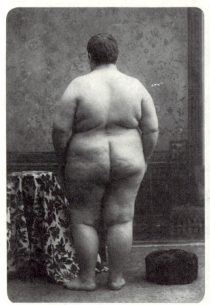

Figure 12.8
Chauncy Morlan (nude posterior)

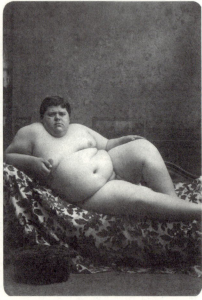

Figure 12.9
Chauncy Morlan (nude reclining)

Charles Eisenmann, ca. 1879–90. Ronald G. Becker Collection, Special Collections Research Center, Syracuse University Library.

Figure 12.10
Charles Eisenmann, ca. 1879–90. *Chauncy Morlan (coat no arms)*/
Ronald G. Becker Collection, Special Collections Research Cen-
ter, Syracuse University Library.

while not overtly figured as being happy, is nonetheless a man destined
to present himself as a commodity and a lucrative one at that. These
nude photographs would have certainly been sold at a high price, and it
seems likely that such a fact was in the mind of Morlan when he posed
for them.

Of further importance for the discussion here, however, is the manner in which these pictures illustrate what I see to be a growing trust

between Morlan and Eisenmann. As emblems of the Levinasian under-standing of reciprocity, these three nude photographs, especially when compared to Morlan's first sitting, point to a growing appreciation, by both photographer and subject, of the relationship necessary to create such images. By the time Morlan sits for his final collection of cartes de visite with Eisenmann, wearing the same coat but without arms to allow the now larger Morlan enough room to wear it, I contend that we see a mature subject, completely at ease with the man he worked with behind the camera (figure 12.10). Of course, seeing these photographs as evidence of a dialogical relationship between Morlan and Eisenmann is a speculation on my part. Nevertheless, it is a speculation, a theory, that I make in order to stretch our understanding of the freak phenom-enon. Levinas's philosophical writings on reciprocity, responsibility, and relational experience, briefly surveyed above, are used here as a new lens—one in which historical freak-performers can gain access to the empowerment felt by people with disabilities today.

Morlan, Wolf, Lesslie, and the unidentified bearded lady were all aware of the fact that they were being photographed—they, in fact, were responsible for the initiating the sessions we have seen here. Moreover, they were also aware of the fact that Eisenmann, among many other photographers at their disposal, was able to create their likenesses in the fashion that they hoped for. As a result, Eisenmann and these freak-performers worked together under the philosophical umbrella of inten-tionality, the third characteristic of the collaborative aesthetic. Certainly, the photos included in this section are testament to the intentionality being discussed: the nonconfrontational yet direct stare of the bearded lady, the aggressive gaze of Lesslie, the many poses and presentations of Wolf, and the pure, unabashed confidence of Morlan all point to a pre-determined, intentional effect of the photographs. Consider the elabo-rate staging of photographs taken of "a very hairy man" (figure 12.11 [a] and [b]). Here we see a clear example of what is meant by intentionality. It is evident that this man, whom none of the archive materials name, is attempting to heighten the exotic nature of his appearance by using the stick and log, the ankle chains, and the backdrops pictured here. He has chosen to do this, and Eisenmann has helped him. On the other end of the spectrum, freak-performer Eli Bowen's desired effect was to prove his equality with his culture (figure 12.12 [a] and [b]). Pictured here in a formal suite, and with his family, the intention seems to be to present a respectable, even typical, likeness. This, too, is made possible, or so it seems, by working *with* Eisenmann.

a

b

Figures 12.11 (a) and (b)
Charles Eisenmann, ca. 1879–90. *Unidentified man with very hairy arms,* 1 and
2/Ronald G. Becker Collection, Special Collections Research Center, Syracuse
University Library.

b

a

Figures 12.12 (a) and (b)

Charles Eisenmann, ca. 1879–90. *Eli Bowen—legless man*, 1 and 2/Ronald G. Becker Collection, Special Collections Research Center, Syracuse University Library.

This final characteristic must be handled with great care—marking another person's intentions can be a mistake of drastic consequence. I again remind my reader that I am working primarily on the landscapes of philosophy and theory, both of which have been informed by historical research. In naming this third element of the collaborative aesthetic as having most to do with intentionality, I am in no way claiming to know exactly the intentions of either Eisenmann or the freak-performers with whom he worked. While one can certainly speculate, as I have above, that economic gains were the intended purpose of these cartes de visite of freak-performers, they remain, in the end, only theoretical conjecture. What is more important than naming the actual intentions of Eisenmann and the freak-performer is simply stating that their work together seems purpose-driven. They are intentional documents. And unlike the medical photographs that came before them, which seem to display the intentions of only one player, the doctor or physician, these examples of the collaborative aesthetic illustrate the intentions of both photographer and subject.

Conclusion

By the middle of the 1890s Charles Eisenmann had closed his studio in the Bowery. By the turn of the century, according to his biographer, Eisenmann had essentially disappeared—no public documents after 1899 show him registered as a photographer or otherwise.[28] With his disappearance went an alternative visual representation of the disabled body. And while many other creators of freak cartes de visite remained in business throughout the first half of the twentieth century, none would ever compare aesthetically or, as I have tried to prove here, philosophically with Eisenmann and his coproducers, the Bowery freak-performers. The collaborative aesthetic that they fostered together was surely a striking moment in the history of the relationship between disability and photography.

That relationship, in fact, seems to be their most valuable contribution. As a definite challenge to the fascination aesthetic of early medical photography, the collaborative aesthetic applied to the photographs taken by Eisenmann and the freak-performers with whom he worked marks a philosophical instance in which, as Levinas hoped for, the self and the Other were connected under the blankets of reciprocity and responsibility.[29] This is what the manner of looking proposed above depends on. What I hope has emerged here is a new identity for the freak-performer, as well as for those individuals who took their pictures. The collaborative aesthetic may be useful in other pictures where disability, nondisability, and the technology and art of photography coincide.

Notes

1. The literature on freaks is quite extensive. For a survey of the work that directly corresponds with this chapter see Rachel Adams, *Sideshow U.S.A.: Freaks and the American Cultural Imagination* (Chicago: University of Chicago Press, 2001); David T. Mitchell and Sharon L. Snyder, eds., *The Body and Physical Difference: Discourses of Disability* (Ann Arbor: University of Michigan Press, 1997); Rosemarie Garland-Thomson, ed., *Freakery: Cultural Spectacles of the Extraordinary Body* (New York: New York University Press, 1996); Robert Bogdan, *Freak Show: Presenting Human Oddities for Amusement and Profit* (Chicago: University of Chicago Press, 1990).

2. For examples of those authors who interpret the historical freak as empowered, see Bogdan; Adams; and Cheryl Marie Wade, "Disability Culture Rap," in *The Ragged Edge: The Disability Experience from the Pages of the First Fifteen Years of* The Disability Rag, ed. Barrett Shaw (Louisville, KY: The Advocado Press, 1994), 16–20.

3. David Hevey, *The Creatures That Time Forgot: Photography and Disability Imagery* (London: Routledge, 1992), 1–3. Hevey argues that, with regard to disability, photography is in itself an oppressive medium because of its extreme subjectivity. Photographs of people with disabilities allow, he argues, a passive approach to issues of objectification, isolation, and oppression. And while he celebrates (through his own photography) the potential for positive photographic representations of people with disabilities, he remains very skeptical about the able-bodied gaze and the images it produces of people who are physically and mentally different.

4. See specifically in this book Martha Stoddard Holmes, "Queering the Marriage Plot: Wilkie Collins's *The Law and the Lady*," and Rebecca Stern, "Our Bear Women, Ourselves: Affiliating with Julia Pastrana."

5. Emanuel Levinas, "Ethics as First Philosophy," in *The Levinas Reader*, ed. Sean Hand (Cambridge, MA: Basil Blackwell, 1989), 84.

6. Emanuel Levinas, *Existence and Existents*, trans. Alphonso Lingis (The Hague: Nijhoff, 1978), 93.

7. See Martin Buber, *I and Thou* (New York: Scribner and Sons, 1958). Levinas himself saw a connection between his own work and that of Buber, yet he was critical of what he saw to be a spiritual idealism in Buber's conceptualization of the I/Other relationship. For more on Levinas's critique of Buber, see Emanuel Levinas, "Martin Buber and the Theory of Knowledge," in *The Levinas Reader*, ed. Sean Hand (Cambridge, MA: Basil Blackwell, 1989).

8. Levinas, "Ethics," 76.

9. Ibid., 77.

10. Ibid.

11. Emanuel Levinas, *Time and the Other*, trans. Richard A. Cohen (Pittsburgh, PA: Duquesne University Press, 1987), 111–13.

12. Ibid., 137.

13. Avril Lansdell, *History à la Carte, 1860–1900* (Cromwell House, UK: Shire Publications, 1985), 7–8.

14. Michael Mitchell, *Monsters of a Gilded Age: The Photographs of Chas. Eisenmann* (New York: ECW Press, 2002), 18.

15. Peter Hamilton and Roger Hargreaves, *The Beautiful and the Damned: The Creation of Identity in Nineteenth-Century Photography* (Burlington, VT: Lund Humphries, 2001), 44–45.

16. Ibid., 43.

17. Lansdell, 9–10.

18. Mitchell, 12.

19. Ibid., 14–18.

20. Ibid., 42.

21. Ibid., 11.

22. Ibid., 33.

23. Levinas, *Time*, 108–10.

24. Ibid., 109–10.

25. Bogdan, 268.

26. Ibid., 270–71.

27. Ibid., 272.

28. Mitchell, 49–50.

29. For more on what I have termed here the "fascination aesthetic" of medical photography, see Hugh W. Diamond, "On the Application of Photography to the Physiognomic and Mental Phenomena of Insanity—May 22, 1856," in *The Face of Madness: Hugh W. Diamond and the Origin of Psychiatric Photography*, ed. Sander L. Gilman (New York: Brunner/Mazel Publishers, 1976), and Stanley Burns, *A Morning's Work: Medical Photographs from the Burns Archive and Collection, 1843–1939* (New York: Twin Palms Publishers, 1998).

NOTES ON CONTRIBUTORS

NADJA DURBACH, associate professor of history, University of Utah, researches the place of the body in nineteenth- and early twentieth-century British culture, particularly in relationship to gender, class, race, and ethnicity. She is the author of *Bodily Matters: The Anti-Vaccination Movement in England, 1853–1907* (Duke University Press, 2005) and several articles that have appeared in *Social History of Medicine*, the *Journal of British Studies*, and *Cultural and Social History*. She is currently completing a book entitled *Displaying Deformity: The Freak Show and Modern British Culture, 1847–1914*.

CHRISTINE C. FERGUSON, lecturer in the Department of English at the University of Glasgow, specializes in late-Victorian literature and culture. Her publications include *Language, Science, and Popular Culture in the Victorian* Fin-de-Siècle: *The Brutal Tongue* (Ashgate, 2006) and articles in *PMLA*, *ELH*, *Victorian Review*, *Nineteenth-Century Contexts*, and the *Journal of Victorian Culture*.

MELISSA FREE, University of Illinois at Urbana-Champaign, is at work on a dissertation entitled "Elsewhere England: Late Colonial South Africa, British Identity, and the Authorial Informant," which examines South African periodicals as well as work by Haggard, Schreiner, and Buchan. She has published pieces on Victorian literature and culture in *Book History* (2006) and *Texas Studies in Literature and Language* (2006).

MARTHA STODDARD HOLMES, associate professor of literature and writing studies, California State University San Marcos, researches the cultural history of the body from Victorian culture to the present. She is author of *Fictions of Affliction: Physical Disability in Victorian Culture* (University of Michigan Press, 2004) and coeditor of *The Teacher's Body: Embodiment, Authority, and Identity in the Classroom* (SUNY Press, 2003). She is working on a book on disability and desire in Victorian fiction.

JOYCE L. HUFF, assistant professor of English, Ball State University, examines the representation of fat in the literature and culture of nineteenth-century Britain and links the development of our current attitudes toward fat to the growth of consumer culture. She is currently working on a book on the depiction of corpulence in Victorian novels and medical discourse. Her principal publications are "Corporeal Economies: Work and Waste in Nineteenth-Century Constructions of Alimentation," in *Cultures of the Abdomen: Diet, Digestion and Fat in the Modern World* (Palgrave Macmillan, 2005), and "A 'Horror of Corpulence': Interrogating Bantingism and Mid-Nineteenth-Century Fatphobia," in *Bodies Out of Bounds: Fatness and Transgression* (University of California Press, 2001).

KELLY HURLEY, associate professor of English at the University of Colorado at Boulder, studies identity, the alien, and the Gothic. She is the author of *The Gothic Body: Sexuality, Materialism, and Degeneration at the* Fin de Siècle (Cambridge University Press, 1996) and *Teaching with the* Norton Anthology of English Literature, *Seventh Edition: A Guide for Instructors* (Norton, 2000), as well as many articles on the Gothic and contemporary film. She is currently at work on a book-length manuscript entitled *Heteromorphosis: Processes of Identify-Formation in Science Fiction–Horror Cinema*.

MEEGAN KENNEDY, assistant professor of English at Florida State University, studies Victorian medicine and science; theory and history of the British novel; fiction of empire; visual culture; and gender theory. She has published articles and reviews in Victorian literature and culture, Victorian studies, and literature and medicine and is currently revising a book manuscript entitled *Rewriting the Clinic: Vision and Representation in Victorian Medicine and the Novel*, which reads nineteenth-century British medical case histories against developments in the British novel.

HEATHER McHOLD, independent scholar, received a Ph.D. in history and a Graduate Certificate in Women's and Gender Studies from Northwestern University in 2003. She researches the history of gender and medicine in Victorian culture with particular emphasis on deformity, the spectacular display of bodies, and contemporary discourse on imperial power. She is the author of "Freaks" in *The Oxford Companion to the Body* (Oxford University Press, 2001), edited by Colin Blakemore and Sheila Jennett.

TIMOTHY NEIL, University of Sheffield, studies Victorian and Edwardian popular culture, particularly early film, fairground, and circus. His current research concerns British migration to rural France, and he is editing a collection of papers on the social archaeology of arborglyphs and graffiti. He has published in *Images, Representations and Heritage: Moving Beyond Modern Approaches to Archaeology* (Springer, 2006), and *The Lost World of Mitchell and Kenyon: Edwardian Britain on Film* (British Film Institute, 2004).

CHRISTOPHER R. SMIT, assistant professor for the Communication Arts and Sciences, Calvin College, is the editor of *Screening Disability: Essays on Cinema and Disability* (University Press of America, 2001). His current book projects focus on disability theology and the disabled body in photography. Smit's essays on disability, media, popular music, and culture can be found in *Disability Studies Quarterly*, *Studies in Popular Culture*, *Journal of Popular Culture*, and several edited collections.

REBECCA STERN, associate professor, University of South Carolina, is the author of *Home Economics: Domestic Fraud in Victorian England* (forthcoming from The Ohio State University Press [2008]). She has also begun work on two new book projects, one on spectacular Victorian bodies and a second on the odd performances of Victorian gerunds and participles. Her articles have appeared in *Nineteenth-Century Literature*, *Victorian Poetry*, *ELH*, and *Nineteenth-Century Studies*.

MARLENE TROMP, professor of English and women's studies, Denison University, researches the "marginal" in Victorian culture, particularly séances, sensation, and freaks; she also studies the *Titanic* disaster. She is the author of *Altered States: Sex, Drugs, and National Identity in Victorian Spiritualism* (SUNY Press, 2006); *The Private Rod: Marital Violence, Sensation, and the Law in Victorian Britain* (University Press of Virginia,

2000); and coeditor of *Beyond Sensation: Mary Elizabeth Braddon in Context* (SUNY Press, 2000).

KARYN VALERIUS, assistant professor of English, Hofstra University, studies gender and embodiment in nineteenth- and twentieth-century literature, popular culture, and science and medicine. She has published articles on reproduction and monstrosity and is writing a book-length project on maternal impressions.

INDEX